AUSTRALIA
Trip Planner & Guide

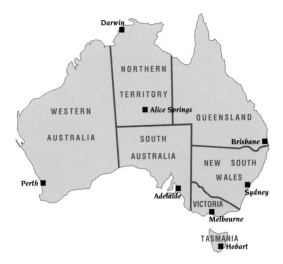

AUSTRALIA
Trip Planner & Guide
Paul Strathern

PASSPORT BOOKS
NTC/Contemporary Publishing Company

This first edition published 1997 by
Passport Books,
An imprint of NTC/Contemporary Publishing Company
4255 West Touhy Avenue, Lincolnwood (Chicago), Illinois 60646-1975
U.S.A.

Conceived, edited, designed, and produced by
Duncan Petersen Publishing Ltd, 31 Ceylon Road, London W14 0PY
from a concept by Emma Stanford

Typeset by Duncan Petersen Publishing Ltd;

Originated by PICA Colour Separation Overseas Pte Ltd, Hong Kong
Printed by GraphyCems, Navarra

ISBN: 0-8442-4898-3

Library of Congress Catalog Card Number: on file

Every reasonable care has been taken to ensure the information in this
guide is accurate, but the publishers and copyright holders can accept
no responsibility for the consequences of errors in the text or in the
maps, particularly those arising from changes taking place after the text
was finalized. The publishers are always pleased to hear from readers
who wish to suggest corrections and improvements.

Editorial director Andrew Duncan
Assistant editors Nicola Davies and Sarah Barlow
Art director Mel Petersen
Design Beverley Stewart, Chris Foley
Maps Chris Foley and Beverley Stewart
Illustrations Beverley Stewart

Photographic credits
All photographs by Jeroen Snijders
except p35, 58, 59, 62, 66, 70, 123, 175, 208, 210, 211, 220, 223,
247, 250, 264, 270, 274, 275, 277
reproduced with the permission of the
Australian Tourist Commission

Paul Strathern was born in 1940 and took a degree in philosophy at Trinity College, Dublin. He has written five novels and worked for more than 20 years as a travel writer, visiting four continents in the course of his work.

He first sailed to Australia in the early 1960s as a crew member on a tramp steamer. This ended up plying the Australian coast for several months, by the end of which half the deckhands had jumped ship, deciding they wanted to live there. Since then, he has returned to Australia several times – as a travel writer, visiting lecturer, and once as representative for an Irish film producer. During the latter trip he travelled all over Australia searching out locations for a film which never materialized.

At various times he has received instruction in the Aussie way of life by a grandmother who trained boxing kangaroos; by an Aborigine obsessed with Wittgenstein; by a Queenslander whose unbeatable roulette system inexplicably failed to break a Gold Coast casino; and by the thirstiest inhabitant of the Northern Territory, who had an unshakeable belief that Crocodile Dundee was his younger brother.

Master contents list

This contents list is for when you need to use the guide in the conventional way: to find out about where you are going, or where you happen to be. The index may be just as helpful.

Conventions used in this guide	12
Something for everyone	13
Australia: an introduction	14
Before you go	16
Getting there	20
Getting around	20
Essential practical information	26
A brief history of Australia	32
Sydney	**42**
Canberra and Region	**58**
New South Wales	**66, 192**
Victoria	**90, 208**
South Australia	**110, 214**
Queensland	**126, 222**
Western Australia	**162, 240**
Northern Territory	**174, 264**
Tasmania	**186, 272**
Index	278

HOWEVER
There is much more to this guide than the region by region approach suggested by the contents list on this page. Turn to page 8 and also pages 10-11.

Australia Overall
- master map

Australia Overall, pages 66-191, is a traveller's network for taking in the whole continent, or large parts of it.

Each 'leg' of the network is a route in its own right, and is covered in a section of its own, starting with an introduction and a simplified map. The sections are numbered – see below – and the numbers are used in cross-references throughout the guide.

The routes are not merely lines on a map. Each features a whole region, and describes many places both on and off the marked trail. Think of the overall routes not only as itineraries, but as interesting ways of describing and connecting the main centres of Australia, and of making travel sense of the continent as a whole.

The overall route network is designed to be used in these different ways:

1 *Ignore the marked route entirely:* simply use the alphabetically arranged gazetteer of Sights and Places of Interest, and the map at the start of each section, as a guide to what to see and do in the region, not forgetting the hotel and restaurant recommendations.

2 *Treat the route as an itinerary,* following it by car or by public transport. You can do sections of a route, or all of it; and you can follow it in any direction. Link the routes to travel the length and breadth of Australia. The introduction to each route summarizes what you you can expect, and gives an idea of how long it will take.

NEW SOUTH WALES

1 *Between Sydney and Port Macquarie*
**Myall Lakes and the
Hunter Valley** 66

2 *Between Port Macquarie and Brisbane*
The Gold Coast 74

VICTORIA

3 *Between Melbourne and Canberra*
Melbourne and Region 90

4 *Between Melbourne and Adelaide*
**The Shipwreck Coast and
Kangaroo Island** 102

SOUTH AUSTRALIA

5 *Between Adelaide and Port Augusta*
**Adelaide, Yorke Peninsula and
Mount Remarkable** 110

6 *Between Port Augusta and Alice
Springs*
South Australia Outback 122

QUEENSLAND

7 *Between Brisbane and Hervey Bay*
**Brisbane and the
Sunshine Coast** 126

8 *Between Hervey Bay and Mackay*
The Capricorn Coast 138

9 *Between Mackay and Cairns*
North to Cairns 150

Western Australia
10 *Between Perth and Kalgoorlie*
The Goldfields 162

11 *Around Perth*
**Perth, Fremantle and Rottnest
Island** 166

NORTHERN TERRITORY
12 *Between Alice Springs and Darwin*
**Darwin and the Northern Territory
Outback** 174

13 *Between Alice Springs and Uluru
(Ayers Rock)*
**Alice Springs,
Uluru and Region** 178

TASMANIA
14 *Around Hobart*
Hobart and Launceston 186

Some practical hints on how to travel red, blue and green are given in the introductory pages and the simplified maps, including key roads and their numbers. Generally, though, there are no absolute rules for going red, blue or green and you are meant to link the places, using a detailed road map, in whatever way suits you best.

The Australia Overall section is ideal for:

■ Planning and undertaking tours of the whole country, or parts.

■ Making the journey to or from your eventual destination as interesting and as rewarding as possible.

■ Linking the in-depth explorations of local sights provided by the Local Explorations section, pages 192-277.

The maps at the start of each section

Are simplified. Use them together with a detailed map.
On the simplified maps:
RED *marks key sights and centres,*
not to be missed.

BLUE *marks important places,*
certainly worth a visit.

GREEN *places are for those who aren't in a hurry and want to experience the region in some depth.*

Contents

The Local Explorations
- master map

The Local Explorations – strategies for exploring all the interesting localities of Australia – complement the regional routes, pages 8-9.

They are designed to be used in these different ways:

1 *Ignore the marked route entirely*: simply use the alphabetically arranged Sights & Places of Interest, and the map at the start of each Local Exploration, as a guide to what to see and do in the area, not forgetting the hotel and restaurant recommendations.

2 *Use the marked route to make a tour* by public transportation (see the transport box), by ferry, or by car. You can do sections of the route, or all of it. (In the introduction it tells you how long you might take to cover everything the quickest way, by car.)

If you are driving, you can generally follow the tour in any direction; usually, the route as marked is an attractive and convenient way to link the places of interest; you may well find other ways to drive it. Always use our map in conjunction with a detailed road map (suggestions are given on each introductory page).

New South Wales

1	The Blue Mountains	192
2	The Coast Between Sydney and Melbourne	196
3	Sydney to Brisbane, Inland	202

Victoria

4	The Grampians - Inland Between Melbourne and Adelaide	208

South Australia

5	Barossa Valley and the Flinders Ranges	214
6	Burra, Clare Valley and Broken Hill	218

Queensland

7	South Queensland Outback	222
8	Central Queensland Outback	226
9	Northern Queensland Outback	230
10	The Far North	234

Western Australia

11	Esperance and the Eyre Peninsula	240
12	South of Perth	246
13	North from Perth	252
14	The Far North-West	258

Northern Territory

15	The Kimberley and Beyond	264

Tasmania

16	The Tasmanian Hinterland	272

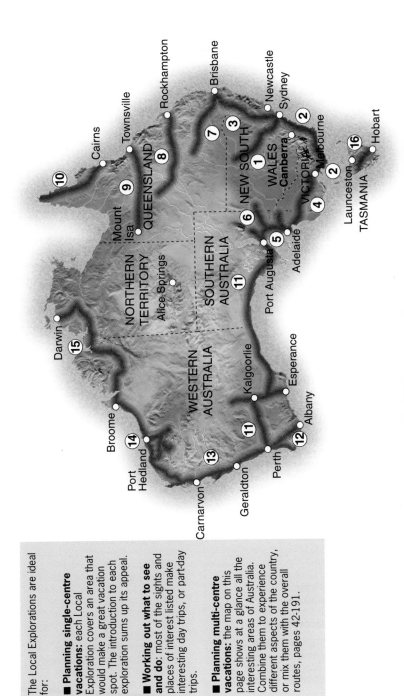

The Local Explorations are ideal for:

■ **Planning single-centre vacations:** each Local Exploration covers an area that would make a great vacation spot. The introduction to each exploration sums up its appeal.

■ **Working out what to see and do:** most of the sights and places of interest listed make interesting day trips, or part-day trips.

■ **Planning multi-centre vacations:** the map on this page shows at a glance all the interesting areas of Australia. Combine them to experience different aspects of the country, or mix them with the overall routes, pages 42-191.

11

Conventions used in this guide

One dollar sign – **$** – or several dollar signs, such as **$$$**, in a hotel or restaurant entry, denotes a price range. Its object is to give an indication of what you can expect to pay.

Bear in mind that accommodation or food offered at any one place may span more than one price range.

Hotels
For a double room for one night in the holiday season:

$	Below A$50
$$	A$50-A$90
$$$	More than A$90

Out of season, prices may drop considerably.
A single room usually costs around two-thirds the price of a double.

Restaurants
A meal for one with an alcoholic drink:

$	Below A$25
$$	A$25-A$60
$$$	More than A$60

Hotels and restaurants
This guide offers a selection of personal recommendations – not exhaustive lists. They have been chosen to represent interest and quality, or to satisfy specific needs, at every price level.

Opening times of restaurants
Most inexpensive restaurants and eateries mentioned in this guide are open all day. Expect minimum hours of 9 am to 9 pm. More expensive restaurants tend to open for lunch and dinner. Expect minimum hours of noon to 2 pm, and 6 pm to 10 pm. Many bars and

⇌ after a heading in **Sights & Places of Interest** means that there is an accommodation suggestion for that place in **Recommended Hotels**.

✕ after a heading in **Sights & Places of Interest** means that there is a suggestion for that place in **Recommended Restaurants**.

licensed hotels only serve dinner between 6 pm and 8 pm.

Unless otherwise stated, restaurants are open seven days a week. Out of season, restaurants sometimes start closing early, take to closing on certain days, and sometimes close altogether. This will often depend upon how business is going.

Opening times of museums and tourist attractions
These vary considerably from place to place, and for this reason are given in the text for every sight where reliable and up-to-date information was available. Even so, it makes sense to enquire at the local tourist office for the times currently in operation.

Distances for routes and tours
These are approximate, and represent the shortest distances you could expect to travel. Since the routes and tours are designed to be travelled in whole, or in part, or indeed not at all, the distances may well be of general interest only.

Credit cards
The most widely recognized cards in Australia are American Express, Diners Club, Master Card and Visa (AE, DC, MC, V). When entries for recommended hotels and restaurants state 'all major cards', it means they accept a *minimum* of these four.

Map legend
↗ after a place name on a map means that the sight or place of interest is covered in detail in another part of the book. Cross references with page numbers are given in the text.

On Australia Overall maps, a **red, blue or green square** by a place name means that sight or place of interest has an entry in the Sights & Places of Interest section. Red means it's a major attraction; blue means it's certainly worth a visit; green means see it if you aren't in a hurry.

■ A **black square** (and no arrow) means that the sight or place of interest is not described in the text and is on the map for orientation only.

Something for everyone

Getting the most from your guide
Here is a *small* selection of ideas for enjoying Australia opened up by this
guide, aimed at a range of needs and tastes. The list is just a start: the guide
offers many, many more ideas for what really matters: suiting yourself. You'll
find that it takes into account not only your tastes, but how much time you
have.

The best surfing in the world
Australia Overall: 7.

One of the world's great railway journeys
Local Explorations: 12.

Meeting the dolphins
Local Explorations: 15.

Dig your own opals
Australia Overall: 6.

The outback, beyond
Local Explorations: 16.

Adventure trails
Local Explorations: 15 *and* 11.

Submarine wonderland
Australia Overall: 9.

Bondi, and Beethoven
Sydney city section.

Gold rush towns
Local Explorations: 4 *and* 12.

Australia:
an introduction

Australia is huge, and utterly different. It's almost as big as the United States, or Europe, yet it has a population of just 16 million – the equivalent of London and Los Angeles together. And most of this 16 million live in suburbs strung out along the one- and-a-half-thousand-kilometre stretch of coast from Adelaide to Brisbane. The interior is vast, but virtually empty. Yet the people who call this wilderness home have been living here in much the same fashion since long before the pyramids were built.

This is a new country, but with a feeling of primeval timelessness at its heart: both elements are part of the Australian heritage. Like the United States, Australia is for the most part a country of immigrants. And like the United States, they have made of their country into something utterly their own. And this is a fitting complement to a land whose geographical isolation has meant that it developed a unique flora and fauna: kangaroos, koala bears, possums, black swans and literally scores of species of exotic birds - the list of uniquely Australian wildlife goes on and on.

To many who live outside Australia, and many who live in it, this is the country of beaches and beer. The 'amber nectar' and the ocean beaches are both famous for their foam, but standing apart from all this froth there are solid - world-class - attractions. The Great Barrier Reef, the Sydney Opera House and Uluru (formerly Ayer's Rock) each, in reality, stunningly surpasses the stereotyped image we have of them from travel brochures.

Then there are Australia's lesser-known attractions. The earliest commercial transport may have been the camel train, but nowadays the continent is crossed by two of the world's greatest train journeys - the Indian Pacific from Sydney to Perth , and the Ghan from Adelaide to Alice Springs.

For years, Aussie chefs were known for little more than inventing peach

Melba and Pavlova cake. Today their work is emerging as the finest in the Southern Hemisphere, with exotic indigenous ingredients including kangaroo and witchety grubs. The influx of New Australians from Southern Europe and South-East Asia has added a touch of exoticism and Mediterranean flare both to the food scene and life generally. Aussie wine now has middle-range vintages comparable with French and Californian counterparts.

Australia is a new country in an ancient setting. It seems to be timeless, yet full of surprises and constantly changing. I first saw Australia in the early 1960s, and each time I go back it continues to astonish me. It was said that anyone who is tired of London is tired of life. Anyone who tires of Australia is tired of living.

Paul Strathern
London, 1996

For overseas visitors

Climate: when to go, and where

The Australian summer begins early in December – Christmas is largely a beach festival. Autumn starts around March, and winter lasts from June to September.

Australia occupies a vast land mass, and straddles several climatic zones – from tropical Darwin in monsoon territory, to cool Tasmania whose climate is similar to that of northern Europe. The desert interior is as hot as the Sahara in summer, and remains pleasantly warm in the winter. Queensland also remains pleasantly warm throughout the year, seldom becoming unbearably hot, even at the height of summer, though it often rains in summer and can get sticky.

Further down the coast, Sydney has agreeably long, hot summers and is seldom chilly in winter. Adelaide is a little warmer, and Melbourne slightly cooler.

On the east coast it rains as much as in Europe, with the heaviest rain in winter. Canberra is up in the mountains: warm enough in summer, but much cooler in winter. Tasmania has slightly cooler summers, but its winters aren't particularly cold. Perth in the west has a microclimate of its own. In summer it's hot, and in winter it's wet and warm. Obviously, the best time for those living in the northern hemisphere to visit Australia is during the northern winter – Australia's summer. But a word of warning: the Australian school summer holidays run from mid-December to the end of January. This is the high season, when prices go up. The popular places tend to be packed.

If you're planning to spend time travelling up north, you should try May, when the dry season starts and the waterfalls are still flowing. Avoid the summer, when the monsoon is on and you can't swim in the sea because of the jellyfish.

	J	F	M	A	M	J	J	A	S	O	N	D
ALICE SPRINGS	33	32	30	25	21	18	18	21	25	29	31	32
BRISBANE	27	27	25	24	22	19	18	20	23	25	26	28
DARWIN	30	30	30	31	30	28	29	30	30	31	31	30
HOBART	20	20	19	15	13	11	10	12	15	17	18	20
PERTH	28	28	25	22	19	17	17	17	18	20	22	25
SYDNEY	23	23	22	20	18	15	15	16	19	20	22	23

These figures are the average maximum temperature in degrees centigrade for each month.

Clothing

Australians tend to dress casually, and only the smartest restaurants require a jacket and tie. It may be hot in the summer, but the weather often goes through abrupt changes, so be sure to bring at least one warm item of clothing. Even in winter, the temperature seldom dips below freezing. But it does rain: be prepared. In the outback, you boil by day and freeze at night, so pack accordingly. You'll also need to take some strong walking shoes if you're planning to trek. Trainers are as useful in Australia as anywhere, but not of course for long walks, or for climbing rocks, or walking over reefs. For the last, sandals are best.

The sun's rays can be exceptionally harmful in Australia. This is said to be because of the country's proximity to the Antarctic hole in the ozone layer. Whether or not that is true, there's no arguing about the effect of the sun. Australia has the highest rate of skin cancer in the world. Even on cloudy days, the rays still get to you. Be sure to pack 15+ sunscreen, and apply it liberally. Take it easy in the sun to begin with, and always reapply your sunscreen after a swim. A broad-brimmed hat gives useful extra protection. Even with all this, you'll probably find a pair of sunglasses useful.

Finally, don't forget the mosquito repellent.

Documentation

All foreign visitors to Australia must have a valid passport. Unless you are a New Zealander, you will also require a visa. Visa application forms can be obtained from your local Australian consulate, embassy or high commission – see the list below. (US visitors can pick up their visas from their local Qantas office, if they fly with that airline.) Three-month visas are issued free; six-month visas cost the equivalent of A$30. (If you think you might stay longer than three months, get a six-month visa before leaving. Extending your visa while you're there will cost you A$200.) All visas are multiple entry, and you will need to show you have a return ticket and enough money to support yourself during your stay, ie A$250 per week minimum.

If you have all your documents with you, you will be able to pick up your visa over the counter. If you apply by post, allow a fortnight *at the least*.

Medical and travel insurance

Medical costs in Australia are not expensive compared with those in Europe or America. Owing to a reciprocal agreement, essential health care is free for citizens of the UK, New Zealand and the Netherlands. But this applies only to *essential* care.

A consultation with a doctor (GP) will cost around A$35. The reciprocal agreement does not apply to dental care. Even if you are covered by the reciprocal agreement *you are strongly advised to buy medical insurance* that will cover the *full* cost of treatment, and the related costs of being flown home.

Medical insurance can be obtained at almost all travel agents, and also at airports. Cover should include medical bills, travel tickets, loss of property, driving accidents and personal injury.

AUSTRALIAN EMBASSIES

Canada Suite 710, 50 O'Connor Street, Ottowa K1P 6L2; tel. (613) 236 0841. Also Toronto and Vancouver.

Germany Godesberger Allee 107, 5300 Bonn 1; tel. (0228) 810 30. Also Berlin and Frankfurt.

Ireland Fitzwilton House, Wilton Terrace, Dublin 2; tel. (01) 76 15 17.

Netherlands Carnegielaan 12, 2517 KH The Hague; tel. (070) 310 82 00.

Switzerland 29 Alpenstrasse, Berne; tel. (031) 43 01 43. Also Geneva.

United Kingdom Australia House, Strand, London WC2B 4LA; tel. (0171) 379 4334.

USA 1601 Massachusetts Avenue NW, Washington DC 20036; tel. (202) 797 3000. Also Chicago, Honolulu, Houston, Los Angeles, New York and San Francisco.

Also, some credit and payment cards operate insurance schemes if you use them to buy your tickets. You won't be able to claim from your insurance company unless you have irrefutable documentary evidence to support your claim. Also, in case of accident or theft, a local police report on the matter is usually essential.

Money

The currency is the Australian dollar, which is abbreviated to $ or, as in this guide, to A$. There are 100 cents to A$1.

Currency comes in the form of A$5, A$10, A$20, A$50 and A$100 bills. Each of these is clearly marked and has a different colour. There are also plastic notes for A$5 and A$10. Coins come as 5 cents, 10 cents, 20 cents, 50 cents, A$1 and A$2.

The wisest way to carry large amounts of money is, of course, in travellers' cheques. These can be exchanged at banks and most post offices. Hotels and tourist offices also change traveller's cheques, but they usually give you a worse rate. It's best to have your traveller's cheques in Australian dollars. British pound and American dollar traveller's cheques are widely acceptable, but you'll need to go to a bank to turn other currencies into Australian cash.

Credit or payment cards are very useful when hiring a car – they are accepted in lieu of a cash deposit. They are also widely accepted in restaurants and hotels. The most widely recognized cards in Australia are American Express, Diners Club, MasterCard (Access) and Visa. See also Conventions used in this guide, page 12.

Import and export

Anyone over 18 may bring into Australia 200 cigarettes (or 250 gms of tobacco or cigars) and 1 litre of alcohol. Otherwise it's mainly common sense. You can't bring in guns or weapons, and don't even think about bringing in even the smallest amount of dope. The customs are also hot on plants which can carry agricultural pests and diseases. This may even be extended to that marvellous ethnic wicker basket which you picked up in an oriental market *en route*, and will certainly apply to any fruit which you intended to eat on the plane.

Local customs: what to expect, how to behave

Australians tend to be easy-going and informal. They pride themselves on their 'matiness'. This means that it's usually easy to strike up a conversation – and you'll learn more about Australia from such friendly chance encounters than any guide book could ever tell you. However, a word of warning. The one thing an Aussie can't stand is being patronised. A superior attitude – whether social, cultural or financial – is quickly sniffed out, and equally quickly put in its place. Poms (the English) are sometimes assumed to be offensive by their mere accent. Others sometimes feel pity for this deprived breed. In such situations it's always best to stress the positive aspects of your reaction to Australia. Any hint of a whinge at once puts you in a stereotyped social category from which it's very difficult to escape.

Australia is, in general, a very liberal and tolerant country. A rich cultural mix, homosexuality, New Age lifestyles and even suburban attitudes are all part of the contemporary Australian scene.

However, racial and sexual intolerance are not unknown. And in the outback you will sometimes encounter social attitudes from the Neolithic era. Especially if you are female, tread warily on entering a local hotel in the outback. The machismo attitude towards drink and sport sometimes extends towards women too. Like their male counterparts, Aussie women tend to be a self-reliant, independent breed – but on occasion you'll find they have to put up with behaviour which falls a long way short of political correctness.

A few words of Strine

'Strine' derives from the way many Australians pronounce the word 'Australian'.

Abo	insulting term for an Aborigine
Amber fluid	Beer (also amber nectar)
Arvo	Afternoon
Banana Bender	Queenslander
Barrack	Cheer on (opposite sense to normal English usage)
Bludger	Someone who doesn't pull their weight, or buy their round of drinks
Blue	A fight, or redhead
BYOB	Bring your own bottle of wine or beer (to a restaurant)
Chunder	Vomit
Come the raw prawn	Have on, deceive
Cozzie	Swimming costume
Crook	Ill
Didgeridoo	Aborigine musical instrument
Decko	Look at
Dinkum	Honest, okay
Dunny	Outdoor lavatory
Esky	Large portable insulated container for keeping beer cold
G'day	'Good day', archetypal Aussie greeting
Gubba	Aborigine word for white person
Jackeroo	Male worker on a sheep or cattle station
Koori	The Aborigine people of south-eastern Australia
Larrikin	Young hooligan
Ocker	Boorish Aussie
Pashing	Kissing, fondling
Perv fashion	Gaze at in a lustful
Pom	Person of English descent
Piss turn	Drinking party
Rollies	Roll-your-own cigarettes
Root	To have sex
Shout	To pay for a round of drinks
Tall poppies	High achievers
Tucker	Food
Sheila	Woman (a word of doubtful political correctness)
Snag	Sausage
Schooner	Large beer glass
Shellacking	Heavy defeat
Station farm	Large cattle or sheep
Sticky beak	Nosey person
Stubby	Small bottle of beer
Walkabout	Missing
Wowser	Party pooper
Whinge	Complain (as in whingeing pom)
Yakka	Work

Getting there

By air

There are two dozen airlines at present flying into Australia. This is a highly competitive route, and you can now get better value in real terms than at almost any time in the past.

The two main entry cities are Sydney and Melbourne, though frequent international flights also arrive at Perth and Brisbane, and others at Hobart and Darwin. Most flights from Europe take a little over 20 hours (what with stops and refuelling). Direct flights from the US West Coast take around 15 hours. There's a huge range of different flights on offer, involving all kinds of stopovers. From Europe you can stop over in the United States, Canada, South America or Hawaii, if you fly westwards. Flying the other way round the world offers even more choice, ranging from Greece and Egypt to Russia, India and South-East Asia. You can also fly out one way, and back the other, on a round-the-world ticket.

There's a wide price range too. The better-known airlines specializing in routes to Australia (such as Qantas, British Airways, Lufthansa and United) tend to be the most expensive. But they also offer the best stopover deals. If you're travelling from Europe and you want a bargain, London is your best bet. Try looking in the small ads, travel sections of the listings magazines or one of the free Australian weeklies (usually available in bars frequented by Aussies). Or ring round the discount flight specialists. In the northern hemisphere spring and early summer, prices sometimes plummet as low as £600 from London to Australia. At other times expect to pay around £200 more for your bargain deal. But if you want to fly around Christmas time, forget about the bargains. This is when the planes are fully booked, and the airlines can ask *real* prices. Expect to pay more than £1,000 and be sure to book well ahead if you want to travel any time during the first two weeks in December.

The cheapest time to travel to Australia from America is during the northern hemisphere summer. Return fares start from around US$1,000 (San Francisco and Los Angeles) and US$2,000 (New York). You can usually get considerable reductions on standard airline prices at discount specialists. Look in the travel sections of any of the main Sunday papers.

There are regular flights from New Zealand to all of Australia's major east coast cities. The best bargains from the discount specialists are around NZ$650 return.

Other ways to Australia

Some drive overland from Europe, through South-East Asia; a few hitch this route; and some have even been known to cycle it. If you're planning to enter either of these exalted categories of traveller, good luck, and be sure to have a long talk with someone who *has* made such a trip.

GETTING AROUND

Australia is 3,000 km from north to south and 4,000 km wide. Public transport in Australia is extensive, but only links the main areas of population and the main tourist spots. Off the beaten track (and most of Australia falls into this category) the only way to get around is by car or hitching.

Railway

The Australian national railway system started life as a monument to colonial planning. In the days when each state was a separate colony, each one applied to London for permission to build its own railway. Permission was duly granted by the Colonial Office, and each state eagerly set about entering the Railway Age. Only when the states joined together to become one nation at the turn of the 20thC was it discovered that each railway had an entirely different gauge from all the others. The Australian network has yet to recover from this feat of perversity. Indeed, until the 1970s, passengers travelling from Sydney to Melbourne still had to get up in the middle of the night and change trains at the state border. And Queensland railways north of Brisbane still run on a different gauge.

Railways (all with the same gauge) now connect all the state capitals and main cities, with the exception of Hobart (which is in Tasmania) and Darwin (which is in the middle of nowhere).

There's also a fairly extensive network of local services. You can travel First Class or Economy, and the XTP expresses reach all of 160 kph. Other trains can be much less fast, in fact, there's no denying it, Australian trains are slow. Indeed, some claim that rail travel in Australia is more a way of getting to meet people than a form of transport.

However, the trains are fairly comfortable: long-distance trains have air-conditioning, sleeping berths and (usually) restaurant cars. (If not, besieged buffet cars are the order of the day amongst those not wise enough to bring their own rations.)

But there is one thing about the Australian railway system that makes it the envy of most railways in the world: its very own Great Epic Journey. This is the famous Indian Pacific, which runs coast to coast from Sydney to Perth; and according to the railway buffs offers one of the greatest railway journeys in the world. It runs through the picturesque Blue Mountains, as well as calling at some of Australia's famous old mining towns such as Kalgoorlie and Broken Hill. Others consider this passage through endless wilderness, with fellow passengers it's impossible to get away from, to be one of the most physically and mentally disabling experiences on Earth. It also contains the longest stretch of continuously straight track in the world: 459 km across the numbing Nullarbor Plain. In fact, the journey is an odd mixture of the sublime

• *Regular internal flights connect Australia's major cities.*

and the soporific. But when you finally make it to your destination the sense of achievement (or relief) may well outweigh any other feeling you may have experienced during the past three days. (Unless, like a Sydney pal of mine, during the course of your journey you have managed to lose one wife and meet up with your next one.) Yes, it will have been three days (and 4,348 km) since you waved farewell to reality.

An almost equally epic journey is the Ghan, which runs from Adelaide to Alice Springs. This is named after the Ghan camel drivers who accompanied Burke and Wills on their early expedition into the interior almost a century and a half ago. In all, the journey is around half as long as the Indian Pacific endurance test.

If you want to submit yourself to the rigours of the Indian Pacific or the Ghan, be sure to reserve well ahead as they're often block-booked. It's always worth booking ahead, even if you're only travelling on an interstate express. And when it comes to rail travel in Queensland, be sure to reserve as soon as you even *think* about travelling – you may even need to reserve a month ahead.

Trains are slightly more expensive than buses, and often not much faster, but they are more comfortable. There are some worthwhile ticket deals for

• Cruise ship port of call, Sydney.

overseas visitors. An **Austrail Pass** allows you to travel over an extended period for a limited cost. Passes run from a fortnight to three months, allowing unlimited travel. A 14-day economy-class pass is A$435; the 90-day pass runs to A$1,125.

A perhaps more convenient bargain is the **Austrail Flexipass**, which allows you eight days of travel within a 60-day period, or 15 days' travel within 90 days. These cost A$320 and A$475 respectively.

A **Kangaroo Pass** allows you to combine rail and bus travel. If you use these passes to travel on trains such as the Indian-Pacific or the Ghan, you'll have to pay a surcharge for a sleeping berth and compulsory meals. You have to purchase these passes at home *before* you set out for Australia. Get the details from your local travel agent.

Bus

This is the cheapest form of public transport, and its extensive services cover much more of the ground than railways. Services are frequent and regular. There are a number of different bus companies, which cover different parts of the country, but this won't involve you in too much complexity: almost all stopping places have just the one bus terminal, out of which all services operate.

The fastest and most frequent bus services operate up and down the east coast, linking anywhere between Melbourne and Cairns. Competition is fierce, and there are occasional price wars. At such times, tickets are sometimes sold at give-away prices.

The railways don't have a monopoly on epic journeys. The western route between Perth and Darwin takes 60 hours and passes through some of the most remote territory in Australia. Even so, you'll be glad of the videos. (Yes, you've come all this way to see *Crocodile Dundee* AGAIN.) Other features of long-distance Aussie bus trips include numb bum, singing drivers and old codgers suffering from verbal incontinence (who always get the seat next to you). A 500-page Patrick White novel (preferably *Voss*), and earplugs, can turn an endurance test into a memorable experience. (The scenery beyond the window illuminates that in the book, and your infrequent conversations with your neighbour ensure that this sublime experience has its essential added ingredient of the ridiculous.)

There's a wide range of bus passes available, but these don't cover all the bus companies. The best is an **Aussie Pass**, which covers the three main interstate companies. The typical price for an Aussie Pass is A$840 for three weeks.

The buses may have an extensive network, but they're not the ideal way to explore remoter territory. If you want some first-hand experience of the outback other than through a bus window, you should try a **minibus** tour. This is very much a growth industry, and all kinds of opportunities are opening up. Typical is a two- to three-day trip in a minibus with around a dozen others. This can either be a tour (where you end up at the same place you started) or a trip (which takes longer than normal between two points, with time to explore). The deal usually includes food and accommodation. Your friendly tour-leader/driver is invariably a fund of fascinating anecdote, local lore and sheer rubbish. Even misanthropes and Patrick White readers will find these great fun. One driver I know even offers you a chance to ride in a balloon, and another is said to offer you a chance to learn how to navigate your way through the wilderness by smell.

If you want to hire a four-wheel-drive vehicle, you'll need to be over 25. Otherwise 21 is the usual age limit. There are a few 'rent-a-wreck' firms where you can pick up a car for only A$20 a day, but these are obviously not so reliable. (A serious consideration, if there's only cousin Ebenezer around to fix your busted gasket.) That old Aussie stand-by, the camper van, can also be hired – for around A$1,000 a week. Third-party insurance and the collision damage waiver are usually included in the price, but be sure to check this *before* you drive off.

Your home driving licence is valid for 12 months' driving in Australia. Petrol usually around 70c per litre, but really remote petrol stations often charge substantially more. The roads in Australia are not too bad between the main

• *The Adelaide to Glenelg tram.*

Car hire

The best way to see Australia is undoubtedly by car. This enables you to see places and people beyond the reach of public transport, and far from civilization – such as the ghost mining towns or cousin Ebenezer. The main international car hire firms – such as Hertz, Avis and Budget – all have offices in major cities and at the airports. Rates are not cheap (around A$80 per day for a small car), but you can save if you hire for a long period. In some cases, it's possible to bargain. It will cost you an extra A$200 if you want to drop the car off at a different place from where you hired it.

centres of civilization, but after that you must be prepared to expect *anything*. Many of the outlying roads and tracks aren't as awful as you might imagine. On the other hand, some have to be seen to be believed. Be sure to ask before setting off into the wide blue yonder down something that *looks* okay on the map. If you're setting out for some remote spot, be sure you have enough fuel, water and food for an emergency. If you're going somewhere *really* remote, tell someone before leaving – so that they can contact rescue services if you don't show up at your destination. One of the worst hazards on the track roads is corrugation – which can go on for miles. This can shake bits out of your car long before it shakes out your false teeth, so drive slowly. In fact, when on tracks, *always* drive slowly. Other hazards to watch out for are potholes (always invisible until the very last moment) and floods (which can turn the remote wilderness on your map into a veritable sea).

Kangaroos can also be a problem, especially at night when they often freeze in the headlights. Though something with even less road sense is that archetypal character who's just driven into town to fill up his tank, and is now fully tanked up and on his way home to a rough ride from the missus. The Aussie authorities have introduced a fierce campaign against drink-driving, but it still accounts for a frighteningly large number of road deaths each year. The random breath test is a popular hobby for the police, and if you've drunk more than the equivalent of one beer you'll make their day.

Otherwise, the rules of the road in Australia are much the same as in Europe or America – except that they drive on the left (assuming the road offers this luxury). Seat belts have to be worn by all drivers, including back-seat ones. One local feature to watch out for: drivers coming on to a road from the right often have priority. Watch out for that pick-up truck coming on to the main road from the dirt track on your right – if he's got priority, you can be sure he'll use it.

The speed limits are marked in kilometres. The limit in most built-up areas is 60 kph. Out on the open road, it's 100 kph. Speed traps are another popular police hobby, and they now have them down to a fine art.

If you're in open country, you'll find much of the traffic exceeding the low limit. If a car coming the other way flashes its lights at you, they're warning you there's a speed trap up ahead. (It's not unknown for a disgruntled driver who's fallen foul of a speed trap to set up a notice warning oncoming drivers.)

Taxis

Empty taxis have a lit-up 'vacant' sign or a light showing on the roof. You can hail one, pick one up at a rank, or book by phone. (You may have to pay a surcharge for the latter.) There are ranks outside most airports, big city bus and railway stations, and by smart hotels. You won't find many cabs cruising outside big city centres. Prices vary, but expect to pay arounnd A$10 for a 5-mile trip. Prices are usually higher at night and at weekends. You'll also have to pay extra for luggage.

Aussie taxi drivers are much the same as those the world over – cussed individualists who are often a mine of fascinating local information and high-octane prejudice. And they can even be helpful, sometimes.

Boat

The only regular boat service (other than local ferries) is the car ferry which runs between Melbourne and Tasmania. This takes around 14 hours and is usually a rough crossing. Unless you're taking a car, it's not worth it – the cheapest ticket is only slightly less than the air fare.

Air

Internal air travel in Australia is quite a bit more expensive than train or bus. But owing to its speed, and the vast distances involved, air is by far the best way to travel if you want to see a fair amount of the whole country.

Through some magic of accountancy, APEX return fares are usually slightly cheaper than single fares. Fares vary, and if you try discount specialists, you may get a bargain. Recent deregulation and the ensuing price wars have resulted in the occasional spectacular reductions (as well as the occasional spectacular airline bankruptcy). At present, booking ahead is the name of the game if you want the greatest reductions. By booking a week in advance you can often save as much as 30 to 40 per cent. Also, if you're not an Australian resident, Qantas will give you a 30 to 40 per cent reduction on all Qantas internal flights if you show your international ticket when booking. Amazingly, this doesn't even have to be a Qantas international ticket. And you can use this offer for as many flights as

• *Filling up before setting out.*

you want. The snag? Your reduction is calculated against the full economy fare – which often means you can still get a cheaper discount ticket elsewhere.

In general, from Sydney to Perth expect to pay between A$450 and $A500. From Sydney to Alice Springs is usually A$25 or so cheaper. Sydney to Brisbane usually costs A$250 to A$200. Expect to pay around A$600 for a flight from Sydney to Darwin, and half this for a flight to Hobart.

There are regular flights connecting all the major Australian cities. This means that cities such as Perth or Brisbane all have at least half a dozen main routes to other cities inside Australia. There's also an extensive route network covering out-of-the-way places, but these tend to use small planes and are relatively expensive.

Internal air flights in Australia are almost invariably non-smoking throughout all seats.

Bicycle

The big cities have several bike rental agencies, and miles of cycling tracks. The country roads are good for cycling too, with little traffic and few hills. You can also load your bike on to most long-distance buses, trains and even internal air flights – usually for a small charge. But be sure to make enquiries about these arrangements when booking your ticket.

Bike helmets are compulsory in Australia.

Hitching

There are two schools of thought about hitching. One says: don't ever. The other firmly maintains that this is one of the best ways to get around, particularly in remote parts.

As usual, both have a point. The recent horrific serial-killer case (all the victims were foreign hitchers, all were buried in the bush) has strengthened the 'never do it' lobby. Women should certainly never hitch alone, and women in pairs should be careful. Also, for some reason, Queensland has a rather poor record of interference with hitchers, especially off the beaten track. That said, hitching can be great in Australia. Drivers are usually friendly, genuinely interested in foreign travellers, and willing to be of assistance to anyone who tells a few yarns (and, inevitably, is willing to listen to rather more). It's not unusual to make genuine friendships on the road in Australia, with people inviting you into their homes and passing on the addresses of mates further down the road. (A capacity for the amber fluid is usually an essential ingredient of such friendships, which are quite likely to be re-activated in a few years time by a return visit, so be prepared.)

By far the best way to arrange a lift is via a youth-hostel noticeboard. This often enables you to fix up surprisingly long lifts but you will have to share the cost of petrol.

Essential practical information

• York Hotel, Kalgoorlie.

Accommodation

In the old days an Australian 'hotel' meant the pub. By law, such hotels also had to have a room where worse-for-wear customers could sleep it off. Room service was provided by a barman dragging you upstairs, and your alarm call was the reverse process which ended in the street in the morning. Not surprisingly, the standard of such accommodation was not the management's main concern. This tradition is still very much alive in Australia, though many such Australian 'hotels' have dispensed with rooms. (Room service now takes place without having to go upstairs.)

Such spots are known as 'licensed' hotels. What you are looking for is known as a 'private' hotel, a guesthouse or a motel.

The Aussies are great travellers, which means there will usually be somewhere to stay no matter where you end up. Even quite small centres of population will have a motel and a campsite on the edge of town, and the central 'hotel' (see above) will provide basic rooms.

Motels are fairly uniform – providing a standard double room with TV and bath for around A$60. In some cases, you'll find one for almost half this price, but such bargains are rare. The price does not include breakfast. In a motel a single room will cost around the same as a double. This is not the case with the small hotels in town and city centres, whose basic rooms are often singles. The price for a single here is around A$30, and expect to pay half as much again for a double. You'll usually have to share a bathroom. Some serve breakfast, some don't. If they do serve breakfast, it's usually good and big.

The same is true of guest houses and private hotels, whose prices are also around A$30 for a single.

If you're looking for somewhere to stay, a sensible place to start is the local bus station. Here there are often direct-dial phones to hotels, or someone behind the counter has a list of places to stay.

There are also modern chain hotels all over the country. As usual, these range from the moderately priced to the laughably overpriced. A medium-range three-star hotel double will cost you around A$120. Choose your amount of stars according to your sense of humour. Big city hotels of this type tend to be rather more expensive than those at holiday resorts. Some of the hotel chains offer attractive deals, as long as you stay at their hotels wherever you go; in fact wherever you stay, the price will drop considerably if you stay for a week.

Apart from smart hotels, there are also resorts. Or at least, they call themselves resorts. In fact, an inexpensive resort is just the same as a motel. The further upmarket you go, the more these resorts resemble their American originals – with some in spectacular settings. Facilities abound, and the bill leaps accordingly. Indeed, some of the luxury resorts on the islands off the Queensland coast are among the finest (and most expensive) millionaires' paradises in the world.

Out in the country, many farms often run bed-and-breakfasts. These are friendly spots, and the breakfast is enough to keep a weightlifter lifting for a week.

A good budget bet in cities is to try one of the colleges. (This only works during the university vacation, of course.) As you'd expect, travelling students get priority (and also pay half price). If there's a vacancy, expect to pay around A$30 for a pleasant basic room and breakfast – the latter is an opportunity for meeting up with people and swapping information.

In holiday areas especially, you'll also find self-catering units. They cover the entire range, beginning at basic cabins. Off-season, you can sometimes get a very good bargain here if you're prepared to do some humorous haggling.

Banks and currency exchange

The best exchange rates are at the

• *Kangaroo Island.*

banks. These are open Monday to Friday 9.30 am to 4 pm, with some extension of these hours in big cities. But just to keep you on your toes, the foreign exchange counter usually closes down at around 3. Bureaux de change are few and far between, but you can usually find somewhere at an airport to change your money or traveller's cheques.

Small centres of population in the outback usually have an Agency, which handles bank business. Though they're not always willing to exchange foreign currency, and anything too obscure will be greeted with extreme suspicion. Years ago I stopped at such a spot with a Belgian friend, who was earnestly assured that his Belgian Franc notes were cunning forgeries as no such currency existed.

Beaches

Australia has more miles of sandy beaches than the whole of Europe. Popular beaches such as Bondi and Manly in Sydney, and Queensland's Gold Coast attract the crowds, but this still leaves miles and miles of unspoiled deserted beach. Surfing is a national obsession, and local radio stations give the state of the surf in their bulletins. But beware of surfing (or swimming) in deserted spots. The surf can be rough, and is likely to have a heavy undertow. If there's no one around swimming or

surfing, there's often a good reason for this.

On the beaches in northern Queensland this reason will often be box jellyfish. These are vicious stingers that can kill you – and by the time you see them you're already being stung by their tendrils, which stretch for metres under the surface. So be sure to ask about what you're likely to find, before plunging into the ocean.

On a happier note, the lifeguards on Australian beaches are said to be the best-looking in the world – according to a recent international survey conducted by students at the University of California (where else?). Those whose object of desire is not a lump of muscle-bound Australian male will probably be pleased to learn that an increasing number of Australian women sunbathe topless these days. Sydney and Perth now even have designated nudist beaches, where those of both sexes can pretend they're not looking.

Beer

Australian beer is of the lager (or pils) type – the celebrated 'amber fluid' that features so frequently in Aussie folklore, songs, conversation, daydreams etc, etc. Beer drinking is like breathing for many Aussies: they are convinced that they'd die without it. Like breath-

27

• *Ettamogah Pub, near Brisbane.*

ing, it has to be done regularly. And after a few days in Australia you'll probably find that you too subscribe to this world view. Australia can be hot, and having a thirst soon becomes part of the human condition.

Aussies drink their beer ice cold. They also go to great pains to keep it that way (until they, or the beer, get drunk). No trip to the beach is properly equipped without a cooler (usually a polystyrene container) packed with ice-cold tinnies or stubbies (cans or bottles).

Aussie beer is mainly around 5 per cent proof – much the same strength as German beer or strong lager in Britain, but stronger than American beer. And for those who don't know about these things: there's more to Aussie beer than just Fosters. Australia has regional beers the way the world has religions. Those who worship one beer would consider it blasphemous to down any other than their own. The famous f-four X (XXXX for those who can't spell) comes from Queensland, Swan from Western Australia and Tooheys from New South Wales. Most other Aussie beers are unheard of outside the country – for the simple reason that the locals have drunk it all before it could be exported. You'll also find draught Guinness in the Irish pubs – where this dark liquid provides a similar service to a blood transfusion.

Pubs and bars are usually open from 11 am to 11 pm. There are regional variations, and hours tend to be somewhat shorter on Sundays.

Breakdowns

In an emergency, dial 000. This is free, and will put you in contact with the police, fire service or ambulance service.

In case of lesser difficulties, you'll probably want to contact one of the motoring organizations.

The Australian Automobile Association is affiliated to the American AAA, and the RAC and AA of Britain, as well as several other similar large automobile associations worldwide. The Australian Automobile Association has sub-branches (with different names) in each state. These are:

Australian Capital Territory: National Road and Motorists' Association; tel. (06) 243 8944.

Queensland: Royal Automobile Club of Queensland; tel. (07) 361 2444.

New South Wales: National Road and Motorists' Association; tel. (02) 260 9222.

Northern Territory: Automobile Association of Northern Territory; tel. (089) 813 837.

South Australia: Royal Automobile Association of South Australia; tel. (08) 202 4500.

Tasmania: Royal Automobile Club of Tasmania; tel. (002) 382 200.

Western Australia: Royal Automobile Association of Western Australia; tel. (09) 421 4444.

Victoria: Royal Automobile Club of Victoria; tel. (03) 607 2137.

Most car hire firms have an emergency number you can ring. This will be displayed on the dashboard of your hire car, or in your folder of documents.

If you break down miles from any phone, try and flag down a passing vehicle. If you're miles from anywhere and there are no passing vehicles, you're still best off staying by your car. This way you have shade, and whatever water and rations you brought with you. If you get desperate, try lighting a tyre. The Australian authorities are understandably paranoid about bush fires, and the sight of smoke rising on the horizon in some deserted spot usually has someone on the scene fairly sharpish. But make sure you don't start your own bush fire – otherwise the rescue services may find they have more important things to do than look after you.

Credit cards
See Conventions used in this guide, page 12.

Cuisine
For years, Australian cooking suffered from the English disease. The aim of all cooks was to reduce food to a taste-less mush. Luckily, this has now large-ly changed. Australian food has some of the finest ingredients you could wish for. Steaks are great, and the seafood is superb. The Aussies also have a few specialities of their own – such as kan-garoo, crocodile and camel. Those who claim to be truly adventurous should test out their nerve on witchetty grubs. Once a mainstay of Aboriginal diet, these small larvae have now started appearing in gourmet restaurants. More to most tastes are carpetbagger steaks – steak stuffed with oysters.

The post-war arrival of continental European immigrants brought about a revolution in the Aussie restaurant scene. Italian and Greek food, Slav dishes and Asian cuisine are now wide-ly available in all main cities, and have begun to spread even further afield.

Eating out in Australia is fairly inex-pensive, and this is helped by the many BYO restaurants. Here you Bring Your Own bottle of wine, barrel of beer or whathaveyou.

Departure tax
As you'll often find, many hospitable Australians don't want you to leave. Unfortunately, this friendly Aussie trait has now become bureaucratized: meaning that everyone over the age of 12 leaving the country must pay a tax of A$20. So don't spend it all on that final farewell party.

Electricity
Australian electricity runs at 240 volts, 50 hertz AC. This is the same as in Britain and most of Europe, but not the same as in America. Plugs are three pin, and you'll need an adaptor – which can be bought at any main city electri-cal store, or sometimes at shops which cater for tourists. If in doubt, ask at your hotel desk.

Embassies and consulates
All the main embassies and high com-missions are in the capital, Canberra. Many countries also have consulates in Sydney and other state capitals. As is often the way with diplomats, these all have varying opening hours, and take holidays (national and Australian) at the slightest opportunity. Except on these holidays, you can usually rely on any embassy being open at least between 10 am and noon on weekdays. Most have slightly longer hours in the morn-ing. Some open after lunch and siesta, others don't bother. After all, as diplo-mats are always explaining: they're not here to look after the likes of us (even if it is us who pay them). They have far more important things to do (most of which are either cocktail parties or much too secret to mention).

Austria Embassy: 12 Talbot Street, Forrest, Canberra; tel. (06) 295 1533.

Canada High Commission: Com-monwealth Avenue, Yarralumla, Can-berra; tel. (06) 273 3844. Consulate: 111 Harrington Street, Syd-ney; tel. (02) 364 3050.

Germany Embassy: 119 Empire Court, Yarralumla, Canberra; tel. (06) 270 1911.

Ireland Embassy: 20 Arkana St, Yarralumla, Canberra; tel. (06) 273 3022.

Netherlands Embassy: 120 Empire Circuit, Yarralumla, Canberra; tel. (06) 273 3111.

New Zealand High Commission: Commonwealth Avenue, Yarralumla, Canberra; tel. (06) 270 4211. Con-sulate: 1 Alfred Street, Circular Quay, Sydney; tel. (02) 247 1999.

Switzerland Embassy: 7 Melbourne Avenue, Forrest, Canberra; tel. (06) 273 3977.

UK High Commission: Common-wealth Avenue, Yarralumla, Canberra; tel. (06) 270 6666. Consulate: Gate-way Plaza, 1 Macquairie Place, Sydney; tel. (02) 247 9731.

US Embassy: 21 Moonah Place, Yarralumla, Canberra; tel. (06) 270 5000. Consulate: 19-29 Martin Place, Sydney; tel. (02) 234 9200.

Byron Bay telephones, New South Wales.

Emergencies

In case of any emergency, the number to ring is 000.

Measurements

Australia converted to the metric system 20 years ago, though many people still use imperial measures when referring to their height or weight (ie 'I'm 6 ft tall and weigh 10 stone' means 'I'm 1.8 m tall and weigh 63.5 kg.')

Australian dress and shoe sizes are different from those in America and continental Europe. Rather than attempt any complex calculations, your best bet is to try on anything before buying it.

1 litre =   1.76 pints (UK) or 1.5 pints (US).
1 kilogram (1,000 grams) = 2.2 lb.
1 kilometre (1,000 metres) = 0.62 miles. To convert kilometres to miles, multiply by five and divide by eight, and vice versa.
1 metre =   3.28 feet.
1 hectare = 2.5 acres.

National holidays

Australia has many national holidays, some of which only apply in certain states. If a holiday falls on a weekend, a day's holiday is usually added – sometimes before the weekend, sometimes after (be sure to check).

• January 1 (New Year's Day).
• First Monday after January 26 (Australia Day).

• First or second Monday in March (Labour Day) – Victoria.
• Second Monday in March (Labour Day) – Western Australia.
• Good Friday and Easter Monday – also Tuesday after Easter in Victoria.
• April 25 (Anzac Day).
• First Monday in May (Labour Day) – Queensland.
• May 1 (May Day) – Northern Territory.
• Third Monday in May (Adelaide Cup) – South Australia.
• First Monday in June (Foundation Day) – Western Australia.
• Second Monday in June (Queen's Birthday) – Queensland, Northern Territory, Victoria.
• First Monday in August (Bank Holiday) – New South Wales.
• First Monday in August (Picnic Day) – Northern Territory.
• First Monday in October (Queen's Birthday) – Western Australia.
•] First Monday in October (Labour Day) – New South Wales, Southern Australia, Australian Commonwealth Territory.
• First Tuesday in November (Melbourne Cup) – Victoria.
• December 25 (Christmas Day).
• December 26 (Boxing Day).

Opening hours

Most shops and businesses in Australia are open between 9 am and 5 pm on weekdays. Many shops have a late night closing (around 9 pm) once a week (usually Thursday or Friday). On

Saturdays shops tend to open at 9 am and close any time between noon and 5 pm. Some shops open on Sundays in tourist spots.

Banks are open 9.30 am to 4 pm Mondays to Fridays. Many stay open until 5 pm on Fridays. In big cities some central branches are open 8 am to 6 pm.

Telephones

IMPORTANT: Owing to the introduction of new technology, Australia is at present overhauling its telephone number system. You may find two extra digits added to the number you wish to dial. Be sure to ask before you dial. In case of difficulty, ring for free details on AUSTEL's information hotline: 1800 888 888.

You can make an international call from most public phones. For an international line dial 0011, followed by your country code, then the telephone number you require (minus the initial 0). Be sure to have a phonecard or a stack of coins ready.

A call to the US or to Europe will cost you approximately A$1.70 per minute at the standard rate, and A$1.30 at the cheaper off-peak rate (during the evening and weekends).

There are a number of new systems operating, including one that enables you to dial an operator in your own country, and one where you can reverse the charges (pay collect), or pay by credit card. For details of these, which now operate to most major countries, see the phone book.

Before you ring, be sure to check the time back home. (See last paragraphs of Time zones, below.)

Time zones

Australia has three separate time zones. Eastern Standard Time oper-

Time zones

ates in Tasmania, Victoria, New South-Wales and Queensland. Central Standard Time is half an hour earlier than this, and operates in South Australia and Northern Territory. Western Standard Time is an hour and a half earlier than CST and operates in Western Australia. This means that when it's noon in Sydney, it's only 11.30 am in Adelaide, and 10 am in Perth.

Australian Eastern Standard Time is nine hours ahead of Continental European Time, ten hours ahead of Greenwich Mean Time (UK), and 15 hours ahead of US Eastern Time.

Now comes the difficult bit. Owing to the rugged individuality of each Australian state, the Daylight Saving Times operated by the different states vary. (Eg Western Australia and Queensland don't add on the hour at all, and others add it in at different times.) Add to this the confusion of European and UK Daylight Saving Times (which of course don't exactly coincide) and the full can of worms becomes apparent. Remember, these little local difficulties can make a difference of up to two hours on the simple calculations in the preceding paragraph. If you wish to ring home at a precise time, consult a local mathematical genius. Otherwise, just accept the fact that you're bound to ring in the middle of the football match.

Tipping

Australia is one of those rare countries where few people expect a tip. If you're feeling generous, and the service has been unusually attentive, round up your bill to the nearest dollar, or leave your loose change. Some smarter restaurants now expect 10 per cent, but taxi drivers will sometimes round your bill down.

Some international dialling codes from Australia:	
Austria	43
Canada	1
Germany	40
Irish Republic	353
Netherlands	31
UK	44
US	1

A brief history of Australia

The Aborigine era

The first human beings probably arrived in Australia around 40,000 years ago. They crossed in migrant waves over the shallow seas which then divided Australia from Indonesia and mainland Asia. Not until around 12,000 years ago did the sea levels rise, stabilizing the present geographical formation of the region.

The Aborigines were a Stone Age people of hunter-gatherers, who developed a unique way of life in the isolation of the Australian subcontinent. Only recently has the full richness of this apparently primitive culture been realized. Over thousands of years, the Aborigines spread across this vast inhospitable territory, following the river systems of the interior. They tended to move in extended families and clans, which gradually developed their own separate identities and languages. Isolation meant that these languages often changed much from their original forms as the population multiplied and spread. By the time Australia was 'discovered' by the Europeans, it is estimated that there were more than 300,000 Aborigines spread out over the entire continent, speaking as many as 300 different languages. These languages could be as disparate as Arabic is from English: the tribes who lived on either side of what is now Sydney Harbour were unable to understand each other.

Yet ties joining the different tribes reached way back into the earliest migrant past. A complex pattern of trading links had long been established – for the exchange of shells and stones of ritual significance, as well as commodities such as ochre and boomerangs. And underlying this network of trading links across the vast distances of the unmapped continent was a more mysterious verbal map of songlines. These traditional memories, passed from generation to generation within families and tribes, provided an intricate map and mythology of the entire continent. The songlines linked natural landmarks, as well as recount-

KEY DATES

Arrival of first human beings in Australia	about 38,000 BC
Australia first 'discovered' by the Portuguese	early 16thC
Spanish explorer Torres sails through Torres Strait	1606
Dampier reaches Australia	1680s
Captain Cook maps eastern coast	1770
First convict shipment arrives under Captain Arthur Phillip	1787
First voluntary immigrants arrive from Britain	1820s
Eyre expedition leaves Adelaide to explore interior	1840
Transportation of criminals from Britain ceases	1853
Burke and Wills expedition attempts north–south crossing	1860
Australians win the Ashes	1882
Commonwealth of Australia formed	January 1, 1901
Immigration Act lays down 'White Australia' policy	1901
Anzac landings at Gallipoli	1915
'Bodyline' cricket series	1932
20,000 Australians taken prisoner by Japanese in Singapore	1942
Australian troops fight in Korea	1950s
Menzies commits Australian troops to Vietnam	1965
Aborigines given vote	1967
Whitlam deposed by Governor-General	1975
Mabo Decision on Aborigine land claims	1992

ing their legendary significance. This was an information superhighway before even the invention of writing – one which was complete and relevant to the physical and spiritual needs of an entire people. It could never be destroyed until the people themselves were destroyed and all memory of it vanished (something which many believe is now well on the way to happening).

Such was the Australia which the Europeans first sighted around 500 years ago. To them, this vast subcontinent was terra nullis – an empty land. It apparently had no maps, no staked-out properties, no borders, and no written laws. But all these existed nonetheless. They were just invisible.

Early European exploration
The first Europeans to set eyes on Terra Australis (The Southern Land) were almost certainly the Portuguese, some time in the early 16thC. Just short of a century later, in 1606, the Spanish explorer Torres sailed through the strait between New Guinea and Cape York, which is now named after him. Around the same time, the first Dutch navigators also began exploring these waters, putting ashore on the barren coast of northern Queensland. More extensive exploration was soon carried out by their fellow countryman Tasman, who discovered a territory which he called Van Diemen's Land (now named after its European discoverer). Tasman mapped vast stretches of the huge island to the north (which he called New Holland) and two large remote islands far to the east, which he also gave a Dutch name (New Zealand). Then in the 1680s the first Pom arrived, in the form of the explorer and part-time pirate William Dampier. Like many Poms to follow, Dampier was not impressed with what he saw and returned to civilization whingeing that Australia was 'an awful place'. The Dutch had come to much the same conclusion, and for 70 years or so everyone did their best to forget about Australia.

In 1770 the British explorer Captain Cook arrived in search of the rumoured 'Great southern land' (in the forlorn hope that this wasn't the awful place the others had come across). On April 19, 1770 Cook's ship, the *Endeavour*,

• An *Aborigine descendant of one of the first Australian settlers.*

reached the south-eastern tip of Australia, which he named point Point Hicks. Nine days later, he put ashore further north at Botany Bay. Here the Poms quickly discovered that the locals just weren't interested in these new arrivals (thus establishing what was to become a long-standing tradition).

Cook continued up the coast, where his ship ran on to a reef off Queensland. For six weeks the crew carried out repairs to the *Endeavour*, establishing a small settlement ashore at what is now Cooktown. Here Cook made further contact with the Aborigines. To him, they appeared to be 'the most wretched people upon the earth', yet he couldn't help noticing that 'they are far more happier than we Europeans'. Cook continued with his explorations, but before he left the subcontinent he raised the Union Jack, claiming it for Britain and naming it 'New South Wales'.

The convicts arrive
The discovery of Botany Bay was a great boon for the British. Here at last was somewhere they could get rid of all their social undesirables. (Previously they'd often been shipped to America, but America had now become independent – forcing British criminals to get

there under their own steam before they were caught.) In 1787, the First Fleet under Captain Arthur Phillip set sail for Australia with 821 convicts on board. Strictly speaking, these were to be the very first Poms: this name originating as an acronym for 'Prisoner Of Mother England'.

On arrival, the British quickly set about establishing hell on earth. Diminishing supplies and Aboriginal attacks, to say nothing of the inhospitable climate and terrain, were bad news for all concerned. The disgruntled guards soon began taking it out on their charges in vicious fashion. And the inmates of the colony – largely muggers, prostitutes, tavern brawlers and other relatively innocent victims of the courts – found it difficult to adapt to their subtropical holiday paradise. But the British were not to be put off by such trifles, and in 1790 the Second Fleet, with 1,000 prisoners clapped in irons, was dispatched to Australia. Of these 267 died en route. Many of the prisoners had been convicted for minor offences, and were officially sentenced to serve seven years 'beyond the seas'. Effectively, however, this meant a life sentence in the most distant exile imaginable at the time – as there was no way back from 'beyond the seas'.

The officers of the New South Wales Corps soon became the leading force in the colony, taking over tracts of land which they began farming. For cheap labour there were always the convicts, who were illegally paid in rum. Successive governors found there was very little they could do to oppose this powerful clique, whose driving force emerged as Lt. Col. John MacArthur. This man was to change the face of Australia for ever. He quickly saw that the territory was ideal for grazing, and imported some merino sheep from South Africa. In 1805, William Bligh was sent out from England as governor. Bligh's highhanded behaviour had already provoked one mutiny, during his period as master of the *Bounty*, and he was soon to repeat this feat as governor of New South Wales. In 1808 Bligh was ousted by the Rum Rebellion, which was largely fomented by MacArthur.

Having only recently succeeded in

• *One of the huge overhanging rocks known as the Balconies, the Grampians, Victoria.*

losing their American colonies, the British had no wish to lose any more of their empire. Colonel Lachlan Macquarie and the 73rd Regiment were sent out to replace Bligh and the New South Wales Corps. MacArthur fled, and the new governor set about bringing some order into the life of the colony.

Macquarie was an astute governor, and not for nothing is he sometimes known as the Father of Australia. He established a more humane regime for

contained a large sea. Others with less geographical knowledge argued that it must be a swamp, a jungle, a vast territory of volcanoes, and so forth. The Aborigines' suggestion that it was largely barren desert was dismissed as primitive imagining.

In 1840, Edward Eyre set off from Adelaide, determined to reach the heart of the continent. His expedition even carried raft-making equipment. After all kinds of troubles, the Eyre

• *Uluru (Ayers Rock), Northern Territory.*

the prisoners; also, prisoners who had served their term and been released (known as Emancipists) were integrated into society and even given public office. By the end of Macquarie's term as governor in 1821, Australia was even attracting a considerable number of voluntary emigrants from Britain.

Macquarie's successor, Sir Thomas Brisbane, reversed this policy, using convicts to do the dirty work of expanding new settlements in recently explored virgin territory. By the 1830s, the British colonization of Australia had spread as far afield as Tasmania, Western Australia and Queensland.

These were all coastal settlements, and inevitably interest soon began to focus on the interior. What lay at the centre of this huge unexplored continent? As is usually the case when nobody has the slightest idea, there were soon several utterly convinced and utterly irreconcilable schools of thought. The geographical experts maintained that the centre of Australia

expedition finally abandoned its trek north at a large barren rock, which he named Mount Hopeless. (Perhaps more apt would have been to call it Mount Eyre, and save the other name for the expedition itself.)

In 1844 the Prussian explorer Doktor Ludwig Leichhardt made it from the Darling Downs in Queensland all the way up to the coast near Darwin. This 2,000-km journey took more than 14 months. Four years later he set off on an even more ambitious expedition to cross the continent from east to west, but was never heard of again. (This expedition was the basis of Patrick White's sublime novel *Voss*). The Aborigines looked upon these expeditions across their mythic lands with curiosity and disdain – often charitably relieving the bedraggled explorers of their lives to prevent further unnecessary suffering.

Yet there were some successes. In 1860 the Burke and Wills expedition set off with a string of camels and made the crossing from Melbourne to the Gulf of Carpentaria. But on the way back it was business as usual: the expedition succeeded in losing its two leaders, and most of the camels escaped. (The camels thrived, and their ancestors can still be seen roaming the desert.)

Meanwhile, also racing across Australia in the hope of picking up the £2,000 prize for the first crossing, John MacDouall Stuart made it as far as the barren lump of rock marking the geographical centre of the continent, which he modestly named Mount Stuart. To the astonishment of all concerned, it looked as if the Aborigines had been right. The heart of Australia was nothing but a vast wilderness of mirage and nebulous myth.

Expansion

While all this serious Victorian exploration was going on, more frivolous types were attracted to specific parts of the interior. In 1851, gold was discovered at Bathhurst in New South Wales. Here was an amber solid which could quench all thirst for years to come: soon everyone who could move was headed for the goldfields. In next-door Victoria, the population became so depleted that a reward was offered for anyone discovering gold in the state. Within a year, one of the largest gold finds ever was made at Ballarat in Victoria, followed by others. Word quickly spread all over Australia, and even overseas. Prospectors were soon flooding in from California and all over Europe at the rate of over 2,000 a week.

In Britain there was a clamour to emigrate to Australia. The government decided in its wisdom that there was no point in sending expert gold-hunters to a land which appeared to be filled with gold, so in 1853 the transportation of criminals to the penal colonies of eastern Australia was officially terminated. (It was 15 years later before the last convicts arrived on the west coast.) By this time, almost 170,000 convicts had been shipped out to Australia.

The continent now began to attract a new type of immigrant. The Chinese were latecomers to the goldfields, many of which were already running out. Much to the consternation of the remaining dogged prospectors, the Chinese soon proved adept at winkling out elusive veins of gold in abandoned claims. The international brotherhood of prospectors quickly united in their hatred of these miserable foreign immigrants, and there were frequent race riots.

As white unemployment began to spread, so racial hatred spread beyond the goldfields. The government soon sensed the drift of public opinion, and imposed punitive taxes on the Chinese, in effect forcing them to leave. Then the government decided to make its intentions plain, and the 1901 Immigration Act instigated the White Australia Policy.

• *Kanowna Cemetery, near Kalgoorlie.*

Yet there were still many people in Australia who definitely weren't white – but were undeniably Australian. There was no possibility of getting the Aborigines to move out to another country, so the authorities decided to try a different tack. In Tasmania the lieutenant-governor ordered his men to round up the entire Aborigine population, who were then herded into a suitably barren patch of land which was designated as a 'reserve'. The cleared land was now fit for civilization. This policy was soon being adopted throughout the continent.

The early 20thC

At the turn of the 19thC, the separate states of Australia finally joined to become a single nation. However, within this federation each of the states insisted upon retaining equal powers, regardless of population. (To this day, Tasmania has as many seats in the Upper House as New South Wales.) On

• *Australia's rich mix of race ... and culture.*

to support a wife and three children.

Australia remained a colony of the British Empire, and as such was dragged into the largely European conflict of the First World War when it broke out in 1914. In the end almost a third of a million Australians were shipped to the other side of the world to fight for the Allies.

This proportionately massive contribution was squandered in tragic fashion. The Australia and New Zealand Army Corps (Anzac) took part in the Gallipoli landings, intended by Churchill to 'knock out Turkey'. The Aussies fought with exceptional bravery but, owing to military planning of extraordinary ineptitude even for British generals, the result was a fiasco. By the end of the war 60,000 Aussies had lost their lives, and almost three times as many had been wounded. To commemorate these sacrifices, and those in ensuing wars, Australians have a public holiday on Anzac Day, the anniversary of the first Gallipoli landings on April 25, 1915.

Post-war Australia continued its rapid

Upper House as New South Wales.) On January 1, 1901 the Commonwealth of Australia came into being, with a Governor-General appointed by Queen Victoria (which meant it was still part of the British Empire). One of the first pieces of legislation passed by the new government was the 1901 Immigration Act. This legalized racial discrimination and de facto defined Australia as a white country, and in practice limited citizenship still further mainly to those of British or Irish stock. Without such measures, Australia might have ended up as Chinese as Hong Kong, or have become a largely multi-European country like America. Obviously, this would have been a great loss to world cricket. (The Australians had already set out and beaten the English at their own game – returning in 1882 with the 'Ashes' of English cricket in an urn.)

Yet during the succeeding decade, the Australian parliament was to introduce some of the most liberal legislation anywhere. In 1902 women received the vote, and five years later a minimum wage was established. This was set at a rate sufficient for a man

development. The famous Flying Doctor Service was introduced to bring medicine to the outback; the Queensland and Northern Territory Air Service was established (now known as Qantas); Sydney Harbour Bridge was started, and Canberra was built as the capital. At the same time, sport was establishing itself as a national obsession, with Australia and individual Australians becoming world-class competitors in many events.

However, relations between Britain and Australia soured over the notorious 'Bodyline' cricket series, which took place in 1932. England bowled for the man, rather than the wicket; they may

• *Memorial on Anzac Hill, Alice Springs.*

have won the series, but they lost countless Australian friends.

The Thirties and Forties
The worldwide Depression of the 1930s hit Australia hard, with unemployment rising to over 30 per cent of the workforce. Poverty forced many on to the road to look for work, and the swagman became a feature of Australian life.

The Second World War exposed Australia's global vulnerability, and once again the Aussies got a raw deal. Australians fought alongside the Allies in the North Africa Campaign, which turned the course of the war against the Germans; but closer to home it was a different story. When the Japanese overran Singapore in 1942, 20,000 Australians were taken prisoner (many of them subsequently died in horrific circumstances building the Burma Railway for the Japanese). As the Japanese rapidly advanced through South-East Asia, it looked as if Australia was doomed to fall. Darwin was bombed, and Sydney attacked by submarines. But the Australians managed to defeat

the Japanese at Port Moresby in New Guinea, thus stemming the tide. From then on it was the Americans who came to Australia's rescue, and the Australians began to understand the reality of their remote bond with Britain.

Despite Britain's lack of help during the Second World War, Australia still retained ties of culture and blood with the Old Country – which politicians, world wars, and even the Bodyline cricket series had not entirely destroyed. It was the wide open spaces of Australia that had attracted the land-hungry Japanese during the Second World War, and Australia quickly drew the appropriate conclusion. Australia was the world's sixth largest country, yet it had a population smaller than that of London. 'Populate or perish' became the policy of the day.

Australia turned to Britain for immigrants, launching a programme allowing British immigrants to sail to Australia for just £10. Disillusioned post-war Brits responded in their tens of thousands. A few whinged, but the rest quickly took to the Aussie way of life. This programme also encouraged many non-British Europeans to try their luck in Australia. The presence of Jews, Greeks and Yugoslavs soon brought a welcome continental spice to the rather bland Aussie social scene.

Post Second World War Australia
The country was now determined to defend itself in the event of renewed expansion by any of its neighbours, and assumed a full role in the politics of the Far East. In the 1950s troops were sent to support the British fighting the communists in Malaya, and Aussies fought alongside the Americans and the British in the war against the communists in Korea.

involvement meant that the Australian outback was used by Britain as a nuclear testing ground. The British attitude towards the Australian interior hadn't changed in almost 200 years. To them, it was still terra nullis. The presence of the Aborigines, and their entitlement to the land, were largely ignored. Admittedly, the white Australians were little better. (Staggeringly, for such a democratic country, it wasn't until 1967 that Aborigines were even included in the national census or allowed to vote.) As a result, the mushroom clouds were soon sprouting in the outback, and large tracts of land alive with invisible songlines now took on a new invisible life: radioactivity.

In 1965 the ageing Liberal Prime Minister Robert Menzies committed Australian troops to support the Americans in Vietnam. This decision split the

• *Barren tracts of the Australian outback.*
• *Eucla. Where to, now?*

country. In 1972 Labor took over under Gough Whitlam, who brought the troops back from Vietnam. He also set about introducing sweeping health and educational reforms, as well as backing a programme of land rights for the Aborigines. This was far too much for the opposition, who did their best to bring the Senate to a standstill. Until this time the Governor-General had been a largely ornamental head of state, much like the Queen of England who appointed him. But in 1975 the Governor-General decided things had gone too far, and removed Whitlam from office. The unelected head of state, appointed by the unelected head of a foreign state, had simply reversed the democratically expressed wishes of the Australian people. Many around the world were astonished that Australia didn't declare itself a republic overnight. In fact, Australians were more interested in the affairs of the moment, and voted in a Liberal-National coalition – which for the next few years restored an element of stability to the political scene.

But 1975 also saw an Australian achievement on the international scene which for once did not involve military bravery or sporting prowess. Australian writer Patrick White was awarded the Nobel Prize for Literature. Australia already had several artists of world-class stature – for example the painter Sidney Nolan and the operatic soprano Joan Sutherland – but White's Nobel Prize set the seal on the country's often maligned cultural status. This also coincided with another social transformation. White openly insisted upon his homosexuality, and this did much to encourage gay Australians to liberate themselves from the crampingly machismo self-image with which the nation had saddled itself. The times they were a-changing, and it wasn't long before even the prime minister was crying on TV. The man responsible for this act of bathos was the ebullient Labor leader Bob Hawke, who took over as prime minister in 1983.

By 1991 the Labor Party decided it had had enough of Bob Hawke's personal confessions, and Paul Keating took over as prime minister. By now Australia was beginning to feel the effects of the worldwide recession, and suffering from the worst unemploy-

ment since the 1930s.

Added to this were various home-grown disasters. A long-term drought was affecting large tracts of eastern Australian farmland, corruption was rampant in the state of Queensland, and Sydney's victorious bid for the 2000 Olympics looked set to bankrupt the entire state of Victoria.

More recently, the government has been forced to come to terms with the difficulties posed by Aborigine land claims. The historic Mabo Decision of 1992 appears to accept these rights, but this will be no easy matter to resolve. At least partly in an effort to distract attention from all these problems, Keating has launched his scheme to turn Australia into a republic.

Despite its seemingly inevitable outcome, this topic is likely to provoke much heated debate. Now that Britain, and more recently the United States, have proved such unreliable economic partners, Australia is being forced to accept its role in the Asian sphere. Yet, understandably, Australians have difficulty seeing themselves as Asians. The eventual breaking of the British tie may well prove crucial in how this far-flung outpost of essentially European civilization comes to see itself.

• *Trying a didgeridoo at The Rocks Market, Sydney.*

Sydney:
introduction

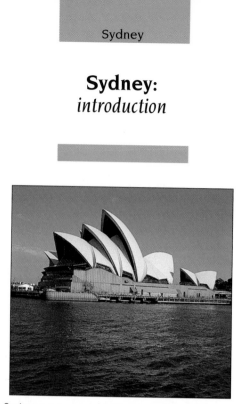

For years Sydney was a secret. Those who stumbled across it were astonished to find one of the most beautifully situated cities in the world. (Only Rio and San Francisco can match it.) They also discovered that Sydney had a lifestyle as sunny and easygoing as California. But this lack of attention also meant that Sydney retained a somewhat inward-looking attitude. Beach-life and beer were the main pastimes of Sydneysiders (as they like to call themselves). Sophistication was an ugly word.

To this day, Sydneysiders retain an essentially down-to-earth view of life. But that famed easygoing attitude, which resulted in a peculiarly restrictive mateyness, has now blossomed into a remarkable liberalism and broadness of taste.

Nowadays, Sydney is renowned throughout the world as a great metropolis. The gayest city in the western Pacific (in every sense of the word), it also has a varied and sophisticated cultural life. Not for nothing is the city's proud new symbol its Opera House. And Sydney's role as host, in the year 2000, to the first Olympic Games of the new millennium, stands as a fitting tribute to a city where sport is virtually a religion, as well as being a form of address. Today Sydney says 'G'day sport' to visitors from all over the world.

Sydney is a big city, with a population of 4 million. If you can, allow at least a week to explore its sights and beaches – and to recover from its hectic nightlife.

• *Darling Harbour.*

A SHORT HISTORY OF SYDNEY

Captain Cook arrived at Botany Bay in 1770, claiming this new land for the British crown. For some unaccountable reason, he named it New South Wales. (Cook had never been to Wales, but even so, he must have realized that Wales didn't look anything like this.)

The British authorities weren't impressed with what they heard about this new land, and decided to use it as a social refuse tip. In 1788, Captain Phillip arrived with the first consignment of convicts, and set up a penal colony at Sydney Cove (just west of the present Opera House, and still the hub of the harbour).

Sydney Cove soon became a going concern. The army officers consigned to the penal settlement had initially looked upon this posting as a kind of hot Siberia. This was not only the end of the world, but the end of all promotion too. In the time-honoured fashion they vented their spleen on the hapless lower ranks, who in turn passed this on (with interest) to the even more hapless convicts.

However, the officers soon found consolation. Here there was land, and to work this land they had an inexhaustible supply of virtual slave labour in the form of the convicts who just had to be paid enough rum to keep them quiet. Many officers made their fortune, carving out large farms for themselves.

In 1819 a way was found through the Blue Mountains, which had formerly pinned the colony to the narrow coastal strip. The opportunities for grabbing yet more land now became considerable as the interior was opened up.

Meanwhile, Sydney was becoming established as a trading port: ships put in with cargo from India and Africa, as well as from Europe. Under the liberal governorship of Lachlan Macquarie, an extensive construction programme was initiated. This included several fine Georgian buildings which remain standing to this day – most notably the Hyde Park Barracks on Macquarie Street. Many of these buildings were the work of the architect Francis Greenway. The multi-talented Greenway was in fact a convict, who had been deported to Australia for forgery – see opposite.

By the 1850s, Sydney had become an attractive, go-ahead city, with a population of 60,000. The first railway on the new continent was built between Sydney and Paramatta as early as 1855, just 25 years after Stephenson's *Rocket* made history in England as the first steam train.

By now the great Australian gold rushes were in full swing. Thousands upon thousands began arriving from all over the world in search of the 'mountain of gold' they had heard about. Some made their fortune, but most were disappointed. However, many of these quickly saw the opportunities for a new life in this new land. By 1890, Sydney's population had multiplied to almost half a million – making it as large as some of the minor European capitals. The pleasant, small city had become a sprawl of cheap and crowded suburban terraces. (Those that remain today are inevitably looked upon as local treasures, their Victorian

THE FORGER WHO BUILT SYDNEY

Despite Governor Macquarie's urgent requests, the authorities in London decided against sending any architects to Australia. A colony like New South Wales had no need for such extravagances. Fortunately, the criminal classes usually include people of all professions, and an architect soon turned up in the colony in the form of Francis Greenway.

Greenway had turned his calligraphic talents from architectural blueprints to forging more ambitious documents, thus earning himself a 14-year holiday at His Majesty's expense. In 1814, Governor Macquarie set Greenway to work designing major buildings for the new Sydney. Many of the city's finest early buildings are his work, the best of which is Hyde Park Barracks. Macquarie also ordered Greenway to build some new Law Courts. Unfortunately, when the building was already half finished there was a change of plan, and Greenway was told to turn it into a church. This is now **St James Church at Queens Square**.

When Macquarie finished his term as governor and sailed back to England, Greenway was left without a protector. An irascible character who didn't suffer fools gladly, he alienated several important people in Sydney, who got him the sack.

By now Greenway had been pardoned, so he went to live on the farm he had acquired outside Sydney. But his jealous enemies continued to pursue him. Greenway was charged with fraudulently gaining possession of his farm. Fortunately, he was able to show the authorities a document which showed that he was entitled to the property, and the charge was dropped. Only after he died was it discovered that this document was a forgery.

Later, Greenway was to achieve the ultimate accolade for a forger, a unique honour which no other country has bestowed upon a man in this profession. He appeared on the A$10 bill, his skilfully depicted portrait presenting a stimulating challege to other members of his profession.

balconies and iron railings lovingly preserved.)

Australia almost went bankrupt in the 1890s, and this hit Sydney hard. The financial centre of Australia was by now Melbourne, which had benefited from the Central Victoria goldfields. But despite valiant ineptitude by the colonial authorities, complete financial disaster was averted. Australia was so rich in natural resources that even the British government couldn't wreck the economy.

Despite this, Sydney's arch-rival Melbourne was now the largest city on the continent, and became the capital of the new Commonwealth of Australia in 1901. But this was only a blip. By the First World War, Sydney was a city of a million people. It may not have been the capital, but there was no doubting now which was Australia's major city – a state of affairs which has remained to this day.

Sydney's importance as a commercial centre has continued to grow, especially now that ties with Britain have eased. Britain has become part of the EC, and Australia has turned to the Pacific. The United States, Japan and the tiger economies of the Pacific Rim are now its leading trading partners and rivals. This diversification of trade has been paralleled by a diversification of Sydney's population. The 'new Australians' are immigrants from southern Europe (particularly from Italy and Greece) as well as from Asia – rather than British or Irish. These latest immigrants have played a big role in transforming what was once a rather uniform and insular social life. Commercially, ethnically and culturally, Sydney is now very much an international city.

IN THIS SECTION

The author's personal introduction to Sydney is on page 42. Practical information on getting in and out of the city, also on getting around once you've arrived, follows on this page.

Because Sydney is pleasant for strolling, we give a guided walking route around the centre, taking in important sights; this starts on page 48. The walk can easily be split into parts, allowing you extra time to visit sights that especially interest you. Sights not covered by this walking route are covered alphabetically under Sights & Places of Interest, starting on page 55.

Hotel and restaurant recommendations are on page 57.

ARRIVING

Sydney's airport, Kingsford Smith Airport, is 8 km south of the city centre. A taxi into town, from the airport to the centre or to Kings Cross, costs around A$20, journey time around half an hour. It's worth paying the extra if you've just endured a long-haul flight.

Kingsford Smith Transport runs a limo service which will take you direct to your hotel. This leaves every half hour or so, and costs less than half the taxi fare.

Buses run into town regularly between 6 am and 10.55 pm. These charge around A$5. No. 300 runs to Central Station and Circular Quay, 350 runs to Central Station and Kings Cross. There is a regular shuttle service between the domestic and international terminals, which are at either end of the airport.

ORIENTATION

The sprawling city of Sydney is divided into two by the wide waterway known as Port Jackson. The two halves are linked at the city centre by the Sydney Harbour Bridge and by the Harbour Tunnel. The main sights, such as Opera House and the historic district known as The Rocks, are on the south shore in the centre of the city.

PUBLIC TRANSPORT

The best way to get around central Sydney is by bus. Get a Metroten ticket, which gives worthwhile savings. It costs around A$5, and enables you to take ten short journeys, or fewer longer ones. For information on the Metroten, and all city transport, ring 954 4422.

Train services from Central Station and Circular Quay are the best way to see the suburbs. There's a monorail service linking Darling Harbour and the city centre: a round-trip ticket costs A$2.50. The ride gives you views of the city centre, even if the monorail itself is something of an eyesore.

If you want to see Sydney Harbour, head for Circular Quay, the terminal for all the main ferry services. These run to the north shore, to Darling Harbour and to many other shoreside destinations. A single ticket is usually around A$3. You can also choose from a range of attractive harbour cruises starting at Circular Quay.

ACCOMMODATION GUIDELINES

Sydney has the wide range of accommodation you'd expect, from top-of-the-range luxury hotels to backpacker hostels. Luxury accommodation is as good, and as expensive, as in any major metropolis. The backpacker hostels can look as if they were designed for the original convict arrivals. In between, prices tend to be rather higher than elsewhere in Australia, but in most places you can expect the usual friendly welcome and honest standards of accommodation. Prices rise during the summer, but there are often bargains to be had out of season.

The main focus for mid- and lower-price accommodation in central Sydney is Kings Cross and the nearby suburbs of Potts Point and Woolloomooloo. Be careful about choosing bargain accommodation in Kings Cross, as some of the cheaper spots can be a bit grim.

More reliable cheap accommodation is to be had in the suburbs. Try the seaside suburbs along the north shore, which are the most pleasant and least distant from the town centre. Bondi Beach, to the south-west of the city centre, also offers a wide range of seaside accommodation.

NEIGHBOURHOODS TO AVOID

Sydney is generally a safe city, but like any sophisticated metropolis it has its unsophisticated elements. A veneer of streetwise savvy is recommended.

Kings Cross is the wildest district in Sydney, with all kinds of entertainments. Inevitably, it's a magnet for certain iron-heads.

Gay and racial abuse are not unknown, but are not the norm. Heavy drinking is a popular local hobby. Make sure that you know what you're doing (and who you're doing it with) before you get involved.

The main central tourist areas are safe at night, but avoid wandering off the beaten track. Just use common sense, and you'll be fine.

• *Monorail, with Sydney Tower behind.*

CENTRAL SYDNEY ON FOOT

This route is over 6 km, and if you stop off to see the sights it can easily last a whole day. If you don't want to spend your entire day sightseeing, divide the walk into segments, and cover these as you wish.

Start at the **Sydney Opera House**. Love it or loathe it, this striking building is now undeniably *the* symbol of the city. Before work on the Opera House began, this prime site was a city tram depot. The prize for the original design of the building was won in 1956 by the Danish architect Jorn Utzon. His scheme was budgeted to cost A$7 million. No sooner had the building work started than the controversy and rows began. Utzon finally resigned from the project in 1963, and a group of local architects took over. The extra people involved meant extra bickering over details as well as the overall plan, thus enabling the building of the Opera House to last another ten years – highly lucrative for all concerned. In 1973 the building was finally opened, having cost a colossal A$102 million, almost *fifteen* times the original estimate. There was an immediate and widespread chorus of howls – most of outrage, but a few of approval.

Opinions differ about what the striking curves of the roofs are meant to represent – ships' sails, nuns' headdresses, two rutting armadillos, and so on. And it was well over two years after the opening before they managed to raise enough money to pay off all the bills.

Nowadays, none of the controversy seems to matter. The Sydney Opera House simply *is*, and its shape is recognized the world over.

The building is more than just an opera house. The **Opera Theatre** seats more than 1,500 spectators, and will set you back at least A$30 a ticket. Well over 2,500 people can fit into the **Concert Hall**, whose revolutionary acrylic rings contribute both to the acoustics of the performances and the acoustics of the controversy. Besides this there are also restaurants, bars and a cinema. And if you don't want to go to a performance, you can always turn up on Sunday morning for the free open-air entertainment which takes place outside the building. This is likely to include anything from high school bands to fire-eaters.

Tours of the building are available from 9 am to 4 pm and last one hour, price A$8.50. The inside is just as exciting (and controversial) as the outside.

From outside the Opera House you

THOMAS MORT

Otherwise known, with little exaggeration, as the 'man who made Australia', Mort was born in Bolton in England in 1816. At 22 he sailed for Sydney, where he started as a warehouse clerk but soon set up in business on his own. After going bust in the shipping trade he made a fortune in wool marketing, starting the first public wool sales in Australia. At the same time he began private experiments freezing meat. Later he made a further fortune mining gold, and built his own docks at Port Jackson. By 1875, his experiments in freezing (and thus preserving) meat had come to fruition. Mort chartered a steamer, installed a refrigeration plant, and filled it with frozen meat to ship to England.

On the eve of the steamer's

departure he threw a grand banquet, which was attended by all the good and the great of Australia. Here he announced that he had solved the problem of how to feed the world. The steamer duly set sail – and broke down. Refrigeration didn't work.

A broken man, Mort retired to his country mansion. He turned his great meat refrigeration plant into an ice-making factory, and died three years later in 1878.

But by now the problems of refrigerated shipment had been solved. Overnight, this transformed world trade – and for almost a century the Australian economy 'rode on the sheep's back'. Mort had been right, and a grateful Australia erected its first public statue to a great Australian.

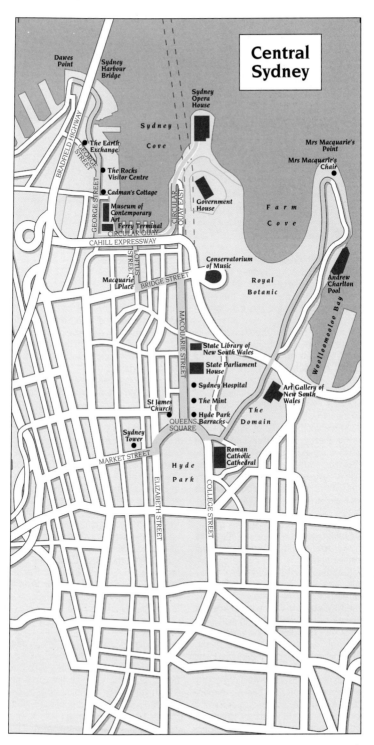

Central Sydney

Dawes Point

Sydney Harbour Bridge

BRADFIELD HIGHWAY

GEORGE STREET

The Earth Exchange

The Rocks Visitor Centre

Cadman's Cottage

Museum of Contemporary Art

Ferry Terminal

CIRCULAR QUAY

CAHILL EXPRESSWAY

LOFTUS STREET

Macquarie Place

BRIDGE STREET

MACQUARIE STREET

Sydney Cove

Sydney Opera House

CIRCULAR QUAY EAST

Government House

Conservatorium of Music

State Library of New South Wales

State Parliament House

Sydney Hospital

The Mint

St James Church

Hyde Park Barracks

QUEENS SQUARE

Sydney Tower

MARKET STREET

ELIZABETH STREET

Hyde Park

COLLEGE STREET

Roman Catholic Cathedral

The Domain

Royal Botanic

Farm Cove

Mrs Macquarie's Point

Mrs Macquarie's Chair

Andrew Charlton Pool

Woolloomooloo Bay

Art Gallery of New South Wales

have a superb **view over Sydney Harbour**. To the west is **Sydney Harbour Bridge**, popularly known as the 'old coathanger'. It used to be the city's symbol. There's more about the bridge below.

From the Sydney Opera House walk south along Circular Quay East. This leads you around the edge of Sydney Cove, on whose far shore the first penal colony was set up more than two centuries ago. Beneath you the Sydney Harbour Tunnel runs beneath the water to the north shore.

At the southern end of Sydney Cove is the **Ferry Terminal**. Ferries and cruises leave here for all over Sydney Harbour – which is nearly 20 km long and in parts as much as 6 km wide. Try the afternoon **Main Harbour Cruise** (*two-and-a-half hours*, A$18) – though simply riding the ferries can prove just as much fun. **Circular Quay** is a busy, bustling spot at all times of day, with heavy traffic and buskers producing similar sounds.

Continue west past the ferry terminal, and then turn right up George Street. On your right you now come to the **Museum of Contemporary Art** (*open 11 am to 6 pm, Wed to Mon, entry A$6*). This may look ordinary on the outside, but it contains some real gems. The museum was opened in 1991 and concentrates on the very latest art (which mostly means anything since the birth of rock and roll). There are more than 4,000 pieces on display, and if you can't find anything to suit your taste here you shouldn't be in a contempo-

• *Sydney Harbour Bridge.*

rary art museum in the first place. On the other hand, it's worth remembering that much of this work wasn't intended to be liked. Duchamp, Christo, Warhol and other controversial 'geniuses' are represented. The **museum shop** has some particularly worthwhile items and cards.

Further up George Street on the right you come to **Cadman's Cottage**. This is the oldest private dwelling in Sydney and dates from 1816. In those days, it was on the beach, and at the front of the house you can still see what was once the sea wall. John Cadman was sent to Australia as a convict for the crime of stealing a horse, and after he had completed his sentence he entered government service. He occupied this modest sandstone house from 1827 for almost 20 years, ending up as government coxswain (in charge of the government boats) – the last man to hold this post. Cadman's Cottage now houses the **National Parks and Wildlife Service of New South Wales Information Centre**. Pick up a few of the pamphlets here – they are a useful aid to planning your trip through the state.

Continue down George Street and you come to **The Rocks Visitor Centre** at No. 104 (*open 10 am to 5 pm*). The Rocks was the site of the original British settlement established by Captain Phillip in 1788, and is named after the sandstone rocks which form Dawes Point. As the colony developed, The

Rocks became a notorious waterfront slum – providing all the amenities expected of such an area. Brawls, mugging, prostitutes and footpads were commonplace. It also proved a breeding ground for that peculiarly Aussie character, the larrikin (see page 53).

The Rocks Visitor Centre contains much information on the skulduggery and wild hoolies of the good old days – which finally came to an end just after the turn of the 19thC. The usual sailor-town diseases were only to be expected of a district such as The Rocks, but when there was an outbreak of the bubonic plague the authorities decided it was time to call a halt to the fun, and much of the old district was bulldozed. Nowadays, parts of the district have been lovingly restored – though without the larrikins and the plague. You can pick up a map of The Rocks at the Visitor Centre.

Further down George Street, on your right, you come to **The Earth Exchange**, (*open 10 am to 5 pm, entry* A$7). This is an educational museum cunningly disguised as a great interactive experience. If you want to witness an erupting volcano or an earthquake, without going through the stressful business of dodging all those falling lumps, this is the place for you. The main theme is geology (this used to be the stuffy old Museum of Geology and Mining), and amongst the minerals and jewels on display upstairs you can see the biggest piece of gold ever found in Australia, the **Jubilee Golden Nugget**. From here continue north towards Dawes Point, beneath the shadow of **Sydney Harbour Bridge**. The bridge links the northern and southern halves of the city, which are divided by the long inlet of Sydney Harbour. The bridge was completed in 1932, when it cost six pence to cross in a vehicle and three pence to cross on a horse. Unlike the Opera House, the Harbour Bridge cost a mere A$20 million – though this bill wasn't finally paid off until 15 years after the Opera House had opened. The bridge carries two railway tracks and eight traffic lanes, which are all supported by the semi-circular spanning arch, not the towers on either side (which are in fact purely for show, serving no structural purpose). The bridge is claimed as the world's widest (as distinct from longest) span,

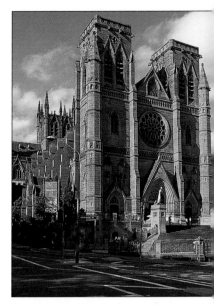

• St Mary's Roman Catholic Cathedral.

and its deck is almost 50 m above the water – though this didn't prove quite high enough for the *Canberra*, which snapped its mast when passing underneath for the first time. The south–eastern tower of the bridge has a viewing platform 200 steps up. This has great views out over the city and the harbour, as well as a small photographic museum, *open 10 am to 5 pm, entry* A$2. A few years back Paul Hogan, of *Crocodile Dundee* fame, used to work as a rigger on the Sydney Harbour Bridge.

Retrace your steps down George Street, then turn left back to the Ferry Terminal. Here cross over and head south down Loftus Street. On your left you will soon see Customs House, which is of no great importance and even less interest. (However, this may all change in a few years, as there are plans to turn the building into an Aborigine Culture Centre.)

Continue down Loftus Street, and on your right you will see the small park called **Macquarie Place**. The statue with its arms akimbo is of Thomas Mort, the first Australian ever to be honoured with a public statue (see page 48). The obelisk here was once the central spot from where all distances from Sydney were calculated.

At Bridge Street turn left, until you

come to the junction with Macquarie Street. The building directly ahead dates from 1819 and used to be the **stables and servants' quarters for Government House**. (The latter is north across Royal Botanic Gardens, behind the trees, and is not open to the public.) The Government House stables now house the **Conservatorium of Music**, which has free lunchtime concerts on Wednesdays during school term-time. The contemporary Australian composer Charles Oliver Jones, whose *Cogs* caused a sensation at the London Proms and later in Berlin and New York, was educated here.

Turn right down Macquarie Street. On your left, after the Royal Botanic Gardens, you come to the **State Library of New South Wales** (*open 9 am to 9 pm, Mon to Fri; 9 am to 5 pm Sat, entry free*). Inside, the floor is covered with a mosaic of one of the earliest maps of Australia – that made by the Dutch explorer Abel Tasman in the 17thC. The Reading Room is closed to the public.

The next building down Macquarie Street is **State Parliament House** (*open 9.30 am to 4 pm, Tues to Thur*). This was once part of the Rum Hospital, which was built for convicts in 1816 out

of three years' profits from the rum trade. (The size of this hospital, which extended all the way down to the old Mint, gives an indication of Aussie rum consumption during the early years of the 19thC.) Initially, the governor used to meet with his advisers in a couple of rooms of the hospital. But as is often the case with advisers, they soon began to multiply and set up committees. More and more rooms were needed for the burgeoning administration, and when New South Wales eventually achieved self-governemnt in the 1840s, the new parliament occupied the whole building. Inside, there are the usual self-aggrandizing portraits of politicians who made it to the top without being found out. The State Parliament sits between February and May, when the Legislative Council Chamber witnesses many a ding-dong masquerading as a debate. The New South Wales legislature prides itself on these knockabout farces, which are open to the public and often provide some of the best entertainment in town. So much so that reservations are usually required: *tel.* (02) 230 2111.

Next door is the Sydney Hospital, and beyond this is the **The Mint**, which was also once part of the Rum Hospital. Work on this building started in 1811, making it the oldest in Australia. In the old days, conditions in the Rum Hospital were generally reckoned to be even worse than those in the penal colony, thus encouraging a fit and healthy life amongst the convicts. Meanwhile, in the hospital, those patients who could still move ate and drank everything they could lay their hands on, ensuring that those who couldn't move soon had no further need of such luxuries. The building was turned into the mint in the 1850s, when the colony of New South Wales first produced its own coins (other than those privately produced by a few industrious locals). Nowadays, the Mint houses a museum which has some stupifyingly dull Victorian exhibits, and some fascinating stamps and coins (*open 10 am to 5 pm daily, half day Wed, entry* A$7).

The next building along Macquarie Street is **Hyde Park Barracks**, which was designed in 1819 by the convict architect Francis Greenway (see page 45). In the original penal colony, the

---

THE GAY AND LESBIAN SCENE
Sydney rivals San Francisco as the gay capital of the world. The main scene is along Oxford Street (known locally as the Golden Mile) in Paddington, and Darlinghurst, south of Kings Cross. The lesbian scene focuses on Leichhardt (known by its fans as Dyke-heart) as well as Paddington and Darlinghurst.

The big event of the gay year is the **Sydney Lesbian and Gay Mardi Gras**, which attracts crowds from all over the gay globe. This takes place throughout February, with parades, a film festival and all kinds of cultural events (for both vultures and battleships). The other big event of the gay year is the **Sleaze Ball,** which blossoms in October. A popular year-round gay meeting spot is the aptly named **Exchange Hotel** at 34 Oxford Street in Darlingurst.

THE LARRIKIN

This uniquely Aussie word describes a young hooligan. It is generally reckoned to be one of the oldest 'Strine' terms, having probably developed in the colony during the early 18thC. As with many interesting coinages, there are several explanations of its origin. The most scholarly (and least plausible) is that it derives from the English 18thC urban slang term a 'leary kinchin'. According to the philologists, this was the equivalent of a young rascal, though these same scholars are forced to admit that where the word 'leary' is concerned, both its origins and meaning are obscure, and that 'kinchen' seems to have been underworld slang for a child (ie again they don't really know). Much more plausible is the usual explanation, that larrikin derives from the popular Irish nickname for anyone called Lawrence ie Larry, with 'kin' being a form of diminutive. However, another plausible explanation has it all down to one man – an Irish policeman who was giving evidence in court. He was describing the behaviour of the defendant, but instead of saying that he was larking about, it came out as 'larrikin'. The clerk of the court copied this down, and it quickly passed into common usage. So much so, that in the early days there were even 'larrikinesses'; districts like The Rocks, in Sydney, soon became notorioius for 'larrikinism'; and a local wag once stood for parliament as a 'larrikinist'.

cons weren't locked up at night – for the simple reason that there was nowhere for them to escape. (Home was the other side of the globe, and anyone straying beyond the settlement fell into Aborigine hands.) But this open-door policy did little to improve nightlife on the streets of Sydney. Few who ventured out without an armed escort were ever heard of again. When Macquarie took over as governor, he decided to institute a more healthy, early-to-bed policy for the convicts. The barracks was commissioned as their new dormitory, and here they were locked up every night. The building itself exhibits the best of Georgian restraint in its clean-cut style. Nowadays, it contains a **museum** (*open 10 am to 5 pm daily, entry* A$7) with many fascinating relics from the old convict days. These include several details of information and fragments of clothing which conjure up a surprisingly vivid picture of what it was really like in those bitter times (not so long ago). There's also a very pleasant café in the courtyard.

At the end of Macquarie Street is Queens Square. On the western side of the square is **St James Church**, another of Greenway's fine buildings. Inside there are many plaques to early explorers and colonial officials who never made it back home.

Continue west to the junction with Elizabeth Street. Then turn south, and take the turn west (ie right) into Market Street. On the right you will now see **Sydney Tower**, which rises from the top of the Centrepoint complex. The tower is 305 m high, and has a viewing gallery at the top (*open* 9.30 *am to* 9.30 *pm daily, entry* A$6). From here you can see out over the entire city, with fine views of the mountains and down the coast. There is also a revolving restaurant at the top, but here you pay heftily for the view as well as the food.

Retrace your footsteps up Market Street, back to Queens Square and Hyde Park Barracks. Just south-east of Hyde Park Barracks is St Mary's, the **Roman Catholic Cathedral**. This impressive Neo-Gothic structure was started at the end of 19thC, and is modelled on Lincoln Cathedral in England. However, certain features – such as the spires on the towers – are missing, owing to the fact that the building still remains to be completed. Right from the start, Sydney always had a large Catholic population, many of Irish descent. In those early colonial days, when the authorities were Protestant and a large proportion of the convicts were Catholic, there was considerable friction between the two sects. This antagonism was lessened by the efforts of Patrick Moran, who became Australia's first cardinal at the turn of the century. Today he is commemorated by a statue outside St Mary's.

• *Manly beach.*

Head north-east from St Mary's Cathedral, and you soon enter the open parkland of **The Domain**, part of the extensive green space that makes the centre of Sydney so pleasant. Continue down Art Gallery Road, and on your right you come to the **Art Gallery of New South Wales** *open 10 am to 5 pm daily, Sun afternoons only, entry free*. This is the largest art gallery in New South Wales, and one of the finest in the land. Unlike so many galleries, it has plenty of space and the collection is not cluttered. The European collection has works from as early as the 11thC, right up to Picasso and beyond. The Australian collection illustrates with particular perception the evolution from early European influences and colonial styles into an unmistakably Australian style reflecting the setting and tradition of the country. With roots further in the past than any of the other collections, the **Aborigine Collection** stands in a class of its own. Here we're all very much outsiders looking in – but to what a world. The gallery also has fine collections of American, Indonesian and Pacific art, and stages many fine international travelling exhibitions; *entry* A$10 *and up*. This should be one of the highlights of your visit – and will tell you even more about the country than that fascinating character who bent your ear at the bar in the outback.

From here continue north into the **Royal Botanic Gardens**, with pleasant ponds, palm trees and hothouses. These gardens were the first land cultivated by the original settlement at Sydney Cove. The initial colonists had brought vegetable seeds and plants from England. Their cold-weather cabbages and the like hardly flourished in the Australian climate, and their cultivators were more used to handling rifles and coshes than wielding hoes. As a result, the first settlement nearly died out through starvation which would have been quite a feat, even for the British colonial authorities, in such a lush and fertile land.

Continue north, keeping Farm Cove to the west (ie your left). At the end of the point you come to **Mrs Macquarie's Chair**. This is named after the wife of the liberal early governor, who had the chair carved out of rock so that she could look out over the waters of Sydney Harbour. The view may have changed over the 150 years since Mrs Macquarie watched the sunsets, but it's still just as spectacular – with the fading red sky ablaze beyond the Opera House and Sydney Harbour Bridge.

This marks the end of your walk, but if you're still feeling energetic, or just want to cool off, you'll find the **Andrew Charlton Pool** halfway down the eastern side of the point, on Woolloomooloo Bay. This open-air salt-water pool is open daily.

SIGHTS & PLACES OF INTEREST

BEACHES

The beaches of Sydney are world famous, and justly so. But this wasn't always the case. Until just before the First World War swimming was actually banned on the beaches between sunrise and sunset. All this came to an end when a local newspaper editor staged a public one-man protest, and walked into the sea fully clothed. The police wisely decided against prosecution. This tradition of clothed bathing lasted some time. For many years, men were not allowed to swim unless their chests were covered. Fortunately this practice has now ceased for men, and is fast dying out for women too.

The ocean beaches north of Sydney begin at **Manly**, which can be reached by ferry. These beaches have good surf, as do those south of Sydney on the coast. The southern beaches are more accessible and quicker to reach from the city centre. These run all the way down to Botany Bay, and by far the best-known is **Bondi**.

All Sydney's ocean beaches are manned by the famous lifeguards. But you are only allowed to swim between the flags. There's good reason for this: the undertow of the surf can be dangerous. Then of course there's the vexed question of sharks. All the ocean beaches have shark nets of some kind, but these don't actually seal off the beach. The fact is, the last fatal shark attack on one of these beaches took place a couple of years before the start of the Second World War. Topless bathing for women is increasingly widespread, but not on all beaches. Just use common sense.

The harbour beaches are more accessible, but don't have surf.

MARKETS

Sydney has several lively street markets. The biggest attraction for tourists is **The Rocks Market** at the northern end of George Street, which takes place at weekends from 10 am to 5 pm. **Paddington Village Bazaar** (known locally as Paddo Market) takes place on Saturdays. This is the place for way-out clothes and general New Ageana.

Balmain Market, 5 km west of

NIGHTLIFE

Sydney is justly renowned for its nightlife, which comes into its own at weekends. Get the *Metro* section of the *Sydney Morning Herald* on Friday for a full listing of the coming week's events.

It goes without saying that Sydney has **pubs** like teenageers have acne. These hotels (ie pubs) can be scenes of heroic drinking sessions and are not for the faint-hearted. However, the sweaty, guzzling mayhem of the weekends can often give way on weekday nights to scenes suspiciously resembling civilization. Most pubs have counter food of some kind, many of them have great live entertainment.

The most historic pub in town is the **Lord Nelson Brewery Hotel** on Kent Street, The Rocks. They've been brewing their own beer here since the early convicts stepped ashore with ocean-sized thirsts. Nearby on Windmill Street is the almost equally historic **Hero of Waterloo**. Also in The Rocks is **Molly Bloom's Bar** on George Street, which often has wild Irish music. Only slightly more sedate is the oompa-pa music at **The Löwenbrau** on Argyle Street. The German ambience here recreates for the locals the atmosphere of the Munich Beer Festival which they visited, but can't remember.

One of the best-known bars in the lively neon-lit entertainment district of Kings Cross is the **Darlo Bar** on Darlinghurst Street. This occupies a small block, but still has them spilling out at the weekends. **The Royal Hotel** near the Five Ways shops on Glenmore Road is a fine old renovated pub, complete with Victorian fittings and a restaurant with a balcony upstairs.

But if you want a fine view, a quiet drink and a bite to eat, try the **Sydney Cove Oyster Bar** on East Circular Quay. Here you can sit outside, watch the boats and sample a schooner of Hahn, the ace local draught beer. On Sunday afternoons they have live jazz.

EVENTS

One of the main cultural happenings of the Sydney year is the **Festival of Sydney,** which takes place throughout January. This features all kinds of artistic events, from grand opera and drama to performance art and buskers.

During the summer there are various **surf festivals** at the beaches. In May and early June there's an **international film festival**. A popular event which attracts huge crowds (of watchers as well as participants) is the 8-km **City to Surf Race**, which takes place between the city centre and Bondi Beach in August.

The final event of the year, which attracts even larger crowds, is the **Sydney to Hobart Yacht Race**, which starts from the harbour at the end of December.

• *Preparing for the Sydney to Hobart Yacht Race.*

town at St Mary's Church, Darling Street, Balmain, is a gem: one of those rare markets which has things you might actually want to buy – from clothes to crafts.

NATIONAL MARITIME MUSEUM,

Darling Harbour; open 10 am to 5 pm, entry A$7. As unconventional inside as it looks outside, this is one of the world's finest naval museums. Here you get everything from early Aborigine dug-outs to the history of Bondi Beach. Outside on the quay is a destroyer and the *Tu Do,* which made it as far as Darwin crammed with Vietnamese boat people.

POWERHOUSE MUSEUM

Harris Street, near Darling Harbour; open 10 am to 5 pm, entry A$5. Housed in a huge old power station is the **Museum of Applied Arts and Sciences**. Here they have a colossal display of anything that's even remotely concerned with science. If you choose to look at what interests you (for instance: brewing, wallpaper, old firepieces) this can be one of the major experiences of your trip. Take up their challenge – 'something for everyone' – and you won't be disappointed.

OTHER SIGHTS

We deliberately give the following a brief mention because we don't think they deserve as much of your time as those described above:

Paddington ('Paddo'): an attractive residential area 4 km east of the city centre with Victorian terraced houses; if you're going there, make for Five Ways, a meeting of several streets with interesting shops, the Royal pub and several good eating places.

Taronga Zoo a short ferry ride from Circular Quay Jetty 5 in a fine harbourside location. It's up a short hill (bus or cable car to top); *open daily 9 am to 5 pm, entry A$14, children A$7.*

Koala Park: on Castle Hill Road, West Pennant Hills, north-west Sydney; *open 9 am to 5 pm, entry A$8, children A$4; train to Pennant Hills Station and then bus No 661 to 665.*

Sydney Aquarium: at the east end of Pyrmont Bridge. Australian specialities including sharks and rays, viewed from underwater walkways; *open daily 9.30 am to 9.30 pm, entry A$13.50.*

St Andrew's Cathedral: across the open space off George Street, built in the 1870s and housing an unusual computerized organ.

RECOMMENDED HOTELS

The Regent, $$; 199 *George Street; tel.* (02) 238 000; *all major cards.*

Best hotel in town, with the best location. Views out over the Opera House and Sydney Harbour Bridge. Superb and tasteful interior decoration on an Australian theme.

The Kendall, $$; 122 *Victoria Street, Potts Point; tel.* (02) 357 3200; *all major cards.*

Excellent Victorian bed-and-breakfast accommodation on the quiet fringe of Kings Cross. Great hospitality and period decoration. Owned by a descendant of the poet Henry Kendall.

The Lord Nelson Brewery Hotel, $$; *Kent Street, The Rocks; tel.* (02) 251 4044; *all major cards.*

This is the oldest pub in town. In the old days it was fairly gruesome; now it has tidied up its act and is merely historic.

Sydney Travellers Rest Hotel, $-$$; 37 *Ultimo Street, Haymarket; tel.* (02) 281 5555; *cards* MC, V.

As good as you'll get at budget price close to the city centre. Rooms range in price; back rooms are quiet.

Manly Paradise Motel, $$; 54 *North Steyne, Manly; tel.* (02) 977 5799; *all major cards.*

If you want moderately priced beach-side accommodation within reach of the city centre, this is the place. They also have self-catering apartments. Manly is just half an hour by ferry from the centre.

Traveller Flats, $-$$; 117 *Victoria Street; tel.* (02) 356 3232; *most major cards.*

Standard self-catering apartments by Kings Cross, yet within walking distance of the Royal Botanic Gardens. Book early and ask for a harbour view.

RECOMMENDED RESTAURANTS

Kables, $$$; 199 *George Street; tel.* (02) 238 000; *all major cards.*

The best restaurant in town, serving superbly imaginative Australian cuisine, and regional variations. Chef Serge Dansereau is at the cutting edge of Aussie *haute cuisine*. Try their exceptional, and surprisngly inexpensive, set lunch menu (**$$**).

Imperial Peking Harbourside, $$$; 15 *Circular Quay, The Rocks; tel.* (02) 247 7073; *all major cards.*

The top Chinese in town, against very stiff opposition.

Sydney Tower Sky Lounge, $-$$; *Centrepoint Tower, Market Street; tel.* (02) 233 3722; *cards none.*

Serves coffees and snacks 300 m up, but without the sky-high prices in the restaurants on Levels 1 and 2, into which you stray at your peril.

Rockpool Oyster Bar, $$; 109 *George Street, The Rocks; tel.* (02) 247 8026; *most major cards.*

Reasonably priced seafood in the heart of Sydney's historic district. The restaurant itself, in the other part of the building, is definitely **$$$**.

Capitan Torres, $-$$; *Liverpool Street; no booking; cards none.*

Not everyone knows Sydney's Spanish district. The *tapas* here are as good (and as inexpensive) as you'll get in Spain.

Museum of Contemporary Art Café, $-$$; *Circular Quay West; tel.* (02) 252 1888; *all major cards; closes* 5.30 *pm.*

Best of the museum cafés by far. Good Australian menu, and the outside tables have great views of the Opera House and the ferries.

The Last Aussie Fishcaf, $$; 24 *Bayswater Road, Kings Cross; tel.* (02) 356 2911; *all major cards.*

Here the Fifties are still alive and jiving to *Peggy Sue*. Assorted seafood, including the famous Fishcaf Curry, which is sure to set you jitterbugging to the Wurlitzer.

Canberra and Region:
introduction

This section centres on the Australian capital Canberra, which is in Australian Capital Territory (ACT). Canberra is a modern architect-designed city whose main business is government. It was first occupied by parliament in 1927, and has an open, suburban feel to it, with a large artificial lake occupying its centre. The New Parliament Building dates from 1988, and is perhaps the nation's modern masterpiece (or monsterpiece, depending upon your taste). Nearby, on the lake shore, is the Australian National Gallery, which has a fine collection of Australian works and a sculpture garden where open-air concerts are staged in summer. These are just some of the capital's sights.

If you feel like doing something different, take a detour west to the Snowy Mountains. In winter they have the best skiing slopes in Australia, and in summer there is great bushwalking, canoeing and swimming.

If you have your own transport, the road linking Sydney with Canberra makes a pleasant journey of about 300 km, easily driven in a day. From Sydney, it quickly ascends through some fine mountain scenery, and then passes into sheep country. You'll need a minimum of a couple of days to see Canberra, and if you want to explore the Snowy Mountains I suggest you set aside another three days.

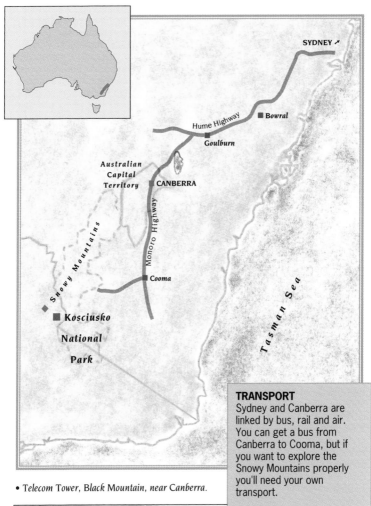

TRANSPORT
Sydney and Canberra are linked by bus, rail and air. You can get a bus from Canberra to Cooma, but if you want to explore the Snowy Mountains properly you'll need your own transport.

• *Telecom Tower, Black Mountain, near Canberra.*

CANBERRA ⊭ ✕

300 km SW of Sydney. The main tourist information office is in the city centre at 67, Northbourne Avenue (toll-free tel. 1800 026 166). Here you can pick up a detailed map of the city. Northbourne Avenue is the main artery which leads S off the Federal Highway into the city centre.

The city centre is known as Civic, and its heart lies Vernon Circle. Canberra's main shopping areas are the pedestrian malls east of the Circle.

Commonwealth Avenue runs south from Vernon Circle to Capital Circle, within which stands Parliament House on Capital Hill. Capital Hill is the summit of the 'parliamentary triangle' formed by Commonwealth Avenue, Kings Avenue and the lake; within it are many of Canberra's most important buildings.

History

Canberra has been the federal capital of Australia since 1927. With a population of more than a quarter of a million, it is still considerably smaller than most of the state capitals. Like Washington DC in the United Sates, its main business is the nation's business, and it even occupies its own federal territory. This is the Australian Capital Territory (ACT), which is not part of any state.

When the separate states of Australia joined together to become a federation in 1901, Melbourne became the national capital. But this was intended only as a temporary measure. The new Australia would have a brand new capital of its own, which owed no allegiance to any of the rival states. It took some years to find a suitable site. In the end, the choice was 2,300 square kilometres of territory in southern New South Wales. This had previously been used for raising sheep, and seemed quite suitable for rearing politicians instead.

A worldwide competition was announced to find an architect to build the new city. This was won by the American town planner Walter Burley Griffin, who was based in Chicago. The powers that be decided to call the new capital Canberra, after the old Aborigine word for the place – which they understood to mean 'meeting place'. This may seem like a happy coincidence, but it turns out that Canberra's founders may simply have been told what they *wanted*

to hear. Subsequent enquiries, too late, discovered that the word Canberra in fact means 'woman's breasts'.

Griffin (who had never seen Canberra) set to work designing a garden city for a population of 25,000. Closeted in his office on the other side of the world in Chicago, Griffin came up with a revolutionary idea. The city would have five separate centres, each devoted to a different function. The result was a collection of suburbs, with little urban cohesion and no living heart. This was to prove particularly apt. Even with its large state capitals, Australia's main centres of population were, and to a large extent remain, essentially suburban in character.

The building of Canberra was interrupted by the First World War. Even after this, progress was slow, as the politicians continued to scheme and to bicker over various details of their future home. Namely, how to pay for it – yet at the same time keep the precise cost of this vast project secret from those who were actually paying for it. Eventually, in 1927, the politicians decided it was time to move in, and the capital officially opened for business.

After all the grand openings, the Depression arrived, and building dwindled to a snail's pace once more. The world looked on in admiration. Long before anyone else, Australia had seemingly solved the problem of what to do about politicians – isolate them in a remote half-built city miles from anywhere. Here they would be entirely free to get on with doing what they knew best: politics.

Not until many years after the Second World War did Canberra begin to come into its own. The National Capital Development Commission (NCDC) was established in 1958, and unlike many such politically appointed commissions, it actually did something. The development of Canberra now began apace. In 1963 the Molonglo River was dammed, creating a lake 11 km long which now forms the central feature of the city. (Other, less revolutionary cities tend to have a central place where people can actually meet.) This stretch of water was named Lake Burley Griffin, after the man responsible for the parts of the city which had not been submerged beneath its surface.

Within ten years, the city's population

had risen from its originally projected 25,000 to more than 100,000 – most of whom were now civil servants and administrators. As we all know, once civil servants have managed to establish this sort of growth in employment, it is very difficult to stop them. Just a quarter of a century later the population of Canberra has leapt by almost 200 per cent – a rate of expansion which leaves even the likes of Mexico City and Rio de Janiero toiling far behind.

Although the main local industry continues to be job creation, Canberra now has other centres of employment besides the government. The city is the home of the prestigious **National University**, whose philosophy department has long been the finest in the southern hemisphere. And tourism is now a growing source of income. Deservedly so – for there's plenty to see in Canberra, even if this is mostly of the 'great capital institutions' variety.

SIGHTS & PLACES OF INTEREST

Canberra's main sights are scattered – seeing them on foot is not a good idea. There are a number of worthwhile bus tours (for details, contact the Canberra Tourist Information Centre, Jolimont Centre, 67 Northbourne Avenue, where many of these tours begin and end).

In fact, the best way to see this city is by bike. Canberra's green spaces are criss-crossed with cycle paths which link up most of the sights, making this the best cycling city in Australia. The most convenient hire service is Dial-a-Bicycle, tel. (06) 286 5463. They will deliver a bike to where you are staying.The hire charge is around A$20 per day, A$60 per week. This includes a helmet, compulsory in Australia.

Sights have been listed in order of interest and proximity to one another, rather than alphabetically.

Australian National Gallery,
Parkes Place; open 10 am to 5 pm daily, entry A$3. This fairly standard 'civic modernist' building houses the **national art collection** (which is separate from the various state collections). The building is linked by an overhead catwalk to the next-door High Court of Australia.

Inside the National Gallery you'll find a wide range of respectable Australian art, lightly seasoned with the usual indifferent or atrocious examples which all national galleries carry as ballast. By popular acclaim, the centrepiece of this collection must be Sidney Nolan's justly famous **Ned Kelly series** – though I think that some of his others are better still. Also not to be missed are the **Arthur Boyds.** The **Aborigine collection** has many peaks (and a few troughs). The bark paintings are superb. There are also works by various European and American big names, and some intriguing pieces of Oceanic origin.

The sculptures aren't quite as good, but they're in a pleasant setting looking out over Lake Burley Griffin. During the summer open-air concerts are staged here in the evenings – apply at the ticket office for the latest schedule. The gallery has an interesting bookshop.

Old Parliament House
King George Terrace. This rather laid-back white neoclassical pile is quintessential 1920s municipal in style, and benefits from its fine site overlooking the lake. From 1927, for more than 60 years, this was the home of Australia's parliament.Unfortunately it's not possible to go in, perhaps because they're still clearing up after parliament's last-night party here in 1988. This monumental thrash lasted until well after daybreak,

SIR DONALD BRADMAN
Donald Bradman was to cricket what Einstein was to physics. What before had been unthinkable was now proved with huge numbers. Indeed, when Bradman started batting, his feats often exercised the mathematicians at the scoreboard as much as they exercised the bowlers and fielders. At the age of 17 he was averaging 100 runs an innings for his local team. Three years later, in 1928, he was playing for Australia. He played for his country for 20 years, during which time he maintained an average of 99.4, and his highest score was 454. Known affectionately as 'the Don', he was always a gentleman both on and off the field.

• *Opposite*: *Parliament House*

and included such high jinks as the prime minister dancing the can-can with the leader of the opposition. Politicians in Canberra have enough practice to be able to hold their liquor very well indeed, leaving even the Aussie press astounded when the drinks bill for this jamboree finally leaked out.

New Parliament Building

Capital Hill; open 9 am to 5 pm daily; reached by 352 and 901 buses from the city centre. This cost over a billion Australian dollars and took almost a decade to build. The result is a striking white building whose architecture attempts a blend of the spectacular and the ordinary, and succeeds in being both. It is the work of Italian architect Romaldo Giurgola, who believes that buildings should blend with their landscape. In keeping with this, part of the roof is covered with earth and grass to make it look like the hilltop it replaced. Meanwhile, above this rises a supported stainless-steel flagstaff, which might perhaps have blended in at Cape Canaveral.

Some of the inside lives up to all expectation. The entrance hall has an **Aborigine mosaic,** as well as panels representing Australian plant life. Other halls and galleries contain many gems, including a huge and highly colourful **Arthur Boyd tapestry,** and **works by**

• *The Carillon, Lake Burley Griffin.*

• *Dome and interior of Australian War Memorial.*

Sidney Nolan, Tom Roberts and Albert Tucker. You can also see a copy of that fundamental democratic document, the Magna Carta – signed by England's bad king John in 1215. Much of this building is intended to have symbolic significance, and a recent political commentator has speculated that perhaps the latter document is intended to show that Australian democracy is a fake. Perish the thought.

Try a visit to the **House of Representatives** or the **Senate** (both within the building) and you'll soon see that this at least *sounds* like a democracy. The decibels rise to a peak at question time, which takes place most days at 2 pm. This is when the Government has to answer questions put by the Opposition: some have said it should be called Answer Time, while others have cruelly suggested that perhaps Lack of Answer Time would be closer to the mark.

Diplomatic District

Yarralumla. Because the city is modern and suburban in character, without any overall defining style, the various diplomatic missions have been allowed to choose their own style when designing their embassies. As a result, the world's nations, both great and small, have shown that Mickey Mouse taste is far from being a uniquely American

DETOUR – **THE SNOWY MOUNTAINS** ✉

In winter these mountains are a popular skiing area. You can expect snow from late June to September. The best base for exploring the region is **Cooma**, which is just over 100 km south of Canberra on the Monaro Highway. This is a small town with a pleasant multicultural feel, owing to the number of immigrants from all over the world who have settled here after working on the Snowy Mountains Hydroelectric Scheme. (The local Avenue of Flags marks the 27 nationalities who worked on the mammoth project.) The main **Visitors Centre** for the Snowy Mountains region is at 119 Sharp Street.

The best skiing in the Snowy Mountains is at **Thredbo**, which is 80 km west of Cooma and almost 1,400 m above sea level. It is a popular and expensive spot. A little down the scale in prices, and in terms of skiing level, is the large twin resort of **Smiggin Holes and Perisher Valley. Mount Selwyn,** up in the north, is also good.

This entire region is part of the **Kosciusko National Park**, which covers a vast 650,000 hectares, making it the largest in New South Wales. This is also worth exploring in summer, when everything is much cheaper. A **chairlift** will take you from Thredbo to within walking distance (6 km) of Mount Kosciusko peak.

Also worth seeing are the **Yarrangobilly Caves,** a huge complex of limestone caverns. These are just outside Kiandra, 115 km north of Cooma on the Snowy Mountains Highway. The all-season lakeside resort of **Jindabyne** lies in the mountains 60 km south-west of Cooma. This resort is entirely new, as the old settlement has now disappeared below the lake. In summer Jindabyne offers canoeing and fishing. In winter, it's one of the better less expensive resorts.

serve. Nation after nation has succeeded in stereotyping itself in a manner which would surely have caused outrage if it had been done by anyone else. (The Americans have their millionaire slave-owner's mansion, the Greeks should be wearing fake togas behind those fake pillars, and the Japanese have their usual crematorium garden.)

Questacon

Parkes Place. This new modernistic **Natural Science and Technology Centre** is picturesquely situated by the banks of Lake Burley Griffin (see below). It is a quintessential hands-on museum, with well over a hundred interactive exhibits for the hyperactive young mind. If the kids are still active after that, let them have a go on the continuous spiral walkway. After this, defeat is inevitable – so make for the café which serves cakes which will prove a good match for those with eyes larger than their stomach.

Lake Burley Griffin

This pleasantly landscaped stretch of water forms the central feature of the city. The best of several parks along its banks is **Commonwealth Park**, at the northern shore to the east. This contains the local oddity: an old house. **Blundell's Farmhouse** is typical of the sheep-rearer's cottages which used to dot this region. It dates from the 1860s. Inside there's a small **museum** (*open 10 am to 4 pm daily, entry* A$3).

Just offshore by the King's Avenue Bridge lies **Aspen Island,** with its carillon (donated by the British government).

At the other end of the park is the **Captain Cook Memorial Water Jet**, which can rise to almost 150 m. I was unable to work out the symbolism of this memorial until a local explained to me that this was what happened to Captain Cook's ship when he first hit Australia and sprung a leak – see page 33.

Black Mountain

Canberra is picturesquely contained within ridges of the Australian Alps, which provide some fine views down over the city. Black Mountain, to the west of town, rises to over 800 m, and can be reached by 904 bus. At the top there's a 200-m telecommunications tower, which has a revolving restaurant. *Tower open 9 am to 10 pm daily, entry* A$3.

SIGHTS IN THE CANBERRA REGION

BOWRAL

90 km SW of Sydney. The Hume Highway passes hereabouts through some spectacular mountain scenery, and then arrives at the rather ordinary town of Bowral. So why mention it? This is the birthplace of Australia's greatest sporting hero – in a nation where sport is the national religion. The greatest cricketer of all time, Sir Donald Bradman (see also page 61), was born here in 1908. The local **cricket ground** is named after him, and there's a **museum** devoted to his exploits.

COOMA 🚗

See Detour – The Snowy Mountains, opposite.

GOULBURN

200 km SW of Sydney. There's been a settlement here since 1833, making this the second oldest inland town in Australia. Right from the start, the main business here has been sheep. In honour of this they've erected a 10-m high sheep, the **Big Merino**. Like a woolly wooden horse of Troy, you can get inside it (where you learn the inside story of the sheep business). At night the Big Merino's eyes glow green in the dark, just like those of the shearers emerging after a long session in the local hotel.

KOSCIUSKO NATIONAL PARK

See Detour – The Snowy Mountains, opposite.

RECOMMENDED HOTELS

CANBERRA

Kythera Hotel, $-$$; 98 *Northbourne Avenue; tel.* (06) 248 7611; *most major cards.*

Pleasant spot north of city centre, with pool. There are a number of other moderately priced hotels along the avenue.

Manuka Park Apartments, $$: *Manuka Circle at Oxley Sreet; tel.* (06) 285 1175; *all major cards.*

Bright modern self-catering apartments, 1 km south-east of Capital Hill.

Acacia Motor Lodge, $$; 65 *Ainslie Avenue; tel.* (06) 249 6955; *most major cards.*

Standard accommodation with bed- and-breakfast, just north-east of the city centre.

COOMA

Swiss Motel, $-$$: *Massie Street; tel.* (064) 52 1950; *cards none.*

Sound basic accommodation at a fair price, in an area which can be expensive.

JINDABYNE

Aspen Chalet, $$-$$$; *Kosciusko Road; tel.* (064) 56 2372; *most major cards.*

It's essential to book in the skiing season. Outside this period, prices drop dramatically.

RECOMMENDED RESTAURANTS

CANBERRA

The Lobby Restaurant, $$; *King George Terrace; tel.* (06) 273 1563; *all major cards.*

Fodder for lobby fodder: a popular haunt of politicians from nearby Capital Hill. Imaginative international menu.

Tosolini's, $-$$; *London Circuit at East Row; tel.* (06) 247 4317; *all major cards.*

Italian café-restaurant where you can also dine outside. The cakes here are the finest in town.

Charcoal Restaurant, $$; 61 *London Circuit; tel.* (06) 248 8015; *all major cards.*

Renowned for years for its great steaks. Popular, so be sure to book.

The Tower Restaurant ($$$); 50 *m up the Telecom Tower on Black Mountain; tel.* (06) 248 6162; *all major cards.*

Fabulous views and a wildly expensive international menu.

Between Sydney and Port Macquarie
Myall Lakes and the Hunter Valley

400 km; map Nelles Australia, 1:400,000

This is the first leg of the long coastal trek from Sydney north to Brisbane. (To find out about the rest of the trail, see Australia Overall: 2. And if you are thinking about travelling the whole eastern coast of Australia, see also Australia Overall: 7, 8 and 9, which take you all the way to Cairns in northern Queensland. If you want to go still further, Local Explorations: 11 describes the stretch north from Cairns to Cape York, the northernmost tip.)

The Pacific Highway north of Sydney passes a number of points of interest. Just outside Gosford lies Old Sydney Town. This is a reconstruction of the city as it was 200 years ago, complete with realistically staged escapes by the convicts, and the occasional hanging.

North of here you come to the industrial port of Newcastle, which is redeemed by its fine beach. Inland is the famous Hunter Valley, which produces some of Australia's finest wines. A tour of this region can be a gastronomic as well a a vinicultural treat.

North of Newcastle you come to the Myall Lakes, a coastal area of outstanding natural beauty. Inland from here is the Barrington Tops National Park, a wooded mountainous region which is also a World Heritage Area. Here you'll find some fine walking trails amongst the forests and the high gullies.

You can travel between Sydney and Port Macquarie in a day, but if you want to stop off to see the Hunter Valley and some of the sights, you should allow three to four days.

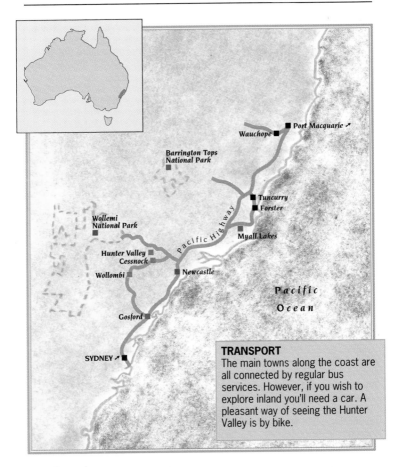

Port Macquarie

Wauchope

Barrington Tops
National Park

Tuncurry
Forster

Wollemi
National Park

Pacific Highway

Myall Lakes

Hunter Valley
Cessnock

Wollombi

Newcastle

Pacific
Ocean

Gosford

SYDNEY

TRANSPORT
The main towns along the coast are all connected by regular bus services. However, if you wish to explore inland you'll need a car. A pleasant way of seeing the Hunter Valley is by bike.

• *Pascific Beach*

SIGHTS & PLACES OF INTEREST

BARRINGTON TOPS NATIONAL PARK ⚏

200 km SW of Port Macquarie. Here you're high in the Great Dividing Range. The peak of Barrington Tops itself is over 1,500 m high. The unspoiled woodland and forests of this mountain region are of such ecological importance that the park has been designated a World Heritage Area. The **main information centre** for the park is at Gloucester River, east of the park, and the best way to get here is via the small town of Gloucester, 60 km inland from Forster-Tuncurry. The national park has some great forest walking trails, but is liable to heavy snow in winter. (It can be pretty chilly up here at all seasons.)

CESSNOCK

See Hunter Valley, this page.

FORSTER-TUNCURRY ⚏

On the coast just N of the Myall Lakes National Park. Twin settlements either side of the passage from Willis Lake to the sea, joined by a bridge. Forster is the larger of the two, and has a **Tourist Information Office** opposite the lake. This is oyster country. To work up an appetite you can swim in the lake or at one of the sea beaches. The lake is also good for **canoeing.**

For thousands of years this region was a thriving Aborigine homeland. In the early years of the 19thC the encroaching colonists and the local Aborigines fought for possession of the land. The result was some gruesome ambushes and bloodthirsty reprisal massacres. At Forster you can take a tour of the locality which brings to life the old Aborigine way of life. Contact Aboriginal Ranger Heritage Tours, tel. (065) 55 5274.

Forster-Tuncurry also makes a useful base for touring the **Myall Lakes National Park** (see page 72), which is south of here.

GOSFORD

Along the N shore of Brisbane Water, just N of Sydney. Even out here you're still just within commuting range of Sydney – and it shows, especially in the house prices. On summer weekends you also get crowds passing through on their way to the beaches further along the coast. The only reason Gosford gets a mention is because there are several things worth seeing in the neighbourhood.

Eight kilometres south-west of Gosford, off the Pacific Highway, is **Old Sydney Town** (*open 10 am to 4 pm Wed to Sun, daily during school holidays, entry A$ 15*). This is a fairly authentic reconstruction of Sydney back in the old convict settlement days – though the atmosphere is somewhat undermined by passing stagecoaches of authentic tourists. Fortunately these are ignored by the authentic 'characters' who roam the set acting out quaintly authentic scenes – the odd attempted escape, the occasional flogging, and other standard examples of British colonial bad behaviour. There's also a zoo.

Also worth a visit is the nearby **Brisbane Water National Park**, just south of Gosford. This has some bushwalks, and if you don't have time to get out and see any Aborigine art in better places, there are also some **rock engravings,** which almost certainly pre-date the pyramids.

HUNTER VALLEY ⚏ ✕

Inland NW from Newcastle. This region is famous for wine and coal. If you wish to visit the coal mines, instead of touring the vineyards and sampling the wine, you should really be reading a different book. But just to set you mind at rest, every now and again (especially in the upper regions of the valley) huge open-cast mines add their touch of colour to the unrelenting greenery. And at Burning Mountain, north of Scone, there's even smoke from a perpetually smouldering subterranean coal seam. (Geologists reckon that this was probably lit by an earthquake – clash of rocks, spark, gas pocket – around the time William the Conqueror was invading Britain.)

Fortunately, the best vineyards are in the lower part of the valley. The chief town here is **Cessnock**, just off the main valley, amidst pleasant rolling countryside watered by running streams. Here you can pick up an excellent map of the Hunter Valley wine region at the local **Tourist Information Centre** on the corner of Wollombi Street and Mount View Road. Harvest time in Australia is around February and

AN ACTIVE CONTINENT

The earthquake which hit Newcastle in 1989 was but a minor episode in Australia's long history of geological transformation.

Australia was originally part of the southern mega-continent Gondwanaland. Over the aeons, this gradually split and drifted apart to form India, Africa, South America, Antarctica – and Australia. At that period it was linked to Asia via a land bridge joining what are now the islands of

Indonesia and the Philippines to South-East Asia. Several times, the entire interior of Australia became flooded, its submarine surface forming the ocean bed. Sand, as well as layers of seashells and crushed coral, are a regularly occurring geological feature of the present-day interior.

Around two million years ago, the interior rose for the last time above the surface of the ocean. Subject to heavy rainfall, it became covered with rich tropical rainforest and jungle (remnants of which can still be found in the occasional sheltered and watered creeks).

Later, the east of the continent was transformed by violent geological turbulence. As a result of this the Great Dividing Range was thrust up just inland of the east coast. When the subsequent Ice Ages came they reached as far north as the Snowy Mountains on what is now the New South Wales – Victoria border. When this ice melted, it

flooded the land which linked Tasmania and New Guinea to the Australian mainland, as well as creating a number of inlets and natural harbours along the coast, the most notable of which is modern-day Sydney harbour.

Nowadays, Australia is comparatively free of violent geological activity, though it's still subject

to the odd warning tremor – as the recent earthquake which hit Newcastle shows only too well.

• *Hunter Valley wines.*

AUSTRALIAN WINE

The origins of the Aussie wine business have long since vanished beneath the centre of Sydney. This is where the first vineyards in the continent were planted, shortly after the colony was established. Alas, the wine produced here wasn't much good, and as Sydney expanded the vineyards were overrun and not replaced. An exception was at the town of **Camden**, which now lies outside the sprawling edges of Sydney on the Hume Highway, just after it starts its long climb into the mountains.

Settlers first reached Camden in 1805, and within 20 years a Scottish family called the Macarthurs was producing a sizeable vintage each year. A decade later vineyards were first planted further north in New South Wales – at Hunter Valley, which runs inland from Newcastle. Not until a couple of decades later did German immigrants begin planting the vineyards of South Australia. These soon expanded and spread. As a result, South Australia is now the major producer of Australian wine. However, New South Wales still continues to produce wine in considerable quantities, and also has a few of the best vintages in the land.

It wasn't until the mid 1960s that the wine business really began to take off in Australia. This was helped by a gradual shift in Aussie drinking habits. Although the massive annual production of beer didn't actually go down, the Aussies still felt capable of taking on board a rapidly increasing amount of wine. And over the past ten years or so, the world has begun to wake up to the quality of this product. Australian Chardonnay is now a byword in Britain, and Australian wines of all kinds have begun making considerable inroads into the US market.

March, and Cessnock stages a suitably bacchanalian **Hunter Valley Vintage Festival** every February

Cessnock makes a useful base if you're planning a comprehensive sampling of the vineyards and their products. There are more than three dozen wineries in the area, mostly a few kilometres to the north-west of Cessnock. (Head for Pokolbin, and take McDon-

• *Vineyards, Hunter Valley.*

alds Road north; at the crossroads with Broke Road there are vineyards in every direction.) Most of these vineyards are open for tasting. Remember, though, that this delightful custom is intended as a prelude to some actual purchasing. These are not charity organizations for roaming oenologists.

(Though you'll find the wine talk here can be as knowledgeable as anywhere, and without too much of the superfluous stronzo.)

Almost all the wineries in the Hunter Valley offer tastings. At the **Golden Grape Estate** on Oakey Creek Road (south-west of Pokolbin) you can see the oldest winepress in Australia, which first began pressing grapes around the time Queen Victoria ascended to the throne. Nearby on Marrowbone Road you'll find **McWilliams Mount Pleasant**, another historic spot which has been renowned for its wine for well over a century. My favourite winery is way off in the Upper Hunter Valley. This is **Reynolds Yarraman** on Yarraman Road, and it is worth searching for. Here you'll find some of the finest wines in the entire region in a superb setting. Families should try **Lindeman's Winery** at Pokolbin, where they also have a children's adventure playground, barbecue and a little wine-making museum.

MYALL LAKES

100 *km* NE *of Newcastle.* Picturesque region of inland lakes and coastal scenery with some excellent beaches, which has become a national park. The best place to pick up information is at **Bombah Point** (10 km from Bulahdelah, which is on the Pacific Highway). From Port Stevens, south of the park, they run **boat trips** through the lakes. The best beach is at **Seal Rocks**, at the northern end of the park. The **lighthouse** here has great sea and coastal views.

NEWCASTLE ⇔ ✕

180 *km* N *of Sydney.* This is the second largest city in New South Wales, with a population of well over a quarter of a million. It's an industrial city, with much the same allure as its namesake in Britain. (In other words, if you come from here it breaks your heart when you're away from it, and does much the same when you get back.)

Newcastle began life in 1804 as a satellite penal colony to Sydney. It was intended for the cream of the convict community – those they just couldn't do anything with, no matter how much they were threatened, thrashed, given cups of tea in bed, and so on. These founder members of the colony soon ensured, with only a little help from their guards,

that it became known as 'The Hell of New South Wales'. Meanwhile, its first official name was only slightly more prepossessing – Coal River. This became the port for the coal which was mined upriver in the Hunter Valley. For years slag heaps, docks and heavy industry contributed to the grime. Then, like the convicts, these began to fade into the background. The place was cleaned up a bit, and modern Newcastle emerged – as busy as ever, but without so much grime. A busy commercial port in Australia is not the same as elsewhere – for a start, there are fine swimming and surfing beaches. There's even a pleasant garden area by the river. And now Newcastle even has a few tourist sights. The **Regional Art Gallery** is on Laman Street, but is really for those culture vultures who are absolutely determined to miss nothing, as well as for lovers on a rainy day who will miss everything. The **Newcastle Regional Museum**, on the other hand, has some interesting interactive technology and is great for children and adults alike. Otherwise, in summer there are cruises around the harbour.

In 1989 Newcastle was the epicentre of the worst earthquake to hit the populated fringe of Australia. Damage was done to buildings, and 12 people were killed. The damage has almost all been cleared up (though you can still detect the odd remnant), and Newcastle continues to improve.

PORT MACQUARIE

See *Australia Overall: 2.*

SYDNEY

See pages 42-57.

WAUCHOPE

20 *km* E *of Port Macquarie.* If you're to find the way here, you'll first have to pronounce it properly – ie 'war-hope'. This small woodland settlement began life in the mid-19thC as a timber town. Now the main activity in the area is a replica of a mid-19thC timber town. This is just 10 km down the road (*open 9 am to 5 pm daily, entry* A$13) at **Timberland**. Here you can see just how the mighty tough lumberjacks set about being mighty tough, venting their pent-up spleen on innocent trees and making voluminous contributions to the wood chip and sawdust industries. Even more

interesting is the replica bakery, where they bake replica Victorian bread.

If you want to see a geniune load of bull, head a couple of kilometres east of town, and here you will come across **Big Bull**, which is advertised as 'the world's largest fibreglass bull'. This doesn't even produce sawdust, but it does have an animal nursery.

Also just east of town is a place where you can hire canoes and paddle down the river.

WOLLEMI NATIONAL PARK

60 km NW of Newcastle. This park occupies the south bank of the Hunter and Goulburn Rivers, just north-west of the main Hunter Valley wine region (see page 68). It has some fine walking trails through mountain scenery, and is just the place to work off all that eating and drinking which was so unavoidable at the wineries. Information on the trails and activities in this park is available at the tourist centres in Cessnock and Newcastle.

WOLLOMBI

40 km N of Gosford. Attractive small village at the western approach to the Hunter Valley wine region. There has been a settlement here for 180 years, and the place still looks much as it did in the old coaching days, when it was an important staging post on the Great Northern Road.

RECOMMENDED HOTELS

BARRINGTON TOPS NATIONAL PARK
Barrington Guesthouse, $$; *Dungong; tel. (049) 95 3212; most major cards.*

This is the closest base for exploring the national park, but even then it's 40 km from the action. Price includes half board.

FORSTER-TUNCURRY
Smuggler's Cove Holiday Village, $-$$; *45 The Lakes Way, Forster-Tuncurry; tel. (065) 54 666; most major cards.*

Cabin accommodation just south of town, convenient for families.

HUNTER VALLEY
During the summer prices rise at weekends, and you have to book ahead. During the week prices can dip considerably.

Wentworth Hotel, $$; *36 Vincent Street, Cessnock; tel. (049) 90 1364; most major cards.*

Accommodation in a pleasant old country pub, which also has a recommendable restaurant.

Vineyard Hill Hotel, $$; *Lovedale Road, Pokolbin; tel. (049) 90 4166; all major cards.*

Tastefully decorated rooms with fine views out over the vineyards.

NEWCASTLE
The Grand Hotel, $-$$; *Church Street; tel. (049) 29 3489; cards none.*

Traditional-style historic watering hole a short walk from the beach.

Newcastle Harbourside Motel; $$; *107 Scott Street; tel. (049) 26 3244; most major cards.*

A friendly welcome from the helpful staff. In the centre of town.

RECOMMENDED RESTAURANTS

HUNTER VALLEY
Old George and Dragon, $$$; *48 Melbourne Street, East Maitland; tel. (049) 33 7272; all major cards.*

Some 30 km east of Cessnock, but well worth the detour. The finest cuisine, in a region noted for its fine cuisine. And wines to match.

Blaxland's Restaurant, $$; *Broke Road, Pokolbin; tel. (049) 98 7724; all major cards.*

Excellent traditional dishes served in historic atmosphere.

NEWCASTLE
Voquet, $$; *Darby Street South; tel. (049) 29 5855; all major cards.*

Smart, but friendly spot specializing in European continental cuisine at reasonable prices.

Between Port Macquarie and Brisbane
The Gold Coast

900 km; map Nelles Australia, 1:400,000

This region has just about everything you could wish for in the way of seaside pleasures. The Gold Coast is a cross between Torremolinos and Miami Beach – with high-rise blocks lining the front and dozens of discos, where the sun shines for 300 days a year, and the surfing never stops. The resorts to the south are quieter, but still have fine beaches and great surf. Those who prefer a less hectic time should visit the remote beaches of South Stradbroke Island, or the hippie colonies of the hinterland of north-east New South Wales. And for that ultimate away-from-it-all experience there's Lord Howe Island, 600 km out in the Pacific.

From Port Macquarie to the northern end of the Gold Coast and Brisbane is at least a couple of days' drive along the Pacific Highway. But if you want to stop off and take in some of the action, allow a week for this route.

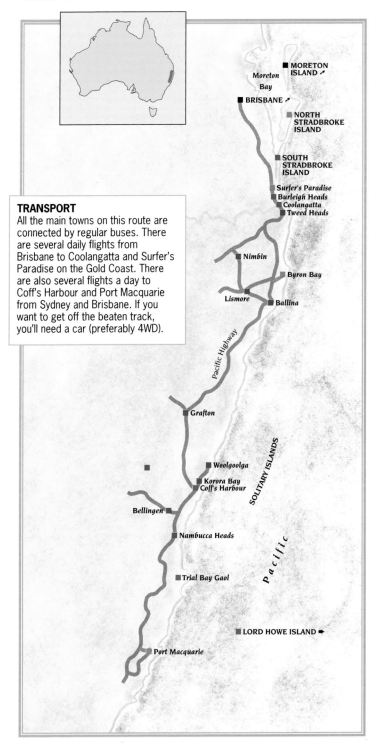

MORETON ISLAND ↗
Moreton Bay
BRISBANE ↗
NORTH STRADBROKE ISLAND
SOUTH STRADBROKE ISLAND
Surfer's Paradise
Burleigh Heads
Coolangatta
Tweed Heads
Nimbin
Byron Bay
Lismore
Ballina
Pacific Highway
Grafton
Woolgoolga
Korora Bay
Coff's Harbour
SOLITARY ISLANDS
Bellingen
Nambucca Heads
Pacific
Trial Bay Gaol
LORD HOWE ISLAND ➡
Port Macquarie

TRANSPORT
All the main towns on this route are connected by regular buses. There are several daily flights from Brisbane to Coolangatta and Surfer's Paradise on the Gold Coast. There are also several flights a day to Coff's Harbour and Port Macquarie from Sydney and Brisbane. If you want to get off the beaten track, you'll need a car (preferably 4WD).

SIGHTS & PLACES OF INTEREST

BALLINA
40 km S of Byron Bay on the Pacific Highway and the coast. Once upon a time there was a gold rush at Ballina. The gold ran out more than 100 years ago, and nothing of any great significance has happened here since. The only remnant of the gold rush is Shaw's Bay Hotel, where drinking has continued uninterrupted since the first nugget was spent over the counter in the 1880s. (I was assured by the barman that they'll still take gold nuggets if you have them.)

Nowadays Ballina is a popular holiday resort, occupying the island at the mouth of the Richmond River. It's famous for its beaches and its bars. Both of these are renowned for their quantities of foam-topped liquid, which the surfers seem to enjoy in equal amounts.

BELLINGEN
W off Pacific Highway at Urunga, just S of Coff's Harbour. This picturesque small town is set in the beautiful Bellingen River valley. Several of the town's buildings are protected by the National Trust. The place has become something of an artistic-hippy colony, though none of its equally picturesque inhabitants is yet being looked after by the National Trust. You can see (and buy) interesting craftwork at the **Yellow Shed** and the **Old Butter Factory**. It's also possible to hire a canoe and head out along the river, which has duck-billed platypuses. Once a month (on the third Sunday), there's a local market where you can buy anything the locals either produce or want to get rid of. (This has a rubbish quotient which is somewhat lower than many other markets of its kind.)

During the summer hundreds of flying foxes nest on **Bellingen Island**.

Bellingen is the setting of one of the final scenes in Peter Carey's novel *Oscar and Lucinda*, which seems set to become an Australian classic.

BURLEIGH HEADS ⊨
10 km S of Surfer's Paradise. Until the 1960s much of the Gold Coast hinterland was still unspoiled rainforest. Now all that's left is the small national park at Burleigh Heads. The park occupies a headland formed by the prehistoric lava flows from the inland volcanoes. There are nature trails through the forest, which is renowned for its exotic birdlife. The sea around the headland is also renowned for its fine surf.

BYRON BAY ⊨ ✕
On the coast 180 km S of Brisbane. Many moons ago Byron Bay was an ordinary little dot on the map, with just a few nondescript wooden houses, an abattoir and a pub. Then the nearby beaches were discovered by the surfers. After them came the hippies – attracted by the laid-back atmosphere and the climate (relaxingly warm in the winter, and really too warm to do anything except 'dig them vibes, man', in the summer). Vegetarian cafés, cool music joints (as well as other sorts of joints) and meditation centres became the order of the day. One shop even boasted a notice: 'Shoplifting is bad for your karma'. The hippies were soon joined by all manner of alternative Australians, hippies who hadn't realized that hippies were meant to be extinct, straightforward pleasure-seekers, and other parody lifestylists. Ironically, the place was then finally 'discovered' by people who had made a fortune out of parodying Australian lifestyles – like the soap stars and Paul Hogan (Crocodile Dundee himself).

Byron Bay remains very much a pillar of alternative Australia, though during the summer it attracts young people of all kinds, some of whom aspire to a hipness they wouldn't dare adopt back at the office in Sydney, and many others who simply aspire to a youth which all too evidently departed a decade or two ago. All this makes Byron Bay a pleasant laid-back spot. The soap starlets mingle all but unrecognized amongst those who pretend they've never seen a soap in their life, and everyone contentedly goes about their daily lack of business. Though how long this magic mix will continue is anybody's guess. The beaches in the region are so beautiful, and the area so ripe for exploitation, that there are the inevitable rumours of a Club Med being set up here in the near future. Then the soap opera will become reality and there will be no room for parody any more.

To the horror of some local purists, there are still plenty of things to do in

CAPE BYRON

This rocky headland, 2 km east of Byron Bay, is the furthest east you can get on the Australian mainland. Several similarly romantic spots have been named after the notorious Romantic poet Lord Byron. This is the exception. The cape was discovered by Captain Cook before Byron was even born, and was named after his more respectable (and almost equally gifted) grandfather John Byron, the celebrated navigator. John Byron believed in journeying further afield than the continental boudoirs which were to become his grandson's favourite field of exploration. Byron senior's expertise as a navigator gained him the nickname 'Foul-weather Jack'. Historians dispute whether this was because he was an expert at getting out of foul weather, or because his presence simply attracted it. Either way, between 1764 and 1766 he circumnavigated the globe – braving typhoons, hurricanes and waterspouts en route. However, one cape he never rounded was Cape Byron. His round-the-world foul-weather odyssey bypassed the calm waters off Cape Byron by several thousand kilometres. (Foul-weather Jack's reputation might not have survived the indignity of being becalmed.)

The lighthouse which now stands on the cape dates from 1901, and its beaming equipment is said to be more powerful than any other in the

• *Cape Byron .*

southern hemisphere. To reach the lighthouse, drive up from Byron Bay to the end of Lighthouse Road. A kilometre or so before the end of this road is Captain Cook's Lookout, where you can head off along the path which leads for 3 km around the headland.

Cape Byron is a favourite spot with sunrise watchers. Also you can often see dolphins playing far out in the ocean. Between mid-June and mid-July you can sometimes see the humpbacked whales on their migration north to spawn, and between mid-September and mid-October they follow the same route back towards the Antarctic.

Byron Bay which don't involve hours on end in the lotus position. The best nearby surfing spots are at **The Pass** (about 1 km east of town in the direction of Cape Byron), and beyond at **Watego's Beach**, where you can often see dolphins. There are several shops in town where you can hire a board, as well as a wetsuit. Adrenalin-addicts will also be attracted to Byron Head for the hang-gliding. If you haven't tried it before, and you really want to know what an 'adrenalin rush' means, contact **Flight Zone** (*tel.* (066) 85 3178), which operates tandem flights where you can gibber with terror beside someone who claims to know what he's doing, high above the beauties of the world you have left far behind.

A marginally less suicidal ambience can be experienced on white-water rafting trips down the Nymboida River further down the coast. Contact **Rapid Action** (*tel.* (075) 30 4088) for details of expeditions, which take place between November and May. After all this you may well feel like visiting **Relax Haven** at the Belongil Beachhouse, out on Childe Street between the Main Beach and Belongil Creek to the west of town. Here you can relax until you're comatose in a flotation tank, and then be massaged back to consciousness.

• *Community centre, Byron Bay.*

• *Cape Byron Beach.*

A couple of kilometres or so offshore are **Julian Rocks**, the best diving spot on this stretch of the coast. For information about trips and equipment, contact **Byron Bay Dive Centre** (9 *Lawson Street*), on the way to Clarks Beach to the east of town.

On the first Sunday of the month there's a market at Butler Street, on the other side of the railway, where you can pick up a suitably exotic range of alternative bargains or bargain alternatives for things you probably never needed in the first place. Either way, it's great fun. See also information on Cape Byron on page 77.

COFF'S HARBOUR ⇔ ✕
130 *km N of Port Macquarie on the Pacific Highway and the coast.* Coff's Harbour is an odd mixture of commercial port and beach resort, set amidst some spectacular coastal scenery. All around there are superb beaches, and behind

town the hills rise to the mountains of the Great Dividing Range.

Coff's Harbour is in the centre of the Banana Coast. To celebrate this fact, a giant concrete banana has been erected on the Pacific Highway a couple of kilometres north of town. This is part of a **banana theme park** (*open 9am to 3pm; entry and ride A$10*), where you can learn all about the banana industry. Features include early pioneer banana-men, caves where Aborigines dreamed of bananas, a video, a ride on an elevated railway through the plantations, and an explanation of what the banana plantations of the space age future will look like. (Alas, even then bananas still won't have zips, apparently.) The kids love it, though the experience may well drive you bananas. If so, be sure to hang on to your sanity long enough to taste their absolutely superb

• *Go bananas at Coff's Harbour.*

banana milk shakes at the end. For these alone, it's worth risking banana-mania tremens.

Coff's Harbour itself has the usual resort jollities, including a **zoo**, 12 km north of town, famed for its wombats, a pet porpoise pool down by the riverfront, a racecourse and a golf course. More fun than any of these are the white-water rafting trips on the Nymboida River (**Whitewater Rafting Professionals** *at* 20 *Moonee Street run day trips for* A$100). Another outlying attraction well worth a look is **George's Gold Mine** (*open* Wed *to* Sun 10.30 *am to* 3.30 *pm; entry* A$7), 40 km north-west in the mountains at Lowanna.

But the real reason for coming to Coff's Harbour is the number of great beaches. **Digger Beach** just north of town is my favourite; maybe because this is where I learned to surf properly (earlier disastrous efforts had been attempted in private on other continents). Here they're experts in teaching the inept to surf – half a dozen lessons for A$75, and if you still can't do it the lessons go on free until either you can, or you can't stand making a fool of yourself in public any longer. (I'm told that the latter factor usually comes into play well before the sixth free lesson.)

At the entrance to the harbour is **Muttonbird Island**, which can be reached by way of the northern harbour jetty. During the summer this is home to nesting Muttonbirds, who return each evening after their day's fishing far out in the ocean. Each April they set out on their amazing migration north. Their route takes them around the entire western Pacific rim, past the Philip-

pines, Japan, and Siberia, to the Aleutian Islands off Alaska. Then it's time to head back once more for the Big Banana.

COOLANGATTA ✕
On the coast 100 *km* S *of Brisbane.* This is my favourite spot on the Gold Coast. It has almost everything you'll find in Surfer's Paradise – including better surf and better beaches – but attracts a less hectic crowd. That said, you can still have a wild old time here. The coastal strip around Coolangatta sprawls either side of the New South Wales border, which means that during the New Year celebrations here they make use of the hour time difference between the two states and bring the New Year in twice.

The state border actually runs through the **Captain Cook Memorial** at Point Danger, where there's a lighthouse and a big bronze globe which shows the details of Captain Cook's 18thC voyages of exploration and discovery.

DORRIGO NATIONAL PARK
NW *of Bellingen.* Follow the road from Bellingen (see page 76) inland up to Dorrigo, where this national park may be comparatively small but its exceptional qualities have placed it on the World Heritage List. Here on the plateau you're more than 300 m above sea level. Apart from the rainforest, the park is also famous for orchids and waterfalls. There are several fine trails through the forest, the best of which is the 6 km Cedar Falls Walk which takes you to a superb waterfall.

If you fancy staying up here for a longer spell, head to the small town of **Dorrigo**, which has a motel and a useful information centre for the park and surrounding region. The road north from Dorrigo takes you past the spectacular **Dangar Falls**.

GRAFTON
On the Pacific Highway 50 *km* N *of Coff's Harbour.* An inland country town on the banks of the Clarence River, Grafton is famous for its Jacaranda Festival, which takes place during the last week in October and the first week in November. A bit long for a jacaranda festival? Not if you know what goes on here for the rest of the year. The person who

sets up an insomnia clinic in Grafton could well corner the market.

To get in the mood, visit **Schaeffer House,** 192 *Fitzroy Street; open Tues to Thurs and Sun 1 to 4 pm; entry* A$3. It contains a small regional museum which is all that one expects of this remarkably persistent species. Guaranteed no excitement here: just a mildly interesting meander through the byways of mundaneness. Then head on down the same street to **Prentice House Art Gallery** at No. 158 (*open Tues to Sat 10 am to 4 pm*).

Now you're ready for a superbly uneventful trip down the wide Clarence River (contact **Clarence River Ferries,** *tel.* (066) 46 6423). After the crass bustle which characterizes so many of the coastal resorts during the high season, Grafton is a genuine tonic. A spot to unwind in: savour it at your leisure.

If you can't do without the sea, head for the adjacent coastline which is part of the **Yuragir National Park**, where you'll find a few remote fishing villages and surfing spots, most of which have a serviceable motel.

KORORA BAY

3 km N of the Big Banana (just outside Coff's Harbour), off Pacific Highway. Follow signs to the coast to reach this superb small sandy bay between the headlands, which is often fairly deserted.

LISMORE

45 km inland from Byron Bay. The main 'city' of north-east New South Wales, Lismore has a population of more than 40,000. Just over a century ago this was a booming timber town, until the lumberjacks became too enthusiastic and put themselves out of business. Now the surrounding countryside is mainly farmland. For some reason this region has long attracted artists and writers, as well as assorted colourful hangers-on. Another unexpectedly lively feature of Lismore is the thirsty life of the students from Southern Cross University.

On the river front you can pick up a cruise, or even take a day trip all the way down to Ballina on the coast (see page 76). Anyone with time to spare

---

LORD HOWE ISLAND ⌫

If you really want to get away from it all, Lord Howe Island, 600 km east of Port Macquarie, is the place to go. The island is only just over 10 km long and 2 km wide, and lies way out in the Tasman Sea almost half way to New Zealand.

Lord Howe Island is named after an 18thC English admiral. Lord Howe played a major role in helping England lose its American colonies, but redeemed himself 20 years later by defeating the French in a battle of no great importance.

The coral reef at Lord Howe Island is said to be the southernmost in the world. For years the island's main income was exporting seeds of the rare Kentia palm tree, which is indigenous to this remote spot. Lord Howe Island even has its own benevolent micro-climate, making it pleasantly warm in winter (never below 15°C) and not too hot in the summer (seldom rising above 25°C).

As you would expect, the place is a paradise. You can swim in the lagoon, surf at Blinkey Beach, snorkel the reef, feed the fish by hand at Ned's Bay, or take a cruise around the island for a view of its two mountains, whose wooded slopes rise sheer from the sea to more than 800 m. For the energetic there are even climbing expeditions to the top of the highest (southern) peak – Mount Gower (875 m). Others may prefer to hire a bike and try to break the island's speed limit (25 kph). You can also hire a motorbike, and there are just a few cars on the island (some of which can be hired). Another mixed blessing comes in the form of the golf course.

Of course there's a snag. Most of us will find it difficult to gain admittance to any paradise, but where earthly paradises are concerned, money always helps. Expect the flight alone from Port Macquarie, the nearest point on the Australian mainland, to set you back well over A$500. Your best bet is a package deal, including accommodation, from Sydney or Brisbane.

• *Near Nimbin*.

should drive north of town into the woods and mountains, past the remote villages of the hinterland, many of which have some pleasantly oddball inhabitants, where you can be sure of seeing (and hearing) some truly breathtaking views. The best-known of these villages is Nimbin (see page 82).

MORETON BAY

At the mouth of the Brisbane River. This protected stretch of water off the coast at Brisbane is almost 100 km long and filled with islands large and small. (You could visit a different one each day of the year and still have a few left over.) From 1867 **St Helena Island** was briefly the location of the notorious Moreton Bay Penal Colony. Later it became a top-security prison for incorrigible escapers. By 1932 most of the prisoners had either escaped or were due to be released, apart from a few hard-core lifers, and the prison was closed down. (The remaining prisoners continued their idle lifestyle at the government's expense elsewhere.) Now it's a national park, with a number of beaches where you too can indulge in the idle life. Another popular beach spot is **Coochie Island** (also known as Coochiemudlo Island), which can be reached by a short ferry ride from Victoria Point on the mainland south-east of Brisbane.

Another island worth visiting is **South Stradbroke Island**. Despite being so close to the Gold Coast, this 20-km-long thin island remains largely unspoiled. Although it is only 1 km wide, its inner scrubland still has kangaroos. The island is popular with fishermen and surfers (the best surf being at the south-eastern beach). Cruise trips run from Surfer's Paradise down the coast: one of the main points of interest for day trippers to this remote spot is the noisy crowded bar at the aptly named **Tippler's Resort**. Contrary to popular myth, survivors of a visit to this watering hole do not get their money back when they return to the mainland if they are still capable of articulating the name of the island.

For Bribie Island and Moreton Island see Australia Overall: 7. For North Stradbroke Island see page 84.

MORETON ISLAND

See Australia Overall: 7, page 35.

NAMBUCCA HEADS

90 km N of Port Macquarie on the Pacific Highway and the coast. Pronounced 'Numbucka' Heads, this is a quiet little resort with a population of just over 6,000. There's an excellent patrolled surfing beach 1.5 km up the coast. The heads themselves have spectacular views along the shore.

An ideal stopover on the Pacific Highway, especially at the height of the season when other places are packed.

NIMBIN 🚄

40 km N of Lismore on country roads, close to Mt Nardi and the Nightcap National Park. Nimbin may only have a popula-

tion of just over 1,000, but this is where it all began. In 1973 the never-to-be-forgotten Aquarius Festival was held here (though many veteran participators insist: 'Anyone who remembers it, wasn't there.'). This event sparked the hippie back-to-the-land movement. In many cases, this movement was just that: many prone long-haired individuals lying with their backs to the land. 'Stay cool, man.' Others, with a more determined attitude towards staying cool, took to growing things especially combustible plants with long pointy green leaves.

Nimbin has never really recovered from the '70s. You'll encounter all kinds

• *Nimbin, still a magnet for alternative lifestyles.*

of quaint things here that you probably thought were extinct – such as communes, bandanas, grimy feet in grimy sandals, making love rather than war with your partner, and laid-back liberal folk with flowing psychedelic clothes. In 1998 they're due to celebrate the 25th anniversary of the original Aquarius Festival, under conditions which they hope will ensure that nobody remembers it for another 25 years.

Cullen Street is the main drag, which of course has its **Rainbow Café**. Other shops are thick with the incense of yesteryear (barely masking the scent of 'Right, sunshine, what's going on here?'). Those who remember the '70s will find themselves returning to the never-never land of their youth – those who managed to avoid this social handicap will find themselves entering an intriguing sociological museum. Did the Age of Aquarius witness the birth of a New Age, or the emergence of a new form of Neolithic Man? You can ponder such deep questions over your 'magik mudpie' and herbal infusion at the Rainbow Café. Other things to see (apart from the hallucinatory)? The **Nimbin Museum** borders closely on the hallucinatory (*open when they feel like it, entry* A$2 *when they're in the mood – "you kinda look as if you should get in free, man"*). A market with a similar attitude towards capitalism and the work ethic opens with remarkable regularity on the fourth Sunday in every month. (How do they remember?) Don't miss this – it's the sort of place where one day Lord Lucan will turn up running a stall.

NORTH STRADBROKE ISLAND ⊯ ✕

At the southern end of Moreton Bay. 'Stradie' is the largest and most popular of the Moreton Bay islands. You can reach it by car ferry or water taxi from Cleveland, which is 15 km east of Brisbane. Most of the island's 3,000 permanent inhabitants are employed at the mineral sand mines, which are towards the lower end of the island. A century ago the island was still joined to South Stradbroke Island (see Moreton Bay, page 82), but in 1896 a hurricane sliced through the sand spit and made two islands.

The ferry puts in at Dunwich, which was first settled in 1828 as a quarantine station for immigrants arriving from Europe. Disaster struck in 1850, when the population was virtually wiped out by cholera.

From Dunwich a sealed road leads out into the island, connecting the other two settlements at Amity Point in the north and Point Lookout in the northeast. The hinterland contains several lakes. **Blue Lake** is excellent for swimming, but you have to walk a couple of kilometres from the road unless you have a 4WD. **Brown Lake** is recommended for swimming and water sports, and **Tortoise Lagoon** is a popular wildlife spot. **Point Lookout** has fine beaches, some accommodation and a number of cafés. There's also great diving offshore at **Shag Rocks**. The island is famous throughout Australia for its excellent fishing, and in August it hosts the Stradie Classic, one of the main events on the Aussie anglers' calendar.

The southern end of the island is mainly given over to swamps and mining.

PORT MACQUARIE ⊯ ✕

On the coast 420 km N of Sydney. This outpost started life in 1821 as a convict settlement at the mouth of the Hastings River, and was intended to house the hard nuts who'd committed second offences in other New South Wales penal settlements, as well as a few prize convicts straight from Britain whose reputation had preceded them. But within a decade the prison authorities decided this was far too pleasant a place for criminal celebrities. The penal colony was disbanded and those who were too hot to handle were moved to a hotter spot. (Britain was pursuing a determinedly anti-Russian policy at the time – the Russians always sent their star prisoners to the coldest spot they could find: Siberia.) After the superstar cons came the pioneer settlers. Unfortunately the old harbour proved unsuitable for large ships, and Port Macquarie never really took off. For 150 years or so the place remained a quiet backwater. Then an even more colourful crowd descended on Port Macquarie – tourists. They were attracted by the miles of sandy beaches, and the unspoiled terrain of forests and mountains inland. For the past 20 years Port Macquarie has continued to expand in a suburban sprawl along the

• *Koala Hospital and Study Centre, Port Macquarie.*

coast, and is now one of the largest resorts in the region, with a population of more than 30,000.

Apart from the superb beaches and unspoiled stretches of the hinterland, there's not much to see in Port Macquarie. Reminders of the old days are few. One of them is **St Thomas's Church**, at the corner of Hay and Williams Streets, which was built by the prisoners in 1828, making it the third oldest church in the country. Its stone blocks were laboriously hewn in traditional convict style. They are held together with a cement made of seashells, pounded into a powder by those crafty cons who quickly recognized a cushy number and volunteered at once for cement-making duties.

Also worth a brief visit is the **Historical Museum** at 22 Clarence Street (*open Mon to Sat 9.30 am to 4.30 pm, Sun 1 to 4.30 pm; entry* A$3), which contains a number of relics from the old days, including the usual costumes which look as if they began life as relics.

Port Macquarie has a large number of koala bears living near town. Unfortunately these woolly fellows have never quite managed to master road drill, so they keep getting involved in car accidents. As a result, Australia's only **Koala Hospital** has been established in the grounds of a fine old house called Roto on Lord Street. Unlike many hospitals, you don't have to be a relative or even a drinking pal to visit the patients. You can visit between 9 am and 4.30 pm; donations welcome (preferably not grapes or copies of the latest Jilly Cooper).

If you're in the mood for a short sortie into unspoiled bush, visit **Kooloon-** **bung Creek Nature Park**, whose entrance is in Horton Street. It may be only 50 hectares, but the trails lead you deep into rainforest and mangroves of sweltering authenticity (but with the heartening reassurance that you're never that far from an ice cold drink).

Just over 20 km west of town, on the other side of the Pacific Highway, is the pleasant woodland village of **Wauchope** (pronounced 'War-hope') (see Australia Overall: 2). Just down the road is **Timbertown**, a reconstruction of an old lumber settlement where they re-enact life as it was in these parts during the mid-19thC.

SOLITARY ISLANDS

Off the coast N of Coff's harbour. These tiny uninhabited islands have been designated a marine park. At this point along the coast the warmer tropical currents from the north meet the cooler southern currents, making the water ideal for a wide range of fish and marine life. There are many dolphins, and during the winter you can often spot whales on

their migration north from the Antarctic. Cruises to the waters around the islands run from Coff's Harbour.

SOUTH STRADBROKE ISLAND
See Moreton Bay, page 82.

SURFER'S PARADISE ⛵ ✕
On the coast 80 km S of Brisbane. This is the big one on the Gold Coast. In a way, its name says it all. The front looks just like Miami Beach, with high-rise blocks lining the esplanade. Indeed, such is the development here that to some extent it defeats its own object. In the late afternoon as the sun sinks to the west, the huge buildings ensure that the beach is plunged into shadow. But no one seems to worry. People come here for the fun as much as the sun. This is the home of the Drive-Thru Bottle Shop, the Cocktail Academy, the Bar-B-Kew Chicken and All-You-Can-Eat Breakfast. And at night you can bop till you drop in the dozens of discos and clubs.

Just like Florida, Surfer's Paradise has a Ripley's Believe It Or Not, a Sea-world theme park with performing dolphins and whales, a Dreamworld theme park (paddle steamers, gold mine, and so on), a Movie World, and its own Gold Coast Indy car race (in March). The only thing missing is Disney World. But to make up for the lack of Goofy and his pals there's always bungee jumping, jet-skiing, day cruises, diving to see wrecks – you name it. And if you can't think of anything else to do, there are always the casino and the bars. The wildest time of year is at Christmas and New Year, when I can guarantee you'll have a holiday you'll never remember. If you're looking for that 'away from it all' holiday, this is the last place in Australia for you.

TRIAL BAY GAOL
80 km N of Port Macquarie, E off Pacific Highway. This gaol (*open 9am to 5pm; entry A$2.50*) was built in the 1880s, by the convicts, for themselves – and it shows. If you must go to gaol, this is about as fine a setting as you could wish for – on a clifftop high above the

• *Surfer's Paradise Beach.*

sea. Prisoners were sent here from the other settlements in order to be trained in practical crafts, but the view must have proved too much of a distraction because within 20 years the place was abandoned. The gaol was briefly reopened in 1914 as an internment camp for 500 Germans – who were thus able to sit out the war looking at the view, while Aussies who weren't so lucky as to be of German descent had to go off and fight. All that now remains is a surprisingly well-preserved stone prison (whose neat prisoner-built walls look suspiciously scalable) – and of course the spectacular nearby views.

TWEED HEADS

On the coast across Cobaki Creek, just S of Coolangatta. Tweed Heads is the southern end of the Gold Coast. Down here it's less hectic, but ironically you often get better surf than at Surfer's Paradise. To all intents and purposes this is now a twin town with Coolangatta, which is north across the border in Queensland (see page 80).

WOOLGOOLGA

27 km N of Coff's Harbour on the Pacific Highway. This small fishing town and resort is known locally as 'Woopi', but it has one distinct feature which sets it apart from other resorts. Many of the local inhabitants are Sikhs – descendants of immigrants who arrived from India more than a century ago. The main place of interest is the **Guru Nanak Sikh Temple** (ask at the Temple Restaurant opposite if you want to pay a visit). At the other end of town is an object called the **Raj Mahal**, which the Sikhs have kindly erected for the benefit of tourists (and in order that the tourists will benefit them). By far the most memorable experience in town is to be had at the **Temple Restaurant**, where their Lamb Vindaloo is as delicious as any you'll get outside the Punjab.

RECOMMENDED HOTELS

BURLEIGH HEADS
Burleigh Beach Tower, $$; 52 *Goodwin Terrace; tel.* (075) 35 9222; *all major cards.*

Balconied rooms with superb sea views, right by the beach. Accommodation consists of pleasant apartments. In high summer ask for one of the top floors, which catch the breeze, as there's no air-conditioning.

BYRON BAY
Cape Byron Resort Motel, $$-$$$; 16 *Lawson Street; tel.* (066) 85 7663; *all major cards.*

Friendly spot with motel-type accommodation, a wide range of facilities, and a location near to the beach. Excellent for children.

COFF'S HARBOUR
Sanctuary Resort, $$; *Pacific Highway; tel.* (066) 52 2111; *cards AE, BC, MC, V.*

The sanctuary of the title has all kinds of tropical birds, as well as kangaroos, and this motel is in the middle of it. On the main road a couple of kilometres south of town.

LORD HOWE ISLAND
Pine Trees, $$$; *tel.* (065) 63 2177; *cards none.*

The oldest hotel on the island, it was started in 1900 and is still run by a direct descendant of the man who opened it. Accommodation in motel-type rooms or cottages in the garden. The lagoon beach begins over the road.

NIMBIN
The Quinns, $; *Falls Road; tel.* (066) 89 1113; *cards none.*

A couple of kilometres south of town. Pleasant bed-and-breakfast accommodation (they also do an excellent full board), with a great place for swimming in the garden.

NORTH STRADBROKE ISLAND
Stradbroke Island Guesthouse, $; 1 *East Coast Road, Point Lookout; tel.* (07) 409 8888; *cards none.*

An inexpensive and welcoming modern guest house on the road as you enter Point Lookout at the north-eastern tip of the island. Surf skis and sand sailers are available free to guests, and they even run a minibus service to and from Brisbane.

PORT MACQUARIE
El Paso Motor Inn, $$; 29 *Clarence Street; tel.* (065) 83 1944; *all major cards.*

A friendly motel, close to the beach, with an excellent restaurant, bar and pool.

SURFER'S PARADISE
Prices for accommodation here fluctuate wildly, according to season. They always rise during school holidays, and peak during the Christmas period. Be sure to book ahead.

The high-rise blocks along the front may seem rather characterless, but the views out over the ocean from their upper rooms are fabulous. Insomniacs and night-owls will be pleased to hear that these views are at their most stunning around dawn.

Bahia Beachfront Apartments,
$$; 154 *Esplanade; tel.* (075) 38 3322; *all major cards.*

This accommodation provides the best deal along the front – especially if you want to economize with a touch of home cooking. On 14 storeys, each apartment has its own balcony.

Bed and Breakfast Lodge, $
26 *Vista Street; tel.* (075) 92 1566; *cards none.*

Fairly basic accommodation, just a couple of minutes from the beach. Serious breakfast discussions about the state of the surf.

RECOMMENDED RESTAURANTS

BYRON BAY
Beach Café, $-$$; *Clark's Beach; tel.* (066) 85 7598; *cards none.*

When it's cold dark winter back in the city, this is the sort of place you dream about – the café on the beach, with the morning waves glistening in the sun as you sip your freshly squeezed exotic fruit juice. On the beach east of town, it is open from 7.30 am till mid-afternoon.

COFF'S HARBOUR
Seafood Mama's, $$; *Pacific Highway, Korora; tel. (066) 53 6733; all major cards.*

About 6 km north of town on the main road, but well worth the journey. They're deservedly renowned for their Italian-style seafood. Try the *fettuccine marinara* for a real treat.

COOLANGATTA
Oskar's on the Beach, $$-$$$; *Marine Parade; tel. (075) 36 4621; all major cards.*

An award-winning restaurant with an exceptionally imaginative menu. Try their green prawns in coconut, coated in beer batter. (If you don't go for this sort of thing, it's not the place for you.) But there's no messing about with the wine list – which is great.

Devotees reckon it's the best restaurant on the entire Gold Coast.

NORTH STRADBROKE ISLAND
The best (and only) place for a night out is:

Stradbroke Hotel, $-$$; *East Coast Road, Point Lookout; tel. (07) 409 8679; cards none.*

At the north-eastern tip of the island, this is the only pub and also has a carvery. There's a great garden looking out to sea, and more or less tolerable live music on Saturday nights.

PORT MACQUARIE
The best place to go for a night out in Port Macquarie is:

Port Macquarie RSL Club, $-$$$; *Park Street; tel. (065) 83 1999; cards accepted vary according to the different establishments within the club.*

This recently opened complex has a variety of eateries, bars and nightclubs. There's a smart restaurant where the seafood is superb, as well as several other less formal places where you can have an cheap meal or a snack. There's also a disco, and a number of bars of varying degrees of sophistication (or lack of it).

If this doesn't sound quite your thing, try:

The Whalebone Wharf Restaurant, $$; *Hastings River Drive; tel. (065) 83 2334; cards none.*

Just west of the town centre, with a romantic view out over Hastings River. Serves excellent locally caught fresh seafood. Closed all day Monday.

SURFER'S PARADISE
For sophisticated dining, try:

Nicholson's, $$$; *Conrad Jupiter's Hotel, Gold Coast Highway, Broadbeach; tel. (075) 92 1133; all major cards.*

Boasts a gourmet menu, with vintage wine list to match. The cuisine is French-orientated, but has several local classics. Smart waiters dispense smooth service amidst chintzy surroundings.

If you fancy a more fiery spot, you need look no further than:

Montezuma's, $-$$; *8 Trickett Street; tel. (075) 38 4748; cards none.*

A small Mexican revolution cunningly disguised as a restaurant. Can get crowded, but it's exceptionally friendly and great fun.

The nightlife in Surfer's Paradise runs the whole gamut from A (awfully nice) to Z (for zonked). In between, there's the huge **International Showroom** at the **Conrad Jupiter's Casino** with the local version of a Vegas floorshow, or **Dracula's** at Hooker Boulevard, where you get a meal served by Dracula and his brides, followed by disco dancing.

Between Melbourne and Canberra
Melbourne and Region

600 km; map Nelles Australia, 1:400,000

Melbourne, the state capital of Victoria, has a population of 3 million, and is an unusual blend of the conservative and the colourful. This was the Victorian city which became Australia's first capital, and it offers many interesting sights. The National Gallery of Victoria, at the Victorian Arts Centre, has the finest collection of Australian art in the land, as well as works by Picasso and Dürer. By contrast, Old Melbourne Gaol is a grim spot. This was where the famous outlaw Ned Kelly was hung in 1880, and they have a ghoulish collection of death masks.

Head north-east from Melbourne along the Hume Highway in the direction of Canberra and you pass, to the south, the Alpine National Park. In winter this is a popular skiing region, and in summer it's known for bushwalking, canoeing and horse riding.

You'll need at least three or four days to do justice to Melbourne. The stretch between Canberra and Melbourne can be covered in two days, but if you want to explore the Alpine National Park, allow at least a couple more. See also Australia Overall: 4 for the area west of Melbourne towards Adelaide.

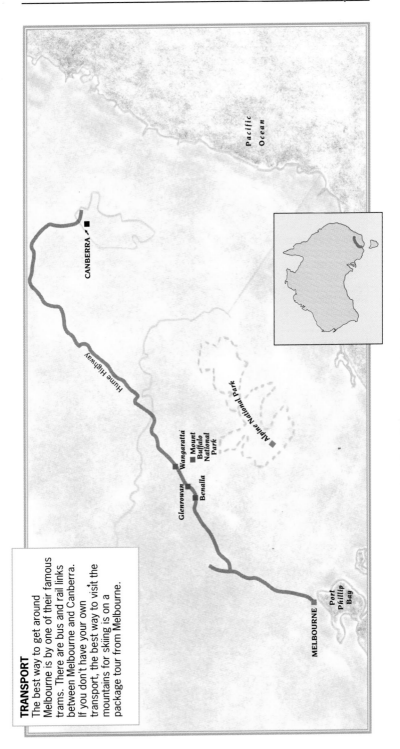

TRANSPORT

The best way to get around Melbourne is by one of their famous trams. There are bus and rail links between Melbourne and Canberra. If you don't have your own transport, the best way to visit the mountains for skiing is on a package tour from Melbourne.

Pacific Ocean

CANBERRA

Hume Highway

Wangaratta

Mount Buffalo National Park

Glenrowan

Benalla

Alpine National Park

MELBOURNE

Port Phillip Bay

SIGHTS & PLACES OF INTEREST

ALPINE NATIONAL PARK ⌂

A 650-hectare national park in the Snowy Mountains, which straddle the eastern Victoria–New South Wales border. In winter this is Australia's skiing territory. There's usually sufficient snow from late June to September. Some of the downhill runs are a little tame compared with the best of their European Alpine counterparts (the mountains aren't so high, or so steep), but there's some great cross-country skiing. The best runs are at Mount Buller and Falls Creek. For the best cross-country skiing, head to Lake Mountain or Lake St Gwinear. In summer the park is justly celebrated for its great bushwalking. You can also go canoeing and rafting here.

The best place to pick up a map and details of activities in the park is at the Tourist Office in Mansfield, 80 km south of Benalla (which is on the main Hume Highway). However, by far the easiest and cheapest way to ski is to join a day or weekend ski package tour from Melbourne. For more information visit the Melbourne Ski Centre at 17 Hardware Street.

BENALLA

100 km NW of Melbourne. A pleasant lakeside stop on the Hume Highway. They have a few Ned Kelly relics in both the Kelly Museum and the local Costume and Pioneer Museum.

CANBERRA

See pages 58-65.

GLENROWAN

200 km NW of Melbourne on the Hume Highway. This is the spot where Ned Kelly made his famous last stand, and the 400 local inhabitants have certainly cashed in on this. You can't miss the giant statue of Ned, clad in his famous mask. They even have a theatre which puts on the Last Stand Show (9.30 *am to* 4.30 *pm daily, entry* A$12), where computerised dummies play out the action. Slightly more authentic is the reconstruction of Ned Kelly's home.

MELBOURNE ⌂ ✕

Melbourne, capital of Victoria, the smallest mainland state of Australia, is also the most crowded state, with a population of four and a half million living in its 230,000 square kilometres – though the term crowded is very much relative where Australia is concerned. Even in Victoria you can still travel for miles in some places without seeing a soul.

History

This region was first occupied more than 40,000 years ago by the Koories, the wandering Aborigine tribes of southeastern Australia. They found the place so fertile and amenable that they even set up a few semi-permanent settlements, remains of which can still be seen. And when it turned cold in winter, they would don cloaks sewn together out of possum skins.

In 1770, Captain Cook arrived off Cape Everard, on the easternmost coast of what is now Victoria. In 1803 a settlement was established at Port Phillip Bay, but this was not a success and the settlers moved across the

---

> **NED KELLY: AUSTRALIAN LEGEND**
>
> Ned Kelly was a bushranger outlaw who came to symbolize free-spirited resistance to the colonial authorities. In the 1870s Ned and his gang specialized in robbing banks and eluding the police posses sent after them. But in a shoot-out at Stringybark Creek, three constables were killed, thus provoking the biggest manhunt in Aussie history. A reward of £1,000 (a colossal sum in those days) was offered for the capture of Ned and his gang. After robbing a bank in Jerilderie, Ned sent a mocking letter to his pursuers, deriding them as 'wombat-headed, magpie-legged sons of English landlords.' In the end the law caught up with him and his gang at Glenrowan, where Kelly emerged in his celebrated iron mask and home-made suit of armour, before being captured and sentenced to hang. Some sympathizers turned up when he was executed at Melbourne Gaol on November 11, 1880. His life and death are now celebrated in rousing folk songs.

Bass Strait to Tasmania.

The first meaningful European occupation of the region began in characteristic style. In June 1835, a land speculator called John Batman crossed the strait from Tasmania and proceded to do business with the local Aborigines. In exchange for a few dozen blankets and knives, 12 red shirts and sundry mirrors and axes, Batman bought 243,000 hectares of land. Upon completing this 'deal' he declared: 'I am the greatest landowner in the world.' He then set about drawing up a document to legitimize his claim. Unfortunately, he now encountered some people even more experienced in sharp practice than himself: the British government. The authorities were unimpressed with Batman's document – instead of legitimizing it, they accused him of trespassing on Crown property. It looked as if Batman had lost his 12 red shirts, and also his briefly-held title as the world's greatest landowner.

But possession is nine-tenths of the law. Batman continued to occupy 'his' property, and was soon joined by hundreds of land-hungry settlers from Tasmania. Two years later, the authorities put a brave face on it and officially recognized the new settlement, though still claiming it as part of New South Wales.

The growing town at the head of St Phillip's Bay was given the name Melbourne, after the British prime minister of the day. (Today, Lord Melbourne is best remembered for his wife Lady Caroline Lamb's scandalous affair with the poet Byron.)

But the new settlers of Melbourne resented being subservient to New South Wales. When the colonial authorities despatched convict ships with the intention of setting up a penal colony at Melbourne, the settlers turned the ships back. They soon decided it was time they formed their own colony. And this they did, naming it Victoria. In 1851, the authorities relented, and the colony of Victoria was declared official.

Just nine days later, on July 10, 1851, gold was discovered up country at Clunes. Within months, much larger deposits had been discovered at Ballarat and Bendigo. The Central Victorian Gold Rush was on. Rumours of a 'mountain of gold' at Bendigo quickly spread back to Britain, and from there across the world. Soon gold-seekers from all over the globe were flooding into Victoria at the rate of tens of thousands a month. By the end of the 1850s the new state's population had multiplied from several thousand to half a million. The senior Australian colony of New South Wales was eclipsed, and Melbourne became established as the financial centre of Australia – a position it was to hold for the next half century.

Meanwhile, out in the rural areas of Victoria, a war was going on. The so-called Black War against the Aborigines began in 1836. For a dozen years or so the Aborigines fought with the grazers and settlers who were encroaching on their land. The death toll amongst the primitively armed tribesmen was high. The Aborigines had developed no immunity against a number of diseases imported by the Europeans, and these too took a heavy toll. It's been estimated that when Batman first set foot ashore at Port Phillip Bay in 1835 there may have been as many as 17,000 Aborigines living in the region. By the time Victoria was recognized as a state 16 years later, this number was down to little more than 2,000.

Many of those who had arrived in Victoria to seek gold were disappointed, but afterwards a large number of them decided to stay on and make a new life for themselves in the colony. As a result of gold-rush prosperity, Melbourne started sprouting grandiose buildings. The city began taking on a distinctly Victorian air. Culture and conservatism became the order of the day amongst the respectable classes. As a result, when Australia became a commonwealth in 1901, respectable Melbourne was chosen as the nation's first capital. Not until 1927 did it lose this title to Canberra.

Nowadays Melbourne (pronounced Mel-b'n) is Australia's second largest city. It only has three-quarters of the population of its rival Sydney (which has almost four million inhabitants). But Melbourne still retains that Victorian air – there's still a distinctly conservative feel to the place, compared with the rest of Australia. Many Victorian bluestone buildings remain amongst the brand-new high-rise blocks. And unlike laid-back Aussies elsewhere, the citizens of Melbourne tend to take life rather more seriously. A higher proportion wear sober suits – and not just because

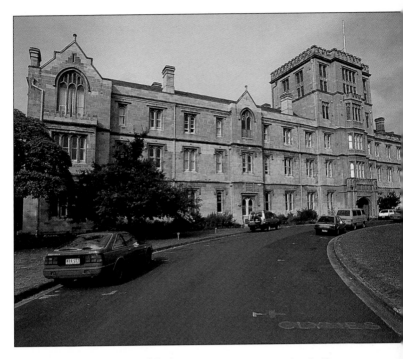

• *One of the many grandiose buildings which gives Melbourne a Victorian air.*

it's colder in winter. Not surprisingly, Melbourne's twin city in the U.S. is Boston. Whereas in Sydney the first question is 'How much money do you make?', in Melbourne they tend to ask: 'What school did you go to?'

Melbourne has no less than five universities, the oldest founded as early as 1855. And it is proud of its traditional colleges, elitist institutions modelled on English public schools. When the American evangelist Billy Graham visited Melbourne in the 1950s, he called it 'the most moral city in the world'. A more typical reaction came from Ava Gardner, when she came to work on the film *On the Beach* ten years later. When asked about the film, she said: "It's a story about the end of the world, and Melbourne sure is the right place to film it."

This was the city which produced Edna Everage (her name echoing the Aussie pronounciation of average) – who was a parody product of suburbia before she became a housewife megastar. Nowadays, Melbourne's image has undergone something of a revamp (much like Edna's) and suburban Melbourne is the location of fictional Ram-

say Street – home of Neighbours. Yet for all the soapy megastar glitz, the old Melbourne is still recognizable. This is also the city which produced media mogul Rupert Murdoch – the man responsible for making the world's tabloids what they are today still likes to project a sober-suited image in public.

Fortunately, Melbourne was given a much-needed influx of life after the Second World War, with the arrival of large numbers of southern European immigrants. This brought in a colourful multi-ethnic mix, with a particularly high proportion of Italians and Greeks. Indeed, Melbourne now contains more Greeks than any city outside Athens. But Melbourne also contains thriving communities of Serbs, Turks, and Lebanese, as well as a large Chinese community whose origins date back to the gold-rush era.

This incongruous mix of old and new, conservative and colourful, makes Melbourne a fascinating place to visit. There's plenty to see here, and experiencing the city will help you make up your own mind about the place.

• *Opposite: Melbourne, tram and rail station.*

95

A walk around central Melbourne

This route, about 2 km, can be covered in an afternoon.

Start at the Victorian Tourism Centre, 230 Collins Street. Here you can pick up a detailed map of the city. The Tourism Centre is in the midst of downtown Melbourne, just east of the main banking district with its glassy skyscrapers and high-rise office blocks.

From the Tourism Centre head east along Collins Street. For 150 years this has been the smartest street in Melbourne. At the junction with Swanston Street, ahead on your right you will see City Square. Ahead on the left is Melbourne Town Hall. Continue across Swanston Street down Collins Street. After the Town Hall, on the same side, is the **Melbourne Atheneum**. This building dates from 1886 and contains a theatre, library and art gallery (*open 8.30 am to 5 pm Mon to Fri, entry free*). This is where Australia's first talking movies were put on.

Further up Collins Street, on your left, you come to the **Scots Church**. In the 1870s a schoolgirl called Helen Mitchell used to sing in the choir here. Later she became an opera singer, and took on the obligatory Italian-sounding name, derived from her native city. In her day, Nellie Melba was the world's foremost prima donna – though she's now best remembered for the rather tired dessert Peach Melba, which is named after her.

Continue down Collins Street, across Russell Street and you enter the chic district known locally as Paris End. This pleasant tree-lined street with its cafés and luxury hotels has the most fashionable shops in town. Look out for discreet Le Louvre at No. 74, where the stars shop.

Continue down Collins Street, over Elizabeth Street, and on your left at No 36 you will see the **Melbourne Club**, the most exclusive club in town.

Just past here you come to the junction with Spring Street. Ahead is the **Treasury Building**, which was built in 1857 by the young whizz-kid architect of the day, 19-year-old J.J. Clark. The heavily fortified vaults of this building were where they kept the ingots that poured in from the goldfields. For obvious reasons, you are not allowed in.

Turn left up Spring Street, and on your left at No. 103 you'll see the famous old **Windsor Hotel**, the greatest of Melbourne's traditional hotels. If you're passing here during the afternoon, be sure to call in for that quintessential Melbourne experience: afternoon tea. The Grand Dining Room of the Windsor Hotel, with its stained-glass domes and chandeliers, claims to be the most elegant in the southern hemisphere.

Continue down Spring Street and on your right is **Parliament House**, which dates from the 1850s. During the first quarter of the 20thC, when Melbourne was Australia's capital, this housed the national parliament. When the state parliament is in session you can visit the public gallery and listen to a riveting debate on the burning issue of the day. Far more interesting are the guided tours, which take place when parliament is not in session.

Continue down Spring Street to its junction with Little Bourke Street. Here, on the corner, is the ornate splendour of the **Princess Theatre**, which was built in 1886. Not long ago this theatre was lapsing into slightly seedy elegance. Then they put on Andrew Lloyd-Webber's *Phantom of the Opera*, and on the proceeds gave the place its present facelift.

Turn left down Little Bourke Street and you're in Chinatown. This has been the home of Melbourne's Chinese community since the gold-era days of the early 1850s. Cross Exhibition Street, and on your right you'll see Cohen Place. Up here you can visit the **Museum of Chinese Australian History** (*open 12 am to 5 pm Thur to Tues, entry A$3*), which is housed in a warehouse. This museum provides an interesting insight into the development of the Chinese community in the state of Victoria, and it is also the home of the Dai Loong, the fearsome 100-legged dragon who plays a big part in the Chinese New Year's Day celebrations.

Retrace your steps to Little Bourke Street, and continue west (right). At the junction with Russell Street turn right. Continue up Russell Street across Lonsdale Street, to the junction with Little Lonsdale Street. Ahead on your left you will now see the **Museum of Victoria** (*open 10 am to 5 pm daily, entry A$5*). This museum has a large collection of exhibits related to local natural history and anthropology. Of particular inter-

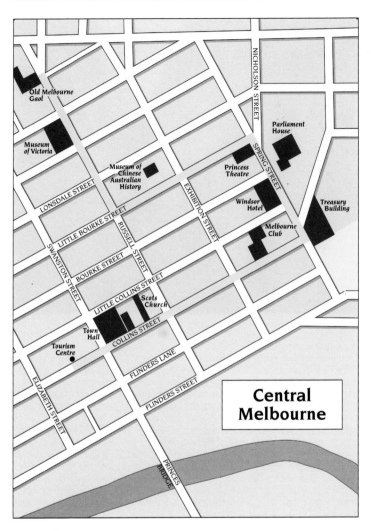

Central
Melbourne

est is the Coorie Exhibition, which illustrates the life of the Aborigine tribes who used to roam Victoria 40,000 years before the arrival of the first Europeans. Other exhibits range from Australia's first car to the stuffed remains of Melbourne's most popular inhabitant during the 1930s. This was the racehorse Phar Lap, who bankrupted many a bookie, and finally won the Melbourne Gold Cup. He was then shipped to the United States, where the mafia were so impressed with his form that they poisoned him – thus causing a rupture in Aussie-US relations which didn't fully heal until the Second World War. (NB: The contents of this muse-

um are due to move soon to a new site south of the river: contact Tourism Centre for details.)

Continue up Russell Street, across La Trobe Street, and on your left you will see the **Old Melbourne Gaol** (*open 9.30 am to 4.30 pm daily, entry A$6*). This grim spot is inevitably one of the oldest in Melbourne, and only passed out of use in 1929. The much-celebrated outlaw Ned Kelly (see page 92) was hung here in 1880, and the star exhibit is his famous metal suit, which he wore as protection against police riflemen. They still have the scaffold on which he was hung, as well as his death mask. In all, more than a hundred outlaws and

• *Old Melbourne Gaol.*

desperadoes of varying innocence were strung up here, and several of the best-known have generously donated their death masks to the exhibition. Each mask has an accompanying outline of how its owner came to be in a position to donate his mask. Don't miss Martha Knorr, the notorious 'baby farmer'. (The authorities made a serious study of these death masks, in the hope of detecting some common feature by which a criminal could be recognized. But since a sizeable portion of the population had arrived in Australia as criminals, their research drew the very opposite of a blank.)

Like many other adventurous souls who have tramped the streets of Melbourne, you'll find this fine old bluestone building marks the end of your walk.

Other Melbourne sights

Queen Victoria Market on Queen Victoria Street (*open 6 am to around midday, Tues, Thur, Fri, Sat, 9 am to 4 pm Sun*) has been held on this spot since the 1870s, and nowadays it remains as busy as it ever was, with more than a thousand stalls selling everything from fruit and vegetables to delicatessen products and cheeses. The wide-ranging produce reflects the city's varied ethnic mix – with ingredients for every-

thing from Greek to Vietnamese cooking. On Sundays it becomes more of a flea market, with plenty of bargains to be had in jeans, cheap clothing and the like. A lively spot, particularly on Saturday mornings.

Royal Botanic Gardens, Kings Domain, are *open daily, sunrise to sunset.* Melbourne's varying climate is ideal for a botanic garden, and this is the best in Australia. It has a huge range of temperate and subtropical flora, as well as a surprising variety of fauna – including all kinds of ducks on the lakes, the odd possum and even a colony of rare fruit-bats which moves in for the summer.

From here you can take a pleasant walk north-west through the park to the banks of the Yarra River, crossing Princes Bridge to Flinders Street Station, where you can have a drink at the famous Young and Jacksons Hotel (see under Recommended Restaurants, page 101).

The **Shrine of Remembrance**, Kings Domain, is a large columned memorial dominating a small hill in the Kings Domain, the large open space which runs east across the river from the city centre. The shrine is partly

• *Opposite: Melbourne's mix of old and new.*

• *Shrine of Remembrance, Kings Domain.*

based on the design of the Parthenon of Ancient Greece. It is a moving tribute to the thousands of Victorians who lost their lives in the two world wars. There is a crypt showing regimental colours, and from the gallery there are fine views of the city.

The Victorian Arts Centre, St Kilda Road, is an arts complex of modern buildings south of the Yarra River at Princes Bridge, opposite Queen Victoria Gardens. There are three main buildings. The Theatres Building has a distinctive 115-m tower, which according to a resident I know looks like 'an anorexic modern version of the Eiffel Tower'. Judge for yourself (many have said far worse). The State Theatre in this building is the home of the Australian Ballet, whose tours of America and Europe have caused a sensation. *Tours noon and 2.30 pm, Mon to Fri, A$8.*

The **Melbourne Concert Hall** by Princes Bridge is home to the Melbourne Symphony Orchestra. When they play the standard classics, they're accused of being too stuffy; but as soon as they play any modern stuff, everyone is up in arms. But you'll find they're easily good enough to ride out this sort of criticism.

I've saved the best till last. Further down the Kilda Road, in a bluestone building that succeeds in being both modern and stuffy, is the **National Gallery of Victoria** (*open 10 am to 5 pm daily, entry A$6, free Mon*).

It has the most comprehensive selection of Australian art in the country. Like the art of any fully developed artistic nation, when they're good, they're very good, but when they're bad... The paintings range from early colonial to the latest contemporary. Best of the former: John Glover. Best of the latter: Sidney Nolan. Also has fine works by Dürer, Blake and Picasso.

The Victorian Arts Centre includes a Performing Arts Museum, and the Sidney Myer Music Bowl, which is across St Kilda Road in the park. In winter this is converted into an ice-skating rink.

Melbourne's suburbs

The pleasant seaside suburb of St Kilda is just 3 km from the city centre – take tram 15 or 16 from Swanston Street. A Sunday morning stroll along the Esplanade, where they have art shows, is a Melbourne institution.

Other outlying districts of interest include Carlton, north-west of the city centre, which is Melbourne's Little Italy, and the lively Greek district at Richmond, west of the city centre. Fitzroy, around Brunswick Street, is an arty district, with plenty of galleries. This lies just north-east of the city centre.

MOUNT BUFFALO NATIONAL PARK ✕

In the Victorian Alps, N of the Alpine national park, 50 km SE of Wangaratta. In winter there's skiing here, especially recommended for family groups. (For further details of skiing in this region, see Alpine National Park, page 92.) In summer you can go riding over the wooded plateau. Lake Catani is pleasant for swimming and fishing.

WANGARATTA ⇌

250 km N of Melbourne. Known as 'Wang' locally, this makes a useful stop on the Hume Highway. Airworld, which is just outside town, has a collection of old aeroplanes (*open 9 am to 5 pm, entry A$6*). Wang has a great Jazz Festival in early November, and is the last resting place of the celebrated bushranger Mad Dog Morgan, whose grave can be seen in the local cemetery.

RECOMMENDED HOTELS

ALPINE NATIONAL PARK

Accommodation tends to be expensive in the mountains during the skiing season, when it's essential to book ahead. In summer, prices drop considerably.

Alberg Hotel, $$-$$$; 53 *Summit Road, Mount Buller Alpine Village; tel.* (057) 77 6260; *most major cards.*

Big resort hotel with wide range of amenities; reputable restaurant.

MELBOURNE
Windsor Hotel, $$$; 103 *Spring Street; tel.* (03) 653 0653; *all major cards.*

Old world luxury at its finest. The building dates from 1883, and still emanates an ambience of Victorian class. I was told that the place was renamed after the Duke of Windsor, when he visited in 1920 as Prince of Wales. The Grand Dining Room is truly impressive.

The John Spencer, $$-$$; 44 *Spencer Street; tel.* (03) 629 6991; *most major cards.*

Victorian-style hotel with wide range of rooms, just west of city centre and by the station.

Olembia Bed and Breakfast, $-$$; 96 *Barkly Street, St Kilda; tel.* (03) 537 1412; *cards none.*

Bright and friendly spot, out at the beachside suburb of St Kilda.

Lygon-Carlton Motel, $-$$; 220 *Lygon Street; all major cards.*

Inexpensive accommodation in lively Little Italy district.

WANGARATTA
Warby Lodge Motor Inn, $$; 55 *Ryley; tel* (057) 21 8433; *most major cards.*

Pleasant motel accommodation. The big plus here is the pool.

RECOMMENDED RESTAURANTS

MELBOURNE
Le Restaurant, $$$; *Regent of Melbourne, 209 King Street; tel.* (03) 670 1881; *all major cards.*

Elegant dining 35 floors up in the Regent of Melbourne. The best seafood in town.

Mask of China, $$; 115 *Little Bourke Street; tel.* (03) 662 2116; *all major cards.*

The best restaurant in Chinatown, specializing in Chiu Chow cuisine.

Electra Greek Tavern, $$; 195 *Lonsdale Street; tel.*(03) 663 4760; *all major cards.*

My favourite restaurant in central Melbourne. Greek cuisine with class. Run by welcoming Mick Spanos from the Aegean island of Mykonos.

Waiters Restaurant, $; 20 *Meyers Place, Bourke Street; tel.* (03) 650 1508; *cards none.*

Good inexpensive Italian food, and plenty of it. Open until midnight; bring your own bottle.

No visit to Melbourne would be complete without seeing the most famous girl in town: Chloe, who greets you clad only in a bracelet in the upstairs bar at **Young and Jackson's Hotel** on Flinders Street. This landmark pub dates from 1853, and Chloe was only 27 when she arrived – after her full-length portrait had been declared indecent at the Melbourne Exhibition of 1880. Raise your eyes from your glass, and judge for yourself.

Out by the sea at St Kilda, amongst the trendy cafés of Acland Street, try Lo Spuntino at number 56. If you fancy something more substantial, try:

Jean-Jacques By-the-Sea, $$; 40 *Jacka Boulevard, St Kilda; tel.* (03) 534 8221; *all major cards.*

Local seafood cooked the French way by a wizard chef, at a price you can afford. What more could you ask?

MOUNT BUFFALO
Mount Buffalo Chalet, $$$; Mt *Buffalo National Park; most major cards.*

An unexpectedly luxurious spot high in the alps, with some superb nearby views. Amenities include croquet on the lawn.

<u>Victoria</u>

Between Melbourne and Adelaide
The Shipwreck Coast and
Kangaroo Island

1,000 km; map Nelles Australia 1:400 000

This section covers the coast between Melbourne and Adelaide, which offers some of the most spectacular ocean scenery in Australia, especially at the Port Campbell National Park.

The Fleurieu Peninsula, just south of Adelaide, is noted for some fine beaches and inland there are vineyards. Offshore you can visit the more remote splendours of Kangaroo Island. East of here lies the Coorong National Park, where the Murray River meets the sea. It is renowned for its pelicans. Between Port Fairy and Cape Otway lies the notorious Shipwreck Coast, with superb cliffs and more good beaches. Geelong, just south-west of Melbourne, is frankly a bit of a disappointment, but nearby Lorne and Apollo Bay easily make up for this.

If you want to cover the entire stretch you should allow three to four days. However, you'll need at least a week if you want to explore.

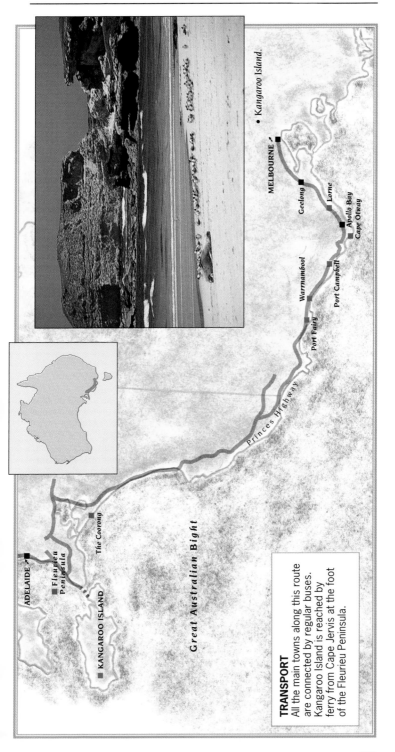

• Kangaroo Island.

MELBOURNE

Geelong

Lorne

Apollo Bay
Cape Otway

Warrnambool

Port Campbell

Port Fairy

Princes Highway

The Coorong

ADELAIDE

Fleurieu Peninsula

KANGAROO ISLAND

Great Australian Bight

TRANSPORT
All the main towns along this route are connected by regular buses. Kangaroo Island is reached by ferry from Cape Jervis at the foot of the Fleurieu Peninsula.

SIGHTS & PLACES OF INTEREST

ADELAIDE
See *Australia Overall: 5, page* 112.

APOLLO BAY 🚢
120 *km* SW *of Melbourne*. Pleasant small fishing port in a picturesque setting with some great surf-pounded beaches nearby. The major attraction here is hang-gliding. Try a course with the West Coast School of Hang Gliding tel. (052) 37 6486, and afterwards you can launch yourself into the air from the nearby 300-m cliffs. Before saying goodbye to it all, you might also fancy going on one of the local fishing trips (tackle provided) or visiting Otway National Park down the coast. This park contains some fine rainforest (watered by more than 200 days of rain a year); the Cape Otway lighthouse; and some excellent views.

CAPE OTWAY
See *Apollo Bay, above*.

COORONG, THE
100 *km* SE *of Adelaide*. This 150-km-long national park marks the divide between the Murray River and the sea. The name comes from the Aborigine word for neck, and the main feature of the park is the Younghusband Peninsula with its high sand dunes. This is bordered by lagoons and salt pans, and the entire area is famous for its large number of pelicans. At the northern end is Lake Alexandrina, where the Murray River flows into the sea. The park itself has no facilities or accommodation, but you can stay at nearby Goolwa on the western shore of Lake Alexandrina – see Recommended Hotels under Fleurieu Peninsula, page 108.

FLEURIEU PENINSULA 🚢 ✕
50 *km* S *of Adelaide*. A pleasant, largely unspoiled, holiday region with some excellent beaches.

The French explorer Baudin arrived here in the early years of 19thC and the peninsula is named after the French marine expert Charles-Pierre Fleurieu (see box, opposite).

The earliest settlers set up as pirates and smugglers, but this thriving business dwindled when the place went legitimate with the establishment of a whaling station at Encounter Bay in 1837. Nowadays, the coastline settlements are mainly devoted to low-key tourism (with only the occasional bed-and-breakfast spot run by a pirate); inland there are thriving vineyards.

The coastline of the peninsula has cliffs and some excellent sandy beaches with plenty of surf. One of these beaches, Maslin (north stretch of Gulf St Vincent shoreline) accounts for the Fleurieu Peninsula's other entry in the history books. It is said to be Australia's first official nudist beach. (Though if Fleurieu was still around, he might well have brought to notice a few earlier Aborigine bathing spots.)

Several of the small towns along the coast have pleasant colonial features. At Victoria Harbour on Encounter Bay there are whales; Goolwa is on Lake Alexandrina close by the mouth of the Murray River and the Coorong (see separate entry); and at Cape Jervis on the tip of the peninsula you can catch the ferry to Kangaroo Island (see separate entry).

GEELONG ✕
On the coast 75 *km* SW *of Melbourne*.
On first sight, Geelong is as attractive as Pittsburg. The main point of interest in this industrial port is the National Wool Museum, which just about says it all. If you want to know about this fascinating product of long woolly grazing, hurry down to the **National Wool Centre** on Brougham Street, *open daily* 10 *am to* 5 *pm, entry* A$7, where you might learn a thing or two you never knew before. Did you know, for instance, that the strand of wool made from one sheep can often extend several times around a cricket field?

However, Geelong also has a few historic houses worth seeing. One of these, the **Corio Villa** at Eastern Beach, was prefabricated out of iron sheets in Scotland. When these bits duly arrived after the long voyage from Glasgow in 1856, they discovered that the instructions on how to assemble the building were missing. Just like many a builder we know, they immediately set to work assembling it by guesswork. Alas, the result is sadly unsurrealistic. For further details of even less interesting local historic buildings, apply at the Tourist Information kiosk on Market Square.

KANGAROO ISLAND ⇔ ✕

Off Fleurieu Peninsula, S of Adelaide.
Reached by ferry from Cape Jervis, at the tip of the Fleurieu Peninsula. The *Philanderer II* takes you across Backstairs Passage.
Kangaroo Island lies just 12 km off the mainland, and is Australia's third largest island (after Tasmania and Melville Island near Darwin). It is 150 km long, 30 km wide, and has over 400 km of coastline. There is much unspoiled scenery. Pleasant beaches (sheltered north, surfing south), can be explored along reasonable unpaved roads. It's windy here, especially in the south (nothing between here and Antarctica). The whole place is refreshingly empty. The very remoteness of the island has long made it popular with Australian wildlife. Over the years this has included escaped convicts, walruses, platypuses, parrots and rare cockatoos. All but the first continue to thrive. Indeed, the last scarlet fantailed glossy black cockatoos, of which

• A *local, Kangaroo Island.*

there are now less than 100 pairs left on the planet, all live on Kangaroo Island.
And of course there are the kangaroos – which even the meat-starved early explorers, rooskinsuited escaped convicts and roaming modern gourmets have not managed to finish off.

Recent archaeological excavations have shown that this spot was inhabited by Aborigines 11,000 years ago, a millennium before it became separated from the mainland.

You can see fairy penguins in **Christmas Cove** west of the ferry harbour, and after dark they often come into town on food sorties. But this is just the start. The best sights are along the south coast. **Seal Bay** has a colony containing literally hundreds of sea lions. (An astonishing 10 per cent of the world's sea lion population waddles and grunts here.) Nearby Vivonne Bay has a beaut of a beach, but only swim near the jetty as there's a dangerous undertow.

Further on you come to **Kelly Hill Caves**. A horse called Kelly inadvertently discovered these caves, disappearing forever into their depths beneath his rider, who managed to scramble to safety. (Some say the caves received their name because his rider swore at him, others because he was grateful.) If you fancy exploring the caves, contact Adventure Caving Tours, tel. (848) 37 231.

The entire western end of the island is occupied by **Flinders Chase National Park**, the largest in the state. Here wildlife such as koalas and emus abound amongst the gum forest. The Visitor Centre is at Rocky River, where they have maps of the best wildlife viewing spots and hiking trails. You can also drive down the bumpy track south to Remarkable Rocks – some of which look like the fossilized remains of large cracked-open dinosaur eggs, and some of which just look remarkable. Here you'll also see seals basking on the rocks, and nearby there's an abandoned lighthouse.

If you haven't brought a car with you to the island, the best way to get around is by moped. Try Kangaroo Island Bike

---

A REDOUBTABLE ARMCHAIR EXPLORER

The 18thC French marine expert Charles-Pierre Fleurieu played a major role in French global exploration. This role was mainly theoretical, but he still managed to pull the carpet out from under a number of renowned non-armchair explorers. In 1790, Fleurieu showed that the Solomon Islands, discovered in 1567 by Medana, were the same as the islands 'discovered' by Carteret in 1767, discovered again by Bouganville in 1768, and discovered again by Shortland in 1788. All of these explorers nearly discovered Australia again too, but it was the French explorer Nicholas Baudin who arrived at a remote peninsula in what is now Southern Australia. He named it after Fleurieu, presumably in the hope that he wouldn't expose this discovery as an error (thus avoiding the headline: 'Fleurieu exposes Fleurieu as mistake').

• *Twelve Apostles, Great Ocean Road.*

Hire, tel. (0848) 31 026) at American Beach. The shoreline of the island has plenty of wrecks, and these are best explored by scuba diving. You can learn to scuba with Adventureland Diving, at Penneshaw, tel. (0848) 31 072).

LORNE ⇌ ✕
On the coast 70 km SW of Geelong. This seaside resort lies below the wooded mountains of the Otway Ranges. Lorne has long been popular with visitors from Melbourne. It retains a certain pre-war elegance, as well as a pleasantly incongruous hippy element. There are good beaches, with excellent surfing, and nearby you can visit the Angahook-Lorne State Park. Here there are bush-walks of varying length and difficulty. Climb to Teddy's Lookout for the best view of the coastline, or set out on a three-hour walk past waterfalls to the picturesque Erskine Falls. You can also drive to the Falls.

The big event here is the Pier to Pub Swimming Race, which takes place every January. The course is just over a kilometre long, and the event is open to all comers – often attracting as many as 2,000 entrants. By the time the last of these gasp and stagger their way to the pub, the victors are sometimes in a similar state.

MELBOURNE
See Australia Overall: 3, page 92.

PORT CAMPBELL ⇌
170 km SW of Melbourne on the coast.
This small coastal town lies on the western edge of the Port Campbell National Park, which has some of the finest

• *'London Bridge', Great Ocean Road.*

coastal scenery you can see anywhere in the world. **The Great Ocean Road**, which travels along the shoreline, lives up to its name with some huge cliffs and dramatic pillars of rock, some of which rise to 100 m above the boiling foam. The best-known of these are the **Twelve Apostles** – though such is the fury of the ocean that these have now been reduced to eight. Another local landmark, called London Bridge, caved in recently stranding some visitors out on the stack – resulting in a dramatic helicopter rescue which grabbed the TV news bulletins. There are several small beaches below the high cliffs, though these are mostly littered with seaweed. One of these can be reached by way of Gibsons Steps. You can also get down to the beach at **Lord Ard Gorge**. In 1878 the iron-hulled sailing ship *Ard George* bringing Irish immigrants to Australia was driven on to the rocks here. There were 53 on board, but only two 18-year-olds survived. These were Tom Pierce, an apprentice officer, and Eva Campbell, the only survivor of her family of eight. The two of them were carried on the waves into the gorge, where Tom managed to drag Eva ashore into a cave. He then scrambled off for help. Despite immense pressure from the newspapers of the day, no romance flourished between them, and Eva eventually returned to Ireland.

Near here you can also walk to a spectacular **Blowhole** and the aptly named **Thunder Cave**.

For further information on the park, call at the Port Campbell National Information Centre, Tregea Street, Port Campbell.

THE SHIPWRECK COAST

The stretch of the south-west Victoria coastline between Cape Nelson and Cape Otway is littered with reefs, unexpected shoals and shallows. For some reason this made it a popular spot with passing mariners, who had managed to sail half way round the world missing everything else. As a result, the area became littered with shipwrecks. During the second half of the 19thC ships were committing the nautical equivalent of hara-kiri here at the rate of two a year. Many salvaged relics and mementoes from these wrecks can be seen in the Flagstaff Hill Maritime Village at Warrnambool.

PORT FAIRY ⇌ ✕

30 km W of Warrnambool, on the coast. A

107

delightful small fishing harbour. Contrary to local legend, it isn't named after an ancient sailor-bar queen. In fact, this picturesque spot was one of the first settlements in Victoria, and dates back to 1826. After the early whalers and sealers came the fishermen, and to this day Port Fairy has one of the largest fishing fleets in the state.

The present town has a population of 2,500 and no less than 50 historic buildings. Head for the Information Centre on Bank Street and they'll give you a map of their Heritage Walk, which takes in most of these buildings. Nearby **Griffiths Island** has a lighthouse and muttonbird colony. This can be reached by a causeway. Many of the original settlers here came from Northern Ireland, and the biggest event of the year is the Port Fairy Folk Festival in early March. This is the best in the land, specializes in Irish and Australian folk, and attracts huge (and very thirsty) crowds.

WARRNAMBOOL ⚓ ✕

On the coast 300 km W of Geelong. The largest town on the south-west coast of Australia, and like many of these towns it has a comparatively long history. Whalers first settled this spot in the 1840s. Forty years later, the British fortified the place with guns – intended to repel a Russian invasion (for which they're still waiting). Nowadays it's a popular holiday spot with some fine beaches and terrific surfing.

In summer Warrnambool attracts a large number of tourists. In winter it attracts larger tourists in the form of right whales, which make their way up from the Antarctic to holiday at Logans Beach. Here, between May and October, you can see them frolicking and spouting. There's even a special viewing platform.

The **Flagstaff Hill Maritime Village** on Merri Street, *open 9.30 am to 4.30 pm daily, entry A$10*, is a reconstruction of a 19thC port around the gun emplacement set up to resist the Russian invasion that never was. Here you can visit the old lighthouse, the fort, and learn about the many shipwrecks along this coast – see box, page 107.

Also worth a visit is the local **Art Gallery** on Timor Street, *open daily 12 am to 5 pm, entry A$2*. This has some fine paintings from the Colonial period and a worthwhile collection of modern prints.

RECOMMENDED HOTELS

APOLLO BAY
Hayley Reef Motor Inn, $$; *Great Ocean Road; tel. (052) 37 6527; most major cards.*
Pleasant motel close to the sea.

FLEURIEU PENINSULA
The City Motel, $-$$; *Ocean Street, Victor Harbour; tel. (085) 52 2455; most major cards.*
A friendly spot in the heart of town, handy for the main historic sights.

River End Resort, $$; *Noble Avenue, 2 km NE of Goolwa; tel. (085) 55 3300; cards none.*
Ecology friendly spot, handy for the cruises on the Murray River, also as a base for exploring the Coorong.

KANGAROO ISLAND – American River
Named after American sealers who put in here in 1803, apparently to build a boat. Nearby Pelican Lagoon is a sanctuary.

Linnets Island Club, $; *American River; tel. (0848) 33 053; cards none.*
Suitably unluxurious accommodation. Pelicans fed around teatime at the quay.

KANGAROO ISLAND – Penneshaw
Where the Cape Jervis ferry puts in.

Sorrento Resort Motel, $$-$$$; *North Terrace; tel. (0848) 31 028; most major cards.*
Pleasant welcoming resort, with abundant facilities (including pool). As good as you'll get on the island. Makes an ideal base for exploring.

LORNE
Erskine House, $-$$; *Mountjoy Parade; tel (052) 89 1205. Cards: MC, V.*
Pleasant guest house where Noel Coward would feel at home amongst the arty interior decoration. Facilities include tennis courts

in the pleasant gardens.

PORT CAMPBELL
Port Campbell Hotel, $-$$; Lord Street; tel. (055) 98 6320; cards none.

A useful base for exploring the National Park. It also has a friendly bar which serves above-average food.

PORT FAIRY
Don't even think of coming here over Labor Day weekend in early March unless you've booked.

At other times your best bet is bed-and-breakfast, of which there are plenty. One of the best is:

The Old Vicarage, $$; 23 College Street; tel (055) 68 1396; cards none.

WARRNAMBOOL
Riverside Gardens Motor Inn, $-$$; Simpson Street; tel. (055) 62 1888; most major cards.

Inexpensive motel accommodation. If this is full there are several reasonable motels out on the Princes Highway.

==

RECOMMENDED RESTAURANTS

FLEURIEU PENINSULA
Sitar Indian Restaurant, $-$$; 12 The Strand, Port Elliot; tel. (085) 54 2144; cards none.

Just the spot for something hot after your hard day riding the waves.

GEELONG
Lamby's Bistro, $$; National Wool Centre, Brougham Street; tel. (052) 26 4660; most major cards.

Guess what's for dinner here? Also has a fairly imaginative menu of less woolly dishes.

KANGAROO ISLAND
The island hardly abounds in recommendable restaurants, so you might want to take a picnic. Best place to pick up ingredients is at Muggleton's General Store, Penneshaw.

Otherwise your best bet is the restaurant at the Sorrento Resort, in Penneshaw (see Recommended Hotels).

LORNE
The place to go in Lorne is:

Kosta's, $$; 48 Mountjoy Parade; tel. (052) 89 1883; cards MC, V.

The menu starts with a Greek base, and branches out to almost everything. The same can be said of the lively ambience and music in the evenings.

PORT FAIRY
Here you will find the oldest continually licensed pub in Victoria, the Caledonian Inn on Bank Street, where they've been slaking giant fishermen's giant thirsts since 1844 without running out of the amber nectar.

Those eclectic souls who actually want to eat something for dinner should try:

Dublin House Inn, $$-$$$; 57 Bank Street; tel. (055) 68 1822; most major cards.

As you'd expect, the seafood here is fresh and served with much fishy wit.

WARRNAMBOOL
Dimitri's, $-$$; 92 Liebig Street; tel. (055) 62 0367; cards none.

Greek menu served with pzazz at this lively spot. There are several other restaurants nearby that are also worth trying.

Between Adelaide and Port Augusta
Adelaide, Yorke Peninsula and Mount Remarkable
330 km; map Nelles Australia, 1:400,000

Many consider Adelaide to be the most beautiful of all Australia's state capitals, with its well laid-out central district and surrounding green parklands. It is a curious mixture of the conservative and the liberal, with a staid history (no convict settlement) and a lively lifestyle. The main attractions here include an excellent art gallery, and some interesting sights nearby. These include Port Adelaide, the historic dockside suburb just 10 km north-west of the town centre; the beaches, which lie a similar distance to the west; and the inland Adelaide Hills with their parks and peaks.

The road to Port Augusta has a couple of sights worth a detour. The Yorke Peninsula, just across Gulf St Vincent from Adelaide, has beaches, a penguin island and a historic copper-mining district. Some 50 km south-east of Port Augusta is Mount Remarkable, which has walking trails, a gorge and some great views.

You can easily travel between Adelaide and Port Augusta in a day, but allow two or three if you want to stop off and see the sights. And it's worth spending at least as long as this in Adelaide itself.

TRANSPORT
There are bus links to all the main sights, but if you want to explore you're better off with a car.

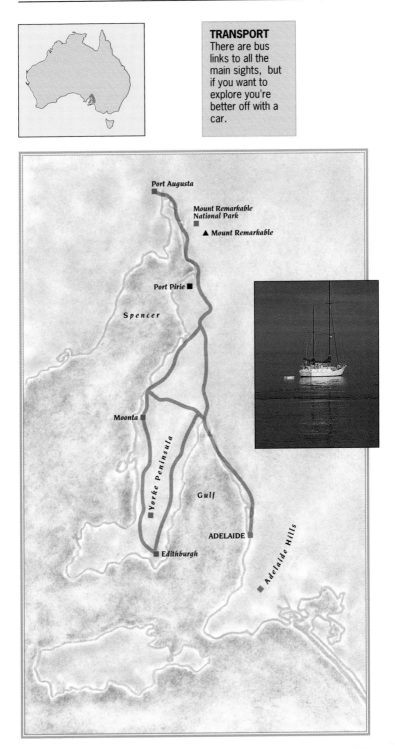

Port Augusta

Mount Remarkable
National Park

▲ Mount Remarkable

Port Pirie ■

Spencer

Moonta ■

Yorke Peninsula

Gulf

ADELAIDE ■

Adelaide Hills

■ Edithburgh

SIGHTS & PLACES OF INTEREST

ADELAIDE ⛵ ✕

SE *corner of South Australia*. Adelaide is laid out on a grid pattern around Victoria Square. Leading north from here is King William Street: at its other end, a five-minute walk away, is the main tourist information office (No. 1, at the junction with North Terrace). Here you can pick up a free map of the city.

History

Right from the start, Adelaide believed in keeping out the riff-raff. Of the early Australian colonies, this was the only one which had no convicts, and from then on it maintained a rather conservative reputation: elegant, but dull. Even today, remnants of this reputation still persist – in the pleasantest possible way, of course. The city is proud of hosting the largest arts festival in Australia. But nowadays it's equally proud of its liberal traditions. (The city had the first legal nudist beach in Australia.)

Adelaide was founded in 1836, and graciously named after the wife of Britain's King William IV. A prime location had been chosen: inland on the flat green banks of the Torrens River, with the attractive foothills of the Mount Lofty Range rising behind. Fortunately, the new colony found a town planner worthy of this site.

Colonel William Light was the son of the founder of Penang (in what is now

> **WARNING**
> At night much of central Adelaide becomes deserted, and is best avoided. Exceptions are the Rundle Street and Hindley Street areas, which are highly recommended for an evening visit. After dark, the parklands around the central area of the city are also best left to the cockatoos and other lurking exotica. You sometimes encounter similar subhuman species on the trains late at night. You're better off travelling by bus where such types tend to become confused when confronted with comparatively sober members of the public.

Malaysia), and had served as an intelligence officer under the Duke of Wellington in his Iberian campaign against Napoleon. Light was appointed as surveyor-general for the new colony, and as he knew little about town planning he chose the easiest scheme of all. Adelaide was laid out on a simple grid pattern, with wide streets and a surrounding area of parkland.

The new colony also benefited from a scheme drawn up by the social idealist Edward Wakefield. Small plots were sold to free settlers, who were guaranteed civil and religious liberty. The aim was to develop a self-supporting colony which wouldn't be dependent upon convict labour. This proved a success, and within a decade the colony was self-sufficient (helped by the discovery of copper in the hinterland). A Victorian colony had been born.

But as with many a Victorian enterprise, there were skeletons in the cupboard. Ironically, William Light was not only illegitimate, but was also of mixed blood – his mother had been a Eurasian woman. Keeping up the family tradition, Light married the illegitimate daughter of the Duke of Richmond; but he preferred to leave her in England, living instead with a local lady. As a result, when he lay on his deathbed in 1839, exhausted by supervising the building of the new colony, he was forbidden the last rites because he was unrepentantly living in sin.

Even the idealistic Edward Wakefield was not all that he appeared. He had initially hatched his plan for the new colony whilst languishing in London's notorious Newgate Prison for running off with an under-age society heiress.

Despite these social stigmas, Adelaide proceeded to become the most genteel city in the land. Amongst the early colonists were a large number of German Lutherans, who were fleeing from religious persecution. In 1856 South Australia became self-governing. The new state may have been a little staid, but it also maintained a firm belief in social justice. In 1894 it became the first place in the world where women were allowed to stand for parliament. They were also granted the vote in the same year, ahead of everywhere except New Zealand.

This liberal tradition has continued. In the early 1970s, the irrepressible Don

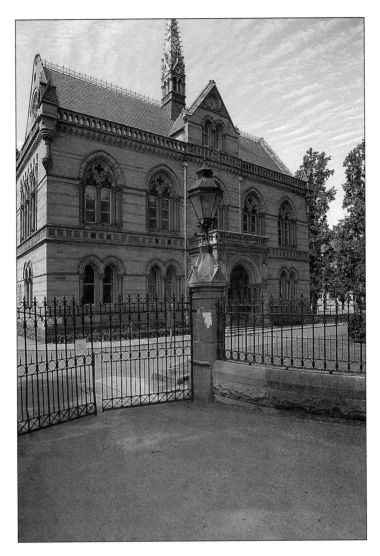

• *Adelaide area .*

Dunstan took over as state premier. Through the ensuing decade, this controversial character proceeded to introduce a wide range of social reforms. Racial discrimination was outlawed, capital punishment was abolished and homosexuality was declared legal.

Nowadays, Adelaide has a population of more than a million. Within easy reach is the largest wine-growing area in the country – which includes internationally famous names such as Barossa Valley. All but two per cent of South Australia's population now live in and around this pleasant, civilized city. But the unforgiving outback is never far away. During the long dry summer of 1983, bush fires raged out of control in the Adelaide hills, threatening the city. And during parched spells, flocks of exotic parrots and cockatoos from the outback sometimes take refuge amidst the greenery of the city parks.

There are plenty of things worth seeing in Adelaide, which is an ideal city for strolling around. Here is a walk which takes in many of the major sights:

•*Supreme Court House*

A walk around Central Adelaide

If you choose to do this entire walk, and see all the sights, it could easily last you a whole day. The main stretch of the walk covers 4 km.

Start plumb in the middle of the city centre at **Victoria Square**. This has a fountain, and is a popular meeting place for local Aborigines. At the southern corner of the square is the Supreme Law Courts Building.

From Victoria Square head south-west down Grote Street and on your left you'll come to the **Central Markets** (*open all day Tues, Thur, Fri and Sat morning*). Besides the usual ripe fruit and riper language of any city produce market, you'll also find some particularly good Malaysian and Chinese take-aways, if you fancy a snack before setting out on the main section of your walk. To do this, return to Victoria Square.

At the northern corner of the square is the **Telecommunications Museum** (*open 10.30 am to 3.30 pm, Mon to Fri, entry free*), which includes some quaint relics from the Pre-Information Super-highway Era.

From here leave Victoria Square by taking the road that leads north: King William Street. This is Adelaide's main street. As you enter the street you will see the Treasury Building on your right, and the GPO on your left. A short dis-

tance further on you will see the **Town Hall** on your right. This neo-Renaissance building dates from 1866, and is said to be modelled on a palace in Florence – which presumably did not incorporate the faces of Queen Victoria and Prince Albert on its façade.

Continue across the junction with Grenfell Street, and on your left, at the corner with Hindley Street, you will see **Edmund Wright House** (*open 9 am to 4.30 pm daily, entry free*). This also is in the ornate Neo-Renaissance style, and was built in 1876 by the same man as was responsible for the Town Hall: Edmund Wright. It was intended as the residence of the Bishop of South Australia . The inside of this building is almost as uninteresting as its outside, but if you're passing by around Wednesday midday you might like to call in here for one of their excellent lunchtime concerts.

From here, cross over to the other side of King William Street and continue north-east down **Rundle Mall**. This is central Adelaide's main shopping area, and has a number of pleasant cafés and arcades. It's also where Adelaide keeps its 'Balls': a shiny silver sculpture of two suitably enlarged balls, one

• *Opposite: University of Adelaide.*

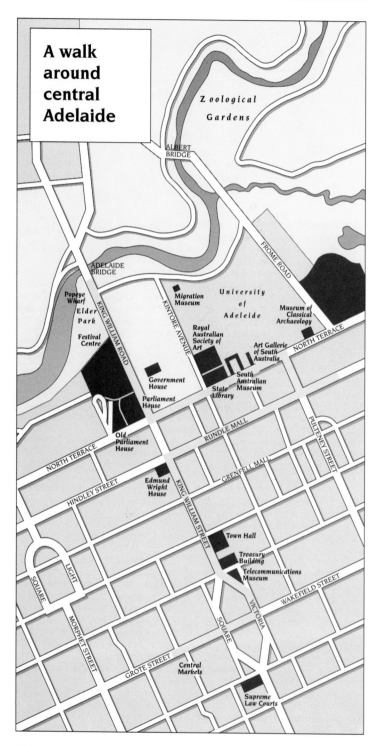

A walk around central Adelaide

Z o o l o g i c a l
G a r d e n s

ALBERT
BRIDGE

FROME ROAD

ADELAIDE
BRIDGE

Popeye
Wharf
Elder
Park

Festival
Centre

KING WILLIAM ROAD

KINTORE AVENUE

Migration
Museum

U n i v e r s i t y
o f
A d e l e i d e

Museum of
Classical
Archaeology

NORTH TERRACE

Royal
Australian
Society of
Art

Art Gallerie
of South
Australia

Government
House

Parliament
House

State
Library

South
Australian
Museum

Old
Parliament
House

NORTH TERRACE

RUNDLE MALL

PULTENEY STREET

GRENFELL MALL

HINDLEY STREET

Edmund
Wright
House

KING WILLIAM STREET

Town Hall

Treasury
Building

Telecommunications
Museum

LIGHT
SQUARE

MORPHET STREET

VICTORIA
SQUARE

WAKEFIELD STREET

GROTE STREET

Central
Markets

Supreme
Law Courts

perched on top of the other. Beyond Rundle Mall you come to lively Rundle Street. This area is even better for open air cafés, and also has a number of smart yuppie bar-restaurants. Here you're liable to be served minimal designer cuisine as minimal as that eaten by designers anywhere, with no expense spared (for you). Non-sophisticates who aren't on expense accounts should head for 205 Rundle Street, the home of the justly famous Austral Hotel. This is popular with students from the nearby university and serves some of the best counter meals you'll find in Australia. (Oh yes, and they also serve beer.)

Rundle Street is also famous for its **East End Market** (*open Fri, Sat, Sun only*). This sells everything from alternative nonsense to pure commercial tat, and some quite worthwhile stuff in between. It is great for the sort of outrageous fashion that it's always so reassuring to see someone else wearing.

Retrace your footsteps back up Rundle Mall to the crossing with Pulteney Street, and here turn right. This quickly brings you to the T-junction with North Terrace. Across the street is the **University of Adelaide**, which opened in 1874. The entire university was originally housed in the neo-Gothic Mitchell building, on whose first floor is the **Museum of Classical Archaeology** (open only during term time, noon to 3 pm, Mon to Fri, entry free). This isn't even as interesting as it sounds, and you're much better off continuing west along North Terrace to the superb **Art Gallery of South Australia** (*open 10 am to 5 pm daily, entry free*).

This is one of the best public galleries in Australia, with a collection ranging from Aborigine and early colonial art to 20thC works. The colonial art may not be world class, but many canvases convey the atmosphere of early Australia in highly evocative fashion. The 20thC collection is world class – and there's more here than Sidney Nolan. They even have works by some of the British Bloomsbury Group, and a cast of the Eros statue which stands in London's Piccadilly Circus.

Next door to the Art Gallery, west along North Terrace, you come to the **South Australian Museum** (*open 10 am to 5 pm daily, entry free*). This has the famous whale skeleton, as well as a collection of extremely interesting Aborigine artefacts. It is the largest collection of its kind in Australia (and, indeed, in the world). Alas for us, but fortunately for the Aborigines, some of the prize exhibits (such as those of religious significance) have now been returned to their rightful owners. But to make up for this there's an interesting video which features the Ngarrindjeri people and their dreamtime story.

By now you might feel in need of a rest, and next door in the **State Library** there's a pleasant magazine room where you can leaf through all the latest Australian magazines and pretend you're doing some important historical research. If you fancy doing some real research here you can look up old papers in the archives.

After your well-earned rest, take a detour right off North Terrace up Kintore Avenue, and on your right you'll see the **Migration Museum**, *open weekends and holidays 1 to 5 pm, entry free*. This museum is unique in Australia, and tells the sad and often bad story of the European settlement of the continent. It is housed in the building which used to be Adelaide's Destitute Asylum, where the immigrants who fell on hard times were forced to lodge. The guided tour (A\$3) is particularly informative.

Retrace your steps back to North Terrace, and turn right (west).

At the junction with King William Street, you will see ahead to your right the classical columned façade of **Parliament House**. This took an astonishing 50 years to build, because no one could agree on whether it should have a dome or not. (The noes won by default, when the building was declared finished in 1939.)

Just beyond this building on North Terrace is the much more interesting **Old Parliament House**, whose interior has now been completely restored (*open Mon to Fri, 10 am to 5 pm, Sat and Sun 12 and 5 pm; entry A\$4*). Don't miss the Assembly Chamber where they debated and voted on the issues of the day, and the Kingston Room where they actually decided who was going to win the vote.

Now retrace your footsteps to the King William Street junction, and turn left (north) up King William Road (the extension of King William Street). Down

• *South Australian Museum.*

here on your left you will see the arty slab of the **Festival Centre**, which contains several theatres and auditoriums for stage and musical productions. On the right of King William Road is Government House.

Continue up King William Road and you come to Elder Park. Ahead is the Adelaide Bridge across the Torrens River. Down by the river's edge on your right is Popeye Wharf. Here you can take a half-hour boat cruise up the river ($5 return), which takes you to the **Zoological Gardens** (*open 9.30 am to 5 pm, longer in summer, entry free*). Those who prefer to paddle their own canoe should cross King William Road to Jolleys Boathouse, where there are boats for hire. This also has a recommendable restaurant ($$), where some may prefer to watch their energetic partners' nautical mishaps while they enjoy their food.

Other sights around Adelaide:

Port Adelaide

This lies 10 km or so west of the city centre. You can reach it by train (from the central station) or by 258/9 buses from North Terrace.

The centre of Port Adelaide has many old balconied buildings, some old sailors' pubs and a number of 19thC streets. There are also several museums. The best is the **South Australia Maritime Museum** at 126 Lipson Street (*open 10 am to 5 pm, Tues to Sun, entry A$7*). Here you can see just what it was like to emigrate on the long voyage to Australia, with reconstructions of steerage accommodation from three different eras. The exhibits also include

a number of old moored ships – one of which, the coaster *Nelcebee*, is said to be the third oldest ship registered at Lloyds of London.

Next door is the **Port Dock Station Railway Museum** (*open daily 10 am to 5 pm, Sat at noon, entry A$6*). No railway buff should miss this one – which has more than a dozen old locos on display, as well as a superb model railway. Those who prefer planes should visit the **Historical Aviation Museum** at 11 Mundy Street, which shows you what the Aussies were flying during the Spitfire era, as well as a display of mementoes from the old days.

On Sundays they have a great flea market at Port Adelaide, and you can also take boat trips around the harbour.

The beaches ✕

Adelaide's most popular beach is at Glenelg, on the coast south-west of the city centre. To get here catch the old tram from Victoria Square, which takes about half an hour. The original settlers of South Australia put ashore here, and there are a couple of sights of historic interest. The harbour has a reconstruction of HMS *Buffalo*, which brought the first settlers (the original was built in India at the beginning of the 19thC). Just down the road you can see the Old Gum Tree, where the proclamation of South Australia was read out in 1836. Glenelg has plenty of guest houses, and several pubs and restaurants, as well as the traditional fish and chip shops. The beach is suitable for swimming and windsurfing, and on summer Sundays you can play at being a sardine. Less crowded, but also less atmospheric, is West Beach, which lies a few miles to the north. My favourite is Henley Beach, which is a little further north still (286/7 buses from North Terrace, just over half an hour's journey). During the week the pubs and restaurants here quieten down somewhat.

Adelaide Hills ⛺ ✕

These lie just 10 km or so inland from the city, forming an enclosing arc. They contain several pleasant parks and gardens, as well as the 'picturesque' German village of Hahndorf.

The easiest spot to reach from the city is the **Cleland Conservation Park** (*open 9 am to 5 pm, entry A$7; buses from the city centre*). This has a wide range of

• *The beach at Glenelg.*

wildlife, and some fine walks. Nearby is the Mount Lofty Lookout, which is over 700 m up and has some fine views out over the city on the plain below.

Just under 10 km north of here is the **Morialta Conservation Park**, with a gorge, waterfalls and some walking trails. (You can get here in just over half an hour from Grenfell Street on the 105 bus.)

Hahndorf lies 30 km south-east of Adelaide. This was founded by émigré Germans who fled from Prussia to escape religious persecution in 1839, and is named after the captain of their ship, Kapitan Hahn; 'Dorf' is the German for village. The village is now a classic tourist spot, complete with Bavarian-

style restaurants and gift shops. (The fact that Prussia is 500 km from Bavaria and has no 'picturesque' architecture is not the point.) However, as anyone who has visited Germany will tell you, it too has a number of fake picturesque villages just like this – so Hahndorf has every claim to be authentic. Go and see the giant cuckoo clock in the **Antique Clock Museum**; and then view the works by the local 19thC artist Hans Heysen at the **Hahndorf Academy**. After this you qualify for a glass or two of authentic locally brewed Pilsner at the suitably rustic bar of the German Arms Hotel. Or head for the German

119

Cake Shop where the kuchen are sufficiently stuffed with cream to be utterly authentic.

(For Fleurieu Peninsula and Kangaroo Island, both south-west of Adelaide, see Australia Overall: 4.)

MOUNT REMARKABLE NATIONAL PARK ⊭

45 km SE of Port Augusta. Drive to the settlement of Wilmington, where an unpaved track leads 10 km to **Alligator Gorge**. There's a walk through this spectacular gorge, whose walls rise sheer in places. Also worth seeing is **Hancocks Lookout**, which is to the north of the park and has fine views out over the gulf. Mount Remarkable itself rises to 969 m and forms part of the southern section of the Flinders Range. To the south it overlooks the small and picturesque settlement of Melrose, once a copper-mining centre, which dates from the early 19thC and is one of the oldest settlements in the entire region.

Information on walks in the area is available from Wilmington Deli, also the Mount Remarkable District Visitor Directory, costing A$2.50 at time of going to press. Camping is permitted in some places – for information and permits, contact the ranger's office at Mambray Creek, tel. (086) 34 7068).

PORT AUGUSTA ⊭ ✕

320 km N of Adelaide on Rt 1. By the 1980s, Port Augusta had become rather a run-down spot. The docks had largely closed down, the railway business was dwindling, and the place was gaining a nasty reputation for crime. But the image of 'Port Gutter', as it came to be known, looks as if it may now be getting cleaner. Port Augusta is, and always will be, a transport centre of strategic importance. Australia's main east–west road and rail links pass through, as do the main links with Alice Springs and the north. Also, its location at the head of the Spencer Gulf makes it the logical port for much of the hinterland region. This all makes Port Augusta about as interesting as it sounds. And yes, you too would probably be best passing on through.

The most interesting spot in town is the **Wadlata Outback Centre** on Flinders Street (*open 9 am to 5.30 pm, Mon to Fri; 10 am to 4 pm at weekends;*

entry A$5.50). This is particularly good on the trials and tribulations of the intrepid (or mad) Victorian explorers of the outback. It also has some excellent displays which elucidate the Aborigine dreamtime and creation myths.

PORT PIRIE

90 km S of Port Augusta. This is the port and smelting centre for the Broken Hill mining district. It looks just as you would expect a busy lead and zinc smelting centre to look, complete with active chimneys; and it has looked much like this for well over 100 years. Bravely, they maintain a Tourist Office at Jubilee Place. Here you can sign up for a tour of the world's largest smelting plant, which takes place at 10 am on Wednesdays and Saturdays. Amazingly, this tour is free.

YORKE PENINSULA ✕

E across Gulf St Vincent from Adelaide. This area is popular with weekenders from Adelaide. It is all rather flat and green and low-key: very much the suburban idea of a pleasant holiday spot. Reasonable fishing, some pleasant beaches for the kids, and Cornish pasties.

Copper was discovered in the north-eastern part of the peninsula in 1859, and this attracted a large number of miners from Cornwall in the west of England. The three towns of Moonta, Kadina and Wallaroo formed what became known as the Copper Triangle. The copper boom petered out in the 1920s, but the region is still known as Little Cornwall. The three towns still have a few relics of the old copper-mining days.

Further south, the coast has a number of beaches. However, the road follows the shore along the opposite east coast, making the beaches here more accessible. From the seaside resort of Edithburgh, at the end of the east coast, you can take a boat trip out to Troubridge Island, which has a colony of Fairy Penguins. From Edithburgh you can also take the picturesque road out to Stenhouse Bay. Just by here, at the tip of the peninsula, is **Innes National Park**. This has some impressive cliffs, excellent surfing beaches (some of which are dangerous for swimmers) and the wreck of the good ship **Ethel**, which foundered here almost a century ago.

RECOMMENDED HOTELS

ADELAIDE

During the Biennial Adelaide Festival accommodation can be very scarce, and it's best to book a long time ahead if you're planning to visit Adelaide during this period.

Adelaide Hilton, $$$; 233 Victoria Square; tel. (08) 217 0711; all major cards.

Luxury accommodation in the heart of the city. All the amenities, including jogging track and pool to work off the effects of their superb restaurant (see Recommended Restaurants).

Plaza Hotel, $-$$; 85 Hindley Street; tel. (08) 231 6371; most major cards.

Grand old hotel just north of city centre, badly in need of refurbishment, hence inexpensive.

City Central Motel, $$; 23 Hindley Street; tel. (08) 231 4049; all major cards.

Standard motel-type accommodation, with a friendly welcome.

ADELAIDE HILLS

Tyele, $$; Stirling; tel.(08) 339 3902; cards none.

Friendly bed-and-breakfast, handy for Cleland Conservation Park and Mount Lofty. Halfway to Hahndorf.

MOUNT REMARKABLE

Mount Remarkable Hotel, $$; Melrose; tel. (086) 66 2119; cards none.

Standard accommodation and friendly staff. Book ahead during summer weekends.

HENLEY BEACH

Meledon Villa, $-$$; 268 Seaview Road; tel. (08) 235 0577; cards none.

Pleasant bed-and-breakfast spot right on the sea front.

PORT AUGUSTA

Poinsettia Motel, $-$$; Burgoyne Street; tel. (086) 42 2856; cards none.

Across the gulf a kilometre or so from town centre, on the corner with the Eyre highway.

YORKE PENINSULA

The Anchorage, $-$$; O'Halloran Parade, Edithburgh; tel. (088) 52 6262; cards none.

Pleasant motel-style accommodation.

RECOMMENDED RESTAURANTS

ADELAIDE

Grange Restaurant, Adelaide Hilton, **$$$**; 233 Victoria Square; tel. (08) 237 0698; all major cards.

Top-of-the-range dining, with first-class menu of Australian cuisine and a dazzling array of wines. Modern, sophisticated atmosphere.

Jolleys Boathouse Restaurant, $$; Jolleys Lane; tel. (08) 223 2891; all major cards; closed for dinner Sun to Tues.

Imaginative menu of Australian cuisine. Views over the Torrens River. A Sunday lunchtime institution, so be sure to book.

Ruby's Cafe, $-$$; 255B Rundle Street; tel. (08) 244 0365; cards MC, V.

Old Bohemian-style market café, with friendly service and a range of local dishes and snacks. BYO.

GLENELG

Colonial Cafe, $-$$; 2 Durham Street; tel. (08) 294 8224; cards none.

Just the place for a pleasant lunchtime snack; they serve more substantial fare in the evenings.

HAHNDORF

German Arms Hotel, $-$$; 50 Main Street; no booking; cards none.

Inn, 150 years old, where they serve their own locally brewed German-style beer. Also has a popular restaurant. German Cake Shop nearby.

PORT AUGUSTA

Basic Foods, $-$$; Commercial Street; no booking; cards none.

Healthy eating, but indeed fairly basic. Apart from this, it's mainly pub food or fish and chips in Port Augusta.

YORKE PENINSULA

Dynasty Room, $-$$; Goyder Street, Kadina; no booking; cards none.

Friendly Chinese restaurant in the Copper Triangle.

Between Port Augusta and Alice Springs
South Australia Outback: Woomera, Coober Pedy and Lake Eyre

1,200 km; map Nelles Australia, 1:400,000

Here is a magnificent journey from the south coast to the heart of Australia at Alice Springs. It runs along the Stuart Highway, which is tarmac all the way – but be careful of the huge lorries which thunder past.

For most of the time you're travelling through desert and wilderness. Some 170 km outside Port Augusta you come to Woomera, at the edge of the secret range where Britain's first atomic bomb was exploded in the early 1950s. Another 370 km down the road you come to Coober Pedy, the famous opal-mining centre which is equally famous for the individualistic characters who mine the opals and live in their own burrowed-out accommodation.

East of here are the large salt flats of Lake Eyre where Donald Campbell broke the world land speed record in 1964.

The distances on this route may be huge, but you should be able to cover it and still see what there is to see in four days.

• Opals.

Transport
The famous Ghan train runs from Adelaide to Alice Springs twice a week. There's also a daily bus between Alice Springs and Port Augusta. If you want to do any off-route exploring, you'll need a 4WD.

■ Alice Springs ↗

• *Coober Pedy, underground home.*

Stuart Highway

■ *Lake Eyre*

■ Coober Pedy

■ Woomera

• *Mining, Cooper Pedy.*

Port Augusta ↗■

Great
Australian
Bight

SIGHTS & PLACES OF INTEREST

ALICE SPRINGS
See *Australia Overall: 13, page 178*.

COOBER PEDY 🛏
370 km N of Woomera on the Stuart Highway. Welcome to the moon. Or so it appears. This is the famous opal-mining centre, and the entire surroundings have been reduced to a lunar landscape by decades of burrowing miners.

But the burrowing isn't all in search of opals. The temperature here often rises above 40°C, the dust is appalling, and the flies are worse. To escape these, the miners burrow entire homes underground. The name Coober Pedy derives from the Aborigine *kupa piti*, which is the equivalent of 'white fellow's burrow'. Some of these underground dwellings are extremely elaborate. There are a couple of underground churches, shops, restaurants, and even some underground motels.

Opals were first found here in 1915, by William Hutchison, who was in fact looking for gold. Servicemen returning from the First World War headed here in droves, and quite a few made it rich.

This region produces most of the world's opals, and still attracts a wide variety of fortune hunters. Coober Pedy's 2,000-strong population is said to include almost three dozen different nationalities. The individual miners tend to be very individual indeed, and all work their own claim. There's a limit of one person per dig, which has kept out big companies.

Try 'noodling' in some of the mounds and you may even strike it lucky with a low-grade opal which has been overlooked. Opals are pretty stones with characteristic opalescent colouring. The superstitious say they're unlucky. Alternatively, you can always buy one. There are dozens of crafty individual salesmen, but you'll probably feel safer dealing with **The Opal Factory** on Hutchison Street.

If you want to learn what it's really like mining here visit the **Old Timers Mine** in Crowders Gully *(open 8.30 am to 6 pm Mon to Sat, 11 am to 6 pm Sun; entry A$1)*.

PORT AUGUSTA
See *Australia Overall: 5, page 120*.

WOOMERA 🛏
170 km NW of Port Augusta on the Stuart Highway. This odd settlement lies at the southern border of the Woomera Restricted Area, better known locally as 'The Range'. It is famous for the fact

LAKE EYRE
This huge dead lake is 400 km north of Port Augusta in one of the most parched regions of Australia. Most of the time the lake is nothing more than a vast salt flat. It was here, in 1964, that Donald Campbell successfully tried for the world land speed record. He eventually reached a speed of 652.37 kph (over 400 mph).

The lake itself is a unique geographical phenomenon. It is situated between two large deserts – the **Sturt Stony Desert** to the east, and the equally forbidding **Simpson Desert** to the north. The lake has a catchment area of over one million square kilometres, which extends well into the Northern Territory and Queensland. Yet despite this, only a trickle of water seeps into the lake. In the last three hundred years it has been filled only three times by floods. The last time was in 1989, when it expanded to almost 150 square kilometres of water. But this soon drained away to leave the usual pristine shimmering sheen of salt flat.

When the floods do come, this entire wilderness region is momentarily transformed. Desert foliage sprouts, flowers bloom in profusion, large flocks of birds fly in, and the surrounding shores are alive with the croaking of frogs. According to the biologists, these frogs exist for the rest of the time underground in a state of hibernation, retaining suffient water beneath their skin to keep them alive. A likely story, but can you think of a better one?

The best way to see the lake is to make it up to Maree, 380 km north of Port Augusta, where they run flights over the lake. Beyond Maree the track is only suitable for 4WD.

that nobody knows what goes on within its 50,000 square kilometres. We know what used to go on there in the 1950s and 1960s: atomic bomb tests and the firing of experimental rockets. Now things are quieter, and a little more mysterious. Indeed, Woomera itself has only been open to the public since 1982.

There's not much to see in town apart from the occasional incongruous Americans who work at the nearby 'Joint Facility'. (In answer to my enquiries, I was told: 'It is what it says it is').

- *Long-haul road trains span the continent.*

Much more informative is the local **Heritage Centre** (*open* 9.30 *am to* 4.30 *pm daily,* Mar *to* Nov *only; entry* A$2.50). The displays and photos here do their best to dispel any air of secrecy, and are interesting both as scientific and as propaganda exhibits. Inevitably the notorious radioactive tests carried out on unwitting soldiers in the 1950s don't feature very prominently – which only makes one wonder what else has been glossed over.

RECOMMENDED HOTELS

COOPER PEDY
Opal Inn Hotel and Motel, $-$$; Hutchison Street; tel. (086) 72 5054; *all major cards.*

The rooms above the pub are cheaper but more basic than the motel rooms.

If you must stay underground, one of the more salubrious spots is:

The Underground Motel, $$; Umoona Road; tel (086) 72 5324; *cards none.*

WOOMERA
Eldo Hotel, $; Kotana Avenue; tel. (086) 73 7867; *cards none.*

ELDO stands for European Launcher Development Organisation: the people who failed to put up a European satellite here. It also has a rather ordinary restaurant.

RESTAURANTS

Even in the desert, every 200 to 300 km you come to a settlement, and there is no such thing as a settlement in Australia without a watering hole for the locals. These hotels invariably serve plates of inexpensive food – some of it fairly reasonable, some indifferent, some awful. These apart, we haven't found eating places in the places covered by this section that are recommendable according to the criteria we apply in *The Versatile Guides.*

Queensland

Between Brisbane and Hervey Bay
Brisbane and the Sunshine Coast

300 km; map Nelles Australia, 1:400,000

Brisbane is the capital of Queensland, and the third largest city in Australia. Though not exactly a holiday resort itself, it's in the middle of some of the finest resort territory in the country. To the north lies the aptly named Sunshine Coast, and to the south lies Australia's answer to Florida, the Gold Coast (see Australia Overall: 2).

The Sunshine Coast starts 50 km or so north of Brisbane, and extends from Bribie Island to Noosa. This stretch of coast is slightly less popular than the more garish Gold Coast. Even so, it attracts the crowds and, in their wake, the developers.

A couple of decades ago the Queensland state legislature abolished death taxes. As a result many retirees from cooler climes down the coast have moved up here, hoping that the Queensland government will eventually go the whole hog and abolish death altogether.

As you would expect, there are miles of fine beaches – with all the opportunities for excellent surfing, swimming, diving and long-distance beach-running which the old folk find so necessary to while away their long leisure hours. There's even great fishing for the youngsters. Caloundra, Maroochydore, Mooloolaba, Noosa – this may sound like the opening line of an Aborigine epic poem, but these are in fact the Sunshine Coast's main resorts.

You can easily drive from Brisbane along the entire length of the Sunshine Coast in a day, and still have time for a couple of beach sorties en route. But if you want to do some serious surfing, explore the islands, and see the sights, you can spend a week here with no difficulty.

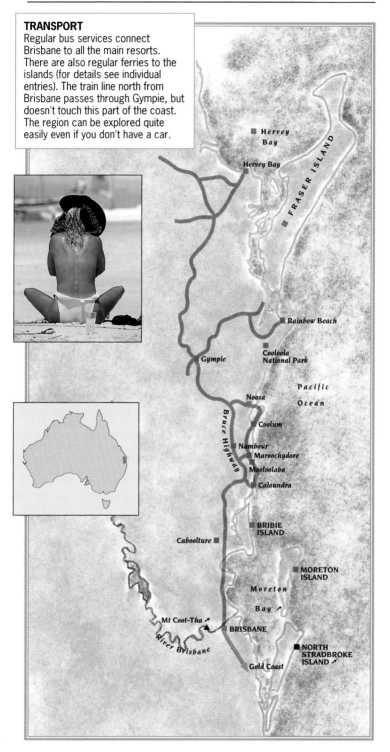

TRANSPORT
Regular bus services connect
Brisbane to all the main resorts.
There are also regular ferries to the
islands (for details see individual
entries). The train line north from
Brisbane passes through Gympie, but
doesn't touch this part of the coast.
The region can be explored quite
easily even if you don't have a car.

Hervey
Bay

Hervey Bay

FRASER ISLAND

Rainbow Beach

Gympie

Cooloola
National Park

Pacific
Ocean

Noosa

Coolum

Bruce Highway

Nambour
Maroochydore

Mooloolaba

Caloundra

BRIBIE
ISLAND

Caboolture

MORETON
ISLAND

Moreton

Bay

Mt Coot-Tha

BRISBANE

River Brisbane

NORTH
STRADBROKE
ISLAND

Gold Coast

SIGHTS & PLACES OF INTEREST

BRIBIE ISLAND

Off the coast 25 km N of Brisbane, at the N end of Moreton Bay. The island is just over 30 km long and joined to the mainland at its southern end by a bridge across the Pumicestone Passage. This end of the island is suffering from creeping development. There are terrific surfing beaches along the island's eastern side, and the north end is largely unspoiled and a favourite local fishing spot.

BRISBANE ⇔ ✕

On the E coast 1,000 km N of Sydney. Brisbane is the state capital of Queensland and has a population of 1.3 million, making it the third largest city in Australia. With its high-rise modern buildings along the waterfront, it looks a decidedly modern city, but it also has many older buildings and a pleasant laid-back feel to it. The climate is subtropical with the lush foliage of mango trees and banana plants sprouting from the gardens. The city spreads over rolling hills and, in the recent boom years, has outgrown its lingering reputation as 'the largest country town on earth'. The Commonwealth Games were held here in 1982, and in 1988 the city staged the World Expo. Despite its size (Brisbane sprawls over more land than any other Australian city), within a few kilometres inland the mountains are covered with subtropical rainforest, and along Moreton Bay and its islands there are miles of superb sandy beaches.

History

The first settlement in the region was the notorious Moreton Bay Penal Colony, which was established in 1824 by John Oxley. When Oxley first put ashore here he found three shipwrecked ex-convicts living amongst the local Aborigines, and they helped him to explore the shoreline, showing him an extensive river which flowed into the bay. This had not previously been marked on the maps, and Oxley named the river after Sir Thomas Brisbane, the governor of New South Wales. Brisbane had sent Oxley on this mission to establish a prison settlement for 'the worst type of offenders'. (It was hoped that the heat would stupefy them, and

lessen their unruly behaviour.) The initial colony at Redcliffe on Moreton Bay was shifted a year later to the banks of the Brisbane River, some 15 km inland.

For the next 15 years, it was living hell for the convicts of the Moreton Bay Penal Colony, and not much better for their disgruntled guards. The convict population rose to almost 1,000, despite disease and the vicious brutality of their keepers. Few managed to escape – the sea was full of sharks, and inland were hostile Aborigines.

In 1839 the notorious colony was at last dispersed, and Moreton Bay was opened up for land-hungry settlers from the south. Yet as the settlers spread inland they encountered fierce resistance from the local Aborigine tribes. In an effort to halt increasing dispossession, the Aborigine tribes united. For almost a decade their leader Dundalli and his warriors harassed the encroaching white pioneers. But it was an uneven struggle. After the pioneer settlers came the cattlemen, driving huge herds north on to the grazing lands of the plateau. In 1859 the Moreton Bay District (the early name for Queensland) became a separate state, and Brisbane was chosen as its capital.

Sugar plantations were soon being established in the north, with Solomon Islanders shipped in to harvest the cane under conditions of virtual slavery. Then came the discovery of gold. Later came the discovery of minerals, and Queensland gradually began to establish itself as a thriving state. Yet Brisbane remained very much a country backwater. This changed somewhat during the Second World War. The US commander General MacArthur established Brisbane as his headquarters during his Pacific campaign against the Japanese. But after the war the Americans left, and life in Brisbane resumed its provincial pace.

In the 1970s the ultra-conservative National Party took over the state government, under the leadership of the maverick Johannes Bjelke-Petersen – known locally as 'Joh'. During the next two decades Joh ran Queensland in his own heavy-handed fashion from the state capital (which became known as 'Johburg'). The police were given a virtual carte blanche, with widespread abuse of civil liberties; nepotism resulted in large-scale corruption; and Joh ran the show, evading all awkward questions with his own characteristic blend of bravado and evasion. Brisbane became the capital of a mineral-rich but socially backward state.

In the end even the smooth-talking Joh couldn't talk his way out of setting up a full-scale enquiry into government malpractice. The Fitzgerald Inquiry was originally intended as a whitewash, but to the consternation of Joh and his government cronies, it insisted upon revealing the truth (which everyone had suspected all along). Corruption was found to be endemic, from the government down.

Joh was out, and the entire state underwent a transformation. The apotheosis of this was the hosting of the World Expo in 1988, which attracted 18 million visitors to the newly revitalized capital. Today, Brisbane continues to thrive and is a vital part of modern Australia – with all its citizens reaping the benefits (and the troubles) of the recent economic ups and downs which have beset the growing commercial centres of the Pacific Rim.

The centre of Brisbane is fairly compact, and where you'll find most of the sights. The main Brisbane Visitor and Convention Centre is on the ground floor of the City Hall in Adelaide Street, with other branches at the airport and in Queen Street Mall. The Queensland Government Travel Centre at the corner of Adelaide and Edward Streets supplies tourist information (and takes bookings) for the whole state.

A walk through Central Brisbane

This walk takes you through the heart of town, past many of the city's landmarks. The walk itself is only a couple of kilometres or so. Brisbane can get hot, and is not an ideal city for long walks, but if you stop off to see the sights on the way this one can easily take an entire afternoon.

Start at the **Old Windmill** (often known locally as the Observatory), which is north of the city centre in Wickham Terrace. The most ancient of the city's old landmarks, on a hill overlooking the heart of town, The Old Windmill is a remnant of the bad old days of the Moreton Bay Penal Colony. It was built in 1828, just four years after the colony had been established. The windmill was intended to grind flour for the colony's

• *Old Windmill.*

bread supply, but right from the start it never worked properly. Its wooden sails were so heavy that they needed a gale to move at all, so convicts were set to work turning the mill. Anyone found guilty of 'insolence' or using 'profane blasphemies' was sentenced to work 14-hour shifts on the notorious treadmill, which earned the windmill the nickname, the 'Tower of Torture'. According to a local historian, the treadmill at the windmill was so draining that 'the steps of the wheels are sometimes literally wet with perspiration'. And those who refused to work were occasionally hung from a gallows, rigged from a wooden sail.

When fire swept the city in 1864 most of the old buildings were burnt to the ground, but the windmill was only partly damaged. Later it became an observatory, and in the 1930s it was used as an experimental television station. Nowadays it remains purely as a grim reminder of the city's early history.

From the windmill set off down the hill south-east along Wickham Terrace towards Edward Street. At Edward Street turn right, continuing across Turbot Street and passing the railway bridge. At the crossing with Ann Street, turn left, and on your right you will see **Anzac Square**, laid in 1930 in memory of the members of the Australia and New Zealand Army Corps (Anzac) who gave their lives in the First World War (most of them fighting bravely against overwhelming odds in the notoriously mismanaged Gallipoli Campaign against the Turks). In the centre of the square is the **Shrine of Remembrance** (*open 11 am to 3 pm, Mon to Fri ; entry free*) with its cupola and sandstone Doric columns, and an everlasting flame. In the crypt beneath the flame is earth from the Gallipoli battlefields, which is designated 'Forever Australia'. From Anzac Square head back (southwest) down Ann Street, cross over Edward Street, and ahead on your left you come to King George Square, overlooked at the far end by **City Hall**, which was built in the 1930s, when it became known as 'Million Pound Town Hall', on account of its excessive cost. Its grandiose Italianate façade (no worse than many similar 'monsterpieces' throughout the world) contains a fascinating permanent reminder of the state's early racist policy. Over the portico is a depiction of Aboriginal life 'dying out before the approach of the white man'. (Even Alabama never managed the likes of this.) Inside is the somnolent **City Art Gallery** (*open Mon to Fri 10 am to 5 pm; entry free*), which occasionally wakes up with travelling shows of work by modern Australian artists. Take the lift up the clock tower to the observation deck for a fine view of the city.

Leave King George Square from the east corner, and continue north-east up Adelaide Street. At the crossing with Edward Street, turn right. Continue south-east down Edward Street until you come to the crossing with Queen Street. Turn left up Queen Street, and on your left you come to the **National Bank Building**. This shrine to the worship of money is one of the finest 19thC buildings in the land – as befits a period when money was taken seriously. Each part of it cost a great deal of money, and is not without meaning. The style dates from the Renaissance period (the era when banking began in earnest), and its fine entrance door is carved from a single piece of wood.

North-east of the National Bank Building, at the junction of Queen and Creek Streets, turn right down Creek Street. At the junction with Elizabeth Street turn right, and on your left you will see **St Stephen's Church**, a splendid neo-Gothic pile, which was completed in 1850, making it the oldest church in Brisbane. According to a local 19thC legend, the building was saved from the ravages of the great 1864 fire, which devastated the city, by a flock of birds in the shape of a cross, followed by a wind that held back the flames. Next door is St Stephen's Catholic Cathedral.

Continue down Elizabeth Street to the crossing with Edward Street, where you turn right, which brings you back to Queen Street. Turn left here into the **Queen Street Shopping Mall**, where you come to shop till you drop. You could be in Dallas or Dortmund (the malls there also have woolly Koalas for sale, haute couture jungle wear for the suburban gardener, and designer deodorants). Those who can resist the roller-coaster and the live lobsters in David Jones food hall should keep an eye open for the buskers. There are at least two geniuses operating here – one of whom mimes a misanthropic old lighthouse keeper in a bombing raid (the other is merely bombed).

Leave the Queen Street Mall by its south-western end. On your left you will now see the **Treasury Building**, which took more than 30 years to build, by which time the state had practically no treasury left to put in it. To recoup their losses, they're now planning to turn it into a casino. It seems this spot was always set aside for losers: it originally housed the officers' quarters of the old penal colony.

Continue south-west down Queen Street, and across the Victoria Bridge over the Brisbane River. Directly ahead you will now see the modern **Queensland Cultural Centre**, which includes a wide variety of sights. Among them, the **Queensland Museum** (*open daily 9 am to 5 pm; entry free*) contains an exciting natural history collection, and some superb fossils dating from millions of years ago to the present (the latter is in uniform in the second gallery, and takes a dim view of noisy kids).

Also part of the Centre, the **State Art Gallery** has some art of the highest quality and some high-octane nonsense. Amongst the former are works by Sidney Nolan and several other Australian artists which would not be out

• *Shrine of Remembrance, Anzac Square.*

A walk through central Brisbane

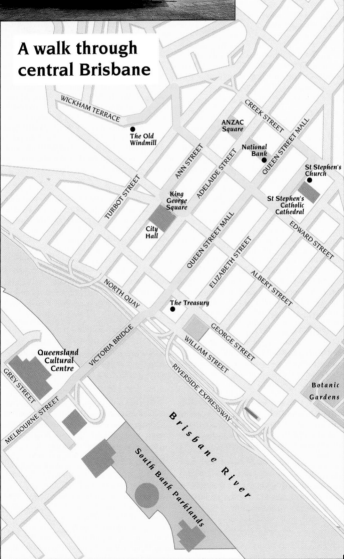

WICKHAM TERRACE

CREEK STREET

ANZAC Square

The Old Windmill

National Bank

QUEEN STREET MALL

St Stephen's Church

ANN STREET

ADELAIDE STREET

TURBOT STREET

King George Square

St Stephen's Catholic Cathedral

EDWARD STREET

City Hall

QUEEN STREET MALL

ELIZABETH STREET

ALBERT STREET

NORTH QUAY

The Treasury

GEORGE STREET

VICTORIA BRIDGE

WILLIAM STREET

Queensland Cultural Centre

RIVERSIDE EXPRESSWAY

GREY STREET

Botanic Gardens

MELBOURNE STREET

Brisbane River

South Bank Parklands

of place in any great 20thC collection. The Aboriginal works on display appear equally varied in quality – but what's good and what's rubbish is more difficult to judge. European standards don't always apply. Finally the **State Library** has some old photos that take you right back into a tough history.

Just to the south-east of the Queensland Cultural Centre, along the bank of Brisbane River, stretch the **South Bank Parklands**, the site of the 1988 World Expo, now a large urban park, where you can wander through various ecosystems, from rainforest to desert and encounter a variety of urban eco-types from candyfloss sellers to buskers. There's also a boat ride along the waterways, cycle paths, a butterfly house and a maritime museum. The site covers more than 15 hectares, which means it isn't quite such a crowded mishmash as it may sound. You can end your walk here with a well-deserved cold drink at one of the many cafés.

Other Brisbane sights

The **Botanic Gardens** in Alice Street were once the convicts' vegetable patch. Most botanical gardens in temperate climates try with varying success to cultivate tropical plants of some sort. As this is the tropics, you might expect them to take up the challenge and try to cultivate a few beetroots and cabbages. But no, this is the real tropical thing, complete with a patch of rainforest, where the trees are outnumbered 20 to one by the toads.

Castlemaine Perkins Brewery (Milton Road, Milton; tel. (07) 361 7322; free tours Mon to Wed) is a must for all lovers of the famous XXXX. The production of this amber fluid is taken very seriously in these parts, and tours must be booked well in advance.

By far the best way to get to the **Lone Pine Sanctuary** (13 km SW of the city centre at Fig Tree Pocket; open 9 am to 4.30 pm; entry A$10) is to take the river cruise from Wharf Road, by Victoria Bridge in the centre of town. (It takes 1½ hours each way, and costs A$13 return.) The most famous inhabitants of this wildlife sanctuary are the koalas, of which there are more than a hundred. They are usually sleeping and farting in the trees (a side-effect of their eucalyptus diet). Those who enjoy fondling flatulent furry animals can have their photo taken with a koala in their arms. Other less attractive (but less malodorous) occupants of the park include dingoes, lizards, wallabies and the notorious Tasmanian Devil. Many of these animals, but not the last mentioned, will allow you to stroke them instead.

Brisbane can get very hot in the summer, and it's quite a distance to the beaches. The best place to cool off is one of the many swimming pools in town, which are open from at least 8 am to 6 pm daily. The best is Spring Hill Baths on Torrington Street (closed May to Aug), one of the oldest in Australia. Otherwise try Valley Pool (open all year), which is in Wickham Street a couple of kilometres north-east of the city centre in Fortitude Valley. This is where the Aussie gold medalists train.

CABOOLTURE

50 km N of Brisbane on Bruce Highway. Despite its name, the most cultured thing about this spot is the milk: this small town is famous for producing yoghurt. The **Abbey Museum of Art and Archaeology** (open Tues, Thur and Sat 10 am to 4 pm; entry A$4) comes a cultural second – with more than 4,000 exhibits of decreasing interest ranging from Ancient Egypt to Victorian Britain.

CALOUNDRA

Seaside resort at the S end of the Sunshine Coast, 50 km N of Brisbane. There was an old man from Caloundra – this may sound like the start of a limerick, but I can't help it – who caught a fish, which had swallowed a fish, which according to him had swallowed yet another fish. After much heated discussion these fish were eventually laid out on the bar of a local hotel. Here it was judged that the third fish, despite being a mere minnow, was too large to have been swallowed by the other two fish. Sid Jackson is now over 80 years old, but still stoutly maintains that he is the only man in Queensland to have caught three fish on the same hook. You'll see him along the streets leading to the beach, wearing a green floppy hat and a baggy tropical shirt (inside the pocket of which is the famous photo of his triple catch). Since his remarkable feat, Sid has given up fishing and done his best to establish himself as a local celebrity. His story is probably the most interesting thing about Caloundra,

THE STORY OF ELIZA FRASER

Fraser Island is named after Eliza Fraser, the Scottish wife of a Victorian ship's captain. Her husband's ship the *Sterling Castle* was wrecked on a reef further up the coast in 1863. Captain Fraser and his wife, along with some of the crew, managed to sail in a lifeboat to Waddy Point, on the north-east coast of Fraser Island. On coming ashore they encountered a group of local Aborigines, who immediately took them as slaves. The shipwrecked survivors endured excruciating conditions (torture, sunstroke, spear prodding, hard work, and so on), and a couple of months later Eliza was put up as a prize amongst the local Aborigine males. It's not quite clear exactly what happened next, but she was eventually rescued by a former convict called John Graham, who was living amongst the Aborigines. Unfortunately the experience had unhinged Eliza. By the time she returned to civilization she was unable, or unwilling, to give a coherent account of her ordeal. Though whether this was due to her mental state or Victorian attitudes towards sex, Aborigines and consorting with a convict, are unclear. A century later this entire episode was imaginatively and sympathetically described by the great Australian writer Patrick White in his novel *A Fringe of Leaves*.

which is otherwise a rather ordinary resort. Since ordinary Aussie resorts are a great deal better than ordinary resorts in most other places, you probably won't be disappointed (and you can always show your snap of Sid – holding up his famous photo – to the folks back home).

Those who prefer their history in more factual form should try the **Queensland Air Museum** (*open Wed, Sat and Sun, 10 am to 4 pm, entry A$4*) at nearby Caloundra Airport. You can also take a boat trip to Bribie Island, which is just across the Pumicestone Passage. Or you can hire a rod, and join

the others trying to emulate Sid Jackson's attempt to get into the Guinness Book of Records (which apparently still isn't responding to his letters).

COOLOOLA NATIONAL PARK

On the coast and inland between Noosa and Rainbow Beach. This has 50 km of beach (OK for 4WD) overlooked by cliffs of coloured sand. Inland, wilderness trails lead you through the woods and scrubland. The Noosa River runs through the park, forming two sizeable lakes – Cootharaba (with its Everglades) and the smaller Cooroibah. You can explore the river and lakes by canoe, or take a cruise (both from Noosa). The best entry points to the park are from Noosa and Rainbow Beach.

COOLUM 🛏

On the coast midway between Noosa and Maroochydore. Coolum has a superb beach and one of the finest health spa resorts anywhere in the world (see Recommended Hotels, page 136).

FRASER ISLAND

Off the coast 140 km N of Brisbane; ferries (called barges) from Urangan (Hervey Bay), River Heads (12 km S) and Inskip Point (10 km N of Rainbow Beach).

If you're taking a car, you'll need a permit, which you can pick up at any local National Parks Office, or at River Heads General Store, which is just before the ferry. But only take a 4WD on to the island, as there are no real roads and anything else just gets bogged down in the sand.

Fraser Island proudly boasts that it's the 'World's Largest Sand Island', gaining it a place on UNESCO's World Heritage List – and unlike many other things taken on by this organization, it looks like surviving.

Fraser Island is 123 km of sand dunes, lakes, isolated settlements, huge beaches, occasional outcrops of volcanic rock, and offshore wrecks. It takes its name from Eliza Fraser, who survived shipwreck and slavery amongst the Aborigines here during the 19thC (see page 133 for a bowdlerized version of this episode).

Thirty years later fate was to wreak a grim revenge on the local Aborigines. The Europeans found that the island's woods contained the rare Satinay tree, whose hard tropical wood is uniquely

HUMPBACKED WHALES

Humpbacked whales spend most of their life in the Antarctic. But once a year they migrate 5,000 km to Hervey Bay where, in the shallow waters protected by Fraser Island, the coast and the southern end of the Great Barrier Reef, they mate and give birth to their young. Like most humans, most animals prefer to do this sort of thing in private – but this is difficult if you're a whale. Especially nowadays, when there aren't many of you left, and everyone wants to know that you're still there. Each year, thousands of humans (most of whom would never dream of watching their own species in such personal acts) make their own annual trek up to Hervey Bay. The whales put on a suitably frisky display of 'breaching' – bursting through the surface and belly-flopping with an enormous splash, like huge ungainly dolphins. Or if they're not feeling so energetic, they'll sometimes spout instead. Then they coyly retire to the privacy of the depths to get on with what they came here for.

Humpbacked whales can weigh up to 40 tons, and are often 15 m long, so they must be feeling fairly frisky when they start breaching. (Imagine something the size and weight of a loaded articulated lorry leaping over a motorway bridge.) Until the 1950s as many as 12,000 humpbacked whales used to make the annual trek to Hervey Bay. By the 1960s the Antarctic whaling fleets had reduced this to less than 200. Fortunately, over the last decade or so this number has more than doubled.

Having failed to denude the island of its woodlands, industry decided to try a different tack. In the 1970s a large mining company bought the mineral rights to the island, and decided to have a go at selling the island's rich mineral sand. As the rich mineral sand was the island, a fierce conservationist campaign was mounted by a local schoolteacher called John Sinclair. Legally, the mining company was quite entitled to alter the geography of Australia in such a fashion. But for once common sense prevailed over the law, and the mining company was forced out.

Now Fraser Island is facing a different threat – from people like us. The rapid increase of tourism is beginning to play havoc with the island's natural beauty. Litter, the erosion of the sand dunes, and destruction wreaked by 4WD vehicles, are all beginning to take their toll. Alas, the best way to cover distance on the island remains by 4WD vehicles, which can be hired at Urangan and Rainbow Beach (you'll need a credit card to cover the A$500 deposit).

The main beach is Seventy Five Mile Beach, which is on the east side of the island. At the northern end of the beach are some picturesque cliffs known as the Cathedrals. Inland you can see the remains of the island's tropical rainforest at Yidney Scrub, and feed the turtles at Bowaraddy Lake. The western shore of the island is largely covered with mangroves. The best places for walking are inland, where there are scores of lakes, some of which are good for swimming. Be careful when swimming from the beaches: the breakers often have an unexpectedly heavy undertow, and sharks are not unknown.

GYMPIE

On Bruce Highway 106 km N of Brisbane. A former gold-mining town, which has now gone to sleep and only wakes up for the annual Gold Mining Festival in October. On the highway there's a suitably somnolent **Mining Museum** (*open 9 am to 5 pm; entry A$4*).

HERVEY BAY ⇔ ✕

On the coast 160 km N of Brisbane, opposite Fraser Island. Hervey Bay doesn't exist – at least, not on the road signs. To get here, follow the signs for Torquay, Pialba, Urangan or Scarness – the rather ordinary beach suburbs

resistant to submarine decay. Woodcutters arrived forthwith, drove off the Aborigines, and began felling the Satinay trees for all they were worth. And they were worth something – enough for them to be shipped half way round the world to Egypt, where Ferdinand de Lesseps made use of the logs to shore up the desert walls of the canal he was building. Fortunately the Suez Canal was finished before the wood ran out.

which have now joined up along the shore to form Hervey Bay. The best beach is at Torquay, but there's no surf anywhere on the bay. Despite this, there are two excellent reasons for coming here. The first is to catch the ferry across to Fraser Island (see page 133). At Urangan you can catch the car ferry or a passenger catamaran. The other reason for coming here is to see the whales.

Hervey Bay is home from home for humpbacked whales. Each winter (between May and September) humpbacked whales from the Antarctic migrate to the sheltered waters of Hervey Bay. Around the time of the annual Whale Festival in August, you can take a day trip out to see the whales. Set out on one of these from the Esplanade at Torquay. (Get there around 8 am, and expect to pay almost A$50.) At other times of year these boats organize day-long fishing expeditions for a similar price.

MAROOCHYDORE ✕

64km N of Brisbane on the Sunshine Coast. The largest town on the Sunshine Coast, Maroochydore has a population of almost 30,000. The coast from here south for the 5 km to Mooloolaba is now practically one long strip of development. Maroochydore has a pleasant beach, the mouth of the River Maroochy and a few small islands. It becomes fairly hectic during the summer. Out of season it's an agreeably quiet spot – with everyone going about their business and paying little attention to the odd surfers going about what appears to be their entire business. Otherwise there are just the oldies and the pelicans – who are cut-throat rivals in the fishing business.

MOOLOOLABA

60 km N of Brisbane on the Sunshine Coast. Mooloolaba, by the Mooloolah River which almost gave it its name, is a lively resort with a fine beach and an esplanade of cafés and restaurants. Nearby is the smart wharf area, with more restaurants overlooking the river – where you can eat seafood and drink enough wine to enable you to pronounce the name of the town and the river consecutively (or just sound as if that's what you're doing).

The only other sight of interest is

Underwater World (*open 9 am to 5 pm; entry A$13.50*), the largest aquarium in Australia, where you can wave to the crocodiles, walk through the shark tank (in a tunnel), and ponder the living versions of fish you have so far only seen on your plate.

The ridge offshore is recommended for diving. According to the persuasive guy who hires out the equipment, you can see stingrays which don't sting and sharks which don't bite. However, my confidence was somewhat undermined by the fact that he still insists you pay before you set out.

MORETON BAY
See Australia Overall: 2, page 81.

MORETON ISLAND
Across Moreton Bay from Brisbane. The island can be reached by catamaran from the quay at Holt Street in Brisbane (around 2 hours each way, and costs A$25). Moreton Bay Island is almost 40 km long, and has miles of sand dunes and fine beaches. But that's practically all there is here. There are roads, but taking a vehicle is costly, you'll need a 4WD, as well as a permit to drive. There is only dormitory accommodation or camping, and it is advisable to bring your own supplies. There are finer beaches elsewhere in this region, which can be just as deserted, and are far more accessible.

MOUNT COOT-THA
See Local Explorations: 3, page 206.

NAMBOUR
On Bruce Highway 60 km N of Brisbane. This small rural town is surrounded by sugar plantations. Nearby, they also grow (and manufacture) pineapples. You want to know what a manufactured pineapple looks like? Head 6 km south of town and you come to the **Big Pineapple**, a 15-m-high fruit made of plastic. Inside you can learn all about how real pineapples are grown, but otherwise it's little more than a bloated photo opportunity. (Angle your camera so that the spiky leaves appear to fountain out of your victim's head.) Six km north of town stands the rival Big Cow. This unlikely pair have proved unexpectedly fertile, giving birth to a local population explosion of oversized progeny – including a giant lawnmower,

monstrous shell, and a bottle of beer the size Aussies dream about (alas, empty).

NOOSA ⋈ ✕

On the coast 80 km N of Brisbane. First came the surfers, attracted by the exceptional high rollers around Noosa Heads. Then the surfers grew up and became high rollers themselves (big city style) returning to turn Noosa Heads into one of the smartest resorts in Australia. In fact, Noosa Heads is only one of three communities which make up Noosa. It is the smart section up by the national park, where the restaurants and fashion boutiques of Hastings Street stand just inland from Laguna Beach. There are nature trails along the cliffs and through the tropical woodlands of the nearby national park. These end up at sandy coves between the headlands, where Alexandria Bay is a popular spot for getting rid of your zebra stripes and showing off that all-over tan. Those who prefer views of a different kind should head for the Laguna Lookout (on the edge of the national park, at the end of Viewland Drive). Cheats can drive up here, others will look upon the spectacular views of miles of beaches and ocean as their well-earned reward for the climb. On the south-eastern side of the headland lies the smart seaside suburb of Sunshine Beach.

West of Noosa Heads, along the mouth of the Noosa River, is Noosaville, where you can rent canoes and take cruises along the Noosa River into the Everglades and lakes of Cooloola National Park (see page 133).

NORTH STRADBROKE ISLAND

See Australia Overall: 2, page 84.

RAINBOW BEACH

On the coast 130 km N of Brisbane. A small town with a population of less than 1,000, which you pass through on the way to the Fraser Island ferry. South of town are the rainbow beach whose coloured sands give the town its name, the rusting wreck of the Cherry Venture which came ashore 20 years ago and has been sinking into the sand ever since, and Cooloola National Park (see page 000). Rainbow Beach is useful as a base for exploring Fraser Island and the Cooloola National Park.

RECOMMENDED HOTELS

BRISBANE

Brisbane has a wide variety of accommodation, ranging from Hilton luxury to backpackers' bed of nails. The more central you get, the higher the price. Prices are liable to drop at the weekends, especially in summer; though during the 'Ekka' (the Brisbane Show) in August you'll be lucky to find a room anywhere.

Annie's Shandon Inn, $-$$; 405 Upper Edward Street; tel. (07) 831 8684; all major cards.
Family-run bed-and-breakfast just five minutes walk from the heart of town.

If you fancy somewhere rather more upmarket, try:

Gazebo Hotel, $$$; 345 Wickham Terrace; tel. (07) 831 6177; all major cards.
On the hill just north of the city centre, with fine views over town. Big bonuses: it's away from the city rush, and has a pool.

Gateway Hotel Brisbane, $$-$$$; 85-87 North Quay; tel. (07) 236 3300; all major cards.
Tastefully decorated rooms, many overlooking the river by Victoria Bridge. Close to all the central sights, with a pool.

COOLUM

Hyatt Regency Resort, $$$; Warran Road; tel. (074) 46 1243; all major cards.
More than 300 apartments, and a championship-standard golf course; more than half a dozen restaurants, ditto swimming pools, tennis courts, squash courts, etc. – all set in 150 hectares of landscaped grounds. You can emerge from here so fit that you need another holiday to recover from it.

HERVEY BAY

Hervey Bay Motel, $-$$; 518 Esplanade, Urangan; tel. (071) 28 9277; cards none.

Standard motel on the front, handy for the ferry to Fraser Island.

NOOSA

This resort can be expensive, and prices shoot up at peak periods. Noosaville has the best inexpensive accommodation (on the riverfront in Gympie Terrace). Best value at the smarter end of town is:

Tingirana, $$; 25 Hastings Street, Noosa Heads; tel. (074) 47 3274; all major cards.

On fashionable Hastings Street, near the beach and all the action.

RECOMMENDED RESTAURANTS

BRISBANE

The best restaurant in town is:

Victoria's, $$$; Brisbane Hilton, Queen Street Mall; tel. (07) 231 3131; all major cards.

Sophisticated dining, with one of the best menus in the land. The cuisine features imaginative Australian dishes with superb continental and Asiatic classics. Be sure to book.

The best French restaurant in town is:

Le Bronx BYO Restaurant, $$-$$$; 722 Brunswick Street; tel. (07) 358 2088; all major cards.

No slavish imitator, the chef here lets his creative talents run riot. The menu includes a series of spectacular dishes which incorporate many Australian ingredients – such as kangaroo – into classic French recipes. Bring your own bottle of vintage wine for a vintage meal.

For less expensive dining, you can always try the buffets and counter meals at some of the central hotels. (The Transcontinental on Roma Street is particularly good.) These allow for Australian-style appetites. The city centre also has no shortage of good cafés, where you can pick up a hearty snack. Try Jimmy's on the Mall – three cafés, all on Queen Street Mall – or:

Ned Kelly's Bushtucker Restaurant, $$; Boardwalk, South Bank Parklands; tel. (07) 846 1880; all major cards.

This claims to be 'the only real bushtucker restaurant in Brisbane'. Certainly there's no denying the authenticity of the decoration and the menu – corrugated iron, timber and kangaroo, witchetty grubs (take your choice as to which is which). As you'd expect, the steaks here are superb. The adventurous will want to try the Moreton Bay Bugs (which are rather like crayfish).

HERVEY BAY

Willy's, $-$$; 410 Esplanade, Torquay; tel. (071) 25 2666; cards none.

Bar-restaurant with live entertainment and a friendly young crowd.

If you fancy somewhere a bit quieter there are several other restaurants just along the Esplanade.

MAROOCHYDORE

BC's Tex Mex, $-$$; 23 Aerodrome Road; tel. (074) 43 5155; cards AE, MC, V.

Popular informal spot, with hot food, cold beer, and suitably tacky decor. Full Mexican range and much Mexican behaviour from the gringo clientele.

NOOSA

Pavilions, $$-$$$; 25 Hastings Street, Noosa Heads; tel. (074) 49 4888; all major cards.

French cuisine with an imaginative Australian flavour. Their lamb dishes are justly renowned, and their wine list is superb. Classy informal atmosphere.

Between Hervey Bay and Mackay
The Capricorn Coast

700 km; map Nelles Australia 1:400,000

This section covers the coastline of central Queensland, which lies opposite the Capricorn group of islands, that forms the southern tip of the Great Barrier Reef. Together with the inshore islands, these have almost everything you'd expect of tropical islands. Some are remote. Many are uninhabited and undeveloped (though it's possible to camp on most of them). Almost all have superb beaches, excellent reef diving and hosts of wild birds. A few have been heavily developed, and a few others are blighted by exclusive luxury resorts.

The islands from the Heron group south to Lady Elliot Island are true reef cays, 80 km or so from the mainland. The Keppel Islands, on the other hand, are the peaks of submerged mountains and lie only 10 km or so from the coast. Besides their superb beaches, several of them also have paths through the rainforests which cover their steep slopes.

The mainland at this point is another matter. There are beaches within reach of all the main towns along the Bruce Highway, but the towns themselves are of little tourist interest. Rockhampton is 'the beef capital of Australia', Mackay is `the sugar capital of Australia', and Bundaberg makes Australia's best-known dark rum. Yes, this is sugar cane and grazing country. The towns are also staging posts for the islands.

If you want to see some of the islands you should allow at least a week to cover this stretch.

Pacific

Ocean

Great Barrier Reef

BRAMPTON
ISLAND

Mackay

Bruce Highway

Yeppoon

KEPPEL ISLANDS

Rockhampton   Rosslyn Bay

TRYON ISLAND

NORTHWEST
ISLAND

WILSON ISLAND

HERON ISLAND

Gladstone   MASTHEAD
ISLANDS

Bruce Highway

LADY
MUSGRAVE
ISLAND

LADY ELLIOT
ISLAND

Bargara

Bundaberg

Hervey
Bay

TRANSPORT

Trains and regular buses connect
all the main towns along the Bruce
Highway. Local buses connect with
the coast, where you can catch the
ferries to the islands. It's also
possible to fly to several islands. A
car is an advantage for exploring
the mainland, but you can't take it
to the islands.

SIGHTS & PLACES OF INTEREST

BARGARA
See Bundaberg, below.

BRAMPTON ISLAND
See Australia Overall: 9, page 152 and Mackay, page 146.

BUNDABERG ⌖
320 km S of Rockhampton, 50 km E off Bruce Highway. Bundaberg is famous all over Australia for the 'polar' hangovers it produces. This is the home of 'Bundie', Australia's best-known dark rum (whose logo is a polar bear). Even those brave (or thick-skulled) souls who claim never to have had a hangover in their life will sing the praises of this place's product. (Yes, there's an unrepeatable song, which goes on for over 20 verses in the version I heard.)

Bundaberg is a centre of the sugar cane industry, and during the harvesting season (July to December) the cane fields are burned off, providing quite a sight. Sometimes, as you travel along the road, huge billowing clouds of smoke obscure the horizon. At night the fires can be spectacular, like the flames of some eerie inferno amidst the dark glowing clouds of smoke.

Bundaberg itself is a small town on the Burnett River, some dozen or so kilometres from the beaches. The closest recommended beach is at **Bargara**. Another popular beach is to the north at **Moore Park**. (Regular buses to both run from Barolin Street, near the Post Office.)

If you're in town between October and January, be sure to visit **Mon Repos** beach, 15 km east of town. In October loggerhead turtles come ashore to lay their eggs here. You'll need patience if you want to watch this: they sometimes only come ashore at the rate of one an hour – but it's an amazing sight. Once they're out of the water, it's all an enormous lumbering effort. (You'd probably lumber a bit too, if you were around 50 years old, lived in a heavy shell, had to dig a pit, lay a hundred or so eggs, and then make it back into the water before dawn.)

After two months in the sand the eggs hatch out. Then the fun really begins. December and January are the best times. Each night it's a mad scramble for the sea, as dozens of tiny hopalongs and tumblers run the gauntlet of the torches and photographers. But don't grouch: in the good old days it was far worse – they were eaten by rats (no need to worry about the rats nowadays: as we all know, rats of any kind – including the human variety – don't like being photographed going about their business). Even so, it's a tough life for a little loggerhead. They're not mature enough to start taking a lively interest in the activity which obsesses all human teenagers for almost 50 years, and their chances of surviving in the ocean this long are less than one in fifty.

There are a couple of sights worth visiting in Bundaberg itself. No trip would be complete without a tour of the **Rum Distillery**, which is on the eastern side of town at Whittered Street (four tours daily; A$3). Aficionados of this dark spirit will be pleased to hear the fumes from the vats are so strong that flash cameras are forbidden, in case they spark a fire. Deep inhalers emerge with a grin, which broadens even further at the sight of the free sample awaiting them at the end of the tour.

Bundaberg has little history, so in 1983 it decided to import some. The famous early aviator Bert Hinkler was born here at the end of the 19thC. In 1921 he flew from Sydney to Bundaberg, setting the world record for the longest continuous flight – 1,270 km. This was no mean feat, when you consider that Blériot had only just managed to cross the English Channel 12 years previously. But Bert Hinkler went on to even more spectacular things. In 1928 he became the first person to fly solo from Britain to Australia. Bert eventually died in Southampton, England, but in 1983 they transported his house back to Bundaberg. You can see it in Young Street, at the junction with Perry Road, across the river in the north of town. If you want to get an idea of Hinkler's achievement, go and look at the reconstruction of his plane, which is in the **Tourist Office** on Bourbong Street.

The coast east of Bundaberg is opposite the southern remnants of the Barrier Reef. From the local airport you can fly the 80 km or so out to two islands: Lady Elliot Island and Lady Musgrave Island (see pages 145 and 146). The latter can also be reached by boat from Port Bundaberg, on the coast north-east of Bundaberg.

Almost 30 km west of Bundaberg on the road to Gin Gin (on Bruce Highway), you can see the **Mystery Craters**. These are rather boring holes in the ground, which haven't been bored anywhere near deep enough to be of much interest to anyone but geologists. They were formed more than 20 million years ago, but were not considered sufficiently interesting until just over 20 years ago, when they were 'discovered' in the middle of a pineapple plantation. Even more boring are the implausible theories about how they were formed. (There's not room for mine here.)

GLADSTONE ⌭

On the coast 110 km E of Rockhampton, E off Bruce Highway. Gladstone is a thriving commercial port with a population of almost 25,000. The locals claim that Gladstone harbour handles more tonnage than the port of Sydney. Otherwise there's not much here, apart from 'the world's largest aluminium plant', which processes bauxite ore mined up in the Cape York Peninsula. It's also very hot, but don't let all this put you off. It is from Gladstone that you can take a boat out to some of the Capricorn Islands, which form the southern outcrop of the Barrier Reef. There are regular services to Wilson Island, the Masthead Islands and the Heron Island Marine Park, which lie 80 km or so offshore (see separate entries for details). For boat timetables, contact the local tourist office (56 Goondoon Street; tel. 079 72 4000).

If you find yourself stuck here with time on your hands, you can catch the local ferry to nearby **Quoin Island**, which has some rather ordinary beaches. Or if you're feeling energetic you can drive 10 km north-west of town to the foot of **Mount Larcom**, and then climb to the summit, which is more than 600 m high. There's a marked trail and there are superb views along the coast from the top.

HERON ISLAND ⌭

70 km E of Gladstone. Heron Island is just 1 km long, and can be reached by catamaran from Gladstone (*A$130 return*). It is famous for its birdlife, and is named after the white reef heron, which can be seen fishing in the reef pools at low tide. It's also a great place for turtles (green and loggerhead) which breed here during early summer. Their eggs hatch in February and March, when you can see the tiny newborn turtles making for the sea. In September you often see humpbacked whales swimming past on their migration route from the Antarctic.

There used to be superb diving on the reef, but this suffered when a new longer jetty was dredged. (Silt kills off coral.) Luckily this has not turned out to be a major disaster: the marine life – including octopus, moray eels, turtles and countless exotic tropical fish – remains as abundant as ever.

The famous (and famously expensive) **Heron Island Resort** occupies the north-east part of the island, which in the old days used to house a turtle canning factory. There's no camping here, and no day tripping. You pay the price – and it's all yours.

NB: At time of writing there's a ban on diving in much of the nearby Wistari Reefs Marine Park. If it's opened up again, be sure to visit: there is some fabulous diving here.

HERVEY BAY

See Australia Overall: 7, page 135.

KEPPEL ISLANDS ⌭ ✕

At the northern end of Keppel Bay, 10 km or so offshore from Rosslyn Bay. In all there are 18 islands in the group, some of which are national parks. By far the biggest and most popular is Great Keppel Island, and it is the only one where you'll find provisions. You can camp on some of the others, but you'll need a QNPWS (Queensland National Parks and Wildlife Service) permit (available from the ferry office in Rosslyn Bay).

Great Keppel Island covers 14 square km and has a dozen fine beaches, which occupy more than 20 km of the island's twisting coastline. Once upon a time a local bright spark who hoped to entice visitors here coined the slogan: 'Get wrecked on Keppel Island.' The idea quickly caught on – and plenty of people did just that. Fortunately, nowadays the island's popularity has spread well beyond those for whom enjoyment equals alcohol. Today if you want to get bombed here, it'll cost you a bomb: the beer isn't cheap any more. Even so, Great Keppel Island is one of

141

THE GREAT BARRIER REEF

There's nowhere in the world quite like the Great Barrier Reef. It originated more than 18 million years ago, though most of the present reef is a mere 2 million years old. More meaningful to non-geologists is the fact that the Great Barrier Reef is more than 2,200 km long – about the distance from London to Athens, or New York to Dallas. The reef starts at Lady Elliot Island in the south (off the coast at Bundaberg) and stretches far up beyond the northern tip of Australia to Papua New Guinea. At some points it's just a few reefs or cays poking up out of the sea, at others it's more than 70 km wide.

The entire reef was made by a tiny primitive polyp (of the *coelenterata* family), a relative of the sea anemone. These apparently insignificant creatures are responsible for the largest structure made by any living creature – which is also the largest living structure in the world. Yes, the Great Barrier Reef is alive and growing. The polyps, which are almost as primitive a life form as you can get outside a rugby scrum, form together in large interlocking colonies (on much the same principle as a scrum). Here, instead of heaving and grunting and punching one another, they excrete lime, and when they die their coagulated skeletons remain as brittle coral.

New polyps then take their place on top of the old skeletons, and over countless millennia this process gradually expands into the reef. The polyps which produce the coral require clear water and a temperate but salty sea. If the water temperature dips below 17°C the coral can't grow, which is why the reef doesn't extend south along the entire eastern coast of Australia. Sunlight is also necessary to the coral-making process, which is why no coral grows lower than 30 m or so below the surface.

The Great Barrier Reef runs along the edge of the Australian continental shelf, sometimes as far as 300 km offshore. The channel between the mainland shore and the reef is comparatively shallow in nautical terms, seldom more than 50 m. The coral foundations of the reef often rise sheer from this depth. But if coral can't grow any deeper than 30 m below the surface, how did this solid foundation of the reef come into being all those millions of years ago? As usual scientists have come up with all kinds of theories, but the fact is no one knows for certain. However, a marine biologist friend of mine thinks there can only be one plausible solution. The sea was shallower at the time when the corals first started to form the Great Barrier Reef, and as the sea level rose, so the corals gradually grew at the same rate. My suggestion that the sea bed may simply have sunk was dismissed out of hand, for baffling scientific reasons which remain beyond my comprehension.

The Great Barrier Reef consists of more than 400 different types of coral, which account for its huge variety of shapes and colours. Spectacular evidence that the reef itself is still alive and growing comes every year after the full moon in early summer. This is when the corals spawn, and their countless tiny eggs scatter through the sea like a suspended submarine blizzard amidst the clear blue water.

If the Great Barrier Reef were just coral, it would still be an aquatic wonderland (and for once this is no clichéd exaggeration). But what makes it even more spectacular is the presence of many thousands of different species of marine life, which have made the reef their home. It has been estimated that more than 10,000 different species inhabit the reef, including more than 2,000 varieties of fish, among them many exotic tropical species. There are dugongs (sea cows), migrating whales from the Antarctic, and of course sharks, which brings us to the dangers of the reef.

For years there used to be legends of unwary fishermen devoured by giant squid, enormous clams which swallowed people whole, octopuses capable of snatching sailors from the decks of ships, and packs of killer 'jaws' which swallowed entire shipwrecked crews turning the sea red. Imaginative depictions of these scenes adorned many a 19thC parlour wall. Yet curiously, all these exotic beasts suddenly vanished around the time when photography was invented.

• *Blue semicircle angel fish, a native of the reef.*

The fact is, there are dangerous species on the reef. But they're not monsters, and they're few and far between. Reef sharks don't eat people. The stingrays may look hideously menacing, but they're shy and tend to avoid divers (and you should avoid disturbing them: that evil-looking tail really can sting). However, if you swim in waters close to the shore you may encounter box jellyfish (sometimes known as sea wasps), which, during the summer, can be a menace on the tropical beaches, and if you're stung badly it can be lethal. Just make sure you ask a local if there are any before having a dip on a beach where no one else is swimming.

Your most likely mishaps are likely to be cuts and grazes suffered from brushing up against coral when you're diving. Grains of coral often remain in the wound, and can cause bad inflammations. Make sure your wound is properly cleaned as soon as you get back. Also, be sure to wear something on your feet. You may not notice a stonefish disguised as a rock, but you'll certainly notice its poisonous spines when you tread on one.

Other dangerous beasties – such as scorpionfish and cone shells – are fairly rare. If in doubt, just leave well alone. There's no need to touch anything: and snapping off bits of coral just means there's less of the reef for the next visitors. (Just think of the years it took to grow that exquisite little twig of coral you fancy as a souvenir. It won't look half so good out of the water, and it'll probably end up in the attic anyway.)

Opinions vary about the overall health of the reef. The experts tend to the opinion that most of it is in fine shape. But there's no avoiding the fact that parts of it are definitely in poor shape. This is largely due to human interference – clumsy anchors, pollution, emptying sewage, souvenir hunting etc. Fortunately for us, there's also an animal scapegoat: the dreaded crown of thorns starfish. Horror of horrors: these tend to appear in sudden swarms and actually devour the coral, although some scientists have suggested that they only swarm because of human-induced imbalances in the marine ecosystem. And apparently they only devour coral in the absence of their usual feeding sources (molluscs, and so on) – which is usually due to pollution.

Despite all this, the Great Barrier Reef remains one of the world's marine marvels. If you dive or snorkel here, it's guaranteed to be one of the highlights of your visit to Australia.

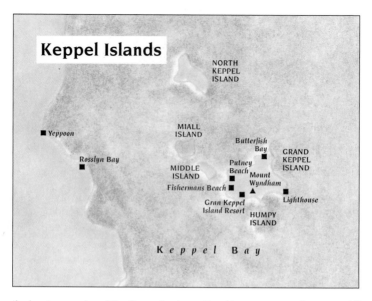

the least expensive of the Queensland offshore holiday spots, and remains one of the best.

At popular **Fisherman's Beach** you'll find all the usual water sports. But you don't have to walk far to find a comparatively deserted spot. There are a number of paths which spread out across the 6-km-long island. You can head for a distant beach (such as Butterfish Bay in the north), climb Mount Windham, or strike out for the lighthouse at Bald Rock Point (which involves a six-hour return walk). Those who haven't come all this way for a commando endurance course may prefer to take a cruise from Fisherman's Bay. At 10 am you can catch the three-hour round-the-island cruise and be back in time for lunch. There are also snorkelling cruises, sunset booze cruises, and so on.

The best snorkelling is half an hour's walk across the headland south of Fisherman's Beach at **Monkey Beach**, where you can also see a reminder of the island's sad (and largely forgotten) history. The shell mounds on this beach are the only remaining traces of the indigenous Aborigine tribe, shipped out as slaves to Fraser Island by early European arrivals.

At the eastern end of the island is the celebrated **Keppel Island Resort** which is owned by Qantas, and was recently refurbished for a mere A$14

million. Here you can easily run up a bill looking much the same as that presented by the builder.

Middle Island is the small island just west of Great Keppel, and is a national park. It has trees, a campsite and a nearby underwater observatory – complete with a genuine Taiwanese junk. Apparently the junk was confiscated for illegal fishing and then sunk to provide a shelter for the local tropical fish. I had no alternative but to believe this story, owing to the intimidating hugeness of the red-faced ranger who told it to me. You are free to doubt such local lore at your peril. The waters around the point are excellent (or notorious) for spotting sea snakes.

The 1-km-wide island just south of Great Keppel, **Humpy Island**, is named for its geographical characteristics. It also has a rather dismal windy campsite.

North Keppel is the second largest island of the group and lies 10 km or so north of Great Keppel. It has a pleasant campsite in the dunes on the northwest of the island by Considine Beach. There's some fine swimming at several beaches, and no real development. Alas, in some parts of the island, residents outnumber visitors by more than 100 to one, though why so many sandflies should have chosen to take up residence in this spot remains a mystery (even to my unimpeachable source).

THE CANE TOAD

Cane toads are such a part of Queensland's mythology that there's even a feature film starring them (intriguingly titled: *Cane Toads: an Unnatural History*). Yet oddly, these local favourites are not real Australians at all.

The cane toad was only brought to Queensland just over 50 years ago. It came from South America, where the Indians are said to have milked its glands to poison the tips of their arrows. The cane toad was imported by the sugar cane plantation owners. They hoped that this warty beast would put an end to the plague of greybeetles which was ruining their crops. But the cane toads didn't take to a diet of greybeetles. They were only interested in doing what any warty toad with a poisonous nature does when he goes on holiday to Queensland. The result was a huge population explosion of cane toads.

This obsessive behaviour has persisted over the decades. And nowadays you can see squashed cane toads on the roads all over Queensland. Indeed, they've begun to spread to neighbouring states where there's no sugar cane at all – and absolutely nothing else to do but breed.

One evening I became involved in a long and complicated discussion about cane toads at the Austral Hotel in Mackay. All were agreed that the cane toad isn't a true Australian. But some went even further, and claimed that it isn't even a toad.

If I can remember the argument correctly: the cane toad is not a true toad – or *bufo*, according to those who know. Someone pointed out – and this seemed to clinch a point which still eludes me – that *bufo* toads are indigenous all over the world, except in Australia (and Madagascar, according to one expert).

The most vociferous of the experts present insisted that the cane toad is really just a variegated toad, rather than a true toad. As far as I could gather, this has something to do with the cane toad's foot size, and its warts (which all agreed are poisonous, though on questioning it turned out that no one had personally verified this in any meaningful fashion).

However, this is not a problem over the entire island.

LADY ELLIOT ISLAND ⋈

80 km NE of Bundaberg. The Capricorn Group of coral reefs and cays form the southern end of the Great Barrier Reef. Lady Elliot Island is at their southernmost tip. The island itself is a small coral cay, less than half a square kilometre in size. The hellish history of Lady Elliot Island is now all forgiven in the interests of its present 'tourist paradise' image.

First the bad news (as history usually is). Through the centuries hundreds of ships have come to grief on the various ray- and shark-infested reefs around here. In an effort to thwart this lemming-like nautical tradition, a lighthouse was built on the island in 1866. But this solitary posting proved so grim that the lighthouse keepers kept committing suicide. Next, the place was discovered by phosphate miners, who did their levelling best to eliminate the island from the map – but were prevented just in time. Meanwhile wild goats had ravaged the last vestiges of local vegetation.

Then came tourism, and Lady Elliot Island was transformed into a natural paradise. All ecologically incorrect goats were banished. In the twinkling of an eye (behind a diving mask) the rays and sharks were transformed into wonders of the deep, turtles were no longer looked upon as mere ingredients for excellent soup, bathers took the place of shipwrecked sailors, and the shrieking scavengers of the sea found themselves transformed into fully-fledged members of a first-class bird sanctuary. What had once been a horror was now billed as a haven of delight, which it really is. Unlike many other similar spots, Lady Elliot Island has not been ruined by luxury. There's no TV, only one telephone, and a luggage limit of 10 kilos (22 lb). The accommodation at the **Lady Elliot Island Resort** is in cabins and permanent safari tents, and the only stand-up entertainers work behind the bar.

The only way to reach the island is by air from Bundaberg (*A$100 return*) or Brisbane. And that's it. The diving is superb, the white coral beach is a delight, and there's excellent wildlife (undersea, in the air, but no goats). Yet despite the lack of luxury, don't expect things to be cheap: nowadays everything is flown in, even the new lighthouse keepers.

LADY MUSGRAVE ISLAND

40 km NW of Lady Elliot Island. Lady Musgrave Island can be reached by a 2-hour catamaran trip from Port Bundaberg (*A$92 return*). This tiny uninhabited island is less than 0.5 km from one end to the other, and is surrounded by a coral reef and a lagoon. It's popular with passing yachts and campers. If you want to camp here, you'll need to get a permit. (Enquire at the ferry office tel. 071 52 9011 well in advance, as campers are limited to 50.) Also, be sure to bring everything you'll need with you (including water). There's no sanitation – only a pit.

As it's so small, the island can become crowded at Christmas and Easter – it has some of the best diving you'll find anywhere on the reef. Outside these peak times, it's just as you'd expect on a remote little dot far out in the Pacific Ocean.

MACKAY ⇔ ✕

330 km N of Rockhampton on Bruce Highway. Mackay is in the middle of a prosperous sugar-cane and mining region, and claims the title: 'Australia's sugar capital'. The sugar terminal at Mackay's port is the world's largest, and sugar has been grown here since the 1860s, when Mackay had the reputation for 'brute force, savage debauchery and disgusting language'. The regulars at the Austral Hotel on Victoria Street told me that sadly it has all changed now – the man who worked on the other side of the bar said he wasn't so sure.

Mackay has a population of around 60,000, many of whom are migrant labourers (including Sicilians and Maltese) who work the cane fields. Despite such a colourful mix, there's not much to do here. However, Mackay is the embarkation point for several islands, including **Brampton Island**, one of the jewels of the coast. This, and other nearby islands, are covered in Australia Overall: 9, page 150.

Apart from this, Mackay's main claim to fame is that the biggest cane toad ever was found here in 1888. On the scales it clocked up a phenomenal 1.8 kilos (for further details of the cane toad, see page 145).

It can get blisteringly hot in Mackay, and it's a long way to the beaches. If you desperately need to cool off you can always try the local swimming pool, which is on the corner of Victoria Street at Milton Street, just a short sweltering walk west of the town centre.

MASTHEAD ISLANDS

70 km E of Gladstone. The Masthead Islands are very small, very remote, and only accessible by charter boat from Gladstone. A restricted number of campers are permitted, who must bring all supplies with them (though it's possible to catch a few fish). A permit from QNPWS is essential. There is a resident population of shrieking terns and great diving off the reef. Strictly for dedicated Robinson Crusoes.

NORTHWEST ISLAND

70 km NE of Gladstone. This is the largest cay in the Capricorn Group, but is completely undeveloped. Campers are strictly limited in numbers, must have a permit from QNPWS, and must bring everything with them.

If you don't fancy camping, it's possible to get here for a day trip (*A$100, including snorkelling equipment*). Boats

• *Beach landing, Great Barrier Reef.*

depart from Rosslyn Bay (see page 148), which is on the coast 50 km north-east of Rockhampton. The island is renowned for its variety of birdlife, and its excellent diving.

ROCKHAMPTON 🚄 ✕
730 km S of Townsville on Bruce Highway.
Rockhampton is on the Tropic of Capricorn (the actual spot is marked by a spire beside the road, on the southern approach to town). This puts Rockhampton on a par with Rio de Janeiro. However, apart from this geographical coincidence there is little resemblance between the two. Rio's Copacabana Beach may be the beefcake capital of Brazil, but Rockhampton has no beach and is simply the 'beef capital of Australia'.

Rockhampton (known locally as 'Rockie') is one of the oldest towns in this part of Australia. Why? Curiously, the place was founded by accident. In 1858 there was a gold rush in this region of central Queensland, but it turned out to be a false alarm. As a result several hundred hard-bitten would-be millionaires found themselves stranded with their packs, shovels and prospecting sieves on the banks of the Fitzroy River. The place developed into a rough-and-ready encampment, which soon became a popular watering hole with stockmen from the surrounding cattle country.

Prosperity hit Rockhampton when they started mining copper at Mount

• *Playing bowls, Rockhampton.*

Morgan, just 40 km south of town. Evidence of this golden era can still be seen in the elegant 1890s sandstone houses along the riverfront.

Other sights include the two famous **bulls**, cast in bronze, which stand on the two main roads into town. The one to the north is a Brahman bull, the breed favoured by the stock-breeders to the north of town, and the one to the south is a Hereford, the breed favoured by the breeders to the south. They were erected by a colourful mayor called Rex Pilbeam, who evidently knew his local citizens better than they realized. Apart from the magnificently proportioned bronze bulls, he made sure that several extra pairs of bull's testicles were also cast. Inevitably one night some boisterous local lads emasculated one of Pilbeam's bulls, and blundered off laughing into the night brandishing their trophies. Next day the lads were astonished to see that a replacement pair had already been stuck back by their prescient mayor.

Rockhampton may be a fairly big town by Australian standards (population getting on for 60,000), but it's in the middle of nowhere. For hundreds of kilometres there's only remote grazing country, with nothing but the empty horizon bubbling in the heat haze.

There are just a couple of things worth seeing here. The **Dreamtime Cultural Centre** (*open daily 10 am to 5.30 pm, entry A$8*) is north of town. This is the heritage centre for the central Queensland Aborigines and Torres Strait Islanders. On show is a curious mix of legend and history. In fact, the two don't really mix at all in the Aborigine past. The history is largely a sad succession of oppression, tragic rebellion and cultural decline. But the legends are something else. Here you get a chance to try and comprehend the complexities and mysteries of Aborigine culture. It's well worth the effort. They are among the last people on earth who remain in touch with the distant origins from which we all spring.

Just over 20 km north of town on the Bruce Highway you come to a settlement called **The Caves**. Around here there are several fine complexes of caves which honeycomb the surrounding limestone (fossilized coral) hills. Most popular are **Olsen's Cave** and **Cammoo** (*both usually open 9 am to 4 pm; entry about A$8 for guided tour*). The caves have the usual astonishing stalactites, petrified rivers of stone, coloured lights and grim commentary. There are also colonies of rare carnivorous ghost bats, who, despite (or perhaps because of) their unobtrusive Draculean lives, are now an endangered species. Those who can't stand grimly humorous commentaries or batty jokes should press on for the **Fitzroy Caves**, which you're allowed to explore on your own. But be warned: these caves are unmarked, unlit and have numerous creepy inhabitants (including bats and spiders).

ROSSLYN BAY

7 km E of Yeppoon, which is 40 km N of Rockhampton. This is the spot where the ferries leave for the justly renowned Keppel Islands (see page 141), which are around 10 km offshore. There are also boats to Northwest Island, which is eight times that distance out on the reef (see page 146).

Behind the terminal the sea winds have sculpted the cliffs into hexagonal columns, which are almost as fascinating to look at as they are to read about. If you've got a long wait for a ferry, head west for the beaches.

TRYON ISLAND

80 km NE of Gladstone. The smallest and remotest of the visited islands in the Capricorn Group, Tryon Island is just 6 hectares, and limited to 30 campers – who are outnumbered 100 to one by the birds (mainly terns, shearwaters and noddies). No regular boats call here. The only access is by charter from Rosslyn Bay. A camping permit and absolute self-sufficiency in supplies and equipment are essential.

WILSON ISLAND

80 km NE of Gladstone. A tiny, isolated national park island, which has a fairly expensive resort and wonderful diving. The tourists here can be as exotic as the birdlife. Reached by catamaran from Gladstone. No day trips.

YEPPOON 🛏 ✕

On the coast 40 km north of Rockhampton. Since before the turn of the century, this is where the folks of Rockhampton have fled to get away from the heat. When the summer temperatures soar in 'Rockie' it's always a little cooler on the coast.

A few kilometres north is the **Capricorn International Resort**, one of the first Japanese developments in Queensland. When it was built several years ago this spot caused a racist furore (a bomb was even set off). Some of this was understandable. Many older generation war veterans had bitter memories of what the Japanese had done to them and their mates in the POW camps of the Burma Road and such like. The rest of the uproar was mainly provincial xenophobia of the ugliest sort, which has fortunately now simmered down.

Nowadays Yeppoon is a pleasant small resort, where Nippons (and even Poms) are quite acceptable. There are fine beaches in the bays for many kilometres to the east. On the eastern outskirts of town you come to **Cooee Bay**, the site of the famous 'Cooee!' competition, where competitors holler from Wreck Point – a taste of what life is like along here.

RECOMMENDED HOTELS

For island resorts see note in Recommended Hotels in Australia Overall: 9.

BUNDABERG
Grand Hotel, $; 89 *Bourbong Street; tel.* (071) 51 24 41; *cards none.*
Basic accommodation in the town centre, just across from the Post Office.

GLADSTONE
Country Plaza International, $$; 100 *Goondoon Street; tel.* (079) 72 1653; *all major cards.*
Not quite as plush as it sounds, but it's in the heart of town and has a pool.

HERON ISLAND
Heron Island Resort, $$$; *book through*: P&O *Resorts,* 160 *Sussex Street, Sydney; tel.* (02) 250 0700; *all major cards.*
Smart away-from-it-all resort, with a range of accommodation from the surprisingly simple to the simply surprising. Plenty to do in the daytime – and refreshingly little 'entertainment' at night. (Did you really come all this way just to listen to a stand-up comedian or watch a Superman video? No, you came to tell tall stories at the bar – and that you can do all night, in the company of the similarly inclined.)

KEPPEL ISLANDS
Great Keppel Island Resort, $$$; *Great Keppel Island; tel.* (079) 39 1744; *all major cards.*
Luxury resort accommodation. Try one of their Oceanview Villas for the view. At night everyone retires to the Shipwreck Bar.

If you fancy somewhere a little more appropriate to island living, try:

Wapparaburra, $-$$; *Putney Beach, Great Keppel Island; tel.* (079) 39 1907; *cards none.*
The campsite here has a number of cabins, and is exceptionally friendly.

LADY ELLIOT ISLAND
Lady Elliot Island Resort, $$-$$$; *book through*: Box 206, *Torquay, Queensland; tel.* (071) 51 6077; *all major cards.*

For once, an island resort that doesn't cost an arm and a leg, though it's far from cheap. Refreshingly basic accommodation away from the hurly-burly.

MACKAY
Pioneer Villa, $-$$; 30 *Nebo Road; tel.* (079) 51 1288; *cards none.*
Small, friendly motel on the Bruce Highway (which becomes Nebo Road here). The big bonus is that they have a pool.

ROCKHAMPTON
Albert Court, $$; *Albert Street; tel.* (079) 27 7433; *all major cards.*
Motel-style accommodation just east of the town centre, with a pool.

YEPPOON
Bayview Tower, $$; *Anzac Parade; tel.* (079) 39 4500; *cards none.*
A welcoming spot, right on the front at the end of main Normanby Street.

RECOMMENDED RESTAURANTS

KEPPEL ISLANDS
Reef Bar and Bistro, $-$$; *Putney Beach, Great Keppel Island; no booking; cards none.*
Lively popular eatery, just back from one of the main beaches.

MACKAY
Austral Hotel, $-$$; *Victoria Street at Peel Street; tel.* (079) 51 3288; *cards none.*
The restaurant here has good steaks, and afterwards you can retire to the bar for a discussion about cane toads (see page 145).

ROCKHAMPTON
Criterion Hotel, $-$$; *Quay Street; tel.* (079) 22 1225; *cards none.*
Just the place for a great steak in the beef capital of Australia. They also do first-rate seafood, and have a friendly bar.

YEPPOON
Strand Hotel, $; *Anzac Parade; no booking; cards none.*
The friendliest joint in town. Recommended for food, drinks, and weekend nightlife.

Between Mackay and Cairns
North to Cairns

750 km; map Nelles Australia, 1:400,000

Here is a journey into the far north of Queensland, where it can be stiflingly hot in summer – with tropical heat and tropical rain; the best time to come is winter. The main attractions of this stretch of coast are the islands and the Great Barrier Reef, both of which have superb diving. Many of the beaches along the coast are spectacularly beautiful: white sands, palm trees and blue, blue sea. But the swimming can be restricted when there are box jellyfish in the region, which is usually during the hot steamy summer (October to May).

Cairns is the main resort town with access to the northern part of the reef, which is closer to the shore up here. Its main competitor to the south is Townsville, which has its own popular island suburb: Magnetic Island. Further south, the Whitsunday Islands are justifiably amongst the most popular in Queensland. They offer both spectacular resorts and undeveloped, remote islands.

If you want to visit a few of the islands you should allow at least a week to cover this stretch.

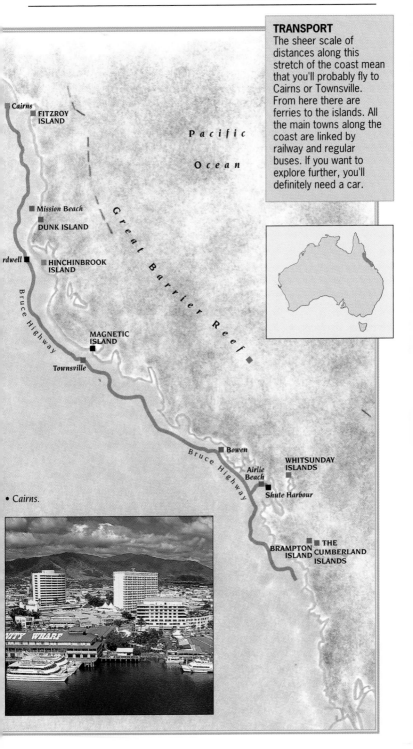

TRANSPORT
The sheer scale of distances along this stretch of the coast mean that you'll probably fly to Cairns or Townsville. From here there are ferries to the islands. All the main towns along the coast are linked by railway and regular buses. If you want to explore further, you'll definitely need a car.

Pacific

Ocean

■ *Cairns*
■ FITZROY
ISLAND

Great Barrier Reef

■ Mission Beach
■ DUNK ISLAND

rdwell ■
■ HINCHINBROOK
ISLAND

Bruce Highway

■ MAGNETIC
ISLAND

Townsville

Bruce Highway ■ Bowen

Airlie
Beach ■
■ WHITSUNDAY
ISLANDS

■ Shute Harbour

• *Cairns.*

BRAMPTON ■ ■ THE
ISLAND CUMBERLAND
ISLANDS

SIGHTS & PLACES OF INTEREST

AIRLIE BEACH ⌂

On the coast 300 km S of Townsville, E off Bruce Highway. A picturesque seaside spot, Airlie Beach has two beaches which are rather disappointing. Also, inshore swimming along this coast can be dangerous from October to April if there are box jellyfish around (be sure to ask before plunging in). But this is the place to stay if you're visiting the Whitsunday Islands (see page 159). The ferry terminal for the islands is at Shute Harbour, just 8 km east down the road.

In the season there are excursion trips to see the whales migrating along the coast from Antarctica (August to October). This is also an excellent spot for learning how to scuba dive, before setting off for the islands. Expect to pay around A$350 for a week-long course, which includes some reef-diving with a qualified instructor. At the end of the course you qualify for a certificate. Try Pro-Dive (tel. (079) 46 6508) on Shute Harbour Road (the main drag).

You may have difficulty finding the sort of accommodation you want during peak season, and also during the Whitsunday Fun Race, which is in September. But you can always call Mandy's Mine of Information (tel. (079) 46 6848), which is on the Airlie Esplanade, just by the junction with Shute Harbour Road.

Most of Airlie Beach's 1,500 or so permanent residents make their living out of the holiday business, and the place has a pleasantly laid-back Californian feel to it.

BOWEN

On the coast 205 km S of Townsville. This small town dates back to 1861, and is now a centre of the fruit and vegetable industry. There are some fine beaches in the bays north of town. Sadly, there are so many more exciting things to see elsewhere along this coast that there's no real reason to stop here.

BRAMPTON ISLAND

Off the coast 50 km NE of Mackay. Brampton is the main island in the Cumberland Group. These islands used to be mountain peaks in prehistoric times, and they have a steep wooded interior. The peak on Brampton rises to more than 200 m,

THE BLACKBIRDERS

Sugar cane has been grown in Queensland for more than 130 years. Harvesting the sugar plantations was backbreaking work, and the owners soon began to employ 'blackbirders' to recruit labour for them. These unscrupulous characters sailed for the Solomon Islands, where they simply rounded up the natives and brought them back to Queensland to work as virtual slaves.

Wages and working conditions on the Queensland cane plantations in the 1860s were pitiful. Slavery on the British West Indian sugar plantations had been abolished as early as 1805, and the continuing campaign of William Wilberforce ensured that slavery as such was outlawed throughout the British Empire in 1825. Yet more than half a century later something suspiciously resembling slavery was flourishing in remote Queensland. This practice was not eliminated until the 1880s, and then only because of widespread white unemployment and growing racism. Blackbirding was then outlawed, and the Solomon Islanders were simply despatched home. Over the following decades their place was taken by cheap immigrant labour from southern Europe, and today the towns in the Queensland sugar belt have long-established communities from such distant spots as Calabria and Sicily in Italy, and the Mediterranean island of Malta.

even though the area of island is just 5 sq km. Inland there are walks through the woods, where you can see a wide range of wildlife – from kangaroos to exotic butterflies. The shoreline has some superb sandy beaches with coral reefs – ideal for swimming and diving. The north-east part of the island is occupied by the Brampton Island Resort, a luxury Polynesian-style holiday centre.

At low tide you can walk across the sandbar to nearby Carlisle Island, whose peak rises to almost 400 m. The other islands in the Cumberland Group are unoccupied, and can only be reached by charter boat from Mackay.

CAIRNS ⇆ ✕

345 km N of Townsville. One hundred and twenty years ago there was nothing else to do here but fish for sea slugs. Now Cairns is a fast-booming resort with an international airport, and the main activity is fishing for tourists.

On my last visit here, an ingenious old hotel owner (who claimed that his ancestors had lived in Queensland since the old days) explained to me why tourists are definitely better for Cairns than sea slugs. "For a start they look nicer," he explained. "Or most of them do, at any rate. And even the worst ones have more taste. Also, you don't have to boil them – they do that for themselves..." At least Cairns hasn't yet become so completely commercialized that they have no time for pulling your leg. How much longer this will last is anybody's guess. The tourist boom didn't hit Cairns until comparatively late, at the end of the 1960s, but it's gone on ever since and shows no sign of abating – with a Hilton, Sheraton and Ramada Inn now all in place.

Cairns (or 'Cans' as the locals call it) is best visited between May and October. The rest of the year it's like a steam bath. The main attractions are the nearby reef, the tropical islands, the Cape York Peninsula and big game fishing. The latter came to worldwide notice when Lee Marvin visited several years back, and since then it has been attracting the modern Hemingway generation. The tuna, marlin and barracuda are as fine as you'll find anywhere.

This is a great place to learn how to dive. Five-day courses take you out to the reef, and at the end you get a cer-

tificate. The cost? Around A\$400 – except when there's a price war on, then you can sometimes pick up amazing bargains. Try Pro-Dive at Marlin Jetty (tel. (070) 31 5255) or Down Under Aquatics, who are at Shop 27, Shield Street (tel. (070 31 3318).

Surprisingly, you have to travel 10 km or so north to the resorts at Palm Cove and Yorkey's Knob for any decent beaches. For stunning snorkelling, you can always try a day trip to Fitzroy Island, 25 km down the coast, where you'll find coral reef just off the main beach. Green Island is the same distance north, but much smaller (only 600 m long). Both islands have woodlands, but they're also popular and can get crowded at high-season weekends. Inland, the terrain rises steeply to the Atherton Tableland, which is mostly above 900 m and refreshingly cooler than the coast. The main attraction here is the small mountain town of Kuranda, some 30 km north-west of Cairns. It can also be reached by a picturesque railway, which winds up through the rolling hills. Once upon a time Kuranda was a lovely spot – now it's a tourist Mecca, complete with market selling souvenirs (not even tacky enough to be interesting).

The rest of the highlands have some stunning scenery, with waterfalls, lakes, forests and even a volcanic crater. This was all untamed jungle until as recently as the gold rush of the 1870s.

CARDWELL

On the Bruce Highway, 200 km S of Cairns. The small coastal town where you catch the boat for Hinchinbrook Island (see page 154). There are also interesting cruises around the island. Cardwell has been here for more than 130 years, making it one of the oldest towns in Queensland. Nothing much has happened here during this period, a tradition which looks set to continue for quite some time.

South of town, the Bruce Highway has some spectacular views out towards Hinchinbrook Island.

DUNK ISLAND

5 km offshore, 20 km S of Mission Beach. Dunk Island is famous as the spot which featured in *The Confessions of a Beachcomber* by Edmund Banfield.

Just before the turn of the century, Banfield found he had a progressive nervous disease and was given only a few months to live. He chucked in his job as a journalist in Townsville and set off to live on Dunk Island. Before this, no European had ever lived on the island. Life in his tropical paradise so agreed with Banfield that he was to live out another 25 years, even finding the time and energy to write his book.

In many ways, the island is still recognizable as the island described by Banfield in the early years of the century. Though nowadays there is an expensive resort (Banfield turns in his grave nearby), and a campsite. But the beaches remain as superb as ever. There's also an exhilarating (but hard) 10-km walk up to the island's peak, through the rainforest, and back along the shore. As you pass by, the wildlife is polite enough to ignore your gaudy plumage and scarlet-hued features – which in no way come up to the standard of theirs.

South of Dunk Island are the tiny **Family Islands**. All but one of these remain completely undeveloped. The one called Bedarra has been turned into a resort for millionaire couples who can't afford their own island, and

• *Railway to Kuranda.*

• Townsville harbour.

have to make up for this social gaffe by paying A$1,200 a day to share one.

FITZROY ISLAND
See Cairns, page 153.

HINCHINBROOK ISLAND 🏝

Off the coast 110 km N of Townsville. This large island (nearly 650 square km) has great beaches and walks. The island scenery is spectacular, with a peak (Mount Bowen) rising to 1,142 m, rainforests along the western shore, miles of bays and sandy beaches along the eastern shore, and mangrove swamps. There's also a host of wildlife, including exotic butterflies. The only snag? Mozzies and sandflies – so be sure to bring plenty of strong insect repellent, especially if you are planning to set off for a few days on the 32-km East Coast Walk, staying at campsites along the way (camping permit and self-sufficiency are essential). Hardy and expert hikers might like to try climbing the peak,

where you can still see the remains of a US plane which crashed into the mountainside during the Second World War.

The best way to see the island is by boat. There are all kinds of trips available from simple day trips with snorkelling, to longer cruises around the coast. They all set out from Cardwell (see page 153).

At the northern tip of the island there's a luxury resort, where you can live in the trees along with fellow rare birds. Accommodation at ground level is also available at similar sky-high prices (see Recommended Hotels, page 161, for details).

The finest sight on the island is Zoe Bay, which also has an idyllic waterfall.

MACKAY
See Australia Overall: 8, page 146.

MAGNETIC ISLAND ✕

10 km N of Townsville, and 40 minutes by regular ferry. This is one of the most popular islands on the Queensland coast, mainly because it's so easy to get to. In fact, it's almost a suburb of Townsville. Despite its popularity, the island is large enough to absorb its many visitors, being more than 8 km long.

Magnetic Island was discovered by Captain Cook in 1770. He named it Magnetic Island because his compass started fluttering off true as he sailed along its coast. The central peak, Mount Cook, rises to 500 m and the island is criss-crossed by many fine walks through the national park and the woods (where there's even a koala park).

The ferries put in first at Picnic Bay, which has fabulous swimming (protected from box jellyfish). The south-eastern side of the island has three settlements overlooking the sea, with a shark aquarium, a reef (great for walking) and bike-hire facilities. There are more than 25 km of road on the island, and even a bus service from Picnic Bay up to Horseshoe Bay in the north.

At Arcadia, the settlement overlooking Geoffrey Bay, they hold cane toad races at 8pm on Wednesdays. The winner gets a kiss from its owner.

MISSION BEACH ⇔ ✕

140 km S of Cairns off Bruce Highway, on the coast. This hot little seaside 'nowheresville' has a permanent population of less than 1,000. And even they are strung out along the palm-lined coast, which boasts some stunning scenery.

Mission Beach is where you catch the boat for Dunk Island (see page 153), or you can go white-water rafting down the nearby Tully River. The small town of Tully, which is on the Bruce Highway some 20 km or so inland, is proud to proclaim itself, 'the wettest place in Australia'. Suggestions that this refers to anything other than the weather are made at your peril.

Unexpectedly, Mission Beach has something of a history. The original mission (to convert the local Aborigines) was set up here in 1914. It did so badly that it was destroyed four years later by an act of God (hurricane), and the Aborigines were left to live in pagan peace.

Further south along the coast at Tam O'Shanter Point, you can see a memorial to the 1848 expedition which started into the hinterland from here. The intention was to reach Cape York, the northernmost point in Australia, by an overland route. Of the unlucky 13 who set off into the shimmering heat haze, only three eventually staggered back hollow-eyed to tell the tale.

SHUTE HARBOUR

See Airlie Beach, page 152.

TOWNSVILLE ⇔ ✕

On the Queensland coast 1,370 km N of Brisbane. This is the second largest city in Queensland (after Brisbane), and has a population of well over 100,000. The original inhabitants were the crocodiles of Ross Creek. In 1864 they were joined by a Scot called John Melton Black, who arrived to found a settlement. This canny entrepreneur had managed to elicit the money for the settlement out of Robert Towns, a Sydney ship's captain with a penchant for financial speculation. The settlement itself was largely built by imported Chinese coolies, who were paid the sort of wages you'd expect for working an 80-hour week on a Scots-run project in the tropics in those days. Many of them suffered severe deprivation (and not just of a financial nature). But in the end the rudimentary settlement was completed, along with a distinctly inadequate harbour.

Although Townsville lacked a good harbour, it soon began attracting trade. The port at Bowen, further down the coast, was cut off by a series of floods, which meant that the stockmen of northern Queensland simply had no other way out. Despite itself, Townsville

> **....CID HARBOUR**
> The anchorage off the west coast of Whitsunday Island, protected by Cid Island, is known as Cid Harbour. This is where a large part of the US Fleet gathered in 1943, before sailing 1,000 km north for the Battle of the Coral Sea. This was the battle that saved Australia from a Japanese invasion, and turned the tide of the Pacific War in the Allies' favour.

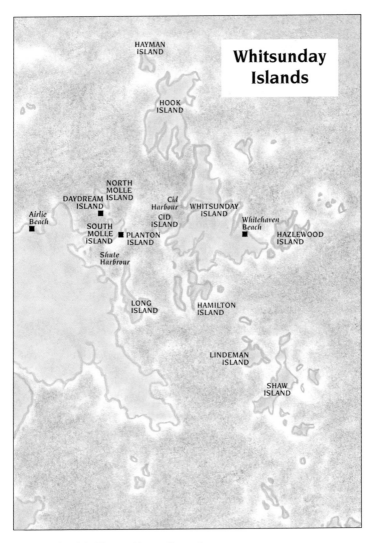

Whitsunday Islands

HAYMAN ISLAND

HOOK ISLAND

NORTH MOLLE ISLAND

DAYDREAM ISLAND

Cid Harbour

WHITSUNDAY ISLAND

CID ISLAND

Airlie Beach

Whitehaven Beach

SOUTH MOLLE ISLAND

PLANTON ISLAND

HAZLEWOOD ISLAND

Shute Harbour

LONG ISLAND

HAMILTON ISLAND

LINDEMAN ISLAND

SHAW ISLAND

began to flourish. Then gold was discovered in the hinterland at Ravenswood and Charters Towers. The inadequacies of Black's original harbour were now exposed to the full rigours of a gold rush. But there was just no other way to get to the goldfields. So Townsville boomed (as best it could).

It is on this foundation of financial acumen (being in the right place at the right time) that modern Townsville's fortunes are based. And it's still in the right place – especially when it comes to taking advantage of northern Queensland's tourist boom. The resort islands and the Great Barrier Reef are all just off-shore.

Alas, things aren't what they used to be. Today Townsville even has a good harbour. And, though most visitors now come in by way of the airport, this shows no signs of silting up.

Townsville has several sights. Undoubtedly the best is the **Great Barrier Reef Wonderland**, which is at the north-eastern end of main Flinders Street, by Ross Creek (*open daily* 9.30 *am to* 5 *pm; entry to all sections* A$18). The Wonderland has a number of different attractions. The most exciting is the world's largest coral-reef aquarium, which contains reconstructions of the

• *Sailing to Whitsunday Islands.*

Great Barrier Reef, complete with all kinds of tropical fish, turtles and rays. To make it even more real and create the right conditions, there's a wave simulator. You can also walk down a glass tunnel through the shark tank. Another tank gives you the opportunity to get a (painless) close-up view of the deadly box jellyfish.

The Omnimax theatre section of Wonderland gives you a 3-D wraparound sensation of all kinds of aquatic experience. Also, don't miss the museum, which has displays of fossils, (including the distinctly uncuddly furry pterodactyl), Aboriginal artefacts and much fascinating information about the life (and history) of northern Queensland. Star exhibit here is the water tank in which Mary Watson escaped from Lizard Island (for her full story see Local Explorations 10, page 237).

Anyone interested in shipwrecks should certainly visit the **Maritime Museum**, which is on the opposite bank of Ross Creek towards the northern end of Palmer Street, and has several exhibits from the famous *Yongala* wreck which went down in a hurricane in 1911, drowning more than 100 passengers.

The shopping centre of town is the Flinders Street Mall. Besides all the usual fun of the retail fair, there's also a lively craft market on Sundays.

For the best view of town, head out to **Castle Hill**, which is just 2.5 km east of the centre. The path to the top is off Stanley Street. The peak is 285 m high and gives you a great view out over the town and sea. On a clear day you can easily see Magnetic Island to the north (see page 155). This is the nearest holiday island, just 10 km from town.

Townsville is one of the best places in Australia to learn how to dive. The most able instructors are at Mike Ball Watersports (252 Walker Street), where they run a variety of courses for around A$400. These include trips out to the reef, and you end up with a certificate of competence (essential if you wish to hire diving equipment elsewhere).

WHITSUNDAY ISLANDS

Offshore from Airlie Beach. This group contains more than 70 islands, and includes many of the finest resorts on the Queensland coast. The islands were

• *Para gliding, Airlie beach.*

discovered on Whit Saturday 1770 by Captain Cook as he sailed up the coast on his great journey of exploration. (He called them the Whitsundays, because he hadn't realized that he had crossed what we now call the International Date Line, so he mistakenly thought it was Sunday.) The individual islands were named after various pals of his in the British admiralty.

Like the other inshore islands along the Queensland coast, these are the peaks of mountain ranges which became submerged in prehistoric times. The islands rise steeply from the sea, their slopes covered with verdant rainforest, and they have an abundance of wildlife.

The Whitsundays offer a bizarre contrast. Several of the islands have been colonized by developers. Parts are pure holidayland, complete with resorts, expensive restaurants and discos. Yet most of the islands remain undeveloped and without permanent inhabitants, and here you can experience some of the finest island scenery in the world.

The Whitsundays are justifiably a major tourist destination. Yet because they are scattered, the islands are capable of absorbing most of the yachts, cruisers, campers and tourist excesses – and still remain spectacular. If you only have time to visit one destination off the Queensland coast, this is probably the best place to come. There's excellent diving and swimming here. Unlike much of Australia's tropical coast, the Whitsundays don't usually attract box jellyfish. But what about that gruesome shark attack which attracted so much publicity in the early 1990s? The truth is, this was the first shark attack ever recorded in the entire history of the Whitsundays – and is said to have been caused by irresponsible divers pestering the shark concerned, until it was finally trapped and baited beyond endurance. So just be nice to any shark you meet, and you should be OK.

The islands are connected by ferries from Shute Harbour. There are also all kinds of other trips on offer – between and around the various islands. Some even last a few days, putting in at different islands for overnight camping. You can find details of these at Mandy's Mine of Information (see Airlie Beach, page 152) or at the various islands.

The largest of the islands is **Whitsunday Island**, which covers more than 100 square kilometres. It has no resort, and is in many ways the best of the entire group. Six-kilometre-long Whitehaven Beach at the south-eastern end is one of the finest you'll see anywhere in Australia (and that's saying something). The southern end of the beach, opposite Hazelwood Island, is superb for snorkelling. There's a campsite here, and at several other of the island beaches. There are also some pleasant walks through the tropical rainforest below the island peak, which rises to more than 400 m. There's no regular ferry service to the island, but most of the cruises put in here.

Hook Island is the second largest of the islands, with daily ferries from Shute Harbour. A number of excellent beaches, some with campsites. There's also a resort at the southern end. Nearby Tara Inlet cuts into the centre of the island like a fjord. On the roof of a cave above a tiny beach here, there are some interesting Aborigine drawings – several cruises put in at this spot.

Daydream Island has the closest resort to Shute Harbour, and is a favourite with honeymooners. The excellent swimming pool, together with those in and around it, are a daydream in themselves.

The northernmost of the islands, **Hayman Island** is the site of an exclusive A\$300 million luxury resort which made the headlines in 1995. It was here that the Aussie-born media supertycoon Rupert Murdoch entertained Tony Blair, the leader of the British Labour Party. This unlikely event signalled a switch in the policy of Murdoch's newspapers, which could well alter the balance of British politics for years to come. Day trippers have long been an extinct species on this island.

There are other attractive resorts on **Long Island** and **Hamilton Island** (which has its own airstrip and high-rise blocks). **Lindeman Island** has a Club Med.

For resort-free trips try North and **South Molle Islands**. Quietest of all is **Planton**, the little island just off South Molle. All of these islands have more or less hardy camping, but can also be visited on day trips.

RECOMMENDED HOTELS

Many of the islands mentioned above have more or less exclusive resorts. These are invariably in the $$$ bracket, but prices sometimes dip slightly out of season. These resorts are usually (if not invariably) booked on a package deal, which often includes everything except drinks. In many cases it also includes your trip from the mainland. Taking all this into account, a bill of A$100+ per person per day can be quite a reasonable deal. Some of the resorts are in the most spectacular and remote situations. But even the ones with comparatively Spartan facilities are never cheap. (Remember, everything has to be flown in to the more remote islands.)

On many islands there is no half-way between resorts and camping. It is advisable to book resort package deals before you set out to the region, at a travel agent in one of the big cities (such as Brisbane or Sydney).

AIRLIE BEACH (SHUTE HARBOUR)
Shute Harbour Motel, $$; *Shute Harbour Road, Shutehaven; tel. (077) 46 9131; all major cards.*

Pleasant motel, next to where the island ferries dock, with views out towards the Whitsunday Islands.

CAIRNS
Yongala Lodge, $$; 11 *Fryer Street; tel. (070) 72 4633; all major cards.*

Typical motel accommodation just west of the city centre, only 100 m from the seafront.

Dreamtime Travellers Rest, $; 4 *Terminus Street; tel. (070) 31 6753; cards none.*

Small guest house just south of the city centre, with a pool. Informal and friendly.

HINCHINBROOK ISLAND
The Hinchinbrook Island Resort, $$$; *Cape Richards; tel. (070) 66 8585; all major cards.*

Some of the accommodation here is in the trees, which are connected by walkways. An island resort which genuinely tries to use its situation, rather than exploit it. A dream, but expensive.

MISSION BEACH
Mission Beach Resort, $$; *Wongaling Beach Road; tel. (070) 68 8288; all major cards.*

In the rainforest, with every facility and several pools. Ideal for children.

TOWNSVILLE
The Summit, $$; 6 *Victoria Street; tel. (077) 21 2122; all major cards.*

On the way up Castle Hill, just 1 km west of the town centre.

RECOMMENDED RESTAURANTS

CAIRNS
The best restaurants in town are in the luxury hotels (Radisson Plaza, Hilton, and so on). For something less expensive, try:

Roma Roulette, $$; 48A *Aplin Street; tel. (070) 51 1076; cards AE, DC, V.*

A friendly spot serving excellent Italian cuisine, run by Antonio. BYO.

Barnacle Bill's, $$; 65 *The Esplanade; tel. (070) 51 2241; all major cards.*

Famous seafood restaurant on the seafront, with a friendly atmosphere.

MAGNETIC ISLAND
Arcadia Hotel Resort, *Arcadia*, **$$**; *cards none.*

A great place for a bite by the pool, on Geoffrey Bay.

MISSION BEACH
Mission Beach Hotel, $-$$; *Wongaling Beach; no booking; cards none.*

Get a first-class inexpensive meal at the bar, or if you prefer something a little more classy, try the bistro.

TOWNSVILLE
Luvit, $; 205 *Flinders Street East; tel. (077) 21 1366; all major cards.*

Excellent cheap pancakes here. Bring your own bottle.

If you fancy something more up-market, there's a wide range of restaurants nearby along Flinders Street East.

<u>Western Australia</u>

Between Perth and Kalgoorlie
The Goldfields

600km; Nelles Australia, 1:400,000

This section covers the long drive down the Great Eastern Highway to the goldfields. In the early 1890s these were the scene of the world's greatest gold rush since San Francisco's in 1849.

Gold was discovered at Coolgardie in 1892. Nowadays, this is almost a ghost town, but many of the old buildings are still standing. A little imagination, and you can still get a feel of what it was like when 15,000 rough and ready prospectors roistered and brawled their way through the bars.

A year later gold was accidentally discovered 40 km north-east at Kalgoorlie by three Irish prospectors. The 'luck of the Irish' rewarded this trio with a slice of the richest square mile in the world, which soon became known as the 'Golden Mile'. By the turn of the 19thC, Kalgoorlie had eight breweries and 93 pubs. Around this time the future US president Herbert Hoover arrived here as a young mining engineer. Staggered by the wild scenes he witnessed, he described the place as just 'three yards inside civilization'. This was indeed the Australian Wild West. Kalgoorlie, together with its twin town Boulder, is still a thriving mining centre retaining its hard-bitten outback traditions.

From Perth to Kalgoorlie it's about 600 km, and there's not much to see on the way. If you're planning to travel all the way east, you can combine this section with Local Explorations: 11. Another alternative is to drive down to Esperance on that same Local Exploration, and then head back west by way of Albany and Local Explorations: 12. Either way, you'll need at least a week for this one.

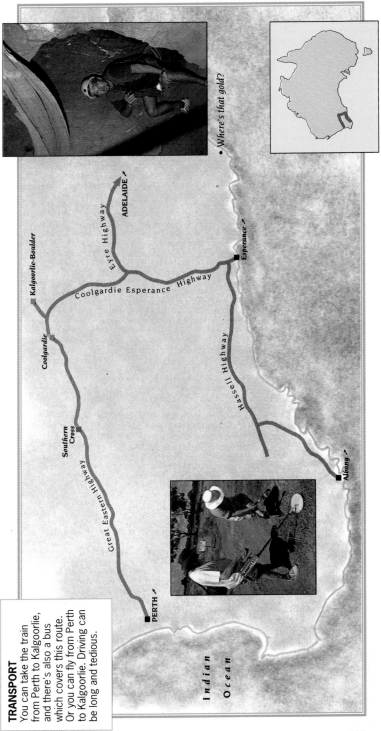

Where's that gold?

ADELAIDE

Eyre Highway

Kalgoorlie-Boulder

Coolgardie Esperance Highway

Esperance

Coolgardie

Hassell Highway

Southern Cross

Albany

Great Eastern Highway

PERTH

TRANSPORT

You can take the train from Perth to Kalgoorlie, and there's also a bus which covers this route. Or you can fly from Perth to Kalgoorlie. Driving can be long and tedious.

Indian Ocean

163

• Hannan's North Historical Mining Complex

their gold and quenching their thirst, the inhabitants also found time to invest their money on no less than two local stock exchanges and read seven daily newspapers. (Gold rushes, like the Wild West, always attracted large numbers of out-of-work hacks.) Five years later, the gold began to run out, and the hacks were forced to return to Grub Street, along with a large number of their readers.

Nowadays, just 1,500 people live here, and the place doesn't even have a bank. Though it does have several incongruously grand public buildings, left over from the great newspaper era. The Old Government Buildings now house the fabulous Goldfields Exhibition, which will provide you with enough fascinating lore and golden nuggets of information with which to bore all your friends back home. (Did you know that there is enough gold in the world's gold reserves to build two Taj Mahals?)

Also worth a visit is the moving local cemetery, which lies on the western outskirts. Coolgardie's main thoroughfare is now named Bayley Street, after the one man who had no need to return here.

ESPERANCE

See Local Explorations: 11, page 243.

KALGOORLIE-BOULDER 🛏 ✕

40 km NE of Coolgardie. These two old goldfield towns were amalgamated in 1989, though Kalgoorlie remains the evocative name and historic centre of attraction.

On 10th June 1893, Paddy Hannan and a couple of his Irish prospecting pals were heading east from Kalgoorlie after a luckless eight months in the goldfields. Their packhorse went lame, and they were forced to camp under a tree (which can still be seen at the top end of Egan Street). When they woke in the morning, Hannan saw that they were in the middle of an undiscovered goldfield. Yahoo.

Another gold rush was soon in full swing. Kalgoorlie boomed and prospectors from far and wide headed for the 'Golden Mile'. Within 15 years Kalgoorlie had a grandiose Town Hall on Hannan Street. Later, they even put up a statue to Hannan outside the Town Hall, and a copy of this still stands there. (The real one was so vandalized

SIGHTS & PLACES OF INTEREST

ADELAIDE

See Australia Overall: 5.

ALBANY

See Local Explorations: 12.

COOLGARDIE 🛏 ✕

560 km E of Perth on the Great Eastern Highway. Coolgardie is a ghost of its former self. In September 1892, the lone prospector Arthur Bayley returned from here bringing with him a bag of gold nuggets. This set off one of the greatest gold rushes the world has ever known. And with reason: Coolgardie turned out to be the richest goldfield in Australia. Within eight years, the population of Coolgardie had multiplied from one Arthur Bayley to 15,000 would-be Arthur Bayleys. The town needed no less than four banks and three entire breweries (not to mention the scores of bars). In between banking that they took it inside.) Hannan Street has several ornate balconied hotels and colonnaded government buildings from the old days, and, unlike Coolgardie, the place is still a thriving town with 25,000 inhabitants. But don't expect civilization – the place has a reputation for outback culture at its most cussed, and they believe in keeping it way. You won't find many poetry readings in the pubs. (However, if you're built like Mike Tyson and feel like giving it a try, the place to go is The Federal at the upper end of Hannan Street.)

The most interesting sight in town is the **Museum of the Goldfields** (*open 10 am to 4.30 pm daily, entry free*) which is at the top of Hannan Street. The British Arms, which stands just beside the museum, used to be famous as the narrowest pub in Australia.

Another must is **Hannan's North Historical Mining Complex** (*open 9.30 am to 4.30 pm daily, entry* A$4), which is north of town. This is an old gold mine which has been transformed into a slightly Disneyworld version of the real thing. But don't miss the underground tour, which is the real thing.

PERTH
See Australia Overall: 11.

SOUTHERN CROSS 🛏
370 km W of Perth. Useful mainly as a break on the long journey to Coolgardie. This was where the first gold was found in 1887, and you can see relics of these times in the **Yilgarn History Museum** on Antares Street (*open 9 am to 4 pm, Mon to Sat, entry* A$1; *closed lunchtime*).

RECOMMENDED HOTELS

COOLGARDIE
Coolgardie Motel, $$; *Bayley Street; tel.* (090) 26 6080; *all major cards.*

Motel accommodation in town centre with a pleasant open-air restaurant (**$$**; same tel.).

Denver City Hotel, $$; *Bayley Street; tel.* (090) 26 6031; *cards none.*

Historic hotel which looks from the outside much as it did in the old days. Inside, it's changed somewhat, and you're unlikely to discover a pouch of gold under your mattress as one guest did in the old days. (According to the yarn: he told his friend, who shot him.) Serves good inexpensive counter meals.

KALGOORLIE
Midas Motel, $$; *409 Hannan Street; tel.* (090) 21 3088; *most major cards.*

A touch of luxury in a tough town. Worth it after the long drive.

York Hotel, $$; *259 Hannan Street; tel.* (090) 21 2337; *all major cards.*

Historic hotel from the old days (it's certainly seen worse days). Authentic rooms now rendered fit for civilized occupancy; prospector-sized breakfasts.

SOUTHERN CROSS
Southern Cross Motel, $$; *Canopus Street; tel.* (090) 49 1144; *cards none.*

Standard motel, with a couple of pubs on nearby Antares Street.

RECOMMENDED RESTAURANTS

COOLGARDIE
See Recommended hotels, this page.

KALGOORLIE
For genuine goldfields fare you should really have a counter meal at one of the hotels. Try the Exchange at 135 Hannan Street, which has a friendly pub clientele ($). For something a little more stylish, try:

Basil's on Hannan, $-$$; *168 Hannan Street; tel.* (090) 21 7832; *cards* AE, MC, V.

Continental ambience with vaguely Italian menu. Bring your own bottle.

Amalfi Restaurant, $$; *409, Hannan Street; tel.* (090) 21 3088; *most major cards.*

Smart Italian, European and Australian food at the Midas Hotel, (see left).

Western Australia
Around Perth
Perth, Fremantle and Rottnest Island

50 km; map Nelles Australia, 1:400,000

Perth is the capital of Western Australia, the country's largest state, and contains more than three-quarters of its population. This is a lively new city, with an ambience and lifestyle much like Southern California. It is closer to Singapore than to Sydney, and this has made these particular Aussies even more self-reliant and individualistic than the rest.

Perth rode high on the boom of the 1980s, with the city centre sprouting smart new high-rise buildings. When the crash came in the early 1990s, it wasn't just the high-flyers who nosedived – plenty of small local investors lost their money too. But Western Australia has real wealth in the form of its huge mineral resources, and Perth soon began to recover.

Perth is within easy reach of the beaches along the Sunset Coast, which runs for 30 km north of the Swan River mouth. South of the river is the seaside town of Fremantle. From here you can catch the ferry to Rottnest Island, 19 km out in the Indian Ocean.

Inland, you can visit the wineries along the Swan Valley, or head up the Northern Highway to the Spanish colonial-style Benedictine monastery of New Norcia.

It's only 20 km from Perth to Fremantle, and you can easily take in the sights in and around the city in three or four days.

But having come this far, it's well worth spending some time getting to know the place and relaxing on the beach.

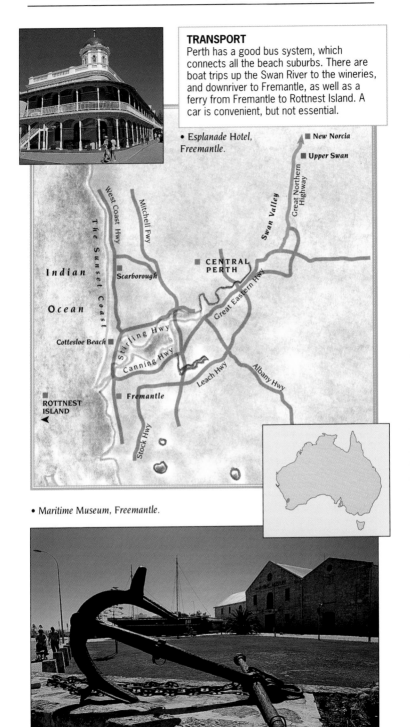

TRANSPORT
Perth has a good bus system, which connects all the beach suburbs. There are boat trips up the Swan River to the wineries, and downriver to Fremantle, as well as a ferry from Fremantle to Rottnest Island. A car is convenient, but not essential.

• *Esplanade Hotel, Freemantle.*

New Norcia

Upper Swan

West Coast Hwy

Mitchell Fwy

Swan Valley

Great Northern Highway

CENTRAL PERTH

Indian

Scarborough

Great Eastern Hwy

Ocean

Stirling Hwy

Cottesloe Beach

Canning Hwy

Leach Hwy

Albany Hwy

Fremantle

ROTTNEST ISLAND

Stock Hwy

The Sunset Coast

• *Maritime Museum, Freemantle.*

SIGHTS & PLACES OF INTEREST

COTTESLOE BEACH
See The Sunset Coast, page 172.

FREMANTLE ⊨ ✕
20 *km* SE *of Perth city centre.* This is where everyone goes to enjoy themselves. 'Freo', as the locals call it, has some fine beaches, plenty of pubs and sidewalk cafés, and all the fun of a seaside resort. The offshore waters were the site of the America's Cup defence in 1987.

Fremantle has always been a lively spot. Its rather grandiose **Town Hall** on High Street dates from 1887, when one of the local councillors was shot dead by a gatecrasher during the opening party. At the other end of the High Street you can see where this ungrateful guest ended up: the Round House. This strange 12-sided building was the city jail, and dates from 1831, which makes it the oldest building in Western Australia.

NEW NORCIA
130 *km* N *of Perth on the Great Northern Highway.* This monastic community was founded by Benedictine monks in 1846, as a mission to convert the local Aborigines. The mission is a rare Australian example of Spanish Colonial architecture. It is named after the birthplace of St Benedictine, the founder of European monasticism, who was born in Italy at the end of 5thC.

The community still flourishes, its monks living a simple life devoted to prayer and agricultural labour. A hundred years ago they planted an olive grove, which today produces some of the finest olive oil in Australia. The original orphanage has now developed into two Catholic Colleges with more than 200 pupils. For some reason, the residence of the boys' college, St Ildephonsus, has sprouted Moslem-style minarets.

Be sure to take the 2-km Heritage Trail, which leads you around the mission. Here you can see the flour mills, the Beehouse down by the river, a museum, a 150-year-old bakery (which makes excellent sourdough bread) and an art gallery (which contains examples of historic and contemporary religious paintings and artefacts, as well as some intriguing old manuscripts).

PERTH ⊨ ✕
T*he capital of Western Australia, situated in the* SW *corner of the state.* Perth used to be known as 'the loneliest city on earth', and with reason. Head west, and there's nothing but 9,000 km of Indian Ocean until you reach Cape Town. Head east, and it's 2,700 km of desert until you reach Adelaide. Around the same time, Perth also acquired a reputation as one of the dullest cities on earth. (A visiting Aussie writer remarked: 'On weekdays Perth strikes me as half-dead – and totally dead on Sunday.')

Nowadays, Perth doesn't feel either boring or lonely. When they defended the America's Cup, the attention of the entire world was focused on Perth – and the only thing that was dull were the heads on the morning after they lost.

Perth is the sunniest city in Australia, and has a pleasant Mediterranean-style climate. In winter it averages around 18°C. In summer it rises to around 29°C, usually kept from any excessive heat by the cooling sea breeze known as the Fremantle Doctor.

Perth accounts for more than three-quarters of the entire population of Western Australia (which covers a larger area than Britain and Germany together).Yet the city still only has just over a million inhabitants.

Nowadays it looks all very modern, with its gleaming concrete and glass high-rise blocks dominating the skyline above the blue waters of the Swan River. Many of these date from the boom era of the 1980s. In those days, some local entrepreneurs thought the sky was the limit. When the boom went bust, a number of these high-profile characters ended up bankrupt or behind bars. But Western Australia's real wealth had, and still has, a very firm foundation. The state has vast mineral resources, much of them yet to be tapped. Up in the remote middle and northern parts of the state, they're literally digging up the earth and shipping it off in hundred-thousand-ton loads to Japan and other industrial nations. If you've owned a Japanese car, you may not have realized that most of its metal probably came from beneath the earth in Western Australia.

Perth has a pleasant easygoing feel, but don't be deceived. Its inhabitants believe in working hard, and playing hard. And this is one of the best environments in the world to do it. Within

A SHORT HISTORY OF WESTERN AUSTRALIA

The Aborigines had been living in Western Australia for more than 40,000 years before it was sighted by the first Europeans, almost certainly Portuguese, some time during the late 16thC.

In a gesture of supreme hubris, the Dutch navigator Dirk Hartog landed on the coast in 1616 and claimed the whole place as Dutch, calling it New Holland. He even left behind a pewter plate nailed to a post recording this fact. This pewter plate duly remained in place on what is now called Dirk Hartog Island, one of the more remote stretches of the 5,000-km-long Western Australian coastline. For some reason, ensuing explorers seem to have missed this notice. Or perhaps they perversely ignored it.

Either way, no one was really interested in this barren lump of land stuck at the end of the Indian Ocean. The Dutch took to using it as a navigational aid. After rounding the Cape of Good Hope, they would make use of the prevailing Westerlies to cross the southern Indian Ocean. When they reached Western Australia, they would turn north along the coast for Batavia (Java). Despite Australia being the largest navigational aid in the world, 'navigators' were soon making a regular habit of sailing slap into it. As a result, most of the early European settlers of Western Australia looked like Robinson Crusoe. Unfortunately, their views on Australia have not come down to us, and can only be imagined.

By the 19thC, the British had begun importing more characters looking like Robinson Crusoe into colonies on the east coast of Australia. These were the first convicts. (And we don't have to imagine what they thought of Australia, because some of them went to immense trouble to record their views on this matter.) The British didn't mind filling up their empire with desperate convicts writing rude tracts about their new home; but when they heard the French wanted to get in, they decided this was going too far. Rumours spread that the French were planning to take over Western Australia, so the British established a colony at Albany in 1826. Three years later Lieutenant-Governor Stirling founded the Swan River Colony in the region of modern Perth. No French turned up, but neither did any further colonists. So the British began shipping in more Robinson Crusoes, in large numbers. But for these convicts, the colony would probably have died.

Then, in the 1890s, gold was discovered in the Western Australian hinterland, and more than 100,000 Robinson Crusoes from all over the world descended on Western Australia in one of the biggest gold rushes the world has ever seen. As a result of this increase in population, Western Australia graduated from a colony to an autonomous state.

Western Australia joined the Commonwealth of Australia in 1901, but this was not a universally popular move. In a referendum held in 1933, almost 70 per cent voted in favour of seceding from the federation. Such feelings were only mollified with the building of the Trans Australian Railway, which gave Western Australia its first tangible link with the rest of the country.

The next big increase in Western Australia's population came as a result of post-war immigration. A large number of these immigrants were Poms, but for the first time in the state's history its new wave of immigrants didn't look like Robinson Crusoe.

A LIGHT IN THE DARKNESS
Paris may be the City of Light, but in 1962 Perth became the 'City of Lights'. When US astronaut John Glenn first orbited the earth, he noticed a single bright light beaming up out of the total darkness of the Western Australian land mass. The citizens of Perth knew they inhabited the loneliest city on earth, and they reckoned that John Glenn might find himself even lonelier out there in orbit. So they decided to turn on every light in the city, just to keep him company. John Glenn was so touched that he christened Perth the 'City of Lights'.

• *Freemantle market.*

easy reach of Perth you'll find great beaches (ideal for both swimming and surfing), some superb vineyards and wineries, a number of small historic towns, as well as hills and forests that are great for walking.

The city itself is situated on the Swan River, at a point where it broadens out to resemble a lake. Much of the riverside is lined with parkland, and there are lakes where you can see black swans (which have been adopted as the symbol of Western Australia). Perth's city centre is around 20 km from where the Swan River enters the sea at Fremantle, which acts as Perth's beach suburb.

There's not much by way of outstanding tourist sights in Perth itself. If you have time on your hands, the best place to go is the **Perth Cultural Centre** on

• *Opposite: Perth, London Court.*

A PERTH CONCOCTION

In 1935, the celebrated Russian ballerina Anna Pavlova visited Perth. She stayed at the Esplanade Hotel (since demolished). For the dinner given after her performance, the hotel's chef, Bert Sachse, created a new dish in her honour. This was a dessert made from whipped egg white, cream, sugar and a variety of fresh fruit, and was named Pavlova in her honour. Pavlova is now served throughout the world wherever anyone has a sickly sweet tooth. Everyone knows who it's named after, but in a recent cookery book I read they claimed that it was invented in Perth, Scotland.

James Street (*open 9 am to 5 pm daily, entry free*). This has a museum with a fine Aborigine Gallery, which will help you understand the often complex and elusive nature of Aborigine culture; it contains some fine Aborigine artefacts. The Marine Gallery includes a superb 25-m skeleton of a blue whale. In other parts of the Centre you can see interesting meteorites, and plenty of fossils.

For those rare souls who are interested in money (rather than how to spend it) there's always the **Perth Mint** (*open Mon to Fri, 9 am to 4 pm, Sat am 10 to 1 pm, entry free*). Here they tell you everything about money except how to spend it. You can even watch the gold being poured, and see replica nuggets such as they found in the gold rush.

If you want to do some shopping, head for the mall complex in the city centre just south of the Railway Station. Running off Hay Street Mall is London Court, a lane of mock-Tudor boutiques.

If you feel the need for open space, try Kings Park, which runs along the shore of the Swan River and is renowned for its flowers in the spring.

If you've got a car, you could drive 5 km west of the city centre to the suburb of Dalkeith. This has the local millionaires' row, complete with glitzy mansions looking out over the Swan River and legal officials trying to deliver court orders.

ROTTNEST ISLAND ✕

19 km off the coast, reached by ferry from Barrack Street, Perth, and from Northport, North Fremantle, or from East Street Jetty, East Fremantle. 'Rotto' is just 10 km long and 5 km wide, and it is the home of the Quokka, a small breed of wallaby. When the Dutch first landed here in 1696, they mistook these beasts for large rats, and named it 'Rat's Nest' island.

In 1893, Rottnest Island gained an unsavoury reputation as a prison settlement for Aborigines. You can still see the old prison buildings, some of which have been turned into a hotel.

Nowadays, the island is best known for its clear swimming waters. Hire a bike and go looking for Quokkas, or go for a glass-bottomed boat trip to see the coral reefs and the wrecks. The Underwater Explorer leaves the jetty at Thomson Bay hourly.

The island pub, known locally as the Quokka Arms, used to be the Governor's residence.

SCARBOROUGH
See The Sunset Coast, below.

SUNSET COAST ⌇

This shoreline stretches 30 km north of the Swan River mouth, and has mile upon mile of sandy beaches. The nearest to Perth city centre is Cottesloe Beach, which can get fairly packed at weekends. The more northern beaches tend to be less crowded, and are popular with surfers. The best of these is Scarborough Beach, a surfers' Mecca.

SWAN VALLEY ✕

This runs north-east from Perth city centre. Take the road north from Guildford along the west bank of the river and follow the Swan Valley Drive up to Upper Swan. This takes you through wine country, where you can taste the local product at the wineries along the route. My favourite is Sandalford Wines, which is directly on West Swan Road – friendly wine and friendly staff.

There are also river tours to the wineries. For details of these (and other boat tours to Fremantle, Rottnest Island and the like) contact the Western Australia Tourist Centre, which is in Forrest Place on Wellington Street just opposite the Railway Station.

UPPER SWAN
See Swan Valley, above.

RECOMMENDED HOTELS

FREMANTLE
Old Bakery, $$; 9, *Little Howard Street; tel.* (09) 335 7531; *cards none.*

Bed-and-breakfast in part of a 19thC bakery.

Ocean View Lodge, $; 100 *Hampton Road; tel.* (09) 336 2962; *cards none.*

Budget accommodation with more than 200 rooms and a pool. Friendly young international crowd, great for meeting people at the barbecue.

PERTH
The New Esplanade, $$-$$$; 18, *The Esplanade; tel.* (09) 221 2190; *all major cards.*

In the centre of town, with superb views out over the Swan River.

Wentworth Plaza, $-$$; 300, *Murray Street; tel.* (09) 481 1000; *all major cards.*

Almost 100 rooms, at a wide variety of prices, right in the heart of town. Choice of restaurants and bars.

SCARBOROUGH BEACH
The beach is dominated by the famous **Observation City Resort Hotel ($$$**; tel. (09) 245 1000). This was built by high-flyer Alan Bond, the man who hit the heights when his boat won the America's Cup in 1983, and landed somewhere else when the banks started asking for their money back. Those who like to keep their feet on the ground will probably prefer:

All Seasons West Beach Lagoon Apartments, $$; 251 *West Coast Highway; tel.*(09) 341 6122; *all major cards.*

Pleasant two-bedroom self-catering apartments with ocean views. Across from the beach, also has pool and imaginative restaurant with a literary theme.

RECOMMENDED RESTAURANTS

FREMANTLE
Left Bank Bar and Café, $-$$; 15 *Riverside Drive; tel.* (09) 319 1315; *all major cards.*

A deservedly popular institution, housed in a century-old building with balcony and views over the river. Worldwide serendipity menu.

Sail and Anchor Pub Brewery, $; 64 *South Terrace; tel.* (09) 335 8433; *cards none.*

Historic (1854) bar with an upstairs brasserie. They have more than a dozen draught beers, some of which are brewed on the premises. A friendly, lively spot.

PERTH
Fraser's, $$, *Fraser Avenue, Kings Park; tel.* (09) 481 7100; *all major cards.*

Aussie and international cuisine, with great views of the Swan River. Outside dining, imaginative ever-changing menu.

Oriel, $-$$; 483 *Hay Street; tel.* (09) 382 1886; *cards* AE, MC, V.

Pleasant café atmosphere, with outside dining in season. Lively spot, with interesting European and local cuisine, and an excellent range of local wines.

ROTTNEST ISLAND
Rottnest Hotel (also known locally as the Quokka Arms), **$-$$**; *Thomson Bay; tel.*(09) 292 5011; *cards* AE, MC, V.

This used to be the governor's residence, now it has a restaurant, as well as a do-it-yourself barbecue area with a good salad bar. Friendly clientele.

SWAN VALLEY
Rose and Crown Hotel, $$; 105 *Swan Street, Guildford; tel.* (09) 279 8444; *all major cards.*

Traditional English inn atmosphere with a beefy British fixed-price menu.

Between Alice Springs and Darwin
Darwin and the Northern Territory Outback

1,500 km; map Nelles Australia 1:400,000

Darwin has some interesting sights, as indeed does Alice – but in between there's not much. And that means not much for a long, long time. The staging posts of the Stuart Highway, such as Tennant Creek and Katherine, are typical hard-bitten outposts of the outback. The characters in the bars are tough, and can be friendly – but don't expect many classical Greek scholars.

On the other hand, you'll find quite a few Greeks in Darwin, which has a rich mix of races and cultures. Darwin is the big city of the fabled Top End, the northern section of the Northern Territory. This is the land of Crocodile Dundee, and you'll soon discover that he was one of its more presentable characters. If you want to visit Crocodile Dundee's natural habitat (and his natural companions), head east from Darwin to the Kakadu National Park. This tropical wilderness has exceptional wildlife, and literally thousands of Aborigine rock-painting sites. Darwin is also an ideal starting point for a visit to the justly renowned Kimberley – see Local Explorations: 15.

It will take you two or three days at least to drive the highway, and you should allow at least four days for exploring once you reach the end.

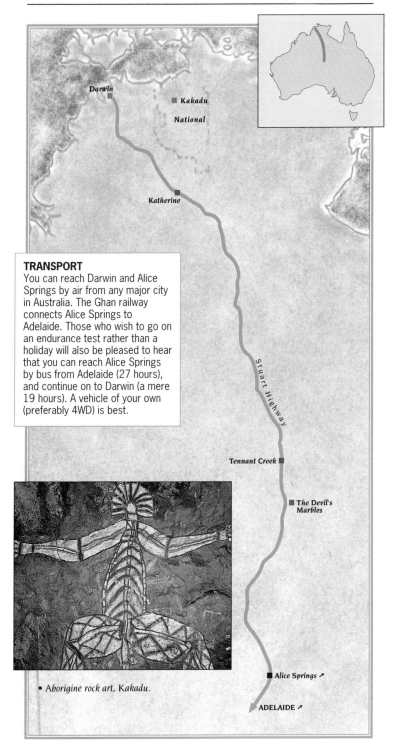

Darwin

Kakadu
National

Katherine

TRANSPORT
You can reach Darwin and Alice Springs by air from any major city in Australia. The Ghan railway connects Alice Springs to Adelaide. Those who wish to go on an endurance test rather than a holiday will also be pleased to hear that you can reach Alice Springs by bus from Adelaide (27 hours), and continue on to Darwin (a mere 19 hours). A vehicle of your own (preferably 4WD) is best.

Stuart Highway

Tennant Creek

The Devil's
Marbles

Alice Springs ↗

ADELAIDE ↗

• *Aborigine rock art, Kakadu.*

ALICE SPRINGS
See *Australia Overall: 13.*

DARWIN ⇌ ✕
On the N coast at the end of the trans-Australian Stuart Highway from Alice Springs. Many places claim to be unique, Darwin undeniably is. Here you're as close to Singapore as you are to Sydney – with desert for over 2,000 km in one direction, and shark-infested sea for almost as far in the other. The climate is impossible: in summer it's the monsoon season, in winter it's drought – with a steady average of 31°C regardless. And every 40 years or so, the place is wiped off the map by a cyclone (last one, 1974).

Yet 70,000 people choose to live here, and these include more races and ethnic groups than anywhere else of a similar size in the world: over 65 at the last count, including Chinese, Vietnamese, Greeks, Italians, Maltese, Lebanese – and when I last visited, at least one Greenlander. (Don't ask: he didn't know why, either.) Between them, this mixed bunch manage to consume more beer per hungover head than anywhere else on the planet. Even other Aussies gasp in admiration as the average Darwin resident downs his average 230 litres of beer a year. (And remember, a sizeable portion of the population are young children who don't drink any beer at all – thus placing an added responsibility on the older children who make up so much of the rest of the population.)

As you might expect, life is somewhat casual up here, with things moving at a relaxed pace and in large shorts.

• *Salt water crocodile — just smiling.*

As a result of the cyclones, Darwin is a predictably modern-looking seaside town. However, jellyfish, crocodiles and brain-frying heat mean that the beaches usually have that away-from-it-all feel.

There are several sights worth visiting. The **Museum of Arts and Sciences** has some superb Aborigine art. You can buy examples of this at the private galleries in town. Try the **Aboriginal Artists Gallery** at 153 Mitchell Street, but don't expect knockdown prices: this is the real thing.

Air buffs should visit the **Darwin Aviation Museum**, which is 8 km south of town on the main highway. Aviation has played a big part in Darwin's history, and here they have everything from a US B-52 bomber to a Japanese plane shot down over Darwin in the Second World War.

Also worth a visit are the reconstructed **Chinese Temple** on Bennett Street (which contains century-old statues from the cyclone-flattened original); and the grim **Fanny Bay Gaol Museum**, which is out on East Point Road. Here they also have relics of the 1972 cyclone, including a half-hour film showing boats that had leapfrogged buildings, lamp-posts flattened along the pavement and residents reduced to a similar state for once by the wind.

DEVIL'S MARBLES
See *Tennant Creek, page 177.*

KAKADU NATIONAL PARK
150 km E of Darwin. This 20,000-sq-km national park covers a huge region of

unspoiled semi-tropical wilderness, with a complete river system, falls, lakes, swamps as big as English counties, forests and mountains. Yes – this is where they filmed the outback scenes in *Crocodile Dundee*. You may not see Hogan, but you'll certainly encounter some even more rare and curious forms of wildlife including black walleroos, sea eagles, jabiru storks, red-eared bats and Whittaker's toads.

Even more exciting are the **Aborigine rock paintings.** No words can convey their sheer variety, wonder and beauty. And figures (for once not currency) can only hint at what you'll see. There are at least 4,000 sites, a few of which are more than 20,000 years old. Some of the wildlife depicted became extinct over 5,000 years ago, and it's known that the Aborigines have been practising this art here for 65,000 years.

KATHERINE

On the Stuart Highway 315 km SE of Darwin. The river here is the first permanent running water north of Alice. You'll find that your main attraction is probably the local public swimming pool, which is out beyond the bus station. The only other place of interest is the **Katherine Gorge**, which lies 15 km north-east of town. This is a spectacularly remote and beautiful series of linked gorges and rapids – good for walking, canoeing and swimming (but ask about the crocs first).

KIMBERLEYS

See Australia Overall: 15.

TENNANT CREEK ⊯ ✕

500 km N of Alice Springs on the Stuart Highway. According to local legend, Tennant Creek started life in 1932 when a lorry broke down at this unpromising spot on the highway. Its cargo was beer and construction materials, both of which were quickly put to use whilst the driver and his mate waited for help.

A year later, gold was discovered here – resulting in the last big Australian gold rush. The two most successful prospectors were a rough-and-ready pair who had only one eye (between them). To you, this may speak volumes for the state of the other gold rushers who made it here. But it's unwise to mention this in any of the 16 licensed premises which serve the 3,500 population. If you want to see how the gold was processed in the old days, visit the **Tennant Creek Battery** at Pecto Road, where they have guided tours of the old crushing plant, April to September only.

Some 90 km south of town, to the east of the highway, you can see the **Devil's Marbles** – hundreds of granite boulders, some huge, scattered over the wilderness. Aborigines identify them as eggs of the legendary Rainbow Serpent Wanambi. Geologists implausibly claim they're all that's left over from some Jurassic mountains.

RECOMMENDED HOTELS

DARWIN
Larrakeyah Lodge, $; *50 Mitchell Street; tel. (089) 81 7550; all major cards.*
Basic accommodation (and fridges) in the centre of town. With pool, but no private baths.

TENNANT CREEK
Pine Tree Motel, $$; *3 Third Street; tel. (089) 72 2533; all major cards.*
Pleasant motel in the centre of town, complete with pool and restaurant.

RECOMMENDED RESTAURANTS

DARWIN
Lindsay Street Cafe, $$; *2 Lindsay Street; tel. (089) 81 8631; cards* MC, V.
Genuinely imaginative cuisine, with Oriental, European and purely Darwinian flourishes. In an old-style Darwin residence.

TENNANT CREEK
For those with a genuine thirst, and the ability to look after its container:

Tennant Creek Hotel, *Paterson Street.*
Generally reckoned as the toughest bar on the highway, fitted out in a style to withstand the Charge of the Light Brigade.

Northern Territory
Between Alice Springs and Uluru
(Ayers Rock)
Alice Springs, Uluru and Region
460 km; map Nelles Australia 1:400,000

A lice Springs is the heart of Australia in more than the geographical sense. It lies right in the middle of the central Australian outback, and the outback plays a central role in the Australian identity: it is part of Australia's heritage, its history and its character. You'll find that Alice Springs, Uluru (Ayers Rock) and the MacDonnell Ranges fulfil all your expectations.

Alice Springs is a pleasant, surprisingly ordinary Australian town, stuck plumb in the middle of some of the most desolate terrain in the world. Beyond the city limits, the red wilderness of the outback begins at once – with a vengeance.

Take a day trip into the MacDonnell Ranges and you'll find remote gorges, waterholes and some astonishing mountain scenery. But the region's main attraction is, of course, Uluru, until 1900 known to everyone except the Aborigines as Ayers Rock. This was a sacred Aborigine site long before Ancient Egyptian civilization began. And its sheer presence, astonishing beauty, and the sense of ethereal wonder it often induces, make it undeniably one of the wonders of the world. For once, the reality far outshines the gloss of the travel posters.

It's possible to see the major sights in this region quite comfortably in four days. If you want to explore in greater depth, allow a week.

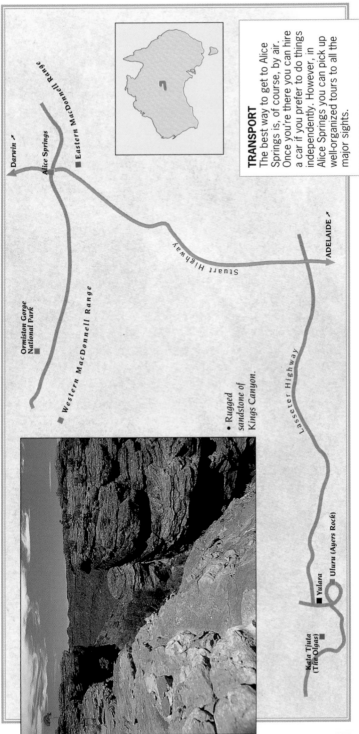

Darwin ↗

Alice Springs

■ Eastern MacDonnell Range

Eastern MacDonnell Range

■ Ormiston Gorge National Park

■ Western MacDonnell Range

Stuart Highway

ADELAIDE ↗

Lasseter Highway

• Rugged sandstone of Kings Canyon.

■ Yulara

■ Uluru (Ayers Rock)

■ Kata Tjuta (The Olgas)

TRANSPORT

The best way to get to Alice Springs is, of course, by air. Once you're there you can hire a car if you prefer to do things independently. However, in Alice Springs you can pick up well-organized tours to all the major sights.

• *The Olgas.*

SIGHTS & PLACES OF INTEREST

ALICE SPRINGS ⚓ ✕
1,500 *km* NW *of Adelaide on the Stuart Highway.* 'The Alice', as it's called, lies plumb in the middle of the Red Centre. In the 1870s, a staging post of the Overland Telegraph Line was established here. This was the brainchild of James Todd, after whom the local river was named. (The local spring was named after his wife Alice.) As a result of Todd's vision, the telegraph line from Adelaide eventually linked up with the submarine cable from Java to Darwin, and for the first time a direct link was established between Australia and Europe. From then on, Britain knew at once when Australian cricket and rugby teams were on their way; though they still haven't yet worked out how to deal with them.

Nowadays, 25,000 people live in Alice Springs, in a town which looks curiously like an ordinary Australian suburb. In summer temperatures can rise to 45°C and can produce an awesome thirst amongst the locals, who often take exemplary precautions long before it reaches this high. And in winter you have to drink to keep yourself warm, with temperatures plunging to 4°C as soon as the sun sets. You can't win.

There's not really much to see in Alice Springs, but there's always something going on. Fireworks, camel races, the Henley Regatta in the dried-out river, a beerfest in the local winery, Rodeo Week, the Verdi Club Beerfest, another beerfest and so forth. Contact the local **tourist office** on the corner of Gregory Terrace and Hartley Street for your gruelling fixture list.

Within easy reach of town there's a **siding** of old locomotives, a **camel farm**, a **winery**, the **old telegraph station** and the **original Alice Springs** where you can picnic under a gum tree. If you're interested in Aborigine art, head down to the **Todd Mall**, where you'll find several galleries. Most of the work on display is the work of local Anangu Aborigines. It's generally of the highest quality, and priced accordingly. My favourites are the dot paintings, which are a recently adapted permanent form of the sand paintings used at sacred ceremonies. In the best of these, you sense a significance which goes far deeper than their more decorative artistic qualities.

KATA TJUTA (THE OLGAS)
50 *km* W *of Uluru (Ayers Rock).* Curious dome-like rock features, whose highest peak, Mount Olga, rises almost to 550 m. Aptly called Kata Tjuta (many heads) by the Aborigines, these rocks were raised by the same geological process as Uluru, their foundations plunging

• *Opposite: Valley of the Winds*

thousands of metres into the earth. Kata Tjuta may well have been seven times their present size, before they were sandpapered by the wind to their present 36 domes.

Try the well-marked **Valley of the Winds walk**, which takes you 6 km through the rocks. Before you set out for Kata Tjuta, be sure to get a map at the nearest ranger station at Uluru – see separate entry.

MACDONNELL RANGES

These spectacular red mountains run in parallel ridge systems through the heart of Australia for several hundred kilometres. They cut from east to west past Alice Springs. Much of the scenery along the MacDonnell Ranges is spectacularly beautiful, with remote gorges, rock faces, spell-binding waterholes (where you can observe the wildlife), trails and wildlife parks.

The Western MacDonnells are the more extensive, and tend to have the more spectacular scenery. Amongst the many sights in the Mac-Donnells are **Standley Chasm**, a nar-

• Opposite:
Standley Chasm,
MacDonnell
Ranges.

• Left and below,
Uluru, (Ayers
Rock).

• Ormiston Gorge.

row gorge which runs between sheer 100-m cliffs; the **Emily & Jessie Gap Conservation Reserve**, which has fine waterholes and Aborigine rock paintings; **Ormiston Gorge** in the **Ormiston Gorge National Park** and **Lone Pine Lookout** with its breathtaking view of the gorge walls and pools.

Even if you have your own transport, the best way to gain a working knowledge of the MacDonnells is to take a tour. Try Cookies, who run full day trips to many of the best spots in the Western MacDonnells, and can be booked from your hotel on tel. (089) 53 4888.

ORMISTON GORGE NATIONAL PARK
See MacDonnell Ranges, page 181.

ULURU (AYERS ROCK) 🏨
460 km SW of Alice Springs. We've all seen the travel poster pictures, but the real thing is something else. At sunset (and to a certain extent at sunrise) the red rock takes on an almost hallucinatory quality as its colour becomes transformed in the frail light. It's easy to understand how the local Aborigines invested the rock, which they call Uluru, with a deep spiritual significance. For

more than 10,000 years (more than twice the age of the Pyramids) this has been a sacred spot. Previously known as Ayers Rock after its 19thC European discoverer, the preferred name is now its original Aborigine one, in line with the new awareness in Australia of Aborigine rights. Even geologically, Ayers Rock is out of the ordinary. The original rock layer was formed over 500 million years ago, when Australia was still part of Africa and India. Since then, movements in the earth's crust have tilted this slab of rock vertically. Ayers Rock rises to almost 350 m, yet it projects twice as deep below the surface, plunging far into the bowels of the earth.

Your point of arrival at Uluru is the **Visitor Centre and Ranger Station** on the road from Yulara, just a couple of kilometres before the rock itself. The **Muruku Art and Craft Centre** here is particularly good, and has a wide range of (largely relevant) Aborigine artefacts. It is probably the best place in the region for Aborigine art at a reasonable price. But you get what you pay for – and it's worth bearing in mind that the best Aborigine art doesn't (and shouldn't) come any cheaper than any other kind of respectable art. Prices for some of the craftwork are less convincing.

Entry to the **Uluru National Park** will set you back a further A$10; the park itself is *open from half an hour before sunrise to just after sunset.*

Those who don't fancy climbing can set off on one of several walks around the rock – details from the Ranger Station. Note: parts of the foot of the rock occupy Aborigine sacred sights and these cannot be visited – they are fenced off. The brochures available at the Ranger Station tell you about the mythological significance of the your particular walk. You can also see some cave paintings. Not surprisingly, many find themselves receptive to the sacred aura of the rock. The complete circuit is around 9 km.

The climb to the peak and back is just over 3 km, and you can usually complete it in less than two hours. The initial climb is by far the hardest, and you get a real sense of achievement when you reach the summit, 867 m above sea level. Here you get a windy wow of a view, and the opportunity to swap climbing stories with other mountaineers. Then it's downhill all the way.

It's no fun coming all this way without taking at least one of the many walks, but the major experience is undoubtedly the sight of the rock itself, especially as it glows and radiates in the sunset.

YULARA

20 km N of Uluru (Ayers Rock). Until the mid-1980s, visiting Uluru involved a certain amount of hardship. There was no accommodation at the site, and the nearest road house was 100 km away. That meant that relatively few people visited the rock (in the decade prior to the Second World War, for example, less than two dozen people climbed to the summit). Nowadays the rock is visited by more than a quarter of a million tourists each year, and some of them stay at the artificial settlement of Yulara. Unlike most such spots, this has retained certain architectural standards, though some of the first buildings, scheduled for demolition, unaccountably remain standing. Don't miss the **police station,** a source of curious pride to its inhabitants.

RECOMMENDED HOTELS

ALICE SPRINGS
Elkira Motel, $-$$; 65 *Bath Street; tel. (089) 52 1222; all major cards.*

A range of rooms, from standard motel up. Good pool and restaurants, children love it.

ULURU (AYERS ROCK)
All hotels and restaurants are confined to Yulara (this page), the tourist reservation 20 km down the road from the rock. At the height of the season this has a population of nearly 6,000, making it the third largest town in the Northern Territories. Here you're a captive audience, and prices at hotels and restaurants tend to be in the **$$-$$$** class. (But of course cheaper for campers and dormitories.) The most reasonable is:

Outback Pioneer Hotel, $$-$$$; *Yulara Drive; tel. (089) 59 2170; all major cards.*

Useful for families. Cabins and lodges (also dormitories, **$**). Pool. Be sure to book well ahead, if you're not coming with a tour.

RECOMMENDED RESTAURANTS

ALICE SPRINGS
The Overlander Steakhouse, $$$; 72 *Hartley Street; tel. (089) 52 2159; all major cards.*

The best restaurant in The Alice. Genuine atmosphere, and superb Northern Territories cuisine (yes, it does exist). This is your chance to try those famous witchetty grubs.

Tasmania
Around Hobart
Hobart and Launceston

200 km; map Nelles Australia, 1:400,000

Tasmania (or 'Tassie', as the locals call it) lies just over 200 km south of Victoria's coastline, across the often turbulent waters of the Bass Strait. It has a temperate climate – wetter and cooler than Australia's, which makes it greener and more picturesque. This also means that it's best to visit in the summer.

Tasmania was discovered by the Dutch explorer Abel Tasman as early as 1642, and was first settled by the British in 1803. Hobart is, in fact, the second oldest city in Australia (after Sydney). Unlike large stretches of Australia, the island still retains much of its past, with many historic buildings and a number of old convict settlements. There are also beaches and tracts of picturesque mountainous hinterland to explore. This is Australia's smallest state, and in many ways its most individual.

The island is around 300 km long and 300 km wide, with a population of 500,000. You can drive from the capital, Hobart, to Launceston in less than three hours, but if you want to see the main sights outside these two centres, and explore the island a little – see Local Explorations: 16 – it's worth allowing three to four days.

GETTING TO TASMANIA

You can fly to Hobart from all the state capitals of Australia, but the best place to fly from is Melbourne.

The ferry *Spirit of Tasmania* runs across the Bass Strait from Melbourne to Devonport, on the north coast. The ferry takes cars, and has all mod cons – including restaurant, cabins and swimming pool. The trip takes 14½ hours, leaving at 6 pm Mondays, Wednesdays and Fridays from Melbourne, and Sundays, Tuesdays and Thursdays from Devonport.

Between November and April there's also a daily SeaCat Service between Port Welshpool on the mainland and George Town, which takes four hours.

Expect to pay around A$450 for a return air flight, or A$250 for the return ferry trip. These prices drop considerably out of holiday season (which coincides with all school holidays).

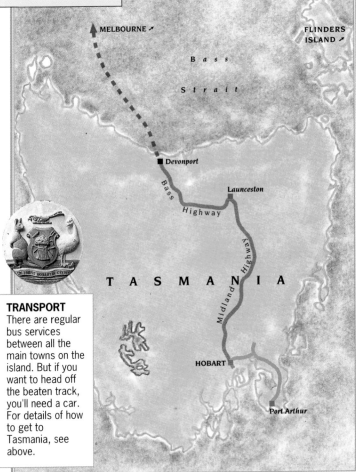

TRANSPORT

There are regular bus services between all the main towns on the island. But if you want to head off the beaten track, you'll need a car. For details of how to get to Tasmania, see above.

SIGHTS & PLACES OF INTEREST

DEVONPORT

58 km NW of Launceston on Rt 1. The uninspiring commercial port where the ferry from Melbourne puts in. You can see the only sight of interest from the deck of the ferry as you come in to land. This is the lighthouse high up on Mersey Bluff, which dominates the west of Devonport. The lighthouse was built in 1889, and its light is visible up to 30 km out to sea.

FLINDERS ISLAND

See Local Explorations: 16, page 276.

HOBART ⌑ ✕

The capital of Tasmania, on the SE coast of the island. Hobart is the second oldest city in Australia (after Sydney), and has a population of more than 200,000. It has a superb seafront setting, with bays, inlets and islands. In the background Mount Wellington rises to over 1,200 m, and its peak is often snow-capped above the wooded slopes.

Hobart began life in 1803 as a grim convict settlement. Many of the colonial buildings from this period still remain. Later, its deep-water harbour made it a base for the Antarctic and South Pacific whaling fleets. Hobart is justly renowned for its pleasant, laid-back atmosphere, but life hots up here in the first week of January during the Syd-

---

FAMOUS NAMES IN TASMANIA

The Norwegian explorer Roald Amundsen reached the South Pole in December 1911, but it wasn't until he reached Hobart that he was able to broadcast this news to the world.

The most famous man born in Tasmania was Erol Flynn, the swashbuckling Hollywood film star. A more recent famous resident was Peter Wright, who wrote *Spycatcher*, the book Maggie Thatcher tried to ban. It was at the Australian court proceedings over this book that Thatcher's envoy Armstrong made the celebrated admission that he had been 'economical with the truth'.

DETOUR – PORT ARTHUR

100 km SE of Hobart. Head east from Hobart across the Derwent River. At Sorrell head south down Arthur Highway to Port Arthur. In the 1830s this was established as the most notorious penal colony on Tasmania. It's on a peninsula which is exposed to the chilling Antarctic winds. This can only be reached by way of a narrow neck of land, which was guarded by chained dogs, and the sea all around was notorious for sharks. More than 12,000 convicts served time here, and most of them quickly decided against embarking on any do-it-yourself reduction in their sentences. The place has been restored to its former hideous glory. You can even see the lunatic asylum, and the Isle of the Dead where more than 1,700 of the inmates ended up. The ill-spelt gravestones here are particularly moving.

---

ney to Hobart yacht race. During this period thousands descend on the city from all over Australia, and some of them even manage to remain in a fit state to watch the finish.

There's plenty to see in and around Hobart. Try a stroll through **Battery Point**, down by the waterfront. Here the old sandstone houses, narrow twisting lanes and pubs still retain a village atmosphere. The main focus of attention round here is **Salamanca Place**, where a number of old warehouses have been transformed into pleasant cafés, boutiques and galleries. On Saturdays they have an open-air market, starting at around 8 am and finishing in the early afternoon. It's particularly interesting for local craftware, and some of the stalls sell imaginative snacks.

This district has a couple of museums – the **Van Diemen's Land Folk Museum** and the **Maritime Museum of Tasmania** – both of which have exhibits and relics from the good old days (which quickly become the bad old days, the more you get to know about them). At nearby **Constitution Dock** you can buy seafood from floating stalls and watch the boats in the harbour. From here you can pick up a number of harbour cruises, the best of which is aboard the *Lady Nelson*, a replica of Matthew Flinders' old sailing ship. It departs at 1 pm, Sat and Sun, from Elizabeth Street Wharf. Those with a sweet tooth should try the **Cadbury Cruise**, which leaves Brook Street pier at 10 *am* Mon *to* Thur for the chocolate factory, inland up the Derwent River.

Nearby is the **Tasmanian Museum and Art Gallery** on Argyle Street, *open daily 10 am to 5 pm, entry free.* This is housed in the city's oldest building, the Commissariat Store, which dates from 1808, and has some interesting historical exhibits from the old convict days. Of particular interest are the rare photos of the Tasmanian tiger, which many believe became extinct in the 1930s. (Recent mysterious sightings, and sav-aged animals, have led some to doubt this.) The art gallery has some fine paintings of the local Aborigines, painted around 150 years ago before they suffered a fate similar to the Tasmanian tiger's.

The city also has a pleasant **Botanical Gardens**, north of the city centre beyond the open space known as Queen's Domain. Here you can stroll in pleasant formal gardens and woodland at the foot of the hill by the Derwent River; *open 8 am to 5 pm, entry free.*

If you want a view, it's just a 20-km drive up to the top of Mount Wellington, from where you can see the entire city laid out below.

LAUNCESTON ⌨ ✕

200 km N of Hobart on the Midland Highway. Known affectionately as 'Lonny' by the locals, its full name is pronounced

---

RECOMMENDED HOTELS

HOBART
Hadley's Orient Hotel, $$; 34, Murray Street; tel. (002) 23 4355; most major cards.
Pleasant traditional hotel close to Franklin Square and the harbour.

Westside Hotel, $$; 156 Bathhurst Street; tel. (002) 34 7884; all major cards.
Smart hotel close to city centre, pleasant staff.

LAUNCESTON
Innkeepers Colonial Motor Inn, $$; 31 Elizabeth Street; tel. (003) 31 6588; all major cards.
Standard motel accommodation. Try nearby Rosie's Tavern for a great night out...

Prince Albert Inn, $$; William Street; tel. (003) 31 1931; most major cards.
Friendly spot whose individualistic decoration includes impressive stuffed beasts. Courteous service.

PORT ARTHUR
Port Arthur Motor Inn, $$; Port Arthur Historic Site; tel. (002) 50 2101; all major cards.
Motel with views of the penal colony. Friendly jailors and pleasant restaurant.

RECOMMENDED RESTAURANTS

HOBART
Aegean Restaurant, $$; 121 Collins Street, tel. (002) 31 1770; all major cards.
Bring your own bottle of wine for a lively Greek evening, complete with belly dancing and plate smashing.

Upper Deck, $$-$$$; Mures Fish Centre, Victoria Dock; tel. (002) 31 2121; most major cards.
The best in town, with a romantic view out over the front. Superb seafood and an excellent wine list.

LAUNCESTON
Fee & Mee, $$-$$$; 190 Charles Street; tel. (003) 31 3195; all major cards.
Award winning restaurant. Try their char-grilled quail.

Shrimps, $$; 72, George Street; tel. (003) 34 0584; most major cards.
Deservedly famous for its succulent fresh seafood, the best in town. Romantic ambience in the evenings.

PORT ARTHUR
See recommended hotels, left.

• Lady Stelfox, *Launceston.*

'Lon-seston'. Surrounded by hills, this is the garden city in the heart of Tasmania. It's a quiet and pleasant spot, with a number of historic houses amongst its many tree-lined parks.

The **Cateract Gorge and Cliff Grounds** is just ten minutes' walk from the centre of town. The dramatic scenery here was caused by a violent earthquake which took place more than 40 million years ago. The park has a

• *Penny Royal Windmill*

• *The Old Umbrella Shop, Launceston.*

hiking trail along the cliffs, as well as a chairlift which claims the longest span in the world (300 m).

Don't miss the **Penny Royal World**, near the river on Paterson Street. This has riverside parklands, historic buildings (including a gunpowder mill where they still fire a cannon), and a paddle steamer trip.

In the centre of town, on George Street, you can visit the Old Umbrella Shop, which dates from the 1860s. Here they have a display which shows how the locals kept themselves dry during the usual weather which has persisted during the last 100 years.

MELBOURNE
See Australia Overall: 3.

• *Opposite: Tasmans Arch.*

New South Wales

The Blue Mountains

800 km; map Nelles Australia, 1:400,000

This is an exploration of the area west from Sydney along the Great Western Highway. You soon begin to climb into the Blue Mountains, the barrier escarpment which encloses the coastal plain, cutting it off from the hinterland.

The Blue Mountains are deservedly popular for their spectacular scenery. This is crossed by some hair-raising bushwalks for men of iron, and also by some spectacular short walks for civilized human beings. There are also many sights – caves, gorges, waterfalls and so forth – which can be reached by road.

Beyond here you pass through Bathurst, the oldest inland settlement in Australia, which was established for convicts who had forfeited the right to enjoy the seaside. You now take the Mitchell Highway north to Dubbo, a pleasant spot with an exceptional zoo and a hearteningly gruesome old gaol for Aussie Wild West desperadoes.

From here the Mitchell Highway continues north-west to Bourke, on the Darling River. Beyond here it's 'Back o'Bourke' – the outback proper. (If you head north to Charleville, you can link up with Local Explorations: 7, which returns you to the coast.)

• Fog in the Blue Mountains

TRANSPORT
There are regular buses all the way along the highway between Sydney and Bourke. To explore the Blue Mountains you'll have to take a tour, if you don't have your own transport.

CHRISTMAS DINNER
In winter when it snows in the Blue Mountains, they have a Yule Festival. At this time, many of the local restaurants serve 'Christmas Dinner' in July.

• *Crimson rosella parrot, Blue Mountains.*

SIGHTS & PLACES OF INTEREST

BATHURST

200 km W of Sydney. The oldest inland settlement in Australia, dating from 1815. Has a number of Victorian buildings. Speed aces will want to try the Mount Panorama Motor Racing Circuit, where they hold the 'Bathurst 1000' each October.

BLUE MOUNTAINS ⊨ ✕

50 km W of Sydney. The Blue Mountains cut off Sydney and the coastal plain from the interior. The first convicts to arrive at Botany Bay, their geography not inspired by their journey halfway round the world, believed that on the other side of these mountains lay 'China and the Indies'. For nearly 20 years no one – escapee or explorer – managed to get beyond this strangely beautiful but impenetrable geographical feature.

The Blue Mountains are really just the beginning of the 1,000-m high inland plateau, which has been fissured with steep valleys and cliffs by aeons of erosion. They received their name from the characteristic blue haze which hangs above them – a poetic feature with a prosaic explanation (oil evaporating from the eucalyptus trees).

The **Blue Mountains National Park** is one of the best, and most popular, in the country. Yet even when the tourist towns here become a traffic nightmare at summer weekends, you're never far from scenery of spellbinding isolation.

Head west from Sydney on the Great West Highway. The Blue Mountains Information Centre is at Glenbrook, and

here you can pick up details of all the activities and sights in the park, as well as maps of the superb bushwalks. Further on, the town of **Springwood** is something of an artists' colony, with several interesting galleries.

If you plan to stay in the Blue Mountains, head on to **Katoomba**, which is the best base. The main sight here is the **Three Sisters**, stone tors which rise spectacularly above Jamison Valley. (These are said to be the daughters of an Aborigine chief, who turned them to stone to prevent their capture by a rival tribe.) Many worthwhile bushwalks – both long and short – start from Katoomba, and even some of the shortest have superb views.

Also worth seeing are the many gorges, some fine caves and also waterfalls.

If you don't fancy driving out here, you can pick up a day rail/bus tour at Sydney Central Station (A$4).

BOURKE ⊨

800 km NW of Sydney. At the end of a 200-km-long straight stretch of the Mitchell Highway, which tests the endurance of even the most saintly driver. Beyond here you're in 'Back o'Bourke' – the outback proper. (Yes, what you've seen on the way was just a foretaste.) After this there's no sealed road, and nothing (but nothing) for hundreds of kilometres in any direction.

Bourke has a population of just over 3,000 hard-bitten humans – who are outnumbered thousands to one by local sheep and cattle, and of course flies, who buzz and thrive in the 40°C plus summer heat.

Bourke itself is a pleasant small town on the Darling River, with the surrounding irrigated land supporting cotton and citrus crops. A hundred years ago, paddle steamers plied up the river to Bourke from the coast by Adelaide.

Frankly, the main attraction of Bourke is the fact that you've made it – and you're well rewarded by an unmistakable feeling of utter remoteness from civilization (which is unmistakably echoed by some of the characters in the local hotels).

If you want to head on north into the Back o'Bourke up the Mitchell Highway, it's just 450 km to Charleville, where you can link up with Local Explorations: 7.

DUBBO 🛏 ✗

400 km NW of Sydney. Australia's Nobel Prizewinning novelist Patrick White named one of his most memorable characters, the Aborigine artist in *Riders in the Chariot*, after this spot. And like the character, there's more to Dubbo than first meets the eye.

Dubbo is a thriving city of 35,000 in the heart of the wheat belt – though cattle and sheep-rearing are also big locally. The main sight in town is **Old Dubbo Gaol** on Macquarie Street, *open 9 am to 4.30 pm, entry A$5.* This was once the main jail for the Aussie Wild West – which was just as wild as its American counterpart, and threw up some sensationally grim characters. The jail itself is just as sensational and ghoulish as you could wish. Don't miss the gallows, along with the lovingly preserved tools of the hangman's trade. In the old cells they have animatronic robots of the former inmates, who at the push of a button recount the dastardly deeds which ensured them 'bed-and-breakfast in Her Majesty's hotel'.

Just down the street is the **Dubbo Museum**, *open 9 am to 5 pm, entry A$4*, which has a range of basically dull exhibits, seasoned with some genuinely thought-provoking items from the old days – primitive stringed instrument, dentist's pliers, and so on.

A couple of kilometres down the road south of town is the **Western Plains Zoo**, *open 9 am to 5 pm, entry A$13.* This claims to be the only free-range zoo in Australia. There's a wide range of the usual Aussie and international animal stars, and all that sometimes separates them from you is a ditch. The zoo has been exceptionally well landscaped with lakes and islands. All is in the best politically correct style – and indeed no animal would dream of eating you unless you're kosher. This really is an enjoyable spot, and there's even a cycling track around the 6-km circuit. Bikes are for hire at the main gate (A$7 for half a day: but forget it if you arrive after 10.30 in summer when it gets HOT.)

KATOOMBA

See Blue Mountains, opposite.

SYDNEY

See pages 42-57.

RECOMMENDED HOTELS

BLUE MOUNTAINS
Three Sisters Motel, $$; *Katoomba Street, Katoomba; tel. (047) 82 2911; most major cards.*

Standard motel accommodation, if you don't fancy any of the smaller bed-and-breakfast spots.

BOURKE
Bourke Riverside Motel, $$; *3 Mitchell Street; tel. (068) 72 2539; most major cards.*

Just the place to sleep off your hero's drink, after having made it to the moon.

DUBBO
Castlereagh Hotel, $-$$; *Brisbane Street; tel. (068) 82 4877; cards none.*

Best of the central hotels. Fairly standard accommodation and standard country breakfast (which will last you all day).

RECOMMENDED RESTAURANTS

BLUE MOUNTAINS
Café Bon Ton, $-$$; *The Mall, Leura; tel. (047) 82 4377; all major cards.*

Everything from cakes and coffee to full-blown Italian cuisine. Bring your own bottle. Leura is a couple of kilometres east of Katoomba.

DUBBO
If you haven't had one before, this is your chance to try a counter meal at a typical country hotel (ie pub). There's one on almost every corner. If you can't make up your mind, try the Civic Hotel on the corner of Trabalgar and Darling Streets (which also has $ accommodation, if you can't find anywhere else). Otherwise try:

Family Eating House, $-$$; *Macquarie Street; no booking; no cards.*

Help-yourself lunch, and standard Aussie fare in the evening.

The Coast between Sydney and Melbourne

900 km; map Nelles Australia, 1:400,000

The Princes Highway heads south-west out of Sydney, along the coast, soon reaching the industrial city of Wollongong. After this the coastal resorts become less crowded. Continuing south you get to Bateman's Bay, Narooma and nearby Central Tilba, then the old whaling port of Eden, where nearby Boydtown once tried to usurp Sydney as the colony's capital.

At Cape Howe you cross into Victoria, where the highway continues west. The south-eastern region of Victoria is known as Gippsland. East Gippsland contains the Wilderness Coast, which is renowned for its superb scenery. After this you reach the Gippsland Lakes, where there's fishing, swimming and wildlife. The big feature of South Gippsland is Wilsons Promontory, site of the most popular national park in the land and the southernmost tip of the Australian mainland.

From here the coast turns north-west towards Phillip Island and the Mornington Peninsula, two holiday regions popular with weekenders from Melbourne.

Just to drive this stretch of coast would take you a couple of days. Allow at least double this if you wish to sample some of the sights.

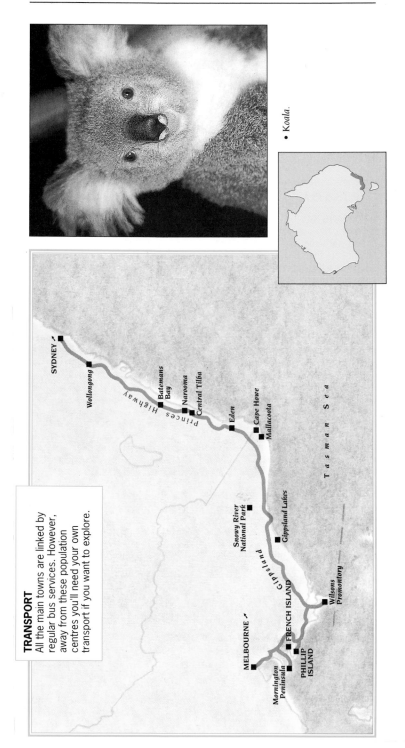

• *Koala.*

TRANSPORT

All the main towns are linked by regular bus services. However, away from these population centres you'll need your own transport if you want to explore.

SYDNEY

Wollongong

Batemans Bay

Narooma

Central Tilba

Princes Highway

Eden

Cape Howe

Mallacoota

Tasman Sea

Snowy River National Park

Gippsland Lakes

Gippsland

Wilsons Promontory

MELBOURNE

FRENCH ISLAND

Mornington Peninsula

PHILLIP ISLAND

- *Windsurfing on the open sea.*
- *Opposite: Ninety Mile Beach.*

SIGHTS & PLACES OF INTEREST

BATEMANS BAY

90 km N of Narooma. An enchanting little fishing settlement on an inlet at the mouth of the Clyde River which becomes a thriving resort in summer. They run river cruises, as well as a steam train to the **Birdland Sanctuary** (*open 9 am to 5 pm daily, entry A$7*), where you can see roos and roosters amongst the trees.

The beaches north of town are popular around sunset with skittish kangaroos, led on by the famous Krazy Kanga. (The locals insist that his legendary feats include a form of surfing, but I didn't stay around long enough either to witness this feat or to have my other leg pulled to kangaroo length.)

CENTRAL TILBA

16 km S of Narooma. Central Tilba and nearby Tilba Tilba are quaint little unspoiled mountain villages, renowned for their craftshops, cheese factories and wineries. They've been making cheese here for more than a hundred years. Visit the oldest cheesemakers, **ABC Cheese Factory** (*open 9 am to 5 pm*) and sample the product. At Tilba Valley Wines you can sample the other ingredient for your picnic.

DANDENONGS, THE

These low blue mountains rise to the east of Melbourne, and are classic day trip country. The mountain sides themselves are mainly wooded (it's the hazy mist that's blue), with walks in the forest, swimming and paddle boats at Emerald Lake, and plenty of tea houses and German-style restaurants en route. A big attraction is *Puffing Billy*, a miniature steam engine that runs from Belgrave to Emerald Lake. Rather more

interesting is the **William Ricketts Sanctuary** (*open 10 am to 4.30 pm, entry A$5*), which is just beyond Kalorama. Here the reclusive artist Ricketts carved sculptures into the rocks, inspired by his affinity with the Aborigines.

EDEN ✕

400 km S of Sydney. This small town began life as a whaling port early in the 19thC. But it nearly became something more. About 9 km south of town on Twofold Bay you can see the remains of one of Australia's great follies. In the 1840s an ambitious English speculator called Benjamin Boyd planned to establish a brand-new settlement here, called **Boydtown**. The aim was to set up a rival to Sydney, which would take over as capital of the colony. As is often the case with such entrepreneurs, a cash flow problem developed and Boyd did a bunk, last heard of somewhere in the South Seas. Boydtown, with its old Seahorse Inn, is still named after him – long after his creditors are dead and forgotten.

Because of its remotenes, Eden doesn't become so crowded as some of the seaside spots nearer to Sydney and Melbourne. Be sure not to miss the **Killer Whale Museum** (*open daily 11 am to 4 pm, entry A$3*). The whaling industry is known for its tall stories, and this museum is no disappointment. Read all about the sailor who in 1891 fell into a whale's mouth and was swallowed whole. He didn't manage to get out until 15 hours later, by which time his hair had turned as white as if he'd seen a ghost. Then there's the story about the killer whale called Old Tom... You can still see real whales making their way up the coast here from Antarctica each spring.

FRENCH ISLAND

See Phillip Island, page 200.

GIPPSLAND AND GIPPSLAND LAKES ⇔ ✕

150 km NE of Wilsons Promontory. This large system of inland waterways, lakes and lagoons is separated from the sea by the sand dunes of **Ninety Mile Beach**. The region is popular with surfers, fishermen and people who just like messing about in boats. Both Sale

and Lakes Entrance on the highway have useful information centres. **Raymond Island** is renowned for its koala bears, and **Rotamah Island** is particularly interesting for birdwatching.

MALLACOOTA ⇔

At SW tip of the Australian mainland. A popular holiday resort on the picturesque Mallacoota Inlet, which is a lake system at the extremity of the coast. The town has only 1,000 permanent inhabitants, and can be badly overrun at the height of the summer season. It stages a respectable **Arts Festival** at Easter, featuring music, drama and sand sculptures.

MELBOURNE

See Australia Overall: 3, page 92.

MORNINGTON PENINSULA ✕

50 km S of Melbourne. This 50-km-long peninsula forms the eastern flank of Port Phillip Bay, and the beach resorts and small fishing ports along its eastern coast are very popular with trippers from Adelaide. (At summer weekends this means real crowds.) By the time you reach **Dromana**, the little coloured beach huts lining the sea have become an almost unending string. Inland at Dromana there's a chairlift up to Arthur's Seat, which has spectacular views over the bay.

At the southern end of the peninsula, the south-facing beaches have good surf. **Sorrento**, at the south-western tip, was the site of the first unsuccessful convict settlement around 1803. At least a couple of the inmates here were later to become rich men and pillars of Melbourne society. Today's wealthy pillars of Melbourne society (not all of whom are unacquainted with convict life) now use Sorrento as their smart resort. From here you can take a ferry across the heads to Queenscliff and complete the circuit of Port Phillip Bay via Geelong (see Australia Overall: 4).

NAROOMA ⇔

380 km S of Sydney. Mention Narooma and oyster-lovers begin to drool. The oyster beds around here produce the supposedly aphrodisiac appetizer by the thousand. The town itself is a small fishing village with some pleasant nearby beaches; there is also canoeing on the Wagonga Inlet. They also run trips

out to the wildlife reserve of Montague Island, where you can dive with the seals and be ignored by fairy penguins.

PHILLIP ISLAND ⇔ ✕

130 km SE of Melbourne. This island is reached by way of a bridge from the mainland. It is popular with holidaymakers from Melbourne, and renowned for its wildlife. The big attraction here is the celebrated **Penguin Parade**. This is conducted with some dignity by dozens (sometimes hundreds) of fairy penguins every evening at Summerland Beach in the south-west of the island. The spectators, alas, are not always so dignified; and at weekends the crowds can be large, over-regimented and the whole thing becomes something of a farce. Try when it's quieter.

Fortunately, there are plenty of other things to see and do on the island. There's swimming and surfing on the southern beaches; Cape Woolamai, in the south-east, has a walking trail; and here you can also see colonies of mutton-birds. These birds migrate from across the Pacific (Japan, Alaska), but it's claimed that they always arrive here precisely on 24th September. Also near here you can see colonies of seals at the rocks off Point Grant.

The main island information office, where they have free maps, is near the ferry at Newhaven. The island's main town is **Cowes**, in the north. Here you can hire a bike at Thompson Avenue. (The only public transport is the tour bus to the Penguin Parade.) From Cowes you can take boat trips to French Island and the seal colonies; and there's also a ferry across to the Mornington Peninsula (see separate entry).

SNOWY RIVER NATIONAL PARK

300 km E of Melbourne. The remote national park here contains some of the finest unspoiled scenery in Victoria. There are a couple of large caves at Buchan, and north of there the road enters some superb wooded mountain wilderness. At McKillops Bridge you can swim in the river, and then take a rafting trip through the gorges, which have rushing water as well as quiet pools. Contact Snowy River Expeditions, tel. (051) 55 9353.

SYDNEY

See pages 42-57.

WILSONS PROMONTORY 🛏

200 km SE of Melbourne. Once upon a time, this promontory was joined to Tasmania, and provided the land bridge for the first Aborigines who inhabited that island. Nowadays, the promontory marks the southernmost point of the Australian mainland, and is renowned for its rocky coastline, fine beaches and miles of excellent walking trails. Inland, the mountains rise to over 750 m. It is impossible to exaggerate the beauty of some of the scenery and remote beaches here, and not for nothing is the national park which occupies this peninsula the most popular in Australia. Fortunately, it is large enough to absorb its many visitors without being seriously spoiled.

The main information centre is at Tidal River, halfway down the west coast. Many of the best walks (both long and short) start from here.

WOLLONGONG

80 km S of Sydney. Thriving industrial city with a population of almost a quarter of a million, and the added attraction of the New South Wales steel industry just down the road at Port Kembla. It ought to be ghastly – but being Australia, it isn't. There are surfing beaches nearby, and the inland hills (Illawarra State Recreation Area) have some fine views. Just a pity that it's all so close to Sydney.

RECOMMENDED HOTELS

GIPPSLAND LAKES
Riversleigh Country Hotel, $$-$$; 1 Nicholson Street, Bairnsdale; tel. (051) 52 6996; most major cards.

Period accommodation and an award-winning restaurant. Ideal base for exploring the lakes.

MALLACOOTA
Mareeba Lodge, $$; 59 Mirrabooka Road; tel. (051) 58 0378; cards none.

Welcoming guest house beyond the noisy centre of town.

NAROOMA
Tree Motel, $$; 13 Princes Highway; tel. (064) 76 2233; most major cards.

Pleasant accommodation on the main road; has a pool.

PHILLIP ISLAND
Rhylston Park Historic Homestead, $$; 190 Thompson Avenue, Cowes; tel. (059) 52 2730; most major cards.

Just south of town in a tastefully restored Victorian dwelling.

WILSONS PROMONTORY
Most of the accommodation on the promontory is limited to campsites. However there are a few flats and cabins available at **Tidal River ($-$$)**; contact the Information Centre, tel. (057) 80 8538. Booking is essential weeks ahead if you want to visit during the school holidays.

RECOMMENDED RESTAURANTS

EDEN
Sea Horse Inn, $-$$; 8 km S of Eden at Boydtown; tel. (064) 96 1361; all major cards.

Historic inn, overlooking the sea. Also has pleasant bed-and-breakfast accommodation ($$).

GIPPSLAND LAKES
At Lakes Entrance:

Sally's, $$; Esplanade; no booking; cards none.

Best food for miles around, especially the seafood; friendly service.

PHILLIP ISLAND
Isola Di Capri, $-$$; 2 Thompson Avenue, Cowes; tel. (059) 52 2435; cards none.

Cheap and cheerful Italian.

MORNINGTON PENINSULA
Delgany, $$$; Nepean Highway, Portsea (beyond Sorrento); tel. (059) 84 4000; all major cards.

Sophisticated dining in what some gourmets claim is Australia's top restaurant. The cuisine is French-based, with some exquisite seafood.

North-East New South Wales
Sydney to Brisbane, Inland

1,000 km; map Nelles Australia, 1:400,000

This route takes you along the New England Highway, which runs through the hinterland between Sydney and Brisbane.

North of Sydney you climb to the New England Plateau. Most of this is over 800 m above sea level, and the weather is cooler than along the coast. It's also much wetter. The main rainy season is during January, when the waterfalls are at their best. Each of the towns you pass through has something different – ranging from the almost English ambience at the university town of Armidale, to 'Australia's country music capital', Tamworth. Off the main highway there are several fine national parks.

However, the finest national parks in this section are on the Scenic Rim, which lies south of Brisbane along the mountains of the Queensland border. Here you'll find spectacular views, long trails through the rainforest, and all kinds of exotic wildlife.

This route is over 1,000 km long, and can be done in two to three days. Allow at least double this if you want to explore the national parks.

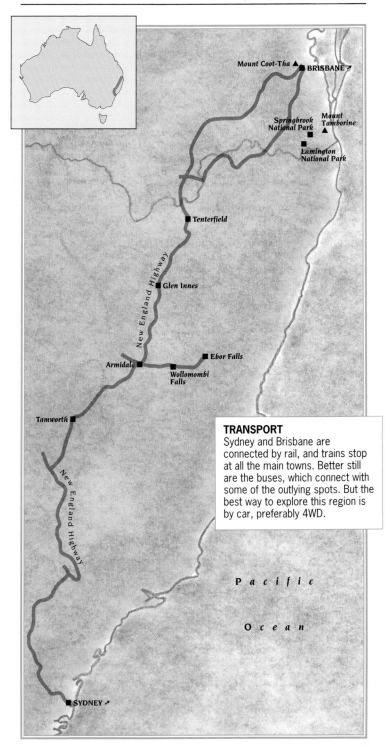

TRANSPORT
Sydney and Brisbane are connected by rail, and trains stop at all the main towns. Better still are the buses, which connect with some of the outlying spots. But the best way to explore this region is by car, preferably 4WD.

SIGHTS & PLACES OF INTEREST

ARMIDALE ⬦ ✕
450 km N of Sydney on the New England Highway. This is a university town, with a population of just over 20,000. It's relatively cool up here on the New England plateau. In the autumn, the leaves turn golden and russet (just like in the other New England) and in winter they even have frosts.

Armidale is the home of the University of New England, as well as several smart private schools, and parts of it have a definite academic feel. There are no less than two cathedrals, several church spires, a number of fine old houses, and the **New England Regional Art Museum**. The latter is a cut above most provincial Australian art museums, but you'd hardly expect it to inspire a brilliant college student to run away to Paris to become an artist. Which is apparently what it did, some years back. This caused a social scandal – the budding artist took the precaution of running off with a young heiress to support him. (Last heard of, they were said to be running a bar in Prague.)

There are several spectacular waterfalls in the region, where the rivers run off the eastern edge of the New England Plateau. The best used to be the

THUNDER EGGS
Known by the geologists as geodes, Thunder Eggs look much like ordinary spherical stones on the outside. When sliced in half they are seen to contain a cavity lined with crystals. Thunder eggs vary in size, but the largest you're likely to find are about the size of a tennis ball. They're formed when cavities in hardened volcanic lava become filled with crystal deposits. After they've been cut in half and the flat inside is polished, it forms a shiny surface with striated layers of coloured agate.

The best place to look for thunder eggs is at Thunderbird Park, near North Tamborine (see entry for Tamborine Mount, page 206). They make good souvenirs.

Wollomombi Falls, which are 45 km east of town in the Oxley Rivers Park. These drop almost 500 m, making them the highest in Australia – but unfortunately they have a tendency to dry up nowadays. A safer bet is the spectacular **Ebor Falls**, some 40 km further on (down the road to Dorrigo). And on the way you get the bonus of passing Point Lookout, with its breathtaking mountain views.

BRISBANE
See Australia Overall: 7.

EBOR FALLS
See Armidale, this page.

GLEN INNES
100 km N of Armidale on the New England Highway. Glen Innes was first settled by two hairy Scotsmen. This fact is commemorated in the local **Land of the Beardies Museum**, which is housed in the old town hospital. Here you can see exhibits and memorabilia from those whiskery times. (Open 10 am to 11 am, 2 pm to 5 pm, Mon to Fri, weekends afternoons only; entry A$4.)

In the late 19thC, Glen Innes became a favourite watering hole with the thirsty bushrangers who roamed these parts having escaped from the penal colonies of the coast. Nowadays, it's well known as a sapphire-mining centre. You can try your luck at hunting for these fabulous blue stones in the nearby Dunvegan Sapphire Reserve.

In October the **Australian Bush Music Festival** is held here – a riotous occasion featuring outback and Aboriginal music, as well as beard-growing competitions and much desperate slaking of thirst. For more information, tel. (065) 32 1359.

LAMINGTON NATIONAL PARK ⬦
90 km S of Brisbane. This national park 850 m up in the MacPherson Range covers over 200 sq km. It straddles the cross-over between two climatic zones, which means that part of it is sub-tropical and part temperate. This makes for a spectacular range of wildlife and vegetation, with many species and plants which were originally unique to the remoter pockets and isolated gorges where they were first discovered. Amongst these is the rare Albert's lyrebird, which is still found nowhere else.

More common (in the purely biological sense) are bush turkeys, bowerbirds, possums and sugar gliders. My favourites are the pademelons, a species of baby wallaby.

Expert botanists will doubtless note the presence of Antarctic Beech Trees, some more than 1,000 years old. This is the furthest north that these trees grow. Others will prefer the parrots, of which over a dozen species are native here.

This remote plateau region has a mysterious history. It's now known that the Aborigines lived here for longer than 6,000 years. However, some time before the Europeans arrived, they suddenly abandoned this entire forested territory. Various reasons have been put forward for the exodus – including mythological omens (such as comets), poisonous plants creeping into their diet, a resurgence of low-level volcanic activity, or the fact that they simply got fed up after a series of prolonged rainy seasons. But the enigma remains unsolved.

Lamington National Park has more

RECOMMENDED HOTELS

ARMIDALE
Cotswold Garden's Motor Inn, $$; 34 Marsh Street, Armidale; tel. (067) 72 8222; all major cards.
Pleasant motel-type accommodation in a building with 'English' gables. On the New England Highway.

Rose Villa Motel, $$; New England Highway; tel. (067) 72 3872; most major cards.
Standard motel accommodation on the main road, north of town.

LAMINGTON NATIONAL PARK
O'Reilly's Guest House, $$-$$$; Green Mountains, an hour's drive up the twisting mountain road from Canungra (Rt 13 – 4WD recommended); tel. (075) 44 0644; all major cards.
This legendary spot 900 m up in the national park is well worth going out of your way to find. It's been run by the O'Reillys for more than 70 years. Here you dine at family tables with fellow hikers and wildlife enthusiasts. The wildlife itself, in the form of wallabies, sometimes dines just outside the window. All beds have electric blankets, which are necessary during the night at this altitude.
The prices are more expensive than you might otherwise expect only because they include full board and a host of activities and trips.

TAMWORTH
Powerhouse Motor Inn, $$; New England Highway, Tamworth; tel. (067) 66 7000; all major cards.
Pleasant friendly motel with an excellent pool and a surprisingly wide range of amenities. Very good for children. If this is full, there are several other motels along the New England Highway nearby.

Central Hotel, $$; Brisbane Street; tel. (067) 66 2160; cards none.
Central location, fair value.

RECOMMENDED RESTAURANTS

ARMIDALE
Jean-Pierre's BYO Cafe, $-$$; East Mall, Armidale; cards none; no booking.
Here you can have a simple snack, or if you prefer something more adventurous, you can try some of Jean-Pierre's excellent French cuisine – and Bring Your Own bottle.

Beardy St Brasserie, $$; Beardy Street; no booking; cards none.
Pleasant spot with Australian and European dishes.

TAMWORTH
The Tamworth Hotel on Marius Street, tel. (067) 66 2923 has the best counter meals and a friendly bar – an ideal spot to start your trawl of the local pubs, which should certainly include the Good Companions on Brisbane Street (for country music memorabilia) and the nearby Imperial (for ready wit – which may be at your expense to begin with, but you're expected to give as good as you get).

than 500 waterfalls. Spread out over the plateau are tracts of open forest, as well as denser rainforest, and there are more than 150 km of well-signposted trails. The two most popular sections of the park are **Binna Burra**, which is renowned for its caves and pademelons, and the forests of the **Green Mountains** region, which has the best views in the entire Scenic Rim. Both of these are accessible by sealed roads from Canungra. Pick up a walking trail guide from a National Parks office.

MOUNT COOT-THA

Just W of Brisbane on Sir Samuel Griffith Drive. Brisbane has one botanic gardens in the centre of the city. This is the other one – and the better of the two. It has been laid out with great care on the lower slopes of Mount Coot-tha, which overlooks the western suburbs. The landscaped gardens take full advantage of the rising terrain, with pine woods on the highest slopes, falling to subtropical rainforest, complete with waterfalls. Below this there's an excellent Japanese Garden, an arid zone, and an atmospherically controlled tropical dome filled with tropical and equatorial plants. The gardens also contain the **Thomas Brisbane Planetarium**, which is the largest in Australia (*entry* A$7); and there's the **Summit Restaurant, $$**; *tel.* 07 3369 9922, which serves cream teas (and other food). The **gardens** themselves are *open 8 am to 5 pm daily, entry free; free guided tours.*

The easiest way to get to the park is by 37a bus, which leaves Anne Street at St George's Square.

SPRINGBROOK NATIONAL PARK

70 km S of Brisbane in the McPherson Range. The National Park is situated on a plateau 900 m up in the mountains, at the eastern end of the Scenic Rim. This area is volcanic, and filled with creeks, pools, waterfalls and caves amongst the rainforest. There are several trails through the extensive park, but you can reach some fine scenery by car – including **Best of All Lookout**, which has stunning views out over the mountains. The main ranger's office and information centre, tel. (075) 33 5147, is at Springbrook. There is another at Natural Bridge. Both have trail maps.

SYDNEY

See pages 42-57.

MOUNT TAMBORINE

40 km S of Brisbane near North Tamborine. This mountain has more than half a dozen parks, many of which have trails which are ideal for bushwalking. The rock formations are volcanic and much of the terrain is covered with rainforest. There are pools, waterfalls and fine views – but much of the walking is tough for the inexperienced. The Visitor Centre is at Doughty Park, North Tamborine, tel. (075) 45 1171.

Of more interest is **Thunderbird Park**, which is 4 km from North Tamborine. Here you can dig for Thunder Eggs (see box, page 204). Mining permits can be obtained on the spot for A$10, and they also hire out buckets and digging equipment. After all this effort you can relax by the waters of nearby Cedar Falls.

TAMWORTH 🚤 ✕

350 km N of Sydney on the New England Highway. Tamworth is the country music capital of Australia, and looks upon itself as the continent's answer to Nashville, Tennessee. It is, of course, nothing of the sort. For a start, it's a much pleasanter place than Nashville. And, needless to say, the music isn't quite in the same class. But this is where you can hear genuine Aussie folk music – whose heroes tend to be much more real than many of their American counterparts. Having now offended all country music fans, no matter where they come from, perhaps I'd better just shut up and tell you that the **Tamworth Country Music Festival** takes place over the Australia Day weekend – at the end of January. During this period, anyone with a Pom accent voicing opinions such as those above could well be placing himself in mortal danger. Just down yer beer and listen.

The Tamworth Country Centre is just south of town (you can't miss it – there's a huge gold guitar in front). Inside the centre there are waxwork effigies of the Oz country greats. There's also a 'Hands of Fame' on the corner of Brisbane Street and Kable Avenue, and a 'Noses of Fame' at Tattersall's Hotel in Peel Street. The best place for country memorabilia is the Good Companions Hotel on Brisbane Street.

• *Spectacular waterfalls can be found in the area south of Brisbane.*

Prior to its country music fame, Tamworth used to be known as the 'City of Lights' – because it was the first city in Australia to install public street lighting – in 1888. The Information Centre, tel. (067) 68 4462, is at CWA Parkby Kable Avenue. Here they have details of the local Heritage Walk.

TENTERFIELD

200 km N of Armidale on the New England Highway. Tenterfield has a population of just 3,000 and may look insignificant, but history was made here. In 1889 Sir Henry Parkes, then prime minister of New South Wales, made his famous Federation speech in Tenterfield. This proposed the union of the Australian colonies, which duly took place 12 years later. Memorabilia commemorating this event can be seen in the little **Museum** at Centenary Cottage (*open 3 to 5 pm, Saturday and Sunday*).

Other nearby attractions include the 200-m **Bald Rock**, which resembles Ayer's Rock and can be climbed; also the 200-m **Boonoo Boonoo Falls**, 30 km north of town.

WOLLOMOMBI FALLS

See Armidale, page 204.

The Grampians - Inland between Melbourne and Adelaide

700 km; map Nelles Australia 1:400,000

North-west of Melbourne you enter what used to be the Central Australian goldfields. In the 1850s, the discovery of gold here sparked one of the biggest gold rushes in history. Ballarat, on the Western Highway, was the site of the famous Eureka Revolt, and it now has a reconstructed old gold town at Sovereign Hill. North of here, on the Calder Highway, is Bendigo, the other great gold-mining centre in the region. Stories of the so-called 'mountain of gold' here spread through the world.

Continue along the Western Highway from Ballarat in the direction of Adelaide and on your right you come to The Grampians (Gariwerd), a mountain region of exceptional natural beauty with plenty of excellent walking.

From here to Adelaide the route is of no great interest and it makes sense to drop down to the coast road. This enables you to take in The Coorong, the picturesque Fleurieu Peninsula and the more remote splendours of Kangaroo Island, all covered in Australia Overall: 4.

You should allow at least three or four days if you want to do justice to it all.

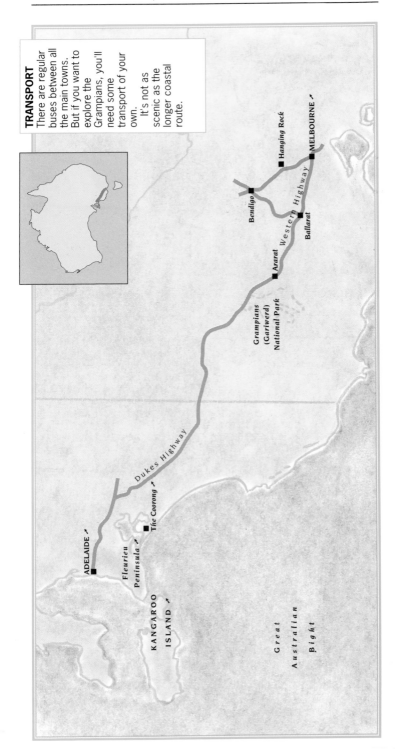

TRANSPORT

There are regular buses between all the main towns. But if you want to explore the Grampians, you'll need some transport of your own.

It's not as scenic as the longer coastal route.

• Sovereign Hill, Ballarat.

SIGHTS & PLACES OF INTEREST

ADELAIDE
See Australia Overall: 5.

ARARAT ⊨
220 km W of Melbourne on the Western Highway. In 1857, a small army of 700 hopeful Chinese diggers was tramping across this region on its way to the Central Victorian goldfields. They seem to have got lost, because the goldfields were the other way. Then one morning they woke up to find that their dreams had come true. They were camped right in the middle of an undiscovered goldfield. At once they all set to work with a will – and were soon recovering gold at the astonishing rate of more than 1,000 ounces a week. Then the gold ran out, so the Chinese turned round and went home to spend their hard-gotten gains in the fleshpots of Shanghai.

This is how Ararat began, and it might have been how it ended, if the sheep grazers hadn't moved in. Today the town and its outlying districts has a population of 8,000 humans and a million sheep. There's not much to see here, apart from the usual left-over Victorian buildings, and the small **Langi Morgala Museum** (*open 2 pm to 4 pm, Sat and Sun, entry A$1*), which has Aborigine artefacts and gold relics on display.

The main Chinese legacy lies north of here at the settlement of Great Western. Here the underground tunnels hewed out by the Chinese in search of gold now contain another valuable export. These are the **Sepelt's Great Western Winery Cellars** on Moyston Road (*open 9 am to 5 pm, Mon to Sat, 12 noon to 5 pm Sun*). The cellars are used for storing the excellent local sparkling wine which we are not allowed to call champagne, but which, claim the makers, tastes better than many which we are allowed to call champagne.

Ararat makes a useful base for touring the nearby Grampians – see page 212.

BALLARAT ⊨ ✕
150 km E of Melbourne. Ballarat is an impressive provincial city with a population of 70,000. Its present Victorian buildings, green avenues and flower beds belie its rough and ready origins in the gold rush of the 1850s. In those heady days, its population grew almost overnight to 40,000, most of whom were forced to live in tents. Over a quarter of the gold from the ore-rich Central Victoria Goldfields was discovered in the region of Ballarat. Not for nothing is one of its main thoroughfares known as Eureka Street – a name which also evokes one of the most violent episodes in Australian history: the Eureka Revolt

GOLD FEVER

In the middle of the 19thC, gold rushes became a worldwide phenomenon. The first great gold rush took place in California in the 1840s. In the 1850s it was Australia's turn. In 1851 gold was discovered for the first time in considerable quantities in Australia – first in New South Wales, then in Victoria. Huge deposits were discovered at Ballarat in 1851, and in the same year the biggest deposits ever were discovered at nearby Bendigo.

Within months, the streets of Sydney were almost deserted, and the middle classes throughout Australia suddenly found themselves suffering from a distinct lack of male servants. The news soon spread worldwide. British and Irish immigrants arrived in their tens of thousands, and forty thousand Chinese turned up. As well as Finns, Russians, Afghans, Filipinos, Japanese, Italians, you name it – they were all hell-bent on becoming 'diggers'.

The population of Victoria mushroomed from 70,000 to more than half a million (while at the same time the population of Australia doubled to more than a million). Gold licenses cost 30 shillings a month – no mean sum in those days, when a week's wages were often far less. (See also The Eureka Revolt, page 212.) This license entitled a digger to a claim of eight square feet. Tent cities sprung up around the gold towns, whose saloons and 'dance halls' soon began witnessing scenes of 'unbridled wickedness'. Diggers who found gold spent, and behaved, with an un-Victorian abandon.

By the 1890s, many of the gold-field settlements had become flourishing towns – with fine streets and resplendent buildings. Banks vied with the saloons, and diggers and ex-prostitutes became mansion owners. Meanwhile, Victoria's state capital, Melbourne, became the largest city in Australia, as well as the country's financial centre.

• *McKenzie Falls, The Grampians.*

of 1854 (see box, page 212).

The site where the rebels erected their stockade has now been turned into a memorial park. Here you can see a diorama which depicts the events of the revolt, and over the street there's a rather disappointing **Eureka Exhibition Museum** (*open 9 am to 5 pm daily, entry A$5*).

However there's nothing disappointing about the main sight in town. This is **Sovereign Hill**, which is a reconstruction of the town during the 1860s gold mining era (*open 9.30 am to 5pm daily, entry A$16*). There are many such exhibitions in Australia, but this is by far the best. Here you can ride in a stage-coach, pan for gold, and see what the old Chinatown was really like. The **Gold Museum** has some fascinating relics, and the **Mine Museum** shows how they worked the gold. At nights there's also a sound and light show depicting the battle at Eureka Stockade, *Mon to Sat, A$ 17, summer only.*

BENDIGO 🛏 ✕

150 km N of Melbourne. Gold was first discovered here in 1851, setting off the Central Victoria Gold Rush. The gold claims here once covered over 300 sq km, and when the surface gold ran out the mining companies moved in and began sinking shafts. There was so

211

much gold at Bendigo that it didn't run out until 1954.

Bendigo is now a large provincial town, but still has legacies of the gold era. The best of the ornate old Victorian buildings are on central Pall Mall – the most ornate of all being the slightly absurd **Shamrock Hotel**. Round the corner in View Street is the local **Art Gallery** (open 10 am to 5 pm, Mon to Fri, 2 pm to 5 pm, Sat and Sun, entry A$2). This has a number of works by painters who lived here in the old days, as well as a varied collection of Australian art.

If you want to visit a local mine, head down the Calder Highway to the corner of Violet Street. Here you can take a tour of the **Central Deborah Gold-mine** (open 9 am to 5 pm daily, entry A$11). This was the last working mine in Bendigo, and you can descend 60 m down a shaft to see the underground galleries. The main shaft plunges through more than a dozen levels to a depth of 500 m. There's also an exhibit of thought-provoking old photographs.

The other main sight is the **Chinese Joss House** at Finn Street in North Bendigo (open 10 am to 5 pm daily, entry A$3). During the gold era this was the local Chinese community's temple. It was built in 1860 and has a highly evocative oriental atmosphere. (What did such people make of their coarse, bewhiskered fellow diggers?) Of particular interest are the figures which symbolize the 12 years of the Chinese lunar cycle (the year of the rabbit, the year of the rat, and so on).

In the centre of town at Bridge Street (which used to be the heart of China-town) there's also a **Chinese Museum**, which contains all kinds of exhibits from the local Chinese processions. These include what is claimed as the world's largest Chinese imperial dragon.

THE EUREKA REVOLT

In 1854 the diggers in Ballarat rebelled against the excessive cost of claim licenses charged by the authorities. They were forced to pay 30 shillings a month (more than a working man's weekly wage), and received next to nothing in return. They were given no protection by the police, who were brutal and corrupt, and often harassed them. There were no roads, no transport, and few civil amenities of any kind. Conditions were squalid beyond belief, and the diggers even have the right to vote.

Eventually 200 diggers, many of Irish descent, staged the only major 'white revolt' in Australia's history. They burnt their licenses, armed themselves and built a makeshift stockade. After barricading themselves into the Eureka Stockade they ran up the Eureka Flag – five white stars and a white cross on a blue background. Armed troops were called in, and during the subsequent confrontation more than 30 men lost their lives. But in the end the diggers won the day. As a result of the Eureka Revolt, claim licenses were abolished, and the diggers also gained the right to vote. Their leader, Peter Lalor, even became an MP.

To this day the Eureka Flag holds a special place in Aussie hearts. It remains a symbol of protest against authority, and is frequently unfurled at demonstrations about almost anything from ecology and nuclear disarmament to pro-republicanism. Many claim that the Eureka Revolt was the start of Australia as an egalitarian society: the beginning of the end of old-style colonialism.

THE GRAMPIANS (GARIWERD) NATIONAL PARK ⇌ ✕

W of Western Highway near Ararat.
These mountains form the southern end of the Great Dividing Range. The Grampians National Park is renowned for its bushwalks, wildlife, mountain scenery, waterfalls and Aborigine art. In spring the mountainsides are covered with flowers.

The National Park Visitor Centre lies 3 km south of Halls Gap (which is just inside the north-eastern entry to the park). Here you can pick up details of the many long and short walks which criss-cross the region. Some of the most accessible walks start from Halls Gap. It is also possible to see much of the national park by car.

Just south-west of Halls Gap is the

Wonderland Range. This contains the Pinnacles, a superb look-out, and close by is the famous Nerve Test Ledge – which has spectacular views for those who can keep their eyes open.

Drive to the **Reid Lookout**, and from here it's just 1-km walk to the balconies, a series of stepped ledges above a truly breathtaking drop, known locally, with good reason, as the Jaws of Death.

The **Victoria Range**, in the western region of the Grampians, is renowned for its many Aborigine rock paintings. Quantity rather than quality is the name of the game here, but this somehow increases their eeriness. This region also contains the Victoria Valley wildlife sanctuary, which contains several rare breeds, as well as the usual hoppers and farters (roos and koalas).

HANGING ROCK
70 km N of Melbourne, close to Woodend. *Picnic at Hanging Rock* was the film which launched Australian movies on to the world market. The actual location is just as picturesque as it looked on the screen, and you can climb to get some fine views.

KANGAROO ISLAND, THE COORONG
And other sites south of Adelaide, *see Australia Overall: 4.*

MELBOURNE
See Australia Overall: 3.

RECOMMENDED HOTELS

ARARAT
Chalambar Motel, $-$$; *Great Western Highway; tel.* (053) 52 2430; *most major cards.*

Fairly basic motel: useful when the Grampians accommodation is all booked out.

BALLARAT
Ballarat Terrace, $$-$$$; *229 Lydiard Street, North Ballarat; tel.* (053) 33 2216; *cards MC, V.*

This century-old house dates from the golden era of Ballarat's prosperity. The accommodation has an authentic Victorian atmosphere, but they only have a few rooms, so be sure to book. No children.

BENDIGO
ANA Downtown Motor Inn, $$; *46 View Street; tel.* (054) 43 9155; *most major cards.*

Plumb in the heart of town; handy for the park and the central sights.

GRAMPIANS (GARIWERD)
Mountain Grand Guest House, $$; *Grampians Road, Halls Gap; tel.* (053) 56 4232; *cards none.*

A soft bed after your hard day's bushwalking. They also have a fine restaurant, and a friendly bar where you can tell everyone your amazing adventures.

RECOMMENDED RESTAURANTS

BALLARAT
Craigs Hotel, $$; *10 Lydiard Street; tel.* (053) 31 1377; *cards none.*

A cut above your average 'hotel' – this has been restored to its former Victorian elegance. Friendly place for a drink, and they also serve acceptable food.

BENDIGO
Shamrock Hotel, $-$$; *Pall Mall; no booking; cards none.*

No trip to Bendigo would be complete without a visit to this historic pile. In the old days they used to wash out the floors in search of gold dust from the miners' boots. Now it has a pleasant bar, café and bistro.

GRAMPIANS (GARIWERD)
Halls Gap is the best place for something to eat. Here you can eat at the **Flying Emu Cafe ($$)**. There's also a café at the general store. The best place to get ingredients for your picnic is at the nearby supermarket.

Barossa Valley and the Flinders Ranges

300 km; map Nelles Australia 1:400,000

The two main sights in this section lie off the road between Adelaide and Port Augusta. The Barossa Valley lies north-east of Adelaide, on the other side of the Adelaide Hills. This is where many of the best wines in Australia originate, and a tour of the wineries here is a vintage treat. There are around 30 wineries to choose from. If you fancy seeing the Murray River (Australia's greatest), head east from Barossa to Loxton, where you can take a boat trip and see the Historic Village.

Running north-east from Port Augusta are the Flinders Ranges. This is prime hiking territory, with some excellent mountain scenery – gorges, peaks and a huge natural basin. The walks here vary from high performance endurance marches to civilized strolls for human beings.

You can cover this ground in less than a day, but it's worth allowing an extra day if you want to look at Barossa Valley in any depth; if you want to walk in the Flinders Ranges, think of setting aside at least two days.

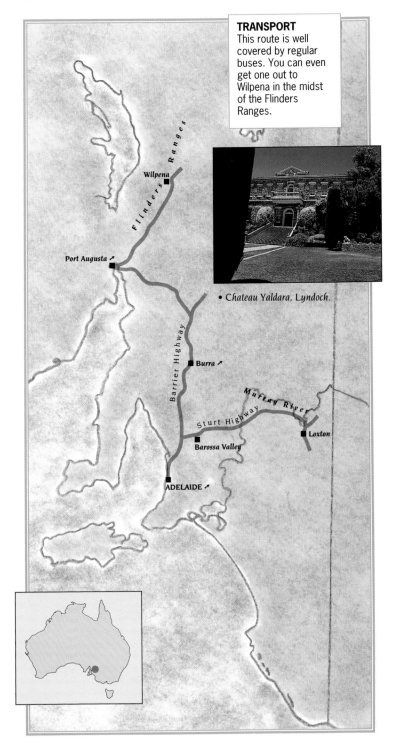

TRANSPORT
This route is well covered by regular buses. You can even get one out to Wilpena in the midst of the Flinders Ranges.

Wilpena

Flinders Ranges

Port Augusta

Chateau Yaldara, Lyndoch.

Barrier Highway

Burra

Murray River

Sturt Highway

Loxton

Barossa Valley

ADELAIDE

SIGHTS & PLACES OF INTEREST

BAROSSA VALLEY 🛏 ✕

60 km NE *of Adelaide*. The Barossa Valley is the best-known wine-growing district in Australia, with well over two dozen wineries. These produce wines ranging from humble but very drinkable plonk to Penfold's Grange Hermitage, which is claimed as Australia's finest.

The region was originally settled by farmers who had fled religious persecution in Prussia (Germany) and Silesia (Poland). These people gave the region its distinctive Lutheran churches and many other German touches which have since been cultivated to enhance the tourist trade. Though curiously, neither Prussia nor Silesia are renowned for their wine.

This entire area was originally known as Neuschlesien (New Silesia), but trying to pronounce this and drink wine evidently proved too much for locals and visitors alike.

You can tour the wineries by car (they're mostly within a 25-km radius), but this means someone has to forego tasting. Far better is to stay overnight in one of the villages, and take a tour – such as Valley Tours, tel. (085) 62 1524. Or you can hire a moped at the Caltex Service Station in Tanunda.

In general, the best wineries to visit are the smaller ones. These have a friendlier atmosphere, which enable you to air your vast vinicultural wisdom with the minimum of public embarrassment. Every winery has its tasting cellar, and there are usually at least half a dozen wines for you to sample. Spittoons are provided for the professionals, who like to demonstrate that they know what they're doing by spitting out what they've tasted. The rest of us, who are also well aware of what we are doing, prefer to complete the process as it was meant to be completed, and then move on to the next one. Always try the white ones first, as they tend to mask your palate less. It's worth going through all the rigmarole of rolling the wine on your tongue and gurgling (before gulping it down) if you want to savour the flavours and taste the differences. And in case you forget, the prime purpose of these tastings is to get you to buy a few bottles of the product. Don't be bashful, you won't be disappointed.

• *Wine produced on the Yaldara Estate. Below,* Hahndorf, Barossa Valley.

Of the towns in the Barossa Valley, **Tanunda** is the most German, with its oompa-pa music and original German cottages. **Lyndoch** has an interesting **Mechanical Music Museum** and the nearby **Barossa Reservoir** with its famous whispering wall; what's said 150 m away reaches your ears as a so-called 'ghostly whisper'. Lyndoch is also the home of the **Chateau Yaldara Estate**, on Gomersal Road. The old mill here has been turned into a neo-rococo chateau but the wine is the real thing. (You can also stay here: see Recommended Hotels, opposite.)

My other favourite wineries are Grant **Burge Wines, Barossa Valley Highway, Jacob's Creek**, which produces the well-known brew, and **Bethany Wines**, Bethany Road. The last is a family-run winery that is probably the most picturesque of them all.

There's always something going on

in the Barossa Valley. Events range from the full-blown Vintage Festival (Easter) to various gourmet events, balloon regattas and other high-octane hot-air jamborees.

BURRA

See Local Explorations: 6.

FLINDERS RANGES 🛏 ✕

These run NE *of* Port Augusta *for* 300 *km.*
It's said that the Flinders Ranges contain some of the oldest rock on earth. Its colours and various indentations make the gorges, ridges and peaks of the Flinders a picturesque treat for hardened hikers and softened strollers alike. According to Aborigine legend, these twisting gorges were carved out by the course of huge dreamtime snake in search of water.

One of the greatest sights in the range is the **Wilpena Pound**, a vast natural basin which occupies almost 100 sq km. This lies in the **Flinders Ranges National Park**, which has several fine gorges and a range of excellent marked walks. Many of these start from just outside Wilpena by the Information Centre, where you can pick up detailed maps for A$8.

If you're not feeling energetic, an exciting way to see the Flinders is to fly. You can pick up flights at Hawker, which is on Rt 47, just 100 km northeast of Port Augusta, tel. (086) 48 4006.

For the southern Flinders see Australia Overall: 5, page 120.

LOXTON ✕

150 *km* E *of* Barossa *Valley.*
Small town on a bend of the great Murray River which flows all the way from the Snowy Mountains to the sea south of Adelaide. Here they have a Historic Village, and the Katarapko Game Reserve, where there's great canoeing. For just under $10 you can take a two-hour boat ride on the river, and afterwards there's always the Australian Vintage Winery to visit.

MURRAY RIVER

See Loxton, *above.*

WILPENA

See Flinders *Ranges, above.*

RECOMMENDED HOTELS

BAROSSA VALLEY

Chateau Yaldara Estate, $$; *Gomersal Road, Lyndoch; tel.* (085) 24 4268; *all major cards.*

The motel is by the winery, and some of the rooms have great views (though these cost more). Amenities include a pool and a pleasant restaurant.

Miners Cottage, $$; Box 28, *Cockatoo* Valley; *tel.* (085) 24 6213; *cards* MC, V.

Superb picturesque cottage beside a billabong on a local farm, complete with pool.

FLINDERS RANGES

Wilpena Pound Motel, $$; *Wilpena; tel.* 1800 805 802; *cards none.*

This has everything from a pool to a good restaurant, and there's also a friendly bar where you can regale the others with tales of your great hike.

RECOMMENDED RESTAURANTS

BAROSSA VALLEY

Lanzerac, $$$; *Menge Road, Tanunda; tel.* (085) 64 2488; *cards* MC, V.

Fine cooking to go with the region's wines. European continental cuisine with an Australian flourish, and a superb wine list.

FLINDERS RANGES

Quorn Mill, $-$$; *Quorn; no booking; cards none.*

Friendly spot in an old converted flour mill. Quorn is the so-called 'Gateway to the Flinders', and has some particularly interesting craft shops.

LOXTON

Loxton Palace, $-$$; East *Terrace; no booking; cards none.*

Aussie-style Chinese cuisine, and a warmer welcome than in many similar oriental outposts.

South Australia

Burra, Clare Valley and Broken Hill

520 km; map Nelles Australia 1:400,000

This section explores the territory north of Adelaide along the Barrier Highway. There are several points of interest just north of Adelaide, and these are covered in Local Explorations: 5. After another 150 km or so you come to Burra, a historic copper-mining town which has a number of well-preserved relics from the old days. Just west of here lies the wine-growing district of Clare Valley, which includes the village of Leasingham, one of my favourite places in Australia, if not the world – see page 221.

After Burra you follow the Barrier Highway through the Benda Range until eventually you come to Broken Hill. This is one of the most famous mining centres in Australia – both historically, and present day. You can don a miner's helmet and descend a deep shaft in a cage. Unexpectedly, Broken Hill is also a thriving art centre. Tour the galleries, and then set out to see the sculptures carved into sandstone. Also of interest is the ghost town of Silverton. This has been used as a set for several films.

It's a long drive out to Broken Hill. Try breaking your journey at Burra on the way out, and visiting the Clare Valley on your way back. Altogether, allow around four days.

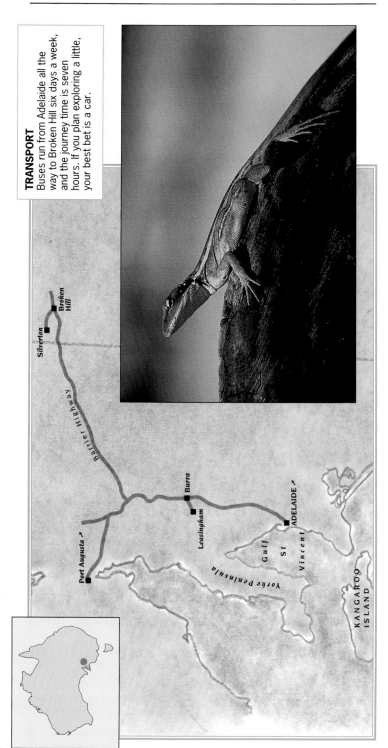

TRANSPORT

Buses run from Adelaide all the way to Broken Hill six days a week, and the journey time is seven hours. If you plan exploring a little, your best bet is a car.

• *Broken Hill.*

=====================================

SIGHTS & PLACES OF INTEREST

ADELAIDE
See Australia Overall: 5.

BROKEN HILL ⇔ ✕
360 km NE of Burra on the Barrier Highway. In winter you freeze here, in summer you boil. And it never rains. (The water has to be shipped in from Menindee Reservoir, 100 km away.) They even need a protective barrier of trees to keep out the dust storms.

But people didn't come here for the climate, they came here to mine. Silver was discovered at Broken Hill in 1885 by a German boundary rider called Charles Rasp. What he discovered was something stupendous. Others mining in the area had missed what was probably the greatest silver, zinc and lead lode on earth. A major mining business has been running here for well over a century – long after the period when most other mining centres had turned into ghost towns.

But business didn't always run smoothly in Broken Hill. To begin with, the profits were huge, but the working conditions were atrocious. This was a one-company town, and it soon also became a one-union town. Clashes became frequent and bitter. But after the miners won the Big Strike of 1919 (which lasted for 18 months) they achieved a revolutionary change in conditions – including a 35-hour week.

A great slag heap is the town's dominant feature, and the grid-patterned streets are mostly named after minerals – such as Mica Street and Cobalt Street. Though local legend has it that Crystal and Beryl Streets are really named after a pair of red-headed Irish twins who worked in the saloons.

So why come here? For a start, the mines have to be seen to be believed. Some plunge over 1,500 m, and even need refrigeration plants (it can reach 60°C at that depth). Try the tour at **Delprat's Mine** (*10.30 am Mon to Fri; two hours, A$20; children not allowed*) where you put on mining gear and descend in a cage. Children may tour **Day Dream Mine**, but that's 20 km north-west of town.

Broken Hill is in New South Wales, but everything mined here is shipped out via Port Pirie, on the coast in South Australia. As a result, Broken Hill considers itself more akin to South Australia, and even keeps South Australian time (which is half an hour later than New South Wales time).

Curiously, the other big feature in Broken Hill is art. There are galleries all over the place (largely filled with work by local artists), there are murals at **Mario's Palace Hotel**, and out in the hills there are sculptures carved out of sandstone. For further details of this thriving art scene contact The Tourist Centre on the corner of Blende and Bromide.

BURRA ⇔ ✕
160 km N of Adelaide. Once upon a time this pleasant small town was a copper-mining hell. Copper was discovered here in 1847, and within a couple of years unemployed miners from Cornwall (England) and Scotland were flooding in. As many as 1,500 of them were forced to live in primitive dugouts down

RECOMMENDED HOTELS

BROKEN HILL
Mario's Palace Hotel, $; Argent Street; tel. (080) 88 1699; cards none.

Fairly basic accommodation. The thing you'll remember about this place is the murals.

BURRA
Burra Motor Inn, $-$$; Market Street; tel. (088) 92 2777; cards none.

Nothing special, but you get a warm welcome and some of the rooms look out over the creek.

RECOMMENDED RESTAURANTS

BROKEN HILL
Papa Joe's, $-$$; Argent Street; no booking; cards none.

Friendly Italian spot, with pasta and miner-sized steaks.

BURRA
As you'd expect in an old mining town, the pubs are the main eating places. If you fancy something a little more elaborate, try the restaurant at the **Burra Motor Inn,** tel. (088) 92 2777 on Market Street.

LEASINGHAM
Crawley's Restaurant, $-$$; Leasingham Village; no booking; cards none.

The place where you can get something to eat to accompany the stunning local wine.

by the creek – and you can still see a couple of these, which have been preserved to chill the hearts of posterity.

In its heyday 5,000 people lived in Burra, and this settlement provided 5 per cent of the world's copper. In the process they dug out what is now known as the **Monster Mine,** a large pit 13 km wide and 6 km long. Then in 1870 the copper ran out, and almost everyone else ran out too. Nowadays, the place has been heavily restored, and is something of a historic spot. You can still see the original **Cornish Miners' Cottages** at Paxton Square. These date from the 1850s. Nearby is the **Market Square Museum,** opposite the Tourist Office. In the latter you can find out about the local **Heritage Trail,** which takes in such wonders as the Monster Mine and **Redruth Gaol** (named after the town in Cornwall, presumably to make the inmates feel at home). The Scottish miners were even less fortunate. When they dug in at the Bon Accord Complex all they discovered was water. But they quickly turned this disaster into profit by selling it to the town water department.

KANGAROO ISLAND
See Australia Overall: 4, page 105.

LEASINGHAM ×
140 km N of Adelaide. This sublime small village is situated in the the Clare Valley, which lies west of the Barrier Highway north of Adelaide. What's so exceptional about this rather ordinary-looking spot? In my opinion this spot produces the most delicious low-medium priced red wine in the world – and it's available all over the world, too. The one with the blended cabernet and malbec grapes is the best, and is available for around £6 (US $9) per bottle. If you're still only thinking about visiting Australia, this'll clinch it. No relatives, or even friends of mine, depend for a living on this wine; nor do I owe a bill at the local Crawley's Restaurant (see Recommended Restaurants, this page) where you can drink your sublime bottle with reasonable food.

PORT AUGUSTA
See Australia Overall: 5, page 120.

SILVERTON
25 km NW of Broken Hill. This is the original Aussie ghost town, which has become so famous that it isn't really a ghost town any more. But at least it looks like one. And it probably did to you, too, when you saw the movies Mad Max II, Razorback or A Town Like Alice, which were all filmed here, along with innumerable advertisements featuring the Australian outback.

This spot once had a population of 3,000, then the silver ran out in 1889. Look over the local jail, with its mementoes of the good old days, take a camel ride around town, then head a further 15 km down the road to the **Umber-umberka Reservoir** for a picnic.

Queensland

South Queensland Outback Inland from Brisbane

1,000 *km; map* Nelles Australia, 1:400,000

The outback has to be seen 'because it's there'. It's also an integral part of Australia and its history – to say nothing of its mythology. The fact that more than 85 per cent of Australians live in suburbs on the coastal rim probably has something to do with this.

If you get no further north than Brisbane, this is your best route into the Queensland outback. You take the Warrego Highway via Toowoomba, heading west across the Darling Downs. On the other side of the mountains you come to grazing territory – mile upon mile of sheep and cattle rearing country, with just a few isolated settlements on the way. This territory also produces some fine wine, as you'll discover when you get to Roma.

If you don't want to go any further west than this, you can detour north from Roma to the Carnarvon National Park (see page 228), which has some of the finest mountain scenery in Queensland, as well as some superb Aborigine rock paintings. From there you can double back to the coast using Local Explorations: 8.

West of Roma you come to Charleville, which is at the end of the Warrego Highway. Beyond here it's another 800 km to the celebrated settlement of Birdsville.

The distances here are vast. If you want to go all the way, you should allow over a week. However, the loop from Roma north to Local Explorations: 8 and then back to the coast can be covered in less than a week, even if you stop to explore.

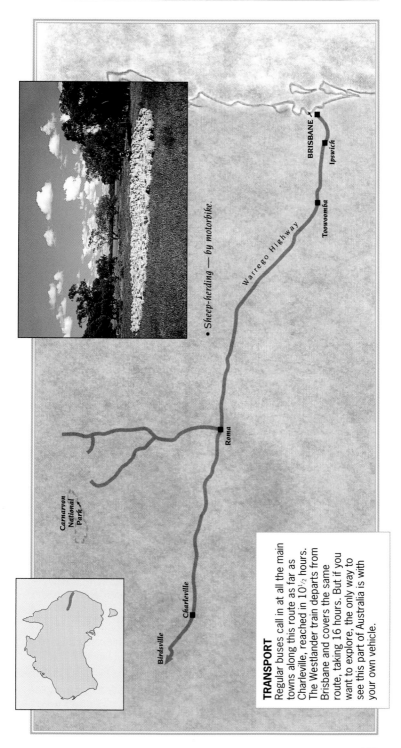

• *Sheep-herding — by motorbike.*

BRISBANE

Ipswich

Toowoomba

Warrego Highway

Roma

Carnarvon National Park

Charleville

Birdsville

TRANSPORT

Regular buses call in at all the main towns along this route as far as Charleville, reached in 10½ hours. The Westlander train departs from Brisbane and covers the same route, taking 16 hours. But if you want to explore, the only way to see this part of Australia is with your own vehicle.

Early colonial architecture, Ipswich.

SIGHTS & PLACES OF INTEREST

BIRDSVILLE

800 km W of Charleville. A tiny settlement, just a dozen kilometres from the South Australia border. It stands at the northern end of the 480-km long Birdsville Track, and is the site of the celebrated Birdsville Hotel. This settlement claims to be 'the remotest spot in Queensland', and it certainly feels like it. In order to get water, they had to drill an artesian well over 1,200 m deep. The water which emerges is too hot to have a bath in. Despite such difficulties, you will find that all fluid intended for human consumption (usually amber in colour) is served at a suitably cool temperature.

For 51 weeks of the year nothing happens in Birdsville. Then on the first weekend in September they hold the **Birdsville Races**. Thousands descend on the settlement, and the Birdsville Hotel once again lives up to its legendary status. Twenty years ago a friend of mine from Melbourne attended these races, and underwent such a gruelling experience (financially and physically) that he swore never to set foot in the outback again. Since then he has travelled widely though all five continents, but his memories of Birdsville have kept him from ever venturing again into the outback.

BRISBANE

See Australia Overall: 7, page 128.

CHARLEVILLE

800 km W of Brisbane on the Warrego Highway. This is the small town at the western end of the Warrego Highway, where it meets the Mitchell Highway, which heads north into the central Queensland outback.

The surrounding region is covered

A MIGHTY MOTH

Today the Darling Downs are ideal grazing country. Yet a little over half a century ago large sections of this region had become infested with impenetrable prickly pear cactuses. Then someone got wind of how they solved this problem in Mexico. A moth with the apposite name Cactoblastis was introduced, and in no time the cactuses were dying off.

According to a story I was told over the bar in Toowoomba, the magnified face of this moth provided Steven Spielberg with the inspiration for ET's endearing but alien features – though in my view he looks much more like a shaved prickly pear cactus.

---

by huge sheep- and cattle-grazing stations, and Charleville is the watering hole for many of the jackaroos who work out in this thirst-inducing terrain. The Corones Hotel has witnessed many prodigious feats of thirst-quenching which have to be seen to be believed. Though a friend of mine was warned by the barman: "You'd best not see it. Just believe it."

IPSWICH

30 km W of Brisbane on the Warrego Highway. A large town at the start of the Darling Downs: its history stretches back to the 1820s, when the first European settlement here was a convict colony, started up as an adjunct to the main colony in Brisbane.

Nowadays the region still has several fine old houses. The best of these is off the road halfway to Brisbane, at **Wacol**. This dates back to 1852 and is a prime example of early Australian colonial architecture; *open 9 am to 5 pm, Wed to Sat, entry A$3.* If you want to explore the older houses in Ipswich, head for the Tourist Information Office in Brisbane Street, where they'll give you a City Heritage Trails pamphlet that maps out several good walks.

ROMA

450 km W of Brisbane on the Warrego Highway. Small town in the centre of cattle- and sheep-grazing country. Almost 100 years ago gas was discovered here – but not enough to start a gas rush. (The outback has witnessed every kind of rush, from gold to tin.) Nowadays, it still supplies Brisbane with gas, by way of a 450-km-long pipeline through the mountains. Thirty years later they struck oil here, but this proved another disappointment – though a small local refinery still supplies the town with its own petrol.

Pre-dating both these finds was the discovery that the local terrain was ideal for vineyards. The best local wine comes from the **Roma Vineyard** just north of town. The wine produced here has been winning prizes since the 1860s. Call in if you feel like tasting (or buying) some. They're open *9 am to 4 pm, Mon to Sat;* off the Carnarvon Road. The town holds a wine festival every November.

Some 150 km north up the Carnarvon road, you come to the spectacular

• *Good grazing, Queensland.*

Carnarvon National Park and Local Explorations: 8 – see page 226.

TOOWOOMBA

150 km W of Brisbane on the Warrego Highway. Largish, rather boring town by the Darling Downs.

RECOMMENDED HOTELS & RESTAURANTS

Settlements in the remoter stretches of the outback can be few and far between. However, most of these spots have a hotel – the local pub – which serves inexpensive food over the counter and usually has a few basic rooms.

Such spots aren't recommendable in the usual sense of the word, but if you're travelling in the outback, they're very much an integral part of the experience. Go easy in these hotels, and you're liable to be befriended by some of the most interesting characters you'll ever meet, in their own modest estimation.

Some outback hotels gain a reputation which spreads far and wide. Amongst these is the legendary Birdsville Hotel in Birdsville, page 224, which has reduced many a strong man to his knees.

Central Queensland Outback Inland from Rockhampton

700 km; map Nelles Australia, 1:400,000

This section explores the country along the Capricorn Highway into the outback. The initial stage crosses the Great Dividing Range, and takes you to the coal-mining centre of Blackwater. By contrast, south-west of here lies the Carnarvon National Park, which has some of the finest mountain scenery in Queensland. There are spectacular walks through the gorges, as well as some of the best Aborigine rock paintings in Australia.

Back on the Capricorn Highway you come to the gemfields. Here you can try your hand at fossicking for your own sapphire or ruby to take home. But be warned: it's hot out here, with temperatures rising to 40°C in the summer.

Further on you come to grazing country and Longreach, which is almost 700 km from Rockhampton – but well worth the journey. This is the home of the Stockmen's Hall of Fame, a superb heritage centre which outlines the long and unique history of the outback.

From here you can retrace your route, or head on via Winton to link up with Local Explorations: 9, Inland from Townsville. Whichever way you choose, allow at least a week.

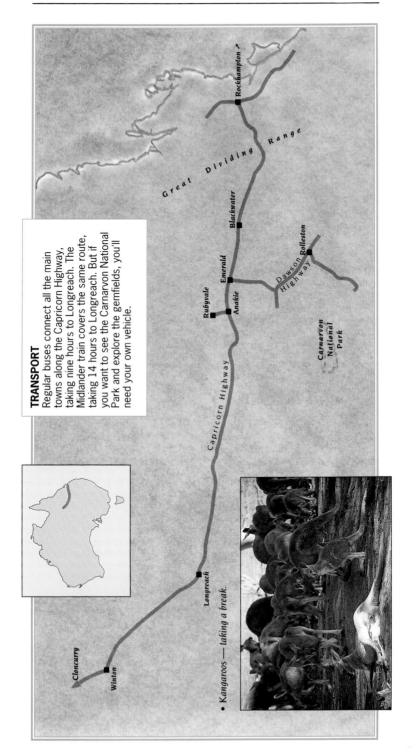

TRANSPORT

Regular buses connect all the main towns along the Capricorn Highway, taking nine hours to Longreach. The Midlander train covers the same route, taking 14 hours to Longreach. But if you want to see the Carnarvon National Park and explore the gemfields, you'll need your own vehicle.

Rockhampton

Great Dividing Range

Blackwater

Emerald

Rolleston

Dawson Rolleston Highway

Rubyvale

Anakie

Carnarvon National Park

Capricorn Highway

Longreach

Cloncurry

Winton

Kangaroos — taking a break.

227

SIGHTS & PLACES OF INTEREST

ANAKIE

40 km W of Emerald. The gem rush began here in the 1870s, and has continued after a fashion ever since – both with large commercial mines and individual prospectors. Yes, there are still a few hardy individualists who manage to make a living out of working claims in this inhospitable territory. Others visit the gemfields on a regular basis – all driven by the hope of finding 'the big one'. It's easy to get hooked.

Visit the Gemfields Information Centre where you can pick up maps of the best nearby spots for fossicking.

BLACKWATER

200 km W of Rockhampton on Capricorn Highway. An open-cast coal-mining town, with all the awesome and fascinating (or grim and depressing) paraphernalia you'd expect of such a spot. Tours of the large **Utah Mine** start at 10 am on Wednesdays.

Further down the road, by contrast, you come to cotton country, where during the autumn harvest everything is flecked with white.

CARNARVON NATIONAL PARK

350 km W of Rockhampton. High up on the Buckland Tableland of the Great Dividing Range, this national park is one of the most popular in Queensland – despite its remoteness. To reach the park entrance, turn south off the Capricorn Highway at Emerald and follow the Dawson Highway to Rolleston. From here follow the Carnarvon Development Road south. For the last 40 km this road is unsealed, and should not be attempted after rain.

This brings you eventually to the Information Centre. From here you can set off on the walk through the **Carnarvon Gorge**, the park's main attraction. The full gorge walk is 19 km, and you'll need to take your own provisions. The gorge rises sheer in many places, and when the top is lost in cloud the spectacular landscape takes on a mysterious beauty, like something out of an ancient legend. Many of the side gorges are even more amazing. You can see Aborigine art at **Cathedral Cave** and the **Gallery**. These are some of the finest and most extensive examples of ancient Aborigine art in all Australia. Aborigines have been decorating these rock faces for more than 3,000 years.

The gorge is renowned for its natural rock gardens, exotic ferns and rare palm trees. It also abounds in marsupial life, and in the shrieks of exotic birds. There are campsites throughout the park, which extends over hundreds of kilometres. Or you can stay at the Oasis Lodge near the entrance, tel. (079) 84 4503. Cabins here cost A$150, but for this you get all meals

---

FOSSICKING FOR GEMS

This is your chance to discover the sapphire or ruby which will pay for your entire holiday (or at least make a miniscule conversation piece for your coffee table). You'll have to buy a license (A$5), and you'll need to hire the necessary equipment (sieve, shovel, pick). These are available at most popular fossicking sites.

Fossicking is good fun, but can be hard work in the heat – the temperature can rise to over 40°C. Alternatively, you can simply try 'specking' (looking for surface finds). The best time for this is during the winter rainy season, when the topsoil washes away and you can (sometimes) catch the glint of what looks like a coloured fleck of glass. Blue is a sapphire, pink a ruby.

As you'd expect, tales of fabulous finds abound. My favourite is the one about the Sydney woman who had a puncture. The garage hand who fixed the tyre found the puncture had been caused by a large ruby. Ownership of the gem was naturally disputed, so they went off to the local hotel to discuss the matter over a few beers. One thing led to another, and they eventually got married, using the ruby for her wedding ring. (As you'll find, credibility is never allowed to get in the way of a good story around these parts.)

and excellent guided tours of the park.

Further west, along unsealed roads, lies the Mount Moffatt section of the park, which has some sturdy hikes though superb mountain scenery.

EMERALD

270 km W of Rockhampton on the Capricorn Highway. A hot and dusty spot which belies its name. The only things worth seeing are the million-year-old fossilized tree trunks outside the Town Hall. Don't be fooled by the name – the main gemfields are 40 km or so west of here around Anakie.

LONGREACH

680 km W of Rockhampton on the Capricorn Highway. Here you're way out in sheepgrazing territory. It's said that the local population (of around 4,000) is outnumbered 300 to 1 by these living carpets.

Longreach has two main claims to fame. The Queensland and Northern Territories Air Service was founded here in 1921. This outpost remained its headquarters for 25 years, by which time it had become Qantas, Australia's national airline.

However, Longreach's main attraction is the **Stockman's Hall of Fame**

• A *woolly gathering*

(*open 9 am to 5 pm daily, entry* A$15). This was opened in 1988, and is housed in an extraordinary architectural wonder. Inside you can see a large range of displays which outline the entire history of the outback, from the mythical Aborigine Dreamtime to the present. Videos, photos and exhibits make this a fascinating repository of outback lore – a region of legends and adventure like no other in the world.

ROCKHAMPTON

See Australia Overall: 8, page 147.

RUBYVALE

55 km W of Emerald. A gem-mining centre which has several good spots for fossicking – see box, opposite, for details of this activity.

RECOMMENDED HOTELS & RESTAURANTS

See note on page 233, in Local Explorations: 9.

Northern Queensland Outback Inland from Townsville

700 km; map Nelles Australia 1:400,000

From Townsville the Flinders Highway leads west across the Great Dividing Range, giving access to northern Queensland outback: one of the most desolate and remote regions of the Australian interior. This is one of the least explored trails of Australia's interior, ideal for those who want to get away from it all. It also contains much history of the 'real' Australia.

This vast and empty region has been mining territory since the middle of the 19thC. It experienced several gold rushes, which attracted footloose gold prospectors from all over the world. Ravenswood is a typical old gold-rush centre, now an atmospheric ghost town.

Further inland you come to the large copper- and lead-mining centres separated from each other by miles and miles of empty outback. Cloncurry is as hot as anywhere in Australia, and Mount Isa produces more lead than anywhere else in the world. At Mount Isa you're almost 1,000 km from Townsville and halfway to Alice Springs.

Travelling from Townsville to Mount Isa will take you at least two days. If you're travelling on to Alice Springs, you'll need a 4WD, a winch, and your own supplies – the direct route will take you a week or so.

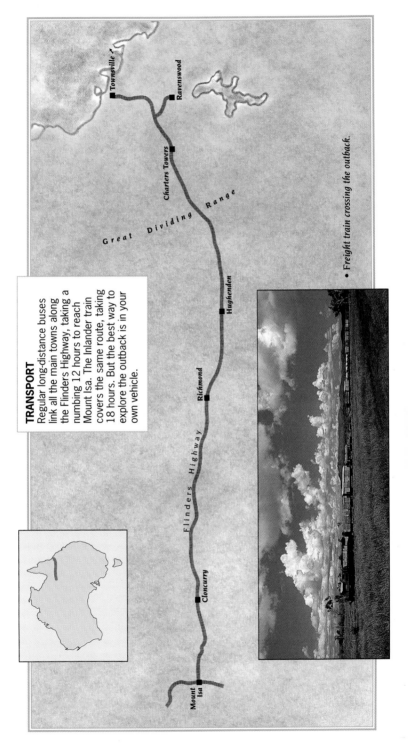

TRANSPORT
Regular long-distance buses link all the main towns along the Flinders Highway, taking a numbing 12 hours to reach Mount Isa. The Inlander train covers the same route, taking 18 hours. But the best way to explore the outback is in your own vehicle.

Townsville

Ravenswood

Charters Towers

Great Dividing Range

Hughenden

Richmond

Flinders Highway

Cloncurry

Mount Isa

• *Freight train crossing the outback.*

• City Hall, Charters Towers.

SIGHTS & PLACES OF INTEREST

CHARTERS TOWERS

140 km W of Townsville on the Flinders Highway. One day in 1871 an Aborigine boy called Jupiter Mosman noticed a glint beneath the water in a nearby creek. Gold. By the end of the decade 30,000 prospectors were burrowing in the ground around Charters Towers. In those days, the town had no name, and was simply known to the locals as The World. The hunt for gold may focus the mind, but it also narrows it somewhat. Eventually, Charters Towers received a name, and they even called its main street after the person who has started it all. Today Mosman Street and central Charters Towers have many reminders of the old days, with several fine colonial buildings, including the Stock Exchange, the School of Mines, the City Hall and the Courthouse. The gold lasted until the early years of this century, by which time Charters Towers had established itself as the beef-trading centre it remains to this day.

A decade or so ago there was a revival in the gold industry, when new mining methods rendered some of the old seams economical. But alas, the days when Mosman Street had 25 pubs and as many bordellos show no signs of returning.

If you fancy seeing how much trouble it took to get even a flake of gold in the old days, head for the **Venus Gold Battery** (*tours 10 am and 2 pm daily*, A$3). This is just half a dozen km east of town. Here you can see a weird and wonderful processing plant, full of defunct machinery, operated for more than a hundred years. Apparently, there are now plans to restore this monster to its former glory.

HOTELS & RESTAURANTS

Charming little hotels and gourmet restaurants have never been a big feature of this part of the outback. However, most settlements, no matter how small, will usually have their 'hotel'. This is, in fact, the local pub, but they serve adequate, inexpensive food and drink. And upstairs they mostly have a few basic rooms – originally intended for their basic patrons who couldn't make it home.

CLONCURRY

400 km W of Hughenden on the Flinders Highway. If you've made it this far, you deserve a medal. Cloncurry was once the world's greatest copper-mining centre. It also claims the record for the highest temperature recorded in Australia – a cool 55°C. (I know of only two other spots in Australia which lay claim to this record.)

In case you're interested: copper was first discovered here in the 1860s, when it was transported out on camel trains. A few years later gold was discovered. News of this spread quickly to those in need of this commodity in Afghanistan and China, causing an Afghan-Chinese gold rush. If you think I'm making this up, go and visit the two foreign cemeteries on the edge of town. Here you can see the graves of the Afghans and Chinese who didn't strike gold (or who did, but then someone struck them).

Cloncurry was so far off the map that it gave the local Reverend John Flynn the idea for the famous Australian Flying Doctor Service, which he founded at Cloncurry in 1928.

Here, you're halfway to Alice Springs.

HUGHENDEN

250 km W of Townsville on the Flinders Highway. It's a long drive to Hughenden, with not much but the wild emus for company in the endless outback. And there's not that much here when you finally arrive. First place to head for is the local swimming pool, which is good and large. This is on Resolution Street beside Allan's Caravan Park.

After that you can try the local

Museum, where they display the reassembled bones of a dinosaur who lived in swamps around here several million years ago. According to one disgruntled local I met, his descendants are still propping up the bar in the Grand Hotel.

MOUNT ISA

900 km W of Townsville. A vast sprawl of mining activity, which produces more lead than anywhere else in the world. Its gougings and burrowings are so extensive that they spread over more than 40,000 sq km. The locals reckon that this makes it the largest city in the world. Tokyo and Los Angeles please take note.

RAVENSWOOD

150 km SW of Townsville. A gold-mining ghost town. Gold was found here in 1868, and yet another Australian gold rush was born. By the early 1870s more than 700 people lived here, and the main street consisted entirely of pubs and dance houses. What? Bearded prospectors in heavy boots whirling to the strains of the Blue Danube waltz? Hardly. Most of the dancing in such establishments was horizontal.

For almost 50 years, the nearby seams of gold and silver continued to produce nuggets, then slivers, then grains, then specks... Until finally it wasn't worth the candle, and even the most hard-bitten of the prospectors moved on.

Nowadays, Ravenswood has a population of around 100 thirsty souls, who manage to support two pubs, one general store and a church. The old Imperial Hotel still boasts swing doors and mirrors dating from the old days. Other buildings have been restored. It doesn't take much to imagine what it must have been like in the so-called golden era. An atmospheric spot.

RICHMOND

110 km W of Hughenden on the Flinders Highway. Plumb in the middle of nowhere. Blink and you'll miss it. However, the hard-bitten locals in the bar are convinced that this is the centre of the universe – and you'd be wise to agree with them.

TOWNSVILLE

See Australia Overall 9, page 156.

233

The Far North
Cape Tribulation, Cooktown, Lizard Island and Cape York

850 km; map Nelles Australia 1:400,000

This section covers (along with Local Explorations: 9) one of the most remote and exciting parts of Australia. It falls naturally into two parts.

First, there is the coastal stretch north of Cairns, taking you up to the Cape Tribulation region. The national park here has superb tropical scenery and beaches. Further north is Cooktown, one of the most historic spots in the land. From here you can visit Lizard Island, which is renowned for diving on the reef.

The second section covers the huge remote vastness of the Cape York peninsula. The roads here are difficult to say the least: they involve river crossings and are only passable during the drier season – approximately June to October: even then, they should only undertaken by experienced 4WD drivers. The best way to see this region is on an organized road tour or sea cruise from Cairns. Don't for one moment imagine that this will be your ordinary package tour: it will be a real adventure.

Distances are vast. It's more than 800 km from Cairns to Cape York, (and then you have to get back again). The tours and cruises last around seven days, and it makes sense to allow a few easy days for recovery in Cairns afterwards.

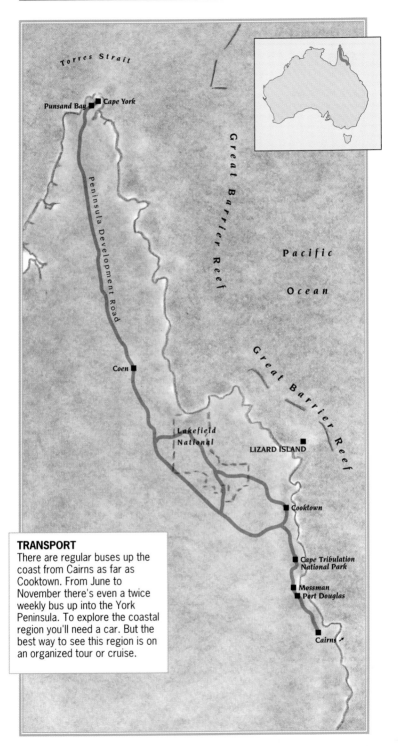

Torres Strait

Punsand Bay ■ ■ Cape York

Peninsula Development Road

Great Barrier Reef

Pacific

Ocean

Great Barrier Reef

Coen ■

Lakefield National

LIZARD ISLAND ■

■ Cooktown

■ Cape Tribulation National Park

■ Mossman
■ Port Douglas

■ Cairns ↗

TRANSPORT
There are regular buses up the coast from Cairns as far as Cooktown. From June to November there's even a twice weekly bus up into the York Peninsula. To explore the coastal region you'll need a car. But the best way to see this region is on an organized tour or cruise.

SIGHTS & PLACES OF INTEREST

CAIRNS
See Australia Overall: 9, page 153.

CAPE YORK ⚓

The northernmost tip of Australia. This is the end of the line, and it's no easy task to get here. You can't just jump into a car and drive. An ordinary car will get you as far as Coen, on the Peninsula Development Road, but here you're still 400 km short of the Cape. From there on, only a 4WD is good enough, and the trip should only be undertaken by those who are experienced in this type of terrain and know how to use a winch. The main trouble is the river beds, and for most of the year these are impassable: you can only be sure of completing this journey between June and October.

By far your best bet is to join one of the tours that set out from Cairns. These last around seven days, taking in most of the sights on the way. Expect to pay around A$1,500 all in – expensive, but it'll be one of the great journeys of your life.

One of the most experienced operators is New Look Adventures, tel. (070) 31 7622. Another great way to see this region, for a similar cost, is to take one of several cruises from Cairns up to Cape York. These also last about a week, and take in many sights (such as Lizard Island) on the way.

And what do you get, when you finally arrive at the end of the line? A view out across the shimmering island-dotted Torres Strait – and that sensational feeling of having done it. Papua New Guinea is over the horizon, just 150 km away.

If you've made it under your own steam, there's a pleasant and not-too-expensive resort with a fabulous beach 9 km west along the coast – as the crow flies. The bad news is that it's 30 km away by road: see Recommended Hotels, page 239.

CAPE TRIBULATION

40 km N of Mossman. This is a spectacularly beautiful stretch of mountainous coast, where the rainforest runs down to the sea. Until recently it was home only to colourful but distinctly backward tribespeople who showed no sign of being able to cope with the 20thC.

These primitive folk dealt in beads, played their own music, and suffered from all the rigours of a paradisiacal existence in the steamy scratchy tropics. Today there are only a few hippies left here – in fact they are almost a protected species.

The region is crossed by unsurfaced roads and tracks, which are well worth exploring. There are also some superb (and not always strenuous) walks through the rainforest – which has been growing uninterrupted in this region for more than 120 million years. These are signposted off the main track. The best is the one to the Cape itself.

The Cape and surrounding area is part of the **Cape Tribulation National Park**. This is entered along the Bloomfield Track, which leads off the Mossman-Daintree road north of Mossman. The region is renowned for its rare and exotic wildlife.

COOKTOWN ⚓

On the coast 200 km N of Cairns.

In 1770 Captain Cook's ship Endeavour came to grief on nearby Cape Tribulation (which might have been called something different if the crew had named it). Cook managed to sail his ship on as far as Cooktown, where he beached it for repairs.

Cook and his expedition were to remain here from June until August 1770. At the time it was the first British settlement on the continent of Australia, and certainly the loneliest European-inhabited spot on earth.

At one point during his stay, Captain Cook asked a local Aborigine the name of a strange long-legged beast which was hopping about in the undergrowth. The Aborigine replied laconically: 'I don't know' – which in the local Aborigine tongue was 'kangaroo'. Or so the story goes. Cook and his men found the Aborigines and their way of life utterly incomprehensible. According to Cook: 'They seemed to set no value on anything we gave them.'

In the light of Cooktown's later history, this is not difficult to understand. For a century after Cook's visit the place remained deserted – apart from the local 'I don't knows' and 'We don't cares.' Then in 1873 gold was discovered in the hinterland 150 km to the south-west, at Palmer River. Cooktown quickly became a gold-rush port, attracting thousands of prospectors – especially from China. Within a year it was the second largest town in Queensland, with a population of more than 30,000. The main activities of this population can be judged from the fact that Cooktown at this time had almost 100 pubs and nearly as many bordellos. Riots became a regular feature, usually as a result of racial bigotry. (All comers vs. the Chinese.) But all good things must one day come to an end: the gold rush petered out within ten years, and everyone left to riot elsewhere.

For the next 100 years nothing happened. Which was very lucky, because at one point the British authorities became convinced that the Russians were going to invade this part of northern Australia. The military took immediate measures to counter this dire threat. An officer in charge of a cannon and three cannon balls was despatched to Cooktown to repulse any invasion force. (This formidable defensive weaponry can still be seen on the front at Endeavour Park – where it might well be a match for the present Russian army.)

Today, the population of Cooktown is less than 1,500, there are only three pubs, no sign that I could detect of any Chinese bordellos, and no one can remember when they last had a proper riot. (Though during the **Discovery Festival**, which is held every June, they stage something pretty similar in the Bottom Pub on Charlotte Street.)

There are a number of low-key sights well worth a visit. The **James Cook Historical Museum** (*open* 10 *am to* 4 *pm daily, entry* A$4) is on the corner of Furneaux Street and Helen Street. This has plenty of bits and pieces from the brief interesting periods in Cooktown's history – including some fascinating remnants from Captain Cook's visit. The nearby **Maritime Museum** is frankly a bit of a disappointment, especially when you consider how many great wrecks there have been along this stretch of coast over the years. (Apparently all the best bits have been pinched by larger museums, so it's not really their fault.)

If you want a fine view, you can always climb up to the **Grassy Hill Lighthouse**, which is on the hill a kilometre or so north of the town centre.

The **Cemetery**, at the other end of

town on McIvor River – Cooktown Road, is a gem. This has the grave of Mary Watson (see Lizard Island, below) and a shrine dating from the old Chinatown days. It also has the tomb of a mysterious woman, apparently of northern European stock, who was found in the late 19thC living quite happily amongst a remote Aborigine tribe on Cape York peninsula. It's thought she might have been a child who had survived a shipwreck and been adopted by the natives. Inevitably, some busybodies decided to rescue her 'for her own good'. But the return to civilization proved so distressing that she died within a year.

LAKEFIELD NATIONAL PARK
80 km NW of Cooktown. From Cooktown you can detour off the main Peninsula Development Road through this national park. It's 150 km before you emerge at the other end, which gives you some idea of its size. This huge wilderness has some fine wetlands and is filled with wildlife of all kinds – from crocodiles to wild pigs. There are camping facilities only in the park, the best spot being at Horseshoe Lagoon.

LIZARD ISLAND
Off the coast 150 km N of Cooktown. Some time in the 1870s Robert Watson and his wife Mary settled on this deserted island. In October 1881, while Robert was out fishing, the island was attacked by Aborigines. Mary Watson, her baby and her Chinese servant, managed to flee, taking to sea in an empty water tank. They attempted to reach the mainland, but were blown off course and only made it as far as a remote island to the north, where they died of thirst. During her ordeal, Mary Watson kept a diary in which she described, in simple everyday terms, the horrendous events which led to her death.

Nowadays, Lizard Island is home to an exclusive resort (said to be popular with detoxed celebs recuperating from a spell in the Betty Ford Clinic). It also has a campsite. The beaches here are amongst the best you'll find off the Queensland coast, and there's great diving on the nearby reef. You can still see the remains of Mary Watson's cottage, and it's possible to climb to the island's highest point, Cook's Look. It was from here that Captain Cook scoured the sea in search of a break in

• *Four-mile beach, near Port Douglas.*

the Great Barrier Reef so that he could reach the open ocean.

MOSSMAN ✕
On the coast, 90 km N of Cairns. Small sleepy town in the sugar-cane region. The only point of interest is the Mossman Gorge 4 km inland, which has some great swimming holes amongst the rapids. There's also a 3.5-km 'Aborigine' walk which takes you through the rainforest past an Aborigine settlement.

PORT DOUGLAS ✕
On the coast 80 km N of Cairns. One of the oldest ports on the coast, which never really made it and lapsed into obscurity for a century or so. Then in the 1980s it suffered from large-scale luxury development. Now it's an odd mix of its old somnolent self (complete with Shipwreck Museum) and a haven for the super-rich (boutiques, expensive resorts and helipad). Curiously, this fragile mix still seems to work and the place is delightful.

PUNSAND BAY
See Recommended Hotels, Cape York, this page.

• *Opposite: Mossman Gorge.*

RECOMMENDED HOTELS

CAPE YORK
Punsand Bay Private Reserve, **$-$$**; *30 km by road from Cape York; tel.* (070) 69 1722; *cards none.*
Literally, the last resort: cabins and permanent tents, with fairly basic facilities. But the beach is fabulous, and the camaraderie amongst those who've made it so far is all you'd expect. An Irish pal of mine still gets Christmas cards from a Sydney mechanic whom he only met here for a day more than ten years ago.

COOKTOWN
Sovereign Hotel, $$; *Charlotte Street, Cooktown; tel.* (070) 69 5400; *cards* AE, MC, V.
Delightful old hotel in the centre of town. Has a pool, and the best bar in town – the famous Bottom Pub.

RECOMMENDED RESTAURANTS

PORT DOUGLAS
Nautilus Restaurant, $-$$; *17 Murphy Street, Port Douglas; tel.* (070) 99 5300; *all major cards.*
The imaginative menu includes some superb Asiatic seafood dishes. Dine out on the terrace under the palm trees. Dinner only.

MOSSMAN
Silly Oaks Lodge and Restaurant, $$; *Finlayvale Road, Mossman Gorge; tel.* (070) 98 1666; *all major cards.*
Here you dine out beneath the stars, overlooking the gorge. Interesting seafood menu, with a tropical slant. The Lodge itself has accommodation in the **$$$** bracket, and a superb rock pool.

Esperance and the Eyre Peninsula

1,620 km; map Nelles Australia, 1:400,000

The Eyre Highway, which skirts the Great Australian Bight, is the main artery of this section. It runs 1,620 km from Port Augusta to Norseman along the edges of the Nullarbor Plain, the wilderness which received its smart Latin-based name, meaning 'no trees', from the first Victorian classics scholars who arrived here. Nowadays, the Nullarbor Plain does in fact have a few trees, though only alongside the road.

First main stop after Kalgoorlie-Boulder is another old gold-mining town, Norseman. Here you can take a detour south to Esperance on the coast. This has some great nearby scenery and beaches, as well as the Recherche Archipelago.

Crossing the Nullarbor Plain you run by the coast after Eucla. Here you can see the spectacular Cliffs of Nullabor, which stretch for hundreds of kilometres along this remote coastline.

Before you reach Port Augusta you come to the Eyre Peninsula, whose small resorts and fine coastal scenery are well worth a detour.

There's no getting away from the fact that this one is a long haul (although that's probably the reason why you chose it in the first place). It can be done in three days, but if you want to explore, allow at least a week.

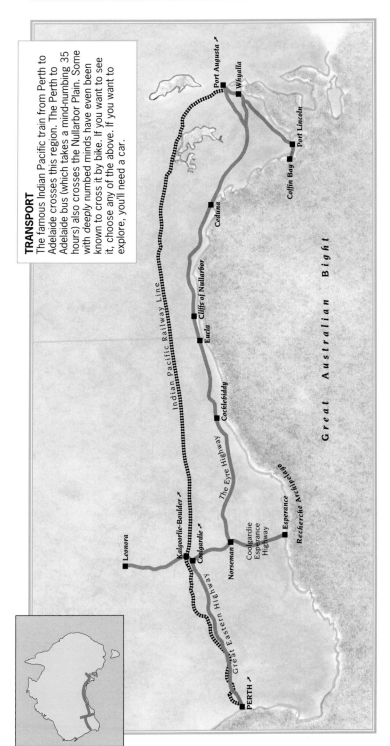

TRANSPORT

The famous Indian Pacific train from Perth to Adelaide crosses this region. The Perth to Adelaide bus (which takes a mind-numbing 35 hours) also crosses the Nullarbor Plain. Some with *deeply numbed minds* have even been known to cross it by bike. If you want to see it, choose any of the above. If you want to explore, you'll need a car.

Great Australian Bight

Port Augusta
Whyalla
Port Lincoln
Coffin Bay
Ceduna
Cliffs of Nullarbor
Eucla
Cocklebiddy
Esperance
Recherche Archipelago
Leonora
Kalgoorlie-Boulder
Coolgardie
Norseman
Coolgardie Esperance Highway
The Eyre Highway
Indian Pacific Railway Line
Great Eastern Highway
PERTH

• *Pelican in flight.*

SIGHTS & PLACES OF INTEREST

CEDUNA

490 *km* E *of Eucla*. This spot marks the end of the long eastward haul across the edge of the Nullarbor Plain. Astonishingly, there's been a settlement in this region since as early as the 1850s, when a whaling station was set up on St Peter Island at the end of Denial Bay. Nowadays, it's a pleasant, sleepy little seaside town with a population of less than 3,000. Nearby there are several swimming coves worth sampling.

Incidentally, 90 km west of here, down on the coast from Penong, is one of the best-kept secrets in the land: **Cactus Beach**. Those hardened surfheads who know such things reckon it has some of the finest wave-riding in Australia.

COCKLEBIDDY

420 *km* E *of Norseman on the Eyre High-way*. This unassuming little settlement in the middle of nowhere has made it into the *Guinness Book of Records*. The Nullarbor Plain has a number of caves near here, the most extensive of which is **Cocklebiddy Cave**. A group of French and Belgian speleologists set the world record for the deepest descent below ground in this cave in 1983.

However, the main attraction hereabouts is the **Eyre Bird Observatory**, which is 50 km away to the south-east. (Continue east down Eyre Highway, then turn south at the sign.) This remote observatory has been set up in the old telegraph station (for many years Western Australia's only communications link with the rest of Australia).

The observatory looks down over sand dunes towards **Twilight Cove** and the sea. Here you can see a large variety of bird species, some which are now becoming increasingly rare. You can only visit this spot if you book ahead, but it's well worth it: $$, full board; tel. (090) 39 3450. They'll collect you from Cocklebiddy, or you'll need a 4WD. There are also some superb walks through the dunes and along the remote wave-pounded shoreline. Twilight in Twilight Cove is an experience you won't forget.

COFFIN BAY 🚤

380 km SW of Port Augusta at the end of the Eyre Peninsula. This tiny grim-sounding resort is in fact named after the American-born British admiral Sir Isaac Coffin, who died in 1839. The nearby cliffs

---

DETOUR – **ESPERANCE** 🚤 ✕
From Norseman you can head 200 km south down the Coolgardie – Esperance Highway to the coast of the Great Australian Bight at Esperance.

This remote spot began life in the 1890s as a port for the goldfields. Now it's a rather ordinary-looking small resort and fishing centre, with an unexpectedly pleasant climate. (The temperature seldom gets above 30°C.) The surrounding landscape is spectacular, with a number of national parks and some superb sandy **beaches**. But a word of warning if you're planning to explore more remote spots along the shoreline. This region is subject to the occasional king wave. These monsters come ashore without warning, and have been known to sweep away the unwary.

Offshore are the hundred or so islands of the **Recherche Archipelago.** In the blue waters around these rocky outcrops, you can see seals, dolphins and migrating whales. The islands are inhabited only by goats, except for **Woody Island**, which is a wildlife sanctuary and can be reached by tugboat cruises. Contact Menzies Marine, tel. (090) 71 1772.

• At *anchor, off Esperance.*

and dune-lined coast have some spectacular beaches and scenery, especially out along the peninsula. This is best explored by 4WD.

COOLGARDIE

See Australia Overall: 10, page 164.

EUCLA 🚤

700 km W of Norseman on the Eyrie Highway. A lonely spot just 12 km from the border with South Australia. The original coastal settlement has been engulfed by sand dunes, and all you can see are its chimneys and the old jetty. The dunes are a fine sight. Nearby is the derelict **Old Telegraph Station,** which was set up in 1877. Other sights include the **Koonalda Cave,** dangerous unless you are a knowledgeable caver; a **concrete sperm whale**; and the famous **sign** which indicates the awesome distances to other (more or less) civilized spots on the globe – a time-honoured photo opportunity.

West of here along the highway are the spectacular **Nullarbor Cliffs**, mile upon mile of one of the world's most desolate coastlines.

KALGOORLIE-BOULDER

See Australia Overall: 10, page 164.

NORSEMAN ⊯

150 km S of Kalgoorlie. If you're heading west across Australia, this is where you pick up your certificate to prove you've crossed the Eyre Highway (available from the Tourist Office at 68 Roberts Street). This settlement, with a population of just 1,500, was named after a prospector's horse, whose statue now stands on Roberts Street. Why all the fuss? Norseman's hoof stumbled on a gold nugget here in 1894. All you'll probably want to see is the swimming pool, which is right by the tourist office.

PERTH

See Australia Overall: 11, page 166.

PORT AUGUSTA

See Local Explorations: 5, page 120.

PORT LINCOLN ⊯ ✕

350 km SW of Port Augusta at the end of the Eyre Peninsula. This is the main tuna fishing centre in Australia, and the largest town on the Eyre Peninsula, with a permanent population of around

---

DETOUR – LEONORA

240 km N of Kalgoorlie. This is a ride down a metalled road into a part of the outback that isn't much visited by tourists. The main sights of interest here are the ghost towns left over from the gold-rush days.

The nearest ghost town to Kalgoorlie is **Kanowna**. This is, in fact, off the route to Leonora, 20 km up the track road that leads north-east from Kalgoorlie-Boulder. It's an eerie spot. At the turn of the century more than 10,000 people lived here, there were over two dozen bars and a dozen trains a day used to call in from Kalgoorlie. Three Irish brothers made it so rich here that they founded a shipping line. Now there's nothing standing but the abandoned railway station, overlooking a heap of rubble. (There's so little building material in this part of the outback that many ghost towns are quickly pillaged of anything that might be of use.)

The road to Leonora itself leads north from Kalgoorlie-Boulder. Around 30 km down the road you come to a nowheresville called **Broad Arrow**. This now has a population of just over a dozen. In the old goldfield days, 2,500 people made a living here. Nowadays, the most hectic scenes are at the local pub when the lads from Kalgoorlie come up on a weekend spree.

Another 25 km down the road you come to **Ora Banda**, which is in much the same state. In a further 70 km you arrive at **Menzies**, where the population reaches into three

figures (just), though it's difficult to tell this at high noon. Here, quite a few structures remain from the old days, when the local population ran to more than 5,000. These buildings include the **Town Hall** with its famous clockless clock tower. Time doesn't just stand still in Menzies, it isn't here at all. Apparently they ordered one from England around the turn of the century, but the ship bringing it to Australia went down in a storm off the Cape of Good Hope. So they ordered another one, but by the time it arrived in Australia the gold had run out, so they couldn't afford to ship it from Perth.

According to a knowledgeable old local, it ended up being used at the Perth's main cricket ground for many years, but this information was greeted with a variety of sceptical noises by his colleagues.

Up the road, **Leonora** is a small mining town with a population of more than 1,000. However, the adjacent settlement of **Gwalia** is now a ghost town. For years the gold mine here was the largest in Western Australia outside Kalgoorlie. For a brief period at the turn of the 19thC it was run by the young Herbert Hoover, who 30 years later became the 31st president of the United States. The mine didn't eventually close down until 1963. (Though there are plans to reopen it, now that the price of gold has risen.) The old mine office houses a museum which has some particularly interesting exhibits.

13,000. The start of the tuna fishing season in January is marked with a wild **Tunarama Festival**, which attracts revellers from as far away as Adelaide. There are a number of old buildings, including **Mill Cottage** which dates from 1866, and a **Maritime Museum**.

Try a cruise 15 km offshore to **Dangerous Reef** which is a haunt of the notorious great white shark. They even organize diving trips, complete with cages to protect these sharks from the lunatics who are willing to swim with them.

Cape Carnot, to the south-west, has some spectacular scenery where the ocean rollers explode through a number of blowholes.

WHYALLA ✕

77 km S of Port Augusta on the Spencer Gulf. This busy steel port is the second biggest town in South Australia, with a population of more than 25,000. If you like steel works (*tours 9.30, Mon, Wed, Sat*), watching bulk carriers and tankers (they also have a thriving gas refinery), and shipping monuments (the

---

THE EYRE HIGHWAY

The Eyre Highway is named after the explorer John Eyre who made the first crossing of southern Australia in 1841. It took him five gruelling months. His partner Baxter was killed by their Aborigine guides, but other Aborigines later led him to a spring which saved his life. Despite this, Eyre wouldn't have survived if he hadn't been lucky enough to come across a French whaling ship in Rossiter Bay. They gave him provisions which enabled him to make it as far as Albany.

---

minesweeper *Whyalla* is the town mascot), then this is the place for you. I enjoyed it, apart from the smog cloud of red dust. I had my last swim at a pleasant local beach here before starting the long drive west down the Eyre Highway, across the Nullarbor Plain: it was particularly pleasant in retrospect, after a thousand or so kilometres.

RECOMMENDED HOTELS

The Eyre Highway across the Nullarbor Plain has regular motels *vast* distances apart, so be sure to plan your journey accordingly. Most offer fairly standard accommodation and have a restaurant where you can eat your heart out over the fact that you set out on this endless wilderness treck.

COFFIN BAY
Coffin Bay Hotel, $-$$; *Coffin Bay; tel.* (086) 85 4111; *cards none.*
Standard accommodation. Be sure to ring ahead during the season.

ESPERANCE
Pink Lake Lodge, $-$$; 85 *Pink Lake Road; tel.* (090) 71 2075; *cards none.*
Standard accommodation, but recommendable.

EUCLA
Amber Motel, $-$$; *Eucla; tel.* (090) 39 3468; *cards none.*
A useful base for exploring the

nearby Cliffs of Nullarbor.

NORSEMAN
Norseman Eyre Motel, $$; *Princep Street; tel.* (090) 39 1130; *cards none.*
Also has a reasonable restaurant.

PORT LINCOLN
Pier Hotel, $; 3 *Tasman Terrace;* (086) 82 1322; *cards none.*
Friendly welcome.

RECOMMENDED RESTAURANTS

ESPERANCE
Peaches Restaurant, $$: 32 *The Esplanade; tel.* (090) 71 3999; *cards none.*
Best for the price in town, with a romantic view.

PORT LINCOLN
Bugs Restaurant, $-$$, *Eyre Street; no booking; cards none.*
Friendly spot; local seafood.

WHYALLA
Spagg's, $-$$; 83 *Essington Lewis Ave; tel.* (086) 45 2088; *cards none.*
Italian cooking with gusto.

Western Australia

South of Perth

400 km; map Nelles Australia 1:400,000

This region used to be Western Australia's best-kept secret. Now the secret is out, and many consider it to be one of the most picturesque regions in the entire continent.

Here there's something for all tastes. The coastline is spectacular, and has beaches which are great for surfing, as well as sheltered sandy coves which are ideal for children. Inland there are some of the classiest vineyards in Australia, producing quality rather than quantity. Margaret River County is a favourite region with Perth's 'mappies' (middle-aged professionals), and the wineries here are now complemented by a liberal sprinkling of gourmet restaurants. Those who fancy something more energetic will want to explore the famous local caves. These extend for miles, some with subterranean lakes and other interesting features.

But the main sight in the region is undoubtedly the historic town of Albany. This was the earliest European settlement in Western Australia, and still retains a distinct atmosphere of its own. Albany is set on a hillside overlooking a protected sound which is larger than Sydney Harbour.

You can see this entire region easily in two or three days, but it's worth allowing double this if you want to sample the sights (and the wine) at your leisure.

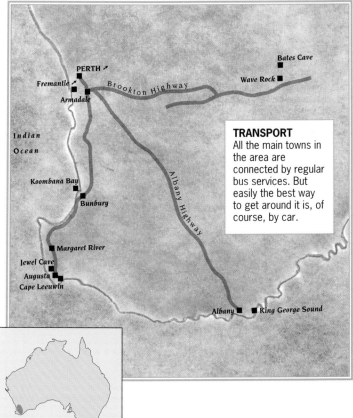

PERTH

Fremantle

Armadale

Brookton Highway

Bates Cave

Wave Rock

Indian Ocean

Koombana Bay

Bunbury

Albany Highway

Margaret River

Jewel Cave

Augusta

Cape Leeuwin

Albany   King George Sound

TRANSPORT
All the main towns in the area are connected by regular bus services. But easily the best way to get around it is, of course, by car.

• *Spectacular rock formations like this bridge adorn the coastline on either side of Albany.*

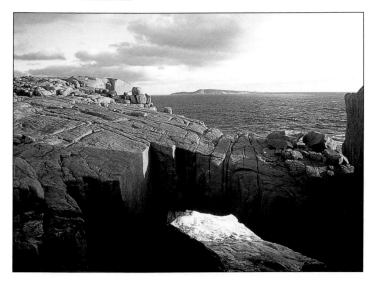

247

SIGHTS & PLACES OF INTEREST

ALBANY ⌀ ✕

On the S coast, 430 km SE of Perth. This is the oldest town in Western Australia. As early as 1791, the British captain George Vancouver anchored in the **King George Sound** (off the present site of Albany), noting that this formed an even larger protected anchorage than Sydney Harbour. But it wasn't until 1826 that the British decided to establish the first European settlement here, to forestall a rumoured French move into the region. On Christmas Day, the barque *Amity* arrived from Sydney with 45 soldiers under the command of Major Lockyer. The settlement was originally called Frederickstown, after one of King George IV's sons. Later, its excellent harbour and strategic position ensured that it became an important port. The Antarctic whaling fleets put in here, and when the age of steam arrived it became an important bunkering port. This was the last point where ships could take on coal before their long voyage across the Indian Ocean to India, on the way back to Europe.

Despite this, Albany grew slowly. As a result, much of its historical character and many of its old buildings have been preserved. To this day, the port only has a population of 20,000. (Compare this with Perth, which was founded three years later, has no real harbour, and yet now has a population of well over a million.)

Albany has a delightful setting, on hillsides overlooking the wide sweep of King George Sound, and there's much to see here.

For the best views, head west of the town centre along Marine Drive, and turn up Apex Drive to **Mount Clarence**. Here you can look out to sea along the coast, and on a fine day you can see as far inland as the peaks of the Stirling Range, which rise to 300 m, over 70 km away. At the top of Mount Clarence is the **Desert Mounted Corps Memorial**. This commemorates the Australians and New Zealanders who gave their lives fighting in the Middle East in the First World War. The original of this bronze memorial was erected in 1932 in Port Said at the entrance to the Suez Canal in Egypt. This was destroyed during the 1956 Suez Crisis, and the memorial here is a recast version. (Only the damaged horse's head was rescued from the original, and this is now on show in the Albany Residence Museum, (see below). The siting of this memorial is particularly apt, as this was the last point in Australia seen by those who set off to fight.

There's another fine view over the harbour from the top of **Mount Melville**, which rises to the west of the town centre. Between July and September you can sometimes see migrating whales spouting out in the sound. At this time of year they also run boat trips to see the whales in the nearby bays. Contact Southern Ocean Charters, tel. (098) 41 7176.

The oldest building in Albany is **Patrick Taylor Cottage** in Duke Street, which dates from 1832. This is now a folk museum, crammed with all kinds of old relics – some of which are intriguing, and some of which should have been thrown away long ago. Another so-called folk museum is housed nearby in the **Old Gaol**, which housed its first guests in 1851. In the old days entry was free, but it now costs you A$2. (But unlike the old days, this also includes an exit ticket.) From here the convicts used to be hired out as virtual slaves to work for nearby landowners.

The highlight of this historic town is undoubtedly the **Albany Residence Museum**, which has some really interesting exhibits from the early maritime days. Alternative-medicine addicts should be sure to see the display devoted to bush medicines used by the Aborigines. (It's often forgotten that the Aborigines were living here long before any of the Europeans turned up. Indeed, their settlement at Oyster Bay is said to be one of the oldest in the region.)

Internet freaks will wish to go and jeer at the **Inter Colonial Communications Museum**, which is housed in the refurbished **Old Post Office**. This contains much steam-age communications bric-a-brac: one day soon the internet and all its attendant paraphernalia will appear much like this.

The coastline on either side of Albany is some of the most spectacular in Australia, with all kinds of exotic natural features – including rock bridges, blowholes and even the occasional beach without a surfer in sight. At **Frenchman's Bay**, the former whaling station has now been transformed into a **whaling museum.**

ARMADALE
Inland on the South Western Highway 30 km S of Perth. Famous as the home of **Pioneer World**, which is a mock-up of a 19thC Australian pioneer village, filled with various mock-up characters. After visiting such a spot, the suspicion grows that some of the real old gold prospectors and the like were equally clichéd characters.

AUGUSTA
On the coast at the SW tip of Australia, 300 km S of Perth. This pleasant small town overlooks the mouth of the Blackwater River. Unexpectedly, this is the third oldest settlement in the whole of Western Australia (after Albany and Perth). There's a small local **museum** (*open 10 am to 1 pm daily, entry A$1*), which has a few interesting bits and pieces.

But there are two much more interesting sights nearby. Some 10 km north-east of here is **Jewel Cave**, which is probably the most exciting of all the many caves in the region. This is renowned for its exquisite helictites. There is a two-hour tour, not for the faint-hearted.

The other point of interest is 10 km south of town: wild and windy **Cape Leeuwin**, the end of this end of Australia. South of here there's nothing between you and the Antarctic 5,000 km away, though it can feel closer on a stormy winter's day. And westwards, there's nothing but 9,000 km of empty Indian Ocean between you and the Cape of Good Hope.

To experience these geographical niceties to the full, you can climb to the top of the **lighthouse** (*open 9 am to 3 pm daily, entry A$3*). Nearby there's also an old waterwheel which is encrusted in salt.

Other intriguing facts: the Dutch were the first to put this stretch of coastline on the map in the early 17thC. The cape itself was named by a Dutch sea captain after his ship ('Leeuwin' means lioness in Dutch). It was from precisely this point in 1851 that Flinders began his mammoth task of mapping the coast of Australia. In 1989

a Perth-based American scientist tested his newly invented laser telescope here. Its beam curved with the surface of the earth so that he could see (and photograph) Antarctica. After patenting this amazing invention, and securing a large grant from the US military for its development, he went missing.

BATES CAVE
See Wave Rock, page 251.

BUNBURY
On the Indian Ocean 170 km S of Perth. Bunbury is the second largest town in Western Australia, but easily the most boring. Head out for the nearby beaches, which are good – especially **Koombana Beach**, where you can often meet friendly dolphins.

CAPE LEEUWIN
See Augusta, this page.

FREMANTLE
See Australia Overall: 11, page 170.

JEWEL CAVE
See Augusta, this page.

KING GEORGE SOUND
See Albany, page 248.

KOOMBANA BAY
See Bunbury, above.

OZKIMO NELL?
During the First World War, the troopships carrying Australian and New Zealand infantrymen to Egypt assembled off the port of Albany. Many of these troops were to die at Gallipoli, and this remote spot was the last they saw of Australia. The same process was repeated a quarter of a century later when the Anzacs (Australia and New Zealand Army Corps) set off to fight against Rommel in the North African desert. According to an aged Aussie war veteran I met at a friend's home in Adelaide, the Anzacs used to sing a long song about the amazing exploits of 'Albany Aggie', whose physical properties rivalled those of the legendary Eskimo Nell.

MARGARET RIVER ⇔ ✕

Inland 100 km S of Bunbury. When you've made your pile in Perth, this is where you retire to live the good life. Margaret River, and the surrounding eponymous county, is a pleasant well-heeled region with plenty of fine wineries, gourmet resturants, some great coastal scenery, a combination of fine surfing and near-by safe sandcastle-building beaches, and some interesting caves. The town prides itself on being something of a cultural centre. Much of this is rather more crafty than arty, but the **Margaret River Pottery** is worth a visit.

A spot that undeniably lives up to its enormous reputation is the **Leeuwin Estate**, which many consider the finest and most picturesque winery in the entire country. This is south-west of town, well signposted off Caves Road at Gnaraway Road. Here they even have a recommendable restaurant, **$$**; tel. (097) 57 6253, so you can try out their wine in ideal circumstances.

About 35 km north of Margaret River at Dunsborough, there's the excellent **Happ's Vineyard**, which is renowned for producing some of the best red wines in the region. Just south-west of here are the **Yallingup Caves.** However, the other worthwhile caves are all towards the coast just south-east of Margaret River. Look out for **Mammoth Cave**, mammoth-sized with mammoth bones, and **Lake Cave**, where a curious formation hangs suspended above the subterranean lake.

PERTH

See Australia Overall: 11.

WAVE ROCK

About 340 km E of Perth outside the small settlement of Hyden. It's a long way to go, but this is probably the most original natural phenomenon in the state. Imagine a tidal wave, petrified just as it's about to break over land. This granite tidal wave is 15 m high and well over 100 m long. The rock has vertical streaking, caused by rain water, which adds eerily to the wave effect. It's a great photo opportunity, and because of its remoteness attracts fewer visitors than one might expect. There are other odd rock formations in the area, such as **Hippo's Yawn**, a short kilome-

tre trek away. Down the road at **Mulka's Cave** and **Bates Cave** there are Aborigine wall paintings.

RECOMMENDED HOTELS

ALBANY
Middleton Beach Guesthouse, $$; *Adelaide Crescent, Middleton Beach; tel.* (098) 41 1295; *cards none.*
Pleasant bed-and-breakfast spot down by the main beach.

MARGARET RIVER
1885 Inn, $$; *Farrelly Street; tel.* (097) 57 3177; *all major cards.*
Historic house with atmospheric interior decoration, and paradise gardens. The restaurant here is wildly expensive, but worth it: haute cuisine and stupendous wine list (**$$$**; *same tel.*)

RECOMMENDED RESTAURANTS

ALBANY
Kooka's, $$; *204 Stirling Terrace; tel.* (098) 41 5889; *all major cards.*
Kitsch paradise on a kookaburra theme in a historic cottage. Imaginative menu with superb fresh seafood. Bring your own bottle.

Earl of Spencer, $; *Earl Street at corner of Spencer Street; tel.* (098) 41 1322; *all major cards.*
Pub in 1870s house which looks down the hill over the harbour: beer, steaks and pleasant company.

MARGARET RIVER
See Recommended Hotels, above, for the best food in town at **$$$** prices. For more modest fare, try:

Margaret River Marron Farm, $-$$; *Wickham Road,* 10 *km S of town; tel.* (097) 57 6329; *cards none; open* 10 *am to* 4 *pm only.*
Marron are local freshwater crustaceans, and the house speciality. You can also tour the farm and have a swim.

• *Opposite: Wave Rock.*

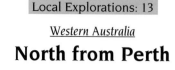

<u>Western Australia</u>

North from Perth

900 km; map Nelles Australia 1:400,000

This section covers the first leg of the 4,500-km-long haul around the coast of Western Australia from Perth to Darwin.

Between Perth and Carnarvon is the Brand Highway, and after Gerald-ton the North West Coastal Highway. These are both sealed all the way.

Although you pass through mile after mile of monotonous outback, there are also a number of spectacular sights en route, and off the high-way. Experiencing the weird wonder of the Pinnacles Desert, walking through the gorges of the Kalbarri National Park and mingling with the dol-phins at Shark Bay are undoubtedly the main attractions of this region. But there are many more – including a 150-year-old Benedictine monastery, some of the most forbidding and remote islands in the world, and a muse-um filled with fascinating relics from centuries-old wrecks. The scant his-tory of this notorious coast is filled with romance and skulduggery, and some of the wrecks have extraordinary tales to tell.

The stretch between Perth and Carnarvon is around 900 km long, and you should allow a week to cover it if you want to see some of the sights.

Warning: before setting out to drive this section, especially if you plan leaving the highway, be sure to read the information on page 23 about car hire and driving on remote and rough outback tracks.

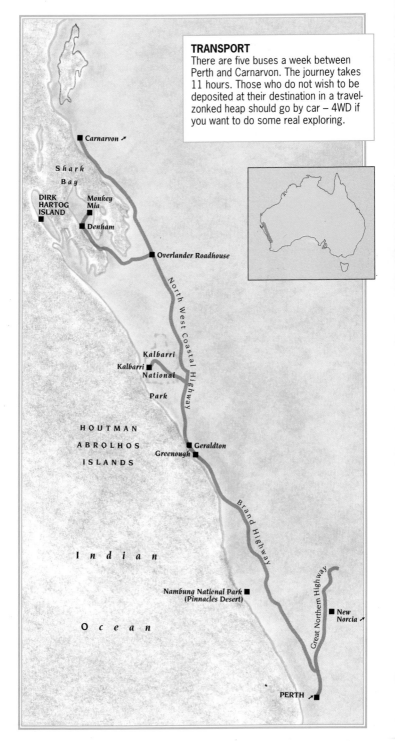

TRANSPORT

There are five buses a week between Perth and Carnarvon. The journey takes 11 hours. Those who do not wish to be deposited at their destination in a travel-zonked heap should go by car – 4WD if you want to do some real exploring.

Carnarvon

Shark Bay

DIRK HARTOG ISLAND

Monkey Mia

Denham

Overlander Roadhouse

North West Coastal Highway

Kalbarri

Kalbarri National Park

HOUTMAN ABROLHOS ISLANDS

Geraldton

Greenough

Brand Highway

I n d i a n

Nambung National Park (Pinnacles Desert)

Great Northern Highway

New Norcia

O c e a n

PERTH

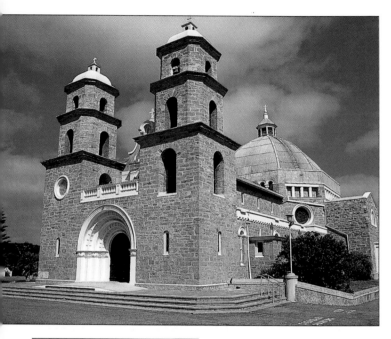

• *St Francis Xavier Cathedral, Geraldton.*

SIGHTS & PLACES OF INTEREST

CARNARVON
See Local Explorations: 14, page 260.

DENHAM AND DIRK HARTOG ISLAND
See Shark Bay, page 256.

GERALDTON 🛏 ✕
420 km N of Perth on the Brand Highway.
This locality has a superb all-year-round climate, miles of fine beaches and some picturesque countryside. In the midst of it all, Geraldton comes as something of a disappointment, with its mundane port and wheat silos. Even the brochure writers are left rather at a loss. ('This thriving centre is the third largest town in Western Australia, with a population of 20,000.') Yet there are a couple of things worth seeing. The architectural glory of Geraldton is the neo-Byzantine St Francis Xavier Cathedral. The interior is an unusual blend of Romanesque and Byzantine – bold and imaginative, or stylized and unoriginal – depending on your taste. The cathedral was completed in 1938, and is the work of Monsignor John Hawes, who spent 25 years on the project. Hawes was an unusual man. He had been an architect before joining the priesthood, and was responsible for the design of several distinctive buildings hereabouts. After he had finally completed his cathedral masterpiece, he left for the Caribbean, where he lived out his days in solitude on a remote island. Even more interesting is the **Maritime Museum** (*open 10 am to 5 pm Mon to Sat, Sun afternoons only, entry free*). This features fascinating relics from a number of old ships which have been wrecked along the coast – including the *Batavia* (see box: Houtman Abrolhos Islands, page 256) and the *Zuytdorp* (see box: A Mystery Solved, page 256).

GREENOUGH
20 km S of Geraldton on Brand Highway.
The big attraction of this small farming community is the **Greenough Historical Hamlet** (*open 9.30 am to 4.30 pm, entry A$2.50*). This consists of a dozen or so buildings which have been restored to their original 19thC splendour (or primitiveness, depending upon your taste). Either way, it's original. This was how they lived in those hard-bitten pioneering days, when the flies outnumbered the humans by a million to one and you couldn't get a bath for love

or money. Gaze and wonder (no need to sentimentalize). And be sure to marvel at the leaning trees up the road – bent by the unending wind – the only thing which kept the flies at bay.

KALBARRI 🛏 ✕

170 km N of Geraldton, on the coast off North West Coastal Highway. Kalbarri is a quiet little resort town with a permanent population of less than 2,000. It has a pleasant protected beach by the mouth of the Murchison River, almost 70 km west off the highway.

Not much happens here, apart from the daily feeding of the pelicans at the local **Fantasyland**; but all around is some of the finest scenery in Western Australia. This is in the Kalbarri National Park, which stretches for scores of miles over the surrounding hinterland. The main landmark here is **Red Bluff**, home of the first two European residents in Australia (see box: Houtman Abrolhos Islands, page 256). A number of unsealed roads run through the park. Also worth a visit are **Rainbow Valley** and **Mushroom Rock**. Off these, trails run through the spectacular gorges and valleys, and you can explore the long and desolate coastline, home to a wide variety of birdlife – as well as some curious wild pigs and some equally curious surfers.

At the Tourist Information Centre on Grey Street you can find details of organized tours in the National Park, as well as walks and helicopter trips.

MONKEY MIA

See Shark Bay, page 256.

NAMBUNG NATIONAL PARK (PINNACLES DESERT)

245 km N of Perth at Cervantes, which is on the coast 50 km E off Brand Highway; entry A$3. The main thing to see here is the **Pinnacles Desert**, which is in the heart of the park. This consists of curious limestone columns which appear to sprout up out of the sand. And oddly, once upon a time they really did sprout. These are in fact the ancient roots of extinct plants which flourished along this coast 30,000 years ago when it was a jungle.

The plants died, and the dead roots fossilized, gradually becoming exposed over thousands of years by the prevailing south-westerly winds. When the first Dutch explorers spotted the Pinnacles as they sailed past, they thought these were the remains of an ancient city. For years it was marked on some ancient maps as such, prompting the German philosopher Leibnitz to speculate that the Chinese may once have colonized this part of Australia.

This spot is popular with day-trippers from Perth, who almost outnumber the columns on high days and holidays. Get here at dawn, when the fine wind-blown sand sometimes creates a mysterious mist, or at golden sunset when the long shadows give the place an eerie archa-

• *The Pinnacles.*

ic atmosphere. This was what the earth was like long before we arrived, and what Perth will probably look like long after we're gone. In spring, the desert becomes a mass of wildflowers. But be warned: the unsealed road is likely to flood after rain.

Along the coastal stretches of the park there are some fine walks over the dunes and the beach, which are home to a huge variety of migrating birdlife.

NEW NORCIA
See *Australia Overall: 11, page 172.*

PERTH
See *Australia Overall: 11, page 168.*

SHARK BAY ⚓ ✕
800 km N of Perth off North West Coastal Highway. Shark Bay is formed by two long spits of land jutting out from the coast. The island which extends beyond the western spit of land – **Dirk Hartog Island** – is the westernmost point in Australia. This is named after the Dutch explorer who landed here and nailed to a post a pewter plate inscribed 'Anno 1616', the first recorded instance of a European setting foot in Australia. (This plate was later pinched by another passing Dutch sailor, and is now on display in the Rijksmusem in Amsterdam – though you can see a replica in the Maritime Museum at Geraldton.)

The entire Shark Bay region is of such ecological importance that it has been designated as a World Heritage and Marine Park. Shark Bay itself is 100 km wide and 200 km long and the only sizeable settlement in the area is **Denham** (population 960), which is on the central spit which juts into the bay. To reach Denham you turn right off the North West Coastal Highway at Over-lander Roadhouse, and then follow the signs for around 130 km. Denham was once a pearl-fishing centre, but now relies on prawns and tourists. From Denham you can take a number of cruises out into the bay, whose glassy water teems with exotic flora and fauna, and whose beaches are a marvel in themselves.

Some 25 km north-east of Denham, on the other side of the peninsula, is **Monkey Mia**, the main tourist destination in Shark Bay. Around thirty years ago, the wife of a local fisherman befriended a bottle-nosed dolphin here,

HOUTMAN ABROLHOS ISLANDS
About 80 km off the coast at Geraldton lie the Houtman Abrolhos Islands. These are genuine desert islands – not your romantic blob of sand with a few sprouting palm trees, but over 50 km of forbidding reefs and barren rocks. And they have a history to match.

In 1629, the Dutch East Indiaman *Batavia* was heading up the coast en route from the Cape of Good Hope to Java. (No, they weren't off course: the expert navigators took the scenic route in those days.) Then the *Batavia* ran aground. The survivors set up camp on what was (and still is) one of the bleakest spots on earth, and despatched a small rescue cutter for Java (over 3,000 km distant). Miraculously, the cutter reached Java, and arrived back three months later with a rescue ship. But by this time the survivors had behaved as survivors often do under such circumstances. They'd mutinied and murdered more than a hundred of their fellow survivors. Civilization was soon restored by the rescuers. The leading mutineers were hanged, and a couple were lucky enough to be left behind on the deserted coast – where they doubtless pondered the error of their ways. Yet these two losers succeeded where many a gifted megalomaniac has failed. They entered the history books: these were the first two permanent European residents in Australia.

Nowadays, the Houtman Abrolhos Islands, of which there are more than 100, provide some of the finest diving on the west coast, with superb tropical fish and exotic reef plants. The islands are also home to many rare species of birds.

Weekend expeditions run from Geraldton, costing around A$250 per person. For details enquire at the Geraldton Tourist Office, which is in the Bill Sewell Complex on Chapman Road.

A MYSTERY SOLVED

In 1927 a stockman discovered a strange carved wooden structure on a cliff 65 km north of Kalbarri. Not until 30 years later was this structure identified as part of the stern from the *Zuytdorp*, a Dutch sailing ship which was known to have been wrecked somewhere along this coast in 1712. A search was made, but no human remains were found – although other evidence indicated that the shipwrecked crew had survived here for several years.

Only recently was this mystery solved. A doctor working amongst local Aborigine children noticed that some of them were suffering from an unusual inherited disorder resulting in defective development of the skin, hair and nails. He finally identified this as Ellis van Creveld Syndrome, a rare genetically inherited disease which had been prevalent in Holland around 300 years ago. The shipwrecked Dutch sailors had seemingly joined up with the local Aborigines, vanishing without trace apart from this curious genetic legacy.

and started feeding it titbits by hand. Dolphins may be intelligent animals, but they obviously can't keep a secret. Within no time, shoals of dolphins were turning up to be fed by hand. Over the years these clever creatures have managed to train human beings to feed them on a regular basis. The trained human beings are now given a uniform and called rangers. Despite gross over-exploitation of this custom (by both humans and dolphins alike), it's still quite a sight. The dolphins usually turn up around 10 am: they may be technically wild, but like any civilized creature they prefer a late breakfast. If you stand knee-deep in the water, a dolphin will occasionally rub up against you so that you can run your hand along its side. (For some, this generates an almost mystical experience; though anyone who has patted a horse may find such fishy contact rather commonplace.)

RECOMMENDED HOTELS

Despite its remoteness, the west coast attracts many visitors at the height of summer, so book ahead.

GERALDTON

Sun City Guest House, $; 184, *Marine Terrace; tel.* (099) 21 2205; *cards none.*

Cheap and cheerful bed-and-breakfast place in the heart of town and close to the sea.

Quality Inn Motel, $$-$$$; *Brand Highway; tel.* (099) 21 2455; *most major cards.*

On the highway at edge of town. Ideal for a rest after a long drive.

KALBARRI

Kalbarri Motor Hotel, $$; *Grey Street, Kalbarri; tel.* (099) 37 1000; *cards none.*

Standard motel accommodation in town centr, close to the ocean.

SHARK BAY

Shark Bay Hotel, $$; *at Denham; tel.* (099) 48 1203; *cards none.*

An established favourite; downstairs is a friendly local pub.

RECOMMENDED RESTAURANTS

GERALDTON

Fiddlers, $$; 103, *Marine Terrace; tel.* (099) 21 6644; *most major cards.*

Excellent value, superb seafood.

Golden Coins, $-$$; 198, *Marine Terrace; no booking; most major cards.*

Best Chinese in town.

KALBARRI

Finlay's Fish BBQ, $; *Magee Crescent, Kalbarri; tel.* (099) 37 1260; *cards none.*

Exceptionally friendly open-air barbecue. Evenings only.

SHARK BAY

Heritage Resort, $$; *Durlacher Street, Denham; tel.* (099) 48 1133; *cards none.*

Easily the best restaurant in town. Good steaks and seafood.

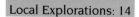

Western Australia

The Far North-West

1,500 km; map Nelles Austrlalia, 1:400,000 km

This section covers a vast territory: from Carnarvon to Broome the North West Coastal Highway runs for 1,500 kilometres. One thing you can be sure of: it's going to be hot. Inland, the summer temperatures can match those of the Sahara.

North of Carnarvon, off the North West Coastal Highway, lies North West Cape. The Ningaloo Reef here is Western Australia's answer to the Great Barrier Reef in Queensland – not so well known, but just as spectacular for diving.

East of here you come to the Pilbara, one of the richest iron-ore mining regions in the world. At places such as Tom Price they hack down entire mountains of the stuff, and load it on to trains for the coast. The mining towns and their ports, such as Port Hedland, are hardly beauty spots but the Pilbara also contains the spectacular gorges of the Karijini National Park. Hiking here beneath remote multicoloured cliffs, cooling off in rock pools with the cries of exotic birds calling through the trees, is for many one of Australia's major experiences.

East of the Pilbara lies Eighty Mile Beach, and beyond this the lively resort of Broome, with its historic Chinatown.

To travel through this region with only a few stops for sightseeing will take you a week. If you want to explore the region properly, going into the Pilbara, you should allow at least a fortnight.

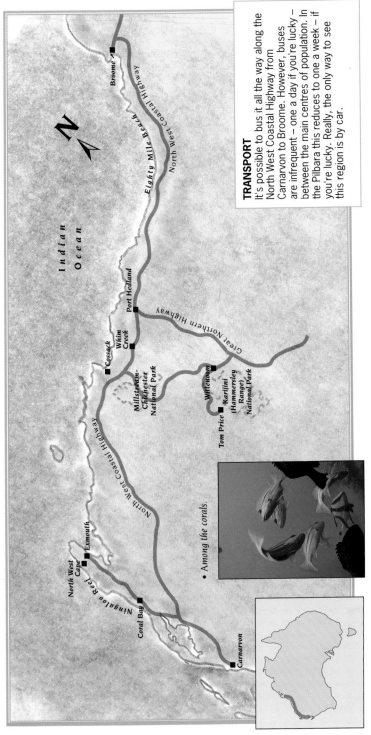

N

Indian Ocean

Broome

Eighty Mile Beach

North West Coastal Highway

Port Hedland

Whim Creek

Cossack

Great Northern Highway

Millstream-Chichester National Park

Wittenoom

Karijini (Hammersley Range) National Park

Tom Price

North West Coastal Highway

Exmouth

North West Cape

Ningaloo Reef

Coral Bay

Carnarvon

• *Among the corals.*

TRANSPORT

It's possible to bus it all the way along the North West Coastal Highway from Carnarvon to Broome. However, buses are infrequent – one a day if you're lucky – between the main centres of population. In the Pilbara this reduces to one a week – if you're lucky. Really, the only way to see this region is by car.

259

SIGHTS & PLACES OF INTEREST

BROOME
See Local Explorations: 15, page 266.

CARNARVON ⊨ ✕
On the coast 900 km N of Perth along the North West Coastal Highway. If you're travelling north from Perth, your arrival here brings you into tropical latitudes and tropical climate. In summer it can get as hot here as anywhere in Australia (and that's saying something). Just to add to the fun, they have the occasional cyclone and flash flood, too. Otherwise nothing much happens. Prawns, bananas and sheep are the main business here – but when you walk down the wide, empty main street you half expect to see John Wayne strolling towards you in a ten-gallon hat. (Carnarvon does have cowboys, but of a different sort: the itinerant labourers who do their best to drink the bars dry.)

A hundred years ago this was where the camel trains used to arrive from the interior, on the long trek from nowhere to nowhere. According to local lore, Robinson Street (the main drag) was built so wide to allow the camel trains to turn around – which sounds unlikely enough to be true.

The Carnarvon Tourist Centre is at the north-eastern end of Robinson Street. Here they'll tiredly try to interest you in something to see in Carnarvon. You can try a conducted tour of a local banana plantation, visit the nearby Bibbawarra Bore (thermal springs with water even hotter in than out), head off to the NASA Satellite Tracking Station (which went out of use 20 years ago), or you can admit defeat and just go and watch the fishermen on One Mile Jetty.

CORAL BAY
On the coast 200 km N of Carnarvon, off the road to Exmouth. Here you're in tropical beach territory, and this tiny resort is as idyllic as it sounds. Easily overrun in high summer, it's pleasantly quiet and warm for the rest of the year. A pleasant spot for diving on the **Ningaloo Reef** (see separate entry, opposite), glass bottom boat trips (contact The Glass Bottom Boat and Sub-sea Explorer tel. (099) 42 5955); and thinking up the ultimate irrefutable philosophy.

COSSACK
On the coast 680 km NE of Carnarvon, just off the North West Coastal Highway. This 'historic ghost town' was once the biggest port along this part of the coast. Pearl fishers, pioneers, gold prospectors and others who had simply lost their way (in life or on the globe) would all put in at Tien Tsin (as it was known in those days). You can still see the Pioneer Cemetery, part of which is given over to the graves of Japanese pearl divers. Many of the buildings here are more than 100 years old, and used to be chained to the ground to stop them becoming airborne during cyclones. The **Courthouse** contains a museum which explains the history of the place, and the **Post Office** is an art gallery. At present this so-called ghost town is undergoing a restoration programme which rather gives the lie to its description. Anyway, even if it is now spookless, it has some fine beaches and there's an interesting **Historic Walk**.

EIGHTY MILE BEACH
Between Port Hedland and Broome. This is just what it says, and, despite decimalization, shows no sign of changing its name to One-Hundred-and-Twenty-Eight-Point-Eight-Kilometre Beach. This is where the Great Sandy Desert, which stretches for 1,000 km inland, meets the sea.

EXMOUTH ⊨ ✕
On North West Cape, 368 km N of Carnarvon. Exmouth sprang into being in 1967, as a service centre for the nearby US Naval Communications Station. The US Navy chose this site for their VLF (Very Low Frequency) transmitter because there's a minimum of cloud (which interferes with VLF transmissions), it's miles from anywhere, and they thought no one would notice. They got two out of three right: protesters were soon on the job.

Exmouth makes a useful base for exploring the **Ningaloo Reef** (see separate entry, opposite), and the lagoons and beaches of the **Cape Range National Park**, which occupies the other side of the North West Cape. Also within easy reach of town is an excellent beach (**Bundegi**, with reef offshore), the 90-year-old wreck of the SS *Mildura*, and the clifftop **Vlaming Head**

Lighthouse, where you feel you can see all the way to India.

The VLF transmitter towers are at the tip of the cape. Trivia fans will be pleased to know that the tallest, at nearly 400 m, is the highest man-made edifice south of the Equator, and taller than the original Empire State Building.

KARIJINI (HAMMERSLEY RANGE) NATIONAL PARK

300 km inland from North West Coastal Highway, S of Port Hedland. This county-sized national park is at the eastern end of the Hammersley Range. It is best known for the spectacular **Pilbara Gorges**, with their coloured cliffs, pools, waterfalls and occasional old abandoned mines. The most spectacular is the **Wittenoom Gorge**, which is in fact just outside the park boundary to the north. **Hammersley Gorge** has some sensational coloured rock formations, and **Red Gorge** is renowned for its breathtaking views. The park is criss-crossed with trekking and adventure trails, but if you set out with your own party (never travel solo) be sure to heed the posted warnings. They mean it: people get killed here, when they don't watch what they're doing. The best way to travel the gorges is to join one of the organized tours which run from Wittenoom. The most famous of these is **Dave's Tour No. 3** (only for the fit and the foolhardy). The same company also runs tours for mere mortals. Contact Dave's Gorge Tours at Wittenoom Bungarra Bivouac Hostel, tel. (091) 89 7026.

Warning: Wittenoom used to be an asbestos mining centre, and there's a warning about this as you enter town. 'I survived Wittenoom' T-shirts are on sale, and you'll probably survive too. If you don't fancy the risk, you can always base yourself on the other side of the park at Tom Price – see separate entry, page 262.

MILLSTREAM-CHICHESTER NATIONAL PARK

80 km inland from North West Coastal Highway head S at turn-off between Roebourne and Whim Creek. This is what the unspoiled interior of Australia was like for thousands of years. Desert, oases of palm trees and lily pools, coloured cliffs and miles of mountain peaks, as well as stretches of tropical vegetation

inhabited by kangaroos, brilliant dragonflies, flying foxes and, inevitably, several unique species of flies. Aborigines also used to live here too, but have since been moved on 'for their own good'.

The main Visitor Centre is in an old converted homestead at Millstream, at the southern end of the park, tel. (091) 84 5144. Here you can pick up maps and details of walks and treks.

Don't miss the **Chinderwarriner Pool** with the famous lilies. This is near the homestead Visitor Centre. From here there are also a number of trails. The best is the one to **Deep Reach Pools**, about 8 km long.

NINGALOO REEF

Runs in a broken string for 250 km along the W coast of North West Cape. This spectacular reef may be smaller and less famous than Queensland's Great Barrier Reef, but it can be equally spectacular. The reef is said to contain 200 different species of coral, and its waters are home to more than twice as many species of fish – from glitter-dust shoals of minnows to turtles that don't get made into soup, and sharks that don't even bite. As near to virtual reality as you can get without donning the techno-gladiator's helmet.

Trips to the reef are organized from Exmouth. Divers should contact Exmouth Dive Centre, Payne Street, tel. (099) 49 1201. All diving equipment can be hired. Ningaloo Coral Explorer at Bundegi Beach runs day cruises – tel. (099) 49 1625.

PILBARA GORGES

See Karijini National Park, this page.

PORT HEDLAND ✕

615 km SW of Broome on the Great Northern Highway. Love it or loathe it, Port Hedland is what the Pilbara is all about. This iron-ore port handles more tonnage than any other in Australia. It's on an island, which is linked to the mainland by a 3-km-long road and rail causeways. The latter carry in the trains of iron ore from the mines in the Pilbara hinterland. These trains can be as long as the causeway, and the entire town is coated in fine red ore dust – which makes your eyes smart, and adds a peculiar flavour to your cigarette if you smoke in the open air.

• *Western Australia, where baking temperatures can match those of the Sahara.*

Where it's not industrialized, much of the coastline is mangrove swamps and grotty inlets with uninviting names such as Stingray Creek. Elsewhere there are ravenous sharks. Other local features include cyclones, summer noonday temperatures that could slay an ox, and ox-like drunks. But if you enjoy industrial moonscapes (as I do), and you're thrilled by the sight of ore carriers the size of felled skyscrapers, registered anywhere from Panama to Piraeus, and manned by crews from Shanghai, Santos or Southampton – this is the place for you. Alas, the Australian mining conglomerate BHP is at present being pressurized by ecologists to clear up its industrial beauty spot – so you'll have to hurry if you wish to experience this (literal) eyesore in all its glory.

TOM PRICE

W of Karijini National Park, 300 km inland from North West Coastal Highway. This is a typical company town, owned lock stock and barrel by Hammersley Iron. It may be no cultural centre, but the massive extent of the mining operations is as awe-inspiring as many a work of art. Basically, these operations consist of digging up a 1,000-m-high mountain (which consists entirely of iron ore) and shipping it to the coast in 3-km-long railway trains. Christo covers mountains in a sheet and calls it art: Hammersley knocks them down and calls it business.

Good as an alternative base for exploring the Karijini National Park.

WHIM CREEK 🏨

100 km E of Cossack on the North West Coastal Highway. This tiny remote spot has little to recommend it but its name – which does not (entirely) describe the reason for its inclusion in this guide. Whim Creek is a historic site: the location of the first big mineral find in the Pilbara region. This vast, largely barren territory covers the mountainous shoulder of north-western Australia, and is now one of the major iron ore exporting regions in the world.

The creek itself winds its whimsical way to the sea at Balla Balla 20 km away.

WITTENOOM 🏨

See Karijini National Park, page 261.

RECOMMENDED HOTELS

CARNARVON
Quality Inn, \$\$; *Robinson Street; tel. (099) 41 1532; cards none.*
The big bonus here is the pool. Also has a reasonable restaurant.

Carnarvon Hotel, \$\$; *Olivia Terrace; tel. (099) 41 1181; cards none.*
Pleasant motel accommodation on the river front.

EXMOUTH
Potshot Hotel Resort, \$\$\$; *Payne Street; tel. (099) 49 1478; all major cards.*
Surprisingly classy, with motel rooms, pool and many amenities. Also has the best restaurant in town.

Exmouth Cape Tourist Village, \$-\$\$; *Murat Road; tel. (099) 49 1101; all major cards.*
Something for everyone – from backpackers' dormitories to chalets for families. Good pool, lively, friendly clientele.

WHIM CREEK
Whim Creek Hotel, \$-\$\$; *tel. (091) 76 4953; cards none.*
This is Whim Creek. The restaurant serves the finest food within 100 km – there are no others.

WITTENOOM
The Old Convent, \$; *Gregory Street; tel. (091) 89 7060; cards none.*
Basic double rooms as well as communal dorms. Nearest restaurant is 40 km away, so be sure to stock up.

RECOMMENDED RESTAURANTS

CARNARVON
Harbour View Cafe, \$\$; *at Small Boat Harbour; cards none; no booking.*
The best seafood in town.

Dragon Pearl, \$\$; *Francis Street; no booking; most major cards.*
Chinese food; a block inland from the river.

EXMOUTH
Sun Cheung, \$-\$\$; *Thew Street; cards none; no booking.*
Apart from the hotel restaurants, the fish-and-chip shops, and the Walkabout Cafe, this is it. Standard Chinese menu, such as is served everywhere from Exmouth in Australia to Exmouth in England.

PORT HEDLAND
Quality Inn, \$-\$\$; *North West Coastal Highway; tel. (091) 72 1222; cards none.*
Friendly hotel-restaurant – out of town and away from the red dust, by the airport.

Western Australia

The Kimberley and Beyond

1,700 km; map Nelles Australia, 1:400,000

The Kimberley is traditionally the last frontier of the Australian continent. Other regions may be remote, and tough, but this is still, in many ways, genuine pioneer territory. One of the reasons for this is the climate. In summer the temperatures rise into the roasting 40s. Then in late November it begins to rain. This is no ordinary rain: it's the Monsoon, and it usually lasts until March. But if you visit in April or September, you'll find a wonderland.

The Kimberley occupies over a third of a million square kilometres – about the same area as France or Texas – yet only 20,000 people live there. It includes mountains which rise to almost 1,000 metres, desert, jungle, gorges with bizarre and beautiful rock formations, great rivers and remote sheep stations.

There are two entry points into the Kimberley: Kununurra, which is on the Victoria Highway just across the border of Northern Territory; and, on the west side, there's Broome, on the Great Northern Highway. To give you an idea of the size of the Kimberley, these two are 1,000 km apart. The road which links them (the Great Northern Highway) is sealed all the way, but at certain spots there are fords. During the rainy season these can sometimes become impassable for several days at a time; and the Fitzroy River, which runs from the heart of the Kimberley to the coast at Derby, can sometimes increase its width from 100 m to 10 km.

Having got this far, you should allow at least a week to cross between Broome and Darwin, and at least a week to explore in between.

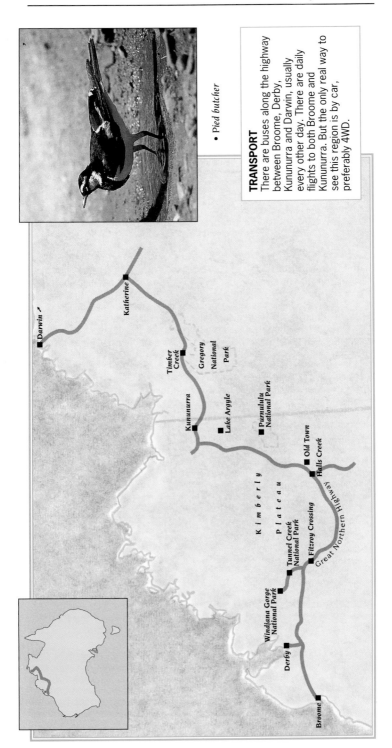

• *Pied butcher*

SIGHTS & PLACES OF INTEREST

BROOME ⇌ ✕

1,500 km NE of Carnarvon on the Great Northern Highway. Broome is a rare delight in these parts. Not only is it a pleasant holiday resort, but it actually has a history, which has given it a distinctive character.

Until the 1870s the local Aborigines were still managing to repel all attempts by Europeans to settle this part of the coast. Then an intrepid intruder discovered that the local beaches were covered in pearl shells. This led to the pearl rush of the 1880s. Overnight Broome became a boom town.

Within 20 years, Broome was 'The Pearl Capital of the World', its pearl shells supplying an astonishing 80 per cent of the world market. (There were comparatively few actual pearls, it was the mother of pearl lining of the shells which provided the lucre.) Four hundred luggers operated from the port – taking with them (or leaving behind dead drunk) as many as 3,000 sailors and divers. Most of these were Asians (Japanese, Malays, Filipinos) and Arabs. An explosive racial mix, they inhabited the area know locally as Chinatown (which did actually have a few Chinese: they usually ran the shops). As is often the case in such waterfront spots, there were often riots: race riots, religious riots, stolen pearl riots, revellers' riots and pure and simple rioters' riots. Then it was time to set sail in the morning to earn enough for the next riot.

After plastic buttons were invented, mother-of-pearl buttons went out of fashion, and the riotous days were over. Those who didn't have enough money to get home remained in Chinatown, which still has a 'rich ethnic mix' (and street signs in five languages).

For several decades this ex-world-capital simply went to sleep. Then the sealed highway linking Broome to the state capital, Perth, arrived at the end of its 2,000-km journey. A few years later, Lord McAlpine arrived. The British peer was so taken with Broome that he financed a one-man revival, and through the 1980s Broome started to become a resort. Fortunately for us (but not Lord McAlpine), he ran into financial difficulties before he could wreck the place, and what remains is a pleasantly developed seaside holiday spot with just enough commercialization for comfort.

If you fancy doing something more than hell-raising in the bars at night, and recovering on the beach during the day, there are several sights worth seeing. **Chinatown** has the world's oldest cinema in continuous use (since 1916), cafés and souvenir shops (some still run by the Chinese). At the end of Frederick Street there's the well-kept old **Japanese Cemetery**. Nearby, if you search around, you'll find the overgrown old Chinese, Malay and Arab cemeteries. Broome also holds an evening market.

For the best beach in the entire north-west, head to **Cable Beach**. This is also virtually the last safe swimming spot: any further north and you're into salt-water croc territory. Cable Beach was the spot where the last link of the London-Australia telephone cable came ashore just 100 years ago. The beach is 5 km east of town on the other side of the headland (regular buses from Carnarvon Street). It stretches for over 20 km and looks as if it was designed for a travel poster (cream sand, sea shading from crystalline clear through jade to deep ultramarine on the horizon). The north end of the beach is for nudist swimming, and on the rest there's all the fun of the fair – including windsurfing, paragliding and even 'camel rides.

At **Gantheaume Point,** the southern limit of Cable Beach, there's a cast of a dinosaur's footprints on the clifftop. The actual petrified prints are in some rocks just offshore, and can only be seen at exceptionally low tides. These prints are said to be 120 million years old.

During the winter season Broome is a lively spot. At the drop of a hat they'll hold a festival. Best of these is the Shinju Matsuri (**Festival of the Pearl**) in September when they hold dragon boat races out in the bay.

For a trip around the bay with a difference, try the *Spirit of Broome* hovercraft, tel. (091) 93 5025. You can also take a moonlit cruise on the pearl lugger *Dampier*. Unromantic types will prefer a blast through the countryside

• *Opposite: Kimberley terrain.*

on a Harley-Davidson.

For details, ask Norm at the tourist office, tel. (091) 92 222, on the corner of Broome Road and Bagot Street. Here they also have details of hikes, birdwatching trips and much more.

DARWIN

See Australia Overall: 12, page 176.

DERBY 🚬

Off the Great Northern Highway, 230 km NE of Broome. The small town of Derby (population 3,200) stands at the mouth of the Fitzroy River, the greatest of the Kimberley rivers, which rises 500 km away on the slopes of Mount Wells (983 m).

Derby is the administrative centre for the regional Aboriginal reservations. Earlier attitudes towards these native Australians was less benevolent here-abouts than it is today. A reminder of those days is the **Boab Prison Tree,** 7 km south of town. Not so long ago, this thousand-year-old tree was used as a lock-up for Aborigines – the maximum number squeezed into its 14-m circum-ference was said to have been 20.

This uncultured European behaviour is brought into sharp contrast by the culture of the people to whom the tree really belongs. Derby has a number of galleries which specialize in Aboriginal

---

STAIRCASE TO THE MOON

This phenomenon occurs at certain points along the coast here. When the full moon rises on a cloudless night, its reflection across the gently rippling shallows of the mudflats appears like a golden stairway. You will find this effect either wonderfully romantic or mystifyingly banal – either way, the locals use it as a great excuse for a celebration.

The best places to see it are from the town beach jetty at Broome (at the end of Robinson Street) or Reader's Point Lookout at Cossack. Witness the phenomenon, and you will discover that wolves and coyotes are not the only species which bay at the moon. At Broome, they also hold a market.

---

art. As with all art, some of this is over-hyped rubbish and some is sublime – with a fair amount in between. (When your assessment of these categories doesn't coincide with the gallery owner's, keep your mouth shut – you're on to a bargain.) The best-known art of the Kimberley features the mysterious Wandjina: see box opposite.

Derby is surrounded by vast mud-flats. During the dry season these are baked solid by the sun, apart from when they are overrun by the occasion-al high tide. During the rainy season they become one huge squelch.

There are organized cruises and trips along the coast. The best of these are run by Buccaneer Sea Safaris, tel. 091 91 1991.

FITZROY CROSSING

On the Great Northern Highway 214 km E of Derby. A nondescript spot, where the road crosses the Fitzroy River. The local **Crossing Inn** is a hundred years old, making it the oldest watering hole in the Kimberley. This has the hard-drinking reputation that you'd expect of such a spot.

Fitzroy Crossing makes a useful base for exploring the **Geikie Gorge,** just 17 km to the north-east. A boat trip takes you through spectacular scenery along a river that has freshwater croc-odiles, stingrays and sawfish. There's also a 2-km walk along the bank.

Some 100 km north-west of Fitzroy Crossing is **Tunnel Creek,** with its 700-m tunnel beneath the mountains. This is where the law finally cought up with the Jundumurra (see Kimberley, page 269). In another 40 km or so you come to **Windjana Gorge**, renowned for its breathtaking scenery, mysteri-ous Aborigine rock paintings of the Wandjina (see box, opposite) and noi-some horse flies.

GREGORY NATIONAL PARK

See Timber Creek, page 270.

HALL'S CREEK 🚬 ✕

On the Great Northern Highway, 520 km E of Derby. Scene of the famous 1895 gold rush, the first in Western Australia. The gold rush attracted more than 1,000 prospectors to this remote spot on the edge of the Great Sandy Desert, and within four years the gold had all but run out. Then news came through that gold had been discovered 1,500 km south at Kalgoorlie – and prospectors left as quickly as they had arrived.

You can still the remants of the gold prospectors' settlement at **Old Town**, in the hills 17 km to the east down the unsealed Duncan Highway. All that's left are abandoned digs, where the odd minuscule nugget is still sometimes discovered; the remains of the post office; the cemetery; and a large mound of empty bottles. Nearby is **Caroline Pool**, where some of the prospectors (occasionally) washed, and you can swim.

Off the road to Old Town, 7 km from Hall's Creek, is the so-called **China Wall**, a curious vein of quartz above a pool. (And it does indeed bear a vague resemblance to the Great Wall of China).

KATHERINE

See Australia Overall: 12, page 177.

KIMBERLEY

Region occupying far NE section of Western Australia. The first European expedition to the Kimberley did not arrive until 1837. Lieutenant George Grey and his men put ashore on the treacherous crocodile-infested coastline, and at once proceeded boldly inland. Next day, Grey was almost drowned trying to swim across the Prince Regent River, emerging minus his trousers.

Not until 40 years later did the first serious European exploration begin. A few settlers followed, setting up sheep stations. But these bold pioneers had overlooked one important fact. This region was already occupied – by the Aborigines. And they didn't want anyone else living there.

The pioneers were soon being attacked by the local Bunuba Aborigines. The police were sent in, but to little avail. By the 1890s, these attacks had been coordinated into a guerrilla campaign by the Aborigine leader Jundumurra, who became known as Pigeon. This nickname was of course only used by his white pursuers – some say on account of his diminutive size, others because of his ability to elude their ambushes by flying away through the undergrowth.

The police eventually captured Jundumurra and dragged him off in chains to Derby. Jundumurra soon escaped,

---

THE WANDJINA

The Aborigine art of the Kimberley is renowned for its depiction of The Wandjina, mysterious beings who control the elements. They are ancestor beings of the Aborigines, who originally came from the sky. A Wandjina is usually painted in human form with black skin and an oval mark on his chest, but has no mouth. Around his head is a halo, which is both his hair and the clouds he controls. The Wandjina appear in many early Aboriginal rock paintings found in the Kimberley, where they are often depicted as giants.

A Jungian psychiatrist has recently claimed that the Wandjina are analagous to the spirits which evolved, in the Western psyche, into the Ancient Greek gods.

---

and later released other Aborigine prisoners. He then got hold of rifles, and began training his men. The police now bought in reinforcements and conducted a full-scale manhunt, using renegade Aborigine trackers brought in from another tribe. The mortally wounded Jundumurra was finally cornered at Tunnel Creek in 1897.

The territory where Jundumurra eluded his squads of determined pursuers remains much the same today as it did 100 years ago (and indeed as it was for thousands of years before Europeans set eyes on Australia). Apart from a few small isolated settlements, nature still runs its course in spectacular fashion. *For particular points of interest in the Kimberley, see separate entries for Derby, Fitzroy Crossing, Hall's Creek, Kununurra, Purnululu National Park and Wolfe Creek.*

KUNUNURRA 🛏 ✕

On Victoria Highway, 172 km W of Timber Creek. Only founded in the late 1950s, to service the construction of the Ord River Dam, 70 km down the road, Kununurra now has a population of more than 4,000, making it the largest settlement in the east Kimberley.

The dam has created **Lake Argyle**, the world's largest artificial lake, which is capable of holding almost ten times

as much water as Sydney Harbour. The former construction camp has been transformed into a tourist resort, complete with cruises on the lake.

In Kununurra itself it's worth visiting the **Waringarri Aboriginal Arts Centre** just north of the town centre on Speargrass Road, and the **gorge at Hidden Valley**, just a couple of kilometres north of town.

If you want to take a two-day **canoe trip** down the Ord River through Lake Kununurra, contact Kununurra Backpackers at 111, Nutwood Crescent, tel. 091 68 1711.

LAKE ARGYLE

See Kununurra, page 269.

OLD TOWN

See Hall's Creek, page 268.

PURNULULU NATIONAL PARK

Some 200 km S of Kununurra, and 50 km E off the Great Northern Highway by 4WD; open April to Dec only. The park contains the **Bungle Bungle Mountains,** which have some of the most spectacular gorges and rock scenery of all Australia. But it's difficult to get to, and the gorges involve some tough hiking. You can pick up a map at the Ranger's Residence, where you pay your A\$20 entrance fee. If you want to see it the easy way, take the A\$125 helicopter ride from Turkey

• *Aborigine rock art, Kimberley.*

Creek on the main highway.

The caves, striped rock formations, creek beaches and palm oases of this region were virtually unknown until the early 1980s, when they were 'discovered' by a roving film crew. They are now on the way to becoming one of the outback's major attractions.

TIMBER CREEK

On Victoria Highway 285 km W of Katherine. Timber Creek consists of little more than the old police station (now a museum), and a couple of pubs with a tourist office in between. The last is inhabited by the redoubtable Max, who runs a boat trip down the Victoria River. The main feature of this trip is Max himself, but the crocs, turtles, local legends (and a few local facts) are also allowed a look in.

South of here, for 150 km, runs the **Gregory National Park.** You can drive for 50 km or so down the road (further if you have a 4WD). Here there's a trail which leads through spectacular remote scenery past a pool which provides the only safe swimming in the park, unless you fancy youself as a Crocodile Dundee.

TUNNEL CREEK

See Fitzroy Crossing, page 268.

WINDJANA GORGE
See Fitzroy Crossing, page 268.

WOOLFE CREEK CRATER NATIONAL PARK
130 km S of Hall's Creek. The meteorite that landed here here aeons ago made an impact big enough to have destroyed any city in the modern world. It left a crater over 800 m wide and 50 m deep, the second largest on Earth.

According to local Aborigine legend, this was where a monstrous serpent emerged from the entrails of the earth. Like many such spots, the facts (and the myths) are rather more interesting than the site itself – unless seen from the air.

After the Earth eventually passes through another large meteorite shower, this is what London, Chicago or Frankfurt could look like.

RECOMMENDED HOTELS

Centres of population are few and far between in this region, but you'll find that each one on the main highway has somewhere to stay. However, few of these are anything special or indeed measure up the criteria we apply for a recommendation in this guide.

BROOME
Quality Tropicana Inn, $$; *Robinson Street; tel. (091) 92 1204; cards AE, MC, V.*
At the corner of Saville Street, within a short walk of Town Beach. A pleasant holiday hotel.

Forrest House, $$; *59, Forrest Street; tel. (091) 93 5067; cards none.*
Bed-and-breakfast at the southern end of town, just 500 m from Town Beach.

DERBY
West Kimberley Lodge, $-$$; *17, Sutherland Street; tel. (091) 91 1031; cards none.*
Adequate standard accommodation, where such a thing is not to be taken lightly.

HALL'S CREEK
Shell Roadhouse, $-$$; *Great Northern Highway; tel. (091) 68 6060; cards none.*
Friendly spot with pleasant rooms; a useful base for exploring the region.

KUNUNURRA
Hotel Kununurra, $$; *Messmate Way; tel. (091) 68 1344; cards none.*
For a bargain, try the motel rooms here.

RECOMMENDED RESTAURANTS

BROOME
Murray's, $$; *Dampier Terrace; cards none.*
The best Chinese food in town, in the old Chinatown.

Charters, Mangrove Hotel, $$; *Carnarvon Street; tel. (091) 91 1303; all major cards.*
Best seafood in town, with great views out over the bay.

The best area for a lively night out in Broome is around Napier Terrace in Chinatown. Here there is a wide choice of restaurants and some lively pubs. The **Roebuck Bay Hotel**, known locally as the Roey by those who have survived it, is generally reckoned to be the liveliest.

HALL'S CREEK
Kimberley Hotel, $-$$; *Roberta Avenue; tel. (091) 68 6101; cards none.*
You can eat bar food at the tables outside; but for something special, try the restaurant, which has a great buffet.

KUNUNURRA
Chopsticks, $$; *Country Club Private Hotel, Coolibah Drive; tel. (091) 68 1024; cards none.*
The classiest restaurant in town, specializing in oriental cuisine to quite a high standard.

The Tasmanian Hinterland

500 km; map Nelles Australia, 1:400,000

Off the beaten track, Tasmania has much to offer: the population of just under half a million is concentrated mainly along the northern and western coasts.

Most of the remote western hinterland is a World Heritage Area. Here you can visit the Cradle Mountain–Lake St Clair National Park, a region of mountains and rainforest that is renowned for its wildlife, including the Tasmanian Devil. South of here lies the Franklin Lower Gordon Wild Rivers National Park, with some fine hiking trails and its notoriously challenging white-water rafting. A useful base for visiting this park is the harbour resort of Strahan, on the west coast, which has beaches and from which you can take boat trips.

The east coast has gentler scenery, but there is some fine hiking along the Freycinet Peninsula. For some weird (but in its own way just as typical) scenery, try Penguin on the north coast. Off the north-west coast lies Flinders Island. For a century, ships foundered here at the rate of more than one a year; now the wrecks entertain scuba divers.

The guide's coverage of Tasmania is completed by Australia Overall: 14, which deals with the island's two main centres, Hobart and Launceston.

Tasmania may be only 300 km at its longest, but if you're planning to explore off the beaten track you should allow at least a week.

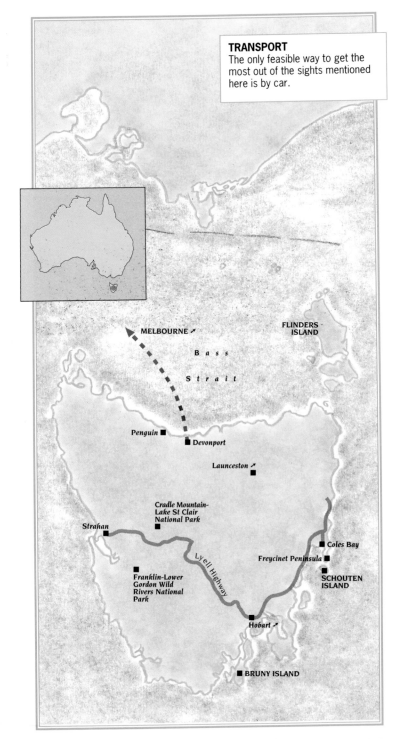

TRANSPORT
The only feasible way to get the most out of the sights mentioned here is by car.

MELBOURNE

FLINDERS ISLAND

B a s s

S t r a i t

Penguin

Devonport

Launceston

Cradle Mountain-
Lake St Clair
National Park

Strahan

Coles Bay

Freycinet Peninsula

SCHOUTEN
ISLAND

Lyell Highway

Franklin-Lower
Gordon Wild
Rivers National
Park

Hobart

BRUNY ISLAND

• Harbour, Coles Bay.

SIGHTS & PLACES OF INTEREST

BRUNY ISLAND 🛏 ✕

To get here take the ferry from Kettering, which is 30 km S of Hobart. Bruny Island is 70 km long and consists of two almost-islands (North Bruny and South Bruny) joined by a narrow isthmus. It's a great place for hiking and lonely beaches. On a sand dune at the start of the isthmus you'll see a monument to Truganini, the last Tasmanian Aborigine. Further on down the isthmus you can sometimes encounter fairy penguins.

Of the two islands, South Bruny has the finest scenery, woodlands and beaches. The best overnight stays are at Allonnah, which is on the west coast of South Bruny.

COLES BAY

See Freycinet Peninsula, page 276.

CRADLE MOUNTAIN–LAKE ST CLAIR NATIONAL PARK

170 km W of Launceston. One of Australia's finest national parks, and part of the World Heritage Area formed by the central Tasmanian wilderness. At either end of the park there are trails which lead past lakes and fine mountain scenery. But the main thing here is the exceptional variety of wildlife, which includes wallabies, wildcats, possums and even the rare and intriguing Tasmanian devil (who's much better in real life than in the ferociously nutty cartoon version).

In the early 1980s, this area was the focus of a world campaign to save it from commercial ruination. This was supported by British TV personality David Bellamy who, along with more than a thousand others, was willing to go to jail to protect this wilderness. They won, but some locals still feel aggrieved, so go easy with your opinions.

FLINDERS ISLAND 🛏

Reached by air from Launceston (and also from Melbourne on the mainland), the island lies 60 km off the NE coast of Tasmania in the Bass Strait. Flinders Island didn't appear on the maps until as late as 1798, when it was charted by Matthew Flinders, who modestly put his name on the map.

Flinders Island quickly became a

• *Opposite: Cradle Mountain.*

THE TASMANIAN ABORIGINES

When the Europeans first settled Tasmania in the early years of the 19thC there were more than 4,000 Aborigine tribesmen living on the island. War erupted between the two communities almost at once. Things got so bad that soldiers were even permitted to hunt down Aborigines like game. By 1829, there were only 135 Aborginies left. These were transported to Flinders Island, where their slaughterers intended to educate them in the benefits of civilization. Seventeen years later, all but 47 had died.

haunt of seal-slaughterers and wreckers, who took to part-time piracy when trade was slack. The island played a similarly iniquitous role in the extermination of the Tasmanian Aborigines (see box, above).

Nowadays, Flinders Island has a permanent population of around a thousand, and the island's wrecks are a great attraction for scuba divers. It also has some superb beaches, a great variety of birdlife, and some great remote bushwalks.

FRANKLIN-LOWER GORDON WILD RIVERS NATIONAL PARK

SE of Strahan, which is on the mid-west coast. The easiest way to see this area of mountains, rivers and unspoiled rainforest is from the Lyell Highway which links Hobart and Strahan. From here you can follow trails into the wilderness and look down over the rivers.

These rivers provide some of the best and most challenging white-water rafting in the world. Adrenalin freaks can apply to Rafting Tasmania, 63 Channel Highway, Taroona; tel. (002) 27 8295. They pride themselves on being the gutsiest white-water outfit of all.

The major feature of this wilderness is **Frenchman's Cap**, which rises to over 1,400 m, with a sheer 500-m-cliff to the summit. Inevitably, this too attracts hardy outdoor types – and that's an understatement. It's a mere five days and 55 km to the summit. The best way to see this spot, and the rivers, is by air from Strahan (see opposite).

FREYCINET PENINSULA 🕭

Midway down E coast. The peninsula contains a national park, which is entered by way of **Coles Bay**, a small fishing town on the edge of Great Oyster Bay. Nearby there are some spectacular red granite cliffs called **The Hazards**, which rise 300 m sheer from the sea.

The peninsula national park has several fine walking trails, where you're likely to encounter all kinds of interesting wildlife. An hour's walk brings you to the spectacular white sandy beach at **Wineglass Bay**. There's a campsite at **Cooks Beach**, and if you want to camp somewhere really remote, try **Schouten Island**, off the end of the peninsula. (To get here ask the fishermen at Coles Bay.)

MELBOURNE

See Australia Overall: 3.

PENGUIN

On the coast, 30 km W of Devonport. The kitsch capital of Tasmania, with a 2-m-high penguin in the local park, and dustbins shaped as penguins lining the main street. (In the pub, they'll tell you the unrepeatable story about the real pen-

THE HUON PINE

This curious-looking tree with its unmistakable trailing coniferous branches is native to Tasmania. Several years ago, it only grew in the south-western extremities of this island, where it thrived on the wet weather and Anarctic winter blasts. In order to adapt to this inhospitable climate, it evolved an exceptionally slow growth rate. As a result, the Huon pine became extremely long-lived, and there are still a few specimens that are more than 2,000 years old. The Huon pine's fine timber was once a prized commodity on Tasmania, and trees were massacred by the early settlers with great enthusiasm. Nowadays, we are much more appreciative of such fine examples of our natural heritage, and Huon pines are mainly used for such essential items as salad bowls and souvenirs.

• *Gordon Rivers.*

guin who came to town in search of a mate.) Penguin has three good beaches and a couple of nearby bird sanctuaries. At **Penguin Point**, you can see plenty of real penguins.

SCHOUTEN ISLAND
See Freycinet Peninsula, page 276.

STRAHAN 🛏 ✕
Middle of the W coast, at the end of Lyall Highway, 260 km from Hobart. The only town on the west coast of the island, this remote spot predictably began life as a settlement for the more dedicated class of criminal. Now it's become one for a similar class of tourist. The town itself is situated on a fine natural harbour. Nearby is 30-km-long **Ocean Beach**, the longest on the island, and famous for its sunsets and its whale skeletons. (Whales are still occasionally washed up here as they migrate north from Antarctica.)

But the big attraction is the nearby **Franklin-Lower Gordon Wild Rivers National Park** – see opposite. On the Esplanade and elsewhere in town you'll find outfits offering a range of organized tours through the park – on foot, on mountain bike, in 4WD. The best way to see the park, if you can afford it, is by air. For this, try Wilderness Air at Strahan Wharf (about an hour and a half for A$100).

RECOMMENDED HOTELS

BRUNY ISLAND
Bruny Hotel, $$; *Main Road, Allonnah, South Bruny; tel.* (002) 93 1148; *cards none.*

Local pub with OK counter meals, which also does bed-and-breakfast.

FLINDERS ISLAND
The plane lands at Whitemark, where you can have bed-and-breakfast at:

Bluff House, $-$$; *Pats River; tel.* (003) 59 2034.

FREYCINET PENINSULA
Freycinet Lodge, $$; *Freycinet National Park; tel.* (002) 57 0101; *cards none.*

Cabins which go down to the sea. There's also a restaurant which has fine views out over Great Oyster Bay.

STRAHAN
Franklin Manor, $$$; *The Esplanade; tel.* (004) 71 7311; *cards* DC, MC, V.

A superb bed-and-breakfast place with fabulous historic decoration and blazing open fire, run by Bernadette Woods from Ireland. In the 19thC habourmaster's house, set in gardens close to the front. Well worth what you pay. See also Recommended Restaurants, below.

RECOMMENDED RESTAURANTS

BRUNY ISLAND
See Recommended Hotels, above.

STRAHAN
Franklin Manor, $$-$$$; *The Esplanade; tel.* (004) 7311; *cards* DC, MC, V.

Haute cuisine served amidst tasteful surroundings. Here they're so civilized that you are allowed to help yourself at the bar and the wine cellar, merely entering your choice in the book.

277

Index

A

Aborigines
  art 180, 184-5, 213,
    228, 251, 268,
    269, 270
  culture 148
Adelaide
  area around 118-20
  central, walk 114-18
  history 112-13
  hotels 121
  restaurants 121
Adelaide Hills 118-20
  hotels 121
Airlie Beach 152
  hotels 161
Albany 248-9
  hotels 251
  restaurants 251
Alexandria Bay 136
Alice Springs 180
  hotels 185
  restaurants 185
Alligator Gorge 120
Alpine National Park 92
  hotels 101
American River 108
Amity Point 84
Anakie 228
Apollo Bay 104
  hotels 108
Ararat 210
  hotels 213
Arcadia 156
Armadale 249
Armidale 204
  hotels 205
  restaurants 205
Aspen Island 64
Augusta 249
Ayers Rock see Uluru
  hotels see Uluru

B

Bairnsdale, hotels 201
Bald Rock 207
Balla Balla 263
Ballarat 210-11
  hotels 213
  restaurants 213
Ballina 76
Bargara 140
Barossa Valley 216-17
  hotels 217
  restaurants 217
Barrington Tops
  National Park 68
  hotels 73
Batemans Bay 198
Bates Cave 251
Bathurst 194
beaches
  Adelaide 118
  Airlie Beach 152
  Bundaberg 140
  Bundegi 260
  Byron Bay 76, 78
  Cable Beach 266
  Cactus Beach 242
  Coff's Harbour 80
  Eighty Mile Beach
    260
  Esperance 243
  Fleurieu
    Peninsula 104
  Fraser Island 134
  Hervey Bay 134-5
  Keppel Islands 144-5
  Koombana Beach
    249
  Myall Lakes 72
  Ninety Mile Beach
    198

Noosa 136
Ocean Beach 277
Port Macquarie 84-5
Sunset Coast 172
Sydney 55
Bedarra Island 154
Bellingen 76
Benalla 92
Bendigo 211-12
  hotels 213
  restaurants 213
Best of All Lookout 206
Big Bull 73
Binna Burra 206
Birdland Sanctuary 198
Birdsville 224
Black Mountain 64
Blackwater 228
Blue Lake 84
Blue Mountains 194
  hotels 195
  restaurants195
Blundell's Farmhouse 64
Bombah Point 72
Boonoo Boonoo Falls
  207
Boulder 164-5
Bourke 194
  hotels 195
Bowen 152
Bowral 65
Boydtown 198
  restaurants 201
Brampton Island 146,
  152-3
Bribie Island 128
Brisbane
  central, walk 129-32
  history 128-9
  hotels 136
  restaurants 137
Brisbane Water National
  Park 68
Broad Arrow 244
Broken Hill 220
  hotels 221
  restaurants 221
Broome 266,268
  hotels 271
  restaurants 271
Brown Lake 84
Bruny Island 274
  hotels 277
Buchan 200
Bulahdelah 72
Bunbury 249
Bundaberg 140-1
  hotels 149
Bunegdi 260
Bungle Bungle
  Mountains 270
Burleigh Heads 76
  hotels 88
Burra 220-1
  hotels 221
  restaurants 221
Byron Bay 76,78
  hotels 88
  restaurants 88-9

C

Cable Beach 266
Caboolture 132
Cactus Beach 242
Cairns 153
  hotels 161
  restaurants 161
Caloundra 132-3
Camden 70
Canberra 58-61
  hotels 65
  region 65
  restaurants 65

sights and places of
  interest 61-4
Canungra 206
Cape Byron 77
Cape Carnot 245
Cape Leeuwin 249
Cape Otway 104
Cape Range National
  Park 260
Cape Tribulation 236
Cape York 236
  hotels 239
Capricorn International
  Resort 148
Capricorn Islands 141
Cardwell 153
Carlisle Island 153
Carlton 100
Carnarvon 260
  hotels 263
  restaurants 263
Carnarvon Gorge 228
Carnarvon National Park
  228-9
Caroline Pool 269
Castle Hill 158
Caves, The 148
Cedar Falls 206
Ceduna 242
Central Deborah
  Goldmine 212
Central Tilba 198
Cessnock 68,71
Charleville 224-5
Charters Towers
  157,232
Chichester 261
China Wall 269
Chinderwarriner Pool
  261
Christmas Cove105
Cid Harbour 156
Cid Island 156
Cleland
  Conservation Park
  118-19
Cleveland 84
Cloncurry 233
Cockleblddy 242-3
Coen 236
Coffin Bay 243
  hotels 245
Coff's Harbour 79-80
  hotels 88
  restaurants 89
Coles Bay 276
Coochie Island 82
Cooee Bay 148
Cooks Beach 276
Cooktown 236-7
  hotels 239
Coolangatta 80
  restaurants 89
Coolgardie 164
  hotels 165
Cooloola National
  Park 133
Coolum 133
  hotels 136
Cooma 64
Cooper Pedy 124
  hotels 125
Coorong, The, national
  park 104
Coral Bay 260
Cossack 260
Cottesloe Beach 172
Cowes 200
  hotels 201
  restaurants 201
Cradle Mountain-Lake
  St Clair National Park
  274

Cumberland Group 152-3

D

Dandenongs, The 198
Dangar Falls 80
Dangerous Reef 245
Darwin 176
  hotels 177
  restaurants 177
Day Dream Mine 220
Daydream Island 160
Deep Reach Pools 261
Delprat's Mine 220
Denham 256
  hotels 257
  restaurants 257
Derby 268
  hotels 271
Devil's Marbles 177
Devonport 188
Digger Beach 80
Dirk Hartog Island 256
Dorrigo National Park 80
Dreamtime Cultural
  Centre 148
Dromana 200
Dubbo 195
  hotels 195
  restaurants 195
Dunk Island 153-4
Dunvegan Sapphire
  Reserve 204
Dunwich 84

E

Ebor Falls 204
Eden 198
  restaurants 201
Edithburgh 120
  hotels 121
Eighty Mile Beach 260
Emerald 229
Emerald Lake 198
Emily & Jessie Gap
  Conservation Reserve
  184
Encounter Bay 104
Esperance 243
  hotels 245
  restaurants 245
Eucla 243
  hotels 245
Exmouth 260-1
  hotels 263
  restaurants 263
Eyre Bird Observatory
  242-3
Eyre Highway 245

F

Falls Creek 92
Family Islands 154
Fisherman's Beach 144
Fitzroy 100
Fitzroy Crossing 268
Fitzroy Island 153
Flagstaff Hill Maritime
  Village 108
Fleurieu Peninsula 104
  hotels 108
  restaurants 109
Flinders Chase National
  Park 105
Flinders Island 274, 276
  hotels 277
Flinders Ranges 217
  hotels 217
  restaurants 217
Forster 68
  hotels 73
Franklin-Lower Gordon
  Wild Rivers national
  Park 276

Index

Fraser Island 133-4
Fremantle 168
  hotels 173
  restaurants 173
French Island 200
Frenchman's Bay 249
Frenchman's Cap 276
Freycinet Peninsula 276
  hotels 277

G

Gantheaume Point 266
Gariwerd 212-13
Geelong 104
  restaurants 109
Geikie Gorge 268
gems, fossicking 228
Geoffrey Bay 156
George's Gold Mine 80
Geraldton 254
  hotels 257
  restaurants 257
Gippsland 198, 200
Gippsland Lakes 198, 200
  hotels 201
  restaurants 201
Gladstone 141
  hotels 149
Glen Innes 204
Glenbrook 194
Glenelg 118
  restaurants 121
Glenrowan 92
Golden Grape Estate 72
Goolwa 104
Gosford 68
Goulburn 65
Grafton 80-1
Grampians 212-13
  hotels 213
  restaurants 213
Great Barrier Reef 142-3
Great Barrier Reef
  Wonderland 157-8
Great Keppel Island
  141, 144
  hotels 149
  restaurants 149
Green Island 153
Green Mountains 206
Greenough Historical
  Hamlet 254-5
Gregory National Park
  270
Griffiths Island 108
Gwalia 244
Gympie 134

H

Hahndorf 119-20
  restaurants 121
Hall's Creek 268-9
  hotels 271
  restaurants 271
Halls Gap 212
Hamilton Island 160
Hammersley Range 261
Hancocks Lookout 120
Hanging Rock 213
Hawker 217
Hayman Island 160
Hazards, The 276
Hazelwood Island 160
Henley Beach, hotels
  121
Heron Island Marine
  Park 141
Heron Island Resort 141
  hotels 149
Hervey Bay 134-5
  hotels 136-7
  restaurants 137

Hidden Valley 270
Hinchinbrook Island 154
  hotels 161
Hippo's Yawn 251
Hobart 188-9
  hotels 189
  restaurants 189
Hook Island 160
Horseshoe Bay 156
Houtman Abrolhos
  Islands 256
Hughenden 233
Humpy Island 144
Hunter Valley 68, 71-2
  hotels 73
  restaurants 73

I

Illawara State
  Recreation Area 201
Innes National Park 120
Ipswich 225

J

Jamison Valley 194
Jewel cave 249
Jindabyne 64
  hotels 65
Julian Rocks 79

K

Kadina 120
  hotels 121
Kakadu National Park
  176-7
Kalbarri 255
  hotels 257
  restaurants 257
Kalgoorlie 164-5
  hotels 165
  restaurants 165
Kangaroo Island 105-6
  hotels 108
Kanowna 244
Karijini National Park
  261
Kata Tjuta 180-1
Katarapko Game
  Reserve 217
Katherine 177
Katoomba 194
  hotels 195
Kelly Hill Caves 105
Keppel Island Resort
  144
Keppel Islands 141,
  144-5
  hotels 149
  restaurants 149
Kiandra 64
Kimberley 269
Kooloonbung Creek
  Nature Park 85
Koombana Beach 249
Koonalda Cave 243
Korora Bay 81
Kosciusko National Park
  64
Kuaranda 153
Kununurra 269-70
  hotels 271
  restaurants 271

L

Lady Elliot Island 145-6
  hotels 149
Lady Musgrave Island
  146
Laguna Beach 136
Lake Alexandrina 104
Lake Argyle 269-70
Lake Burley Griffin 64
Lake Cave 251

Lake Eyre 124
Lake Mountain 92
Lake St Clair 274
Lake St Gwinear 92
Lakefield National Park
  237
Lamington National Park
  204-6
  hotels 205
Launceston 189-90
  hotels 189
  restaurants 189
Leasingham 221
  restaurants 221
Leonora 244
Leura, restaurants 195
Lindeman Island 160
Lindeman's Winery 72
Lismore 81-2
Lizard Island 237-8
Lone Pine Lookout 184
Lone Pine Sanctuary
  132
Long Island 160
Longreach 229
Lord Ard Gorge 107
Lord Howe Island 81
  hotels 88
Lorne 106
  hotels 108-9
  restaurants 109
Loxton 217
  restaurants 217
Lyndoch 216
  hotels 217

M

MacDonnell Ranges
  181,184
Mackay 146
  hotels 149
  restaurants 149
McWilliams Mount
  Pleasant 72
Magnetic Island 156
  restaurants 161
Mallacoota 200
  hotels 201
Mambray Creek 120
Mammoth Cave 251
Mansfield 92
Maree 124
Margaret River 251
  hotels 251
  restaurants 251
Marine Parks
  Heron Island 141
  Solitary Islands 85-6
Maroochydore 135
  restaurants 137
Maslin 104
Masthead Islands 146
Melbourne 90-1, 93-5
  central, walk 96-8
  history 92-3
  hotels 101
  restaurants 101
  sights 98-100
  suburbs 100
Melrose 120
Menzies 244
Middle Island 144
Millstream-Chichester
  National Park 261
Mission Beach156
  hotels 161
  restaurants 161
Mon Repos beach 140
Monkey Beach 144
Monkey Mia 256-7
Monster Mine 221
Montague Island 200

Mooloolaba 135
Moonta 120
Moore Park 140
Moreton Bay 82
Moreton Island 135
Morialta Conservation
  Park 119
Mornington Peninsula
  200
  restaurants 201
Mossman 239
  restaurants 239
Mount Bowen 154
Mount Buffalo National
  Park 100
  restaurants 101
Mount Buller 92
Mount Clarence 248
Mount Cook 1566
Mount Coot-Tha 206
Mount Isa 233
Mount Kosciusko 64
Mount Melville 248
Mount Moffatt 229
Mount Olga 180
Mount Remarkable
  National Park 120
  hotels 121
Mount Selwyn 64
Mount Tamborine 206
Mulka's Cave 251
Murray River 217
Muruku Art and Craft
  centre 184
Mushroom Rock 255
Muttonbird Island 80
Myall Lakes National
  Park 72

N

Nambour 135-6
Nambucca Heads 82
Nambung National Park
  255-6
Narooma 200
  hotels 201
National Parks
  Alpine National Park
    92
  Barrington Tops
    68, 73
  Blue Mountains194
  Brisbane Water 68
  Burleigh Heads 76
  Cape Range 260
  Cape Tribulation 236
  Carnarvon 228-9
  Cooloola 133
  Cradle Mountain-Lake
    St Clair 274
  Dorrigo 80
  Flinders Chase 105
  Flinders Ranges 217
  Franklin-Lower Gordon
    Wild Rivers 276
  Grampians 212-13
  Gregory 270
  Innes 120
  Kakadu 176-7
  Karijini 261
  Kosciusko National
    Park 64
  Lakefield 237
  Lamington 204-6
  Millstream-Chichester
    261
  Mount Buffalo100
  Mount Remarkable
    120, 121
  Myall Lakes 72
  Nambung 255-6
  OrmistonGorge 184
  Otway 104

Index

Port Campbell 106-7
Purnululu 270
Snowy River 200
Springbrook 206
The Coorong 104
Uluru 185
Wollemi 73
Woolfe Creek Crater 271
Yuragir 81
New Norcia 168
Newcastle 72
hotels 73
restaurants 73
Nimbin 83-4
hotels 88
Ninety Mile Beach 198
Ningaloo Reef 261
Noosa 136
hotels 137
restaurants 137
Noosaville 136
Norseman 244
hotels 245
North Keppel Island 144-5
North Molle Islands 160
North Stradbroke Island 84
hotels 88
restaurants 89
North Tamborine 206
Northwest Island 146-7
Nullarbor Cliffs 243

O

Ocean Beach 277
Old Sydney Town 68
Old Town, Hall's Creek 269
Olgas, The 180-1
Ora Banda 244
Ormiston Gorge National Park 184
Otway National Park 104

P

Palm Cove 153
Penguin 276-7
Penneshaw 108, 109
Penong 242
Perisher Valley 64
Perth 168, 170-2
hotels 173
restaurants 173
Phillip Island 200
hotels 201
restaurants 201
Pialba 134
Picnic Bay 156
Pilbara Gorges 261
Pinnacles Desert 255-6
Planton Island 160
Point Lookout 84,204
Pokolbin 72
Port Adelaide 118
Port Arthur 188
hotels 189
Port Augusta 120
hotels 121
Port Campbell 106-7
hotels 109
Port Douglas 239
restaurants 239
Port Fairy 107-8
hotels 109
restaurant 109
Port Hedland 261-2
restuarants 263
Port Kembla 201
Port Lincoln 244-5
hotels 245
restaurants 245

Port Macquarie 84-5
hotels 88
restaurants 89
Port Pirie 120
Portsea, restaurants 201
Punsand Bay 239
Purnululu National Park 270

Q

Queenscliff 200
Quorn, restaurants 217

R

Rainbow Beach 134
Rainbow Valley 255
Ravenswood 157, 233
Raymond Island 200
Recherche Archipelago 243
Red Bluff 255
Red Gorge 261
Reid Lookout 213
Relax Haven 78
Reynolds Yarraman 72
Richmond (Queensland) 233
Richmond (Victoria) 100
Rockhampton 147-8
hotels 149
restaurants 149
Roma 225
Rosslyn Bay 148
Rotamah Island 200
Rottnest Island 172
restaurants 173
Rubyvale 229

S

St Helena Island 82
St Kilda 100
restaurants 101
Scarborough Beach 172
hotels 173
Scarness 134
Schouten Island 276
Seal Bay 105
Seal Rocks 72
Seventy Five Mile Beach 134
Shag Rocks 84
Shark Bay 256-7
hotels 257
restaurants 257
Shipwreck Coast 107
Shute Harbour 152
hotels 161
Silverton 221
Simpson Desert 121
Smiggin Holes 64
Snowy Mountains 64
Snowy River National Park 200
Solitary Islaneds 85-6
Sorrento 200
South Molle Islands 160
South Stradbroke Island 82
Southern Cross 165
hotels 165
Sovereign Hill 211
Springbrook National Park 206
Springwood 194
Staircase to the Moon 268
Standlay Chasm 181, 184
Stenhouse Bay 120
Stockman's Hall of Fame 229
Strahan 277

hotels 277
restaurants 277
Sturt Stony Desert 124
Sunset Coast 172
Sunshine Beach 136
Surfer's Paradise 86
hotels 88
restaurants 89
Swan Valley 172
restaurants 173
Sydney 42-3
beaches 55
central 48-54
history 44-5
hotels 57
nightlife 55
restaurants 57
sights and places of interest 55-6

T

Tamworth 206-7
hotels 205
restaurants 205
Tanunda 216
restaurants 217
Tennant Creek 177
hotels 177
restaurants 177
Tenterfield 207
Thomas Brisbane Planetarium 206
Thredbo 64
Three Sisters 194
Thunderbird Park 206
Tidal River, hotels 201
Tilba Tilba 198
Timber Creek 270
Timberland 72
Timbertown 845
Tippler's Resort 82
Tom Price 263
Toowoomba 225
Torquay 134,135
restaurants 137
Tortoise Lagoon 84
Townsville 156-8
hotels 161
restaurants 161
Trial Bay Gaol 86-7
Troubridge Island 120
Tryon Island 148
Tully 156
Tuncurry 68
hotels 73
Tunnel Creek 268
Tweed Heads 87
Twilight Cove 243

U

Uluru 184-5
hotels 185
Umberumberka Reservoir 221
Upper Swan 172
Urangan 134,135
hotels 136-7
Utah Mine 228

V

Valley of the Winds walk 181
Venus Gold Battery 232
Victoria Harbour 104
Victoria Range 213

W

Wacol 225
Wadlata Outback centre 120
Wagonga Inlet 200
Wallaroo 120
Wangaratta 100

hotels 101
Waringarri Aboriginal Arts centre 270
Warrnambool 108
hotels 109
Watego's Beach 78
Wauchope 72-3, 85
Wave Rock 251
Western Australia, history 169
Whim Creek 263
hotels 263
Whitsunday Islands 158-60
Whyalla 245
restaurants 245
wildlife sanctuaries, Birdland Sanctuary 198
Lone Pine Sanctuary 132
William Ricketts Sanctuary 198
Wilmington 120
Wilpena Pound 217
hotels 217
Wilson Island 148
Wilsons Promontory 201
hotels 201
Windjana Gorge 268
Wineglass Bay 276
wineries 68,70, 71-2, 172, 198, 210, 221, 225, 251, 2161-7
Wittenoom 261
Wollemi National Park 73
Wollombi 73
Wollomombi Falls 204
Wollongong 201
Wonderland Range213
Woody Island 243
Woolfe Creek Crater National Park 271
Woolgoolga 87
Woomera 124-5
hotels 125

Y

Yallingup caves 251
Yarralumla 63-4
Yarrangobilly Caves 64
Yeppoon 148
hotels 149
restaurants 149
Yorke Peninsula 120
hotels 121
Yorkey's Knob 153
Yulara 185
hotels 185
Yuragir National Park 81

Z

Zoe Bay 164